BARCELONA

CONTENTS

Rick Steves®

BARCELONA

INTRODUCTION

If you're in the mood to surrender to a city's charms, let it be in Barcelona. Spain's second city bubbles with life in its narrow Barri Gòtic alleys, along the pedestrian boulevard called the Ramblas, in the funky bohemian quarter of El Born, and throughout the chic, grid-planned new part of town called the Eixample. Its Old City is made for seeing on foot, full of winding lanes that emerge into secluded squares dotted with palm trees and ringed with cafés and boutiques. The waterfront bristles with life, overlooked by the park-like setting of Montjuïc. Everywhere you go, you'll find the city's architecture to be colorful, playful, and unique. Rows of symmetrical ironwork balconies are punctuated with fanciful details: bay windows, turrets, painted tiles, hanging lanterns, flower boxes, and carved reliefs.

As the capital of the Catalan people, Barcelona is full of history. You'll see Roman ruins, a medieval cathedral, twisty Gothic lanes, and traces of Columbus and the sea trade. But by the late 19th century, the city had boomed into an industrial powerhouse, and became the cradle of a new artistic style—Modernism. Pablo Picasso lived in Barcelona as a teenager, right as he was on the verge of reinventing painting; his legacy is today's Picasso Museum. Catalan architects, including Antoni Gaudí, Lluís Domènech i Montaner, and Josep Puig i Cadafalch, forged the Modernista style and remade the city's skyline with curvy, playful fantasy buildings—culminating in Gaudí's over-the-top Sagrada Família, a church still under construction. Salvador Dalí and Joan Miró join the long list of world-changing 20th-century artists with ties to this city.

Today's Barcelona is as vibrant as ever. Locals still join hands and dance the everyone's-welcome *sardana* in front of the cathedral every weekend. Neighborhood festivals jam the events calendar. The

Map Legend

↳ Viewpoint	✈ Airport	Tunnel
↟ Entrance	ⓣ Taxi Stand	Pedestrian Zone
ⓘ Tourist Info	Ⓣ Tram Stop	Railway
WC Restroom	Ⓑ Bus Stop	Ferry/Boat Route
⛫ Castle	Ⓜ Metro Stop	Tram
⛪ Church	Ⓟ Parking	Stairs
▪ Statue/Point of Interest	🍦 Gelato	Walk/Tour Route
⊠ Elevator	Park	Trail

Use this legend to help you navigate the maps in this book.

cafés are filled by day, and people crowd the streets at night, pausing to fortify themselves with a perfectly composed bite of seafood and a drink at a tapas bar. Barcelona's lively culture is on an unstoppable roll in Spain's most cosmopolitan and European corner.

ABOUT THIS BOOK

Rick Steves Barcelona is a tour guide in your pocket.

In this book, you'll find the following chapters:

Orientation to Barcelona includes specifics on public transportation, helpful hints, local tour options, easy-to-read maps, and tourist information. The "Planning Your Time" section suggests a schedule for how to best use your limited time.

Sights in Barcelona describes the top attractions and includes their cost and hours.

Four **Self-Guided Walks** cover Barcelona's most enjoyable neighborhoods: the Ramblas promenade, historic Barri Gòtic, trendy El Born, and a Modernista paradise, the Eixample.

The **Self-Guided Tours** lead you through Barcelona's most fascinating museums and sights: the Cathedral of Barcelona, the Picasso Museum, and two architectural gems, Gaudí's Sagrada Família and Park Güell.

Sleeping in Barcelona describes my favorite hotels, from good-value deals to cushy splurges.

Eating in Barcelona serves up a range of options, from inexpensive tapas bars to fancy restaurants.

Barcelona with Children includes my top recommendations for keeping your kids (and you) happy.

Shopping in Barcelona gives you tips for shopping painlessly and enjoyably, without letting it overwhelm your vacation or ruin your budget.

Key to This Book

Updates

This book is updated regularly—but things change. For the latest, visit www.ricksteves.com/update.

Abbreviations and Times

I use the following symbols and abbreviations in this book:

Sights are rated:

▲▲▲	Don't miss
▲▲	Try hard to see
▲	Worthwhile if you can make it
No rating	Worth knowing about

Tourist information offices are abbreviated as **TI,** and bathrooms are **WC**s. To categorize accommodations, I use a **Sleep Code** (described on page 173).

Like Europe, this book uses the **24-hour clock.** It's the same as ours through 12:00 noon, then keeps going: 13:00, 14:00, and so on. For anything over 12, subtract 12 and add p.m. (14:00 is 2 p.m.).

When giving **opening times,** I include both peak-season and off-season hours if they differ. So, if a museum is listed as "May-Oct daily 9:00-16:00," it should be open from 9 a.m. until 4 p.m. from the first day of May until the last day of October (but expect exceptions).

If you see a ✪ symbol near a sight listing, it means that sight is described in far greater detail elsewhere—either with its own self-guided tour, or as part of a self-guided walk.

For **transit** or **tour departures,** I first list the frequency, then the duration. So, a train connection listed as "2/hour, 1.5 hours" departs twice each hour and the journey lasts an hour and a half.

Nightlife in Barcelona is your guide to fun, including classical concerts, nightclubs and after-hours hangouts, flamenco performances, and jazz clubs.

Barcelona Connections lays the groundwork for your smooth arrival and departure, covering transportation by train, plane, and bus (with detailed information on Barcelona's Sants train station and El Prat de Llobregat airport), plus the basics on the city's cruise ship docks.

Day Trips from Barcelona covers nearby sights: Sitges, Montserrat, Figueres, and Cadaqués.

Barcelona: Past and Present gives the background of this city and its region, including a timeline of Barcelona history, information about famous Catalans, and a rundown of contemporary events.

Practicalities is a traveler's tool kit, with our best advice about money, sightseeing, staying connected, and transportation (trains, buses, car rentals, driving, and flights). There's also a list of recommended books and films.

The **appendix** has nuts-and-bolts information, including useful phone numbers and websites, a festival list, a climate chart, a handy packing checklist, and Spanish and Catalan survival phrases.

Browse through this book and select your favorite sights. Then have a *meravellós* trip! Traveling like a temporary local, you'll get the absolute most out of every mile, minute, and dollar. As you visit places I know and love, I'm happy that you'll be meeting my favorite Catalans.

Planning

This section will help you get started planning your trip—with advice on trip costs, when to go, and what you should know before you take off.

TRAVEL SMART

Your trip to Barcelona is like a complex play—it's easier to follow and really appreciate on a second viewing. While no one does the same trip twice to gain that advantage, reading this book in its entirety before your trip accomplishes much the same thing.

Design an itinerary that enables you to visit sights at the best possible times. Note holidays, specifics on sights, and days when sights are closed or most crowded (all covered in this book). You can wait in line at the Sagrada Família, or get advance reservations and bypass the queue without breaking a sweat. Day-tripping to the Dalí Theater-Museum in Figueres on Monday during the off-season is a waste, since it's closed. Be careful on the first Sunday of the month; some sights such as Palau Güell and the Catalan Art Museum are jammed because they're free. To get between destinations smoothly, read the tips in the Practicalities chapter on taking trains and buses, or renting a car and driving. A smart trip is a puzzle—a fun, doable, and worthwhile challenge.

When you're plotting your itinerary, strive for a mix of intense and relaxed stretches. Every trip—and every traveler—needs slack time (laundry, picnics, people-watching, and so on). Pace yourself. Assume you will return.

Update your plans as you travel. You can carry a small mobile device (phone, tablet, laptop) to find out tourist information, learn the latest on sights (special events, tour schedules, etc.), book tickets and tours, make reservations, reconfirm hotels, research transportation connections, and keep in touch with your loved ones. If you don't want to bring a pricey device, you can use guest computers at hotels and make phone calls from landlines.

Enjoy the friendliness of the Spanish people. Connect with the culture. Set up your own quest for the best square, cloister, tapas bar, or whatever. Slow down and be open to unexpected experiences. Ask questions—most locals are eager to point you in their idea of the right direction. Keep a notepad in your pocket for noting directions, organizing your thoughts, and confirming prices. Wear your money belt, learn the currency, and figure out how to estimate prices in dollars. Those who expect to travel smart, do.

TRIP COSTS

Five components make up your trip costs: airfare, surface transportation, room and board, sightseeing and entertainment, and shopping and miscellany.

Airfare: A basic round-trip flight from the US to Barcelona can cost, on average, about $1,000-2,000 total, depending on where you fly from and when (cheaper in winter). If Barcelona is part of a longer trip, consider saving time and money in Europe by flying into one city and out of another; for instance, into Barcelona and out of Paris. Overall, Kayak.com is the best place to start searching for flights on a combination of mainstream and budget carriers.

Surface Transportation: A 10-ride Metro card costs about $15. For round-trip train rides to day-trip destinations, allow about $11 for Sitges, $26 for Montserrat, and $45 for Figueres. To travel between El Prat airport and Barcelona, figure (one-way) $6 by train, $8 by bus, or $50 by taxi.

Room and Board: You can manage comfortably in Barcelona on $130 a day per person for room and board. This allows $5 for breakfast, $15 for lunch, $25 for dinner, and $85 for lodging (based on two people splitting the cost of a $170 double room). Students and tightwads can enjoy Barcelona for as little as $80 a day ($45 for a bed, $35 for meals and snacks).

Sightseeing and Entertainment: It's worth considering the $42 Articket BCN sightseeing pass, which admits you to seven museums, including the recommended Picasso Museum, Catalan Art Museum, and Fundació Joan Miró (for more information, see page 24). Otherwise, figure about $20 per major sight (Picasso Museum-$15, La Pedrera-$23, Sagrada Família-$21), and $10 for others. An evening concert at the Palace of Catalan Music costs about $30-40 per person. An overall average of $30 a day works for most people. Don't skimp here. After all, this category is the driving force behind your trip—you came to sightsee, enjoy, and experience Barcelona.

"You're Not in Spain, You're in Catalunya!"

This is a popular nationalistic refrain you might see on T-shirts or stickers around town. Catalunya is *not* the land of bullfighting and flamenco that many visitors envision when they think of Spain (best to visit Madrid or Sevilla for those).

The region of Catalunya, with Barcelona as its capital, has its own language, history, and culture. Its people—10 million strong—have a proud, independent spirit. Historically, Catalunya ("Cataluña" in Spanish, sometimes spelled "Catalonia" in English) has often been at odds with the central Spanish government in Madrid. The Catalan language and culture were discouraged or even outlawed at various times in history, as Catalunya often chose the wrong side in wars and rebellions against the kings in Madrid. In the Spanish Civil War (1936-1939), Catalunya was one of the last pockets of democratic resistance against the military coup of the fascist dictator Francisco Franco, who punished the region with four decades of repression. During that time, the Catalan flag was banned—but locals vented their national spirit by flying their football team's flag instead.

Three of Barcelona's monuments are reminders of royal and Franco-era suppression. Citadel Park (Parc de la Ciutadella) was originally a much-despised military citadel, constructed in the 18th century to keep locals in line. The Castle of Montjuïc, built for similar reasons, has been the site of numerous political executions, including hundreds during the Franco era. The Sacred Heart Church atop Tibidabo, completed under Franco, was meant to atone for the sins of Barcelonans during the civil war—the main sin being opposition to Franco. Today, many Catalans favor breaking away from Spain, but the central government has vowed to block any referendum on independence (see page 273).

To see real Catalan culture, look for the *sardana* dance or an exhibition of *castellers* (both described on page 45). The main symbol of Catalunya is the dragon, which was slain by St. George ("Jordi" in Catalan)—the region's patron saint. You'll find drag-

INTRODUCTION

ons all over Barcelona, along with the Catalan flag—called the Senyera—with four horizontal red stripes on a gold field. Nineteenth-century Catalan Romantics embraced a vivid story about the origins of their flag: In the ninth century, Wilfred the Hairy—a count of Barcelona and one of the founding fathers of Catalunya—was wounded in battle. A grateful neighboring king rewarded Wilfred's bravery with a copper shield and ran Wilfred's four bloody fingers across its surface, leaving four red stripes. While almost certainly false, this legend hints at the nostalgic mood in 19th-century Barcelona, when the Renaixença (Catalan cultural revival) prodded historians to dig deeply into their medieval past to revive obscure historical figures and lend legitimacy to the resurgent Catalan nation.

The Catalan language is irrevocably tied to the history and spirit of the people here. After the end of the Franco era in the mid-1970s, the language made a huge comeback. Schools are now required by law to conduct all classes in Catalan; most school-age children learn Catalan first and Spanish second. While all Barcelonans still speak Spanish, nearly all understand Catalan, three-quarters speak Catalan, and half can write it.

Most place names in this book are listed in Catalan. Here's how to pronounce the city's major landmarks:

Plaça de Catalunya	PLAH-sah duh kah-tah-LOON-yah
Eixample	eye-SHAM-plah
Passeig de Gràcia	PAH-sehj duh GRAH-see-ah
Catedral	KAH-tah-dral
Barri Gòtic	BAH-ree GOH-teek
El Born	el BORN
Montjuïc	mohn-jew-EEK

When finding your way, these terms will be useful:

exit	*sortida*	sor-TEE-dah
square	*plaça*	PLAH-sah
street	*carrer*	kah-REHR
boulevard	*passeig*	PAH-sehj
avenue	*avinguda*	ah-veen-GOO-dah

For more Catalan words, see the survival phrases on page 321.

Shopping and Miscellany: Figure roughly $3 per coffee, ice-cream cone, or soft drink. Shopping can vary in cost from nearly nothing to a small fortune. Good budget travelers find that this category has little to do with assembling a trip full of lifelong and wonderful memories.

WHEN TO GO

Sea breezes off the Mediterranean and a generally warm climate make Barcelona pleasant for much of the year. Late spring and early fall offer the best combination of good weather, light crowds, long days, and plenty of tourist and cultural activities. You'll encounter hot, humid weather and the biggest crowds in July and August, and some shops and restaurants close down in August. Winter temperatures are far from freezing, but rainfall is abundant.

KNOW BEFORE YOU GO

Your trip is more likely to go smoothly if you plan ahead. Check this list of things to arrange while you're still at home.

You need a **passport**—but no visa or shots—to travel in Spain. You may be denied entry into certain European countries if your passport is due to expire within three months of your ticketed date of return. Get it renewed if you'll be cutting it close. It can take up to six weeks to get or renew a passport (for more on passports, see www.travel.state.gov). Pack a photocopy of your passport in your luggage in case the original is lost or stolen.

Book rooms well in advance if you'll be traveling during peak season (July-Sept) or on any major holidays (see page 314).

You'll need **reservations** if you want to visit Barcelona's Casa Lleó Morera or the Salvador Dalí House near Cadaqués (see page 260). To minimize your time in lines, reservations are recommended for these Barcelona sights, especially in the busy summer months: Picasso Museum, Sagrada Família, Casa Batlló, La Pedrera, Palau Güell, and Park Güell (see "Sight Reservations and Advance Tickets," page 25).

Call your **debit- and credit-card companies** to let them know the countries you'll be visiting, to ask about fees, request your PIN code (it will be mailed to you), and more. See page 278 for details.

Do your homework if you want to buy **travel insurance.** Compare the cost of the insurance to the likelihood of your using it and your potential loss if something goes wrong. Also, check whether your existing insurance (health, homeowners, or renters) covers you and your possessions overseas. For more tips, see www.ricksteves.com/insurance.

If you're taking an **overnight train,** especially to international destinations, and you need a sleeping berth *(litera)* on an exact

Barcelona Almanac

Population: Approximately 1.6 million.

Languages: Spanish and Catalan are the two official languages of Catalunya, but Catalan is the preferred language in schools and offices. Catalan is not a dialect of Spanish, but an independent language.

Currency: Euro (€)

City Layout: The tangled Gothic Quarter (Barri Gòtic) lies at the heart of the city, edged by the connected boulevards of the Ramblas. The more orderly Eixample district spreads north of the old city, while unassuming Barceloneta spills along the seafront. Looking down over it all is the big Montjuïc hill.

Tourist Tracks: Every year, 7.5 million people visit Barcelona. The bustling center for tourists and locals is the Ramblas, which sees more than 150,000 people daily. Avinguda del Portal de l'Angel is Spain's most walked street, trod upon by 3,500 pairs of feet every hour.

Architecture: Barcelona is home to the Modernista style championed by Catalan architect Antoni Gaudí, whose most famous work is the Sagrada Família church. Nearly 30 of his buildings are scattered throughout the greater Barcelona area.

Fun in the Sun: Until 1992, when the city hosted the Olympic Games, Barcelona had only one small beachfront area, in Barceloneta. Other waterfront property was taken up by industrial purposes. For the Olympics, the seaside was reconstructed, and the city shoreline is now spanned by nine beaches along a three-mile stretch.

Soccer: Futbol Club (FC) Barcelona has the largest privately owned stadium in the world, with a seating capacity of 100,000. Every year, more than 1.5 million people visit its museum.

The Average Jordi: The average Barcelonan is 41 years old, will live to age 81, and is likely Catholic. The majority (62 percent) of Barcelona's residents were born in Catalunya.

date—consider booking it in advance through a US agent (such as www.ricksteves.com/rail), even though it may cost more than buying it in Spain.

All **high-speed trains** (AVE) in Spain require a seat reservation, but it's usually possible to make arrangements in Spain just a few days ahead unless it's a holiday weekend. (For more on train travel, see Practicalities.)

If you're planning on **renting a car** for travels beyond Barcelona, bring your driver's license and get an International Driving Permit (see page 300).

INTRODUCTION

If you plan to hire a **local guide,** reserve ahead by email. Popular guides can get booked up.

If you're bringing a **mobile device,** download any apps you might want to use on the road, such as translators, maps, and transit schedules. Check out **Rick Steves Audio Europe,** featuring hours of free travel interviews and other audio content about Spain (via the Rick Steves Audio Europe free app, www.ricksteves.com/audioeurope, iTunes, or Google Play; for details, see page 307).

Check the **Rick Steves guidebook updates** page for any recent changes to this book (www.ricksteves.com/update).

Because **airline carry-on restrictions** are always changing, visit the Transportation Security Administration's website (www.tsa.gov) for a list of what you can bring on the plane and for the latest security measures (including screening of electronic devices, which you may be asked to power up).

Traveling as a Temporary Local

We travel all the way to Spain to enjoy differences—to become temporary locals. You'll experience frustrations. Certain truths that we find "God-given" or "self-evident," such as cold beer, ice in drinks, bottomless cups of coffee, and bigger being better, are suddenly not so true. One of the benefits of travel is the eye-opening realization that there are logical, civil, and even better alternatives. A willingness to go local ensures that you'll enjoy a full dose of Spanish hospitality.

Europeans generally like Americans. But if there is a negative aspect to the Spanish image of Americans, it's that we are loud, wasteful, ethnocentric, too informal (which can seem disrespectful), and a bit naive.

While Spaniards look bemusedly at some of our Yankee excesses—and worriedly at others—they nearly always afford us individual travelers all the warmth we deserve.

Judging from all the happy feedback I receive from travelers who have used this book, it's safe to assume you'll enjoy a great, affordable vacation—with the finesse of an independent, experienced traveler.

Thanks, and *bon viatge!*

Rick Steves

Back Door Travel Philosophy

From *Rick Steves Europe Through the Back Door*

Travel is intensified living—maximum thrills per minute and one of the last great sources of legal adventure. Travel is freedom. It's recess, and we need it.

Experiencing the real Europe requires catching it by surprise, going casual..."Through the Back Door."

Affording travel is a matter of priorities. (Make do with the old car.) You can eat and sleep—simply, safely, and enjoyably—anywhere in Europe for $125 a day plus transportation costs. In many ways, spending more money only builds a thicker wall between you and what you traveled so far to see. Europe is a cultural carnival, and time after time, you'll find that its best acts are free and the best seats are the cheap ones.

A tight budget forces you to travel close to the ground, meeting and communicating with the people. Never sacrifice sleep, nutrition, safety, or cleanliness to save money. Simply enjoy the local-style alternatives to expensive hotels and restaurants.

Connecting with people carbonates your experience. Extroverts have more fun. If your trip is low on magic moments, kick yourself and make things happen. If you don't enjoy a place, maybe you don't know enough about it. Seek the truth. Recognize tourist traps. Give a culture the benefit of your open mind. See things as different, but not better or worse. Any culture has plenty to share.

Of course, travel, like the world, is a series of hills and valleys. Be fanatically positive and militantly optimistic. If something's not to your liking, change your liking.

Travel can make you a happier American, as well as a citizen of the world. Our Earth is home to seven billion equally precious people. It's humbling to travel and find that other people don't have the "American Dream"—they have their own dreams. Europeans like us, but with all due respect, they wouldn't trade passports.

Thoughtful travel engages us with the world. In tough economic times, it reminds us what is truly important. By broadening perspectives, travel teaches new ways to measure quality of life.

Globetrotting destroys ethnocentricity, helping us understand and appreciate other cultures. Rather than fear the diversity on this planet, celebrate it. Among your most prized souvenirs will be the strands of different cultures you choose to knit into your own character. The world is a cultural yarn shop, and Back Door travelers are weaving the ultimate tapestry. Join in!

ORIENTATION TO BARCELONA

Bustling Barcelona is geographically big and culturally complex. Plan your time carefully, carving up the metropolis into manageable sightseeing neighborhoods. Use my day plans to help prioritize your time, and make advance reservations for sights (or get a sightseeing pass) to save time waiting in lines. For efficiency, learn how to navigate Barcelona by Metro, bus, and taxi. Armed with good information and a thoughtful game plan, you're ready to go. Then you can relax, enjoy, and let yourself be surprised by all that Barcelona has to offer.

BARCELONA: A VERBAL MAP

Like Los Angeles, Barcelona is a basically flat city that sprawls out under the sun between the sea and the mountains. It's huge

(1.6 million people, with about 5 million people in greater Barcelona), but travelers need only focus on four areas: the Old City, the harbor/Barceloneta, the Eixample, and Montjuïc.

A large square, **Plaça de Catalunya,** sits at the center of Barcelona, dividing the older and newer parts of town. Below Plaça de Catalunya is the Old City, with the boulevard called the Ramblas running down to the harbor. Above Plaça de Catalunya is the modern residential area called the Eixample. The Montjuïc hill overlooks the harbor. Outside the Old City, Barcelona's sights are widely scattered, but with a map and a willingness to figure out public transit (or take taxis), all is manageable.

Here are overviews of the major neighborhoods:

Old City (Ciutat Vella): This is the compact core of Barcelona—

ORIENTATION

Greater Barcelona

ideal for strolling, shopping, and people-watching—where you'll probably spend most of your time. It's a labyrinth of narrow streets that once were confined by the medieval walls. The lively pedestrian drag called the **Ramblas**—one of Europe's most entertaining streets—goes through the heart of the Old City from Plaça de Catalunya to the harbor. The Old City is divided into thirds by the Ramblas and another major thoroughfare (running roughly parallel to the

Barcelona Neighborhood Overview

GRÀCIA

Park Güell

EIXAMPLE

LA PEDRERA

SAGRADA FAMÍLIA

PASSEIG DE GRÀCIA

CASA BATLLÓ

Citadel Park

OLD CITY

EL BORN

Plaça de Catalunya

VIA LAIETANA

CATHEDRAL

PICASSO MUSEUM

BARRI GÒTIC

LAS RAMBLAS

SANTS STATION

EL RAVAL

BARCELONETA

Plaça d'Espanya

FUNDACIÓ JOAN MIRÓ

Port Vell

Not to Scale

MONTJUÏC

CRUISE PORT

Mediterranean Sea

← To Airport

ORIENTATION

Ramblas), Via Laietana. Between the Ramblas and Via Laietana is the characteristic **Barri Gòtic** (BAH-ree GOTI-teek, Gothic Quarter), with the cathedral as its navel. Locals call it simply "El Gòtic" for short. To the east of Via Laietana is the trendy **El Born** district (a.k.a. "La Ribera"), a shopping, dining, and nightlife mecca centered on the Picasso Museum and the Church of Santa Maria del Mar. To the west of the Ramblas is the **Raval** (rah-VAHL), enlivened by its university and modern-art museum. The Raval is of least interest to tourists (and, in fact, some parts of it are quite dodgy and should be avoided).

Harborfront: The old harbor, **Port Vell,** gleams with landmark monuments and new developments. A pedestrian bridge links the Ramblas with the modern Maremagnum shopping/aquarium/entertainment complex. On the peninsula across the quaint sailboat harbor is **Barceloneta,** a traditional fishing neighborhood with gritty charm and some good seafood restaurants. Beyond Barceloneta, a gorgeous man-made **beach** several miles long leads east to the commercial and convention district called the **Fòrum.**

Eixample: Above the Old City, beyond the bustling hub of Plaça de Catalunya, is the elegant Eixample (eye-SHAM-plah) district, its grid plan softened by cut-off corners. Much of Barcelona's Modernista architecture is found here—especially along the swanky artery Passeig de Gràcia, an area called **Quadrat d'Or** ("Golden Quarter"). Beyond that is the **Gràcia** district and Antoni Gaudí's **Park Güell.**

Barcelona: From Small to Sprawl

The city of Barcelona has grown with its history. The original Roman town from the time of Christ was contained inside the knot of streets clustered around today's cathedral and enclosed by an oval-shaped ring of Roman walls (stretching basically southeast from the square in front of the cathedral).

When Rome fell (around A.D. 476), the Christian Visigoths made the cathedral the center of town, and the populace remained huddled inside the Roman walls. During the Dark Ages, the city was ruled briefly by Moors (714-801) and Franks (ninth century). When the Counts of Barcelona unified Catalunya (10th century), the city began expanding. They built churches outside the Roman walls (or *extra muro*), each a magnet gathering a small community. By 1250, they needed to build a larger wall to contain these new settlers. This medieval wall stretched from Plaça de Catalunya to the sea, embracing the whole Old Town. The hilltop of Montjuïc—outside the residential area—was topped with a harbor-guarding fortress.

Barcelona is a good example of how a city's architectural heritage rises and falls with economic times. In the 14th century, when the Mediterranean was the epicenter of trade, Barcelona thrived. That's why there are a lot of Gothic buildings here. After 1492, when the Age of Discovery opened up new sea routes, trade shifted to the Atlantic and away from Mediterranean ports. The following centuries saw little grand building in Barcelona.

Then, in the 19th century, Barcelona bounced back, powered by the Industrial Revolution. By 1850, the city was bursting at the seams. The outer wall was torn down and replaced by circular boulevards (named Rondas, meaning "to go around"). The city expanded in a regimented grid of modern boulevards—an urban waffle known as the Eixample. With affluence came big shots with big egos and plenty of money to finance the Modernista architectural wonders that now grace the city.

In 1992, Barcelona hosted the Summer Olympics, which quickly accelerated modernization and stoked Barcelona's economy. In a brilliant move, organizers of the games housed much of the one-time rush of visitors on huge cruise ships. It seems this helped jump-start a thriving cruise ship industry. In 1992, 70 cruise ships called here. Today Barcelona is one of the leading cruise ports in Europe, and last year the city hosted over 800 (much bigger) ships.

A big issue for the character of the city today is the impending end of rent control for landowners and their tenants in the city center. If, as threatened, the ceiling is lifted, many of the charming shops that add so much character to the old quarter will be driven out of business, replaced by branches of much mightier corporate retailers.

Today, Barcelona's population sprawls beyond city maps, creating a greater metropolitan area of some 5 million people—more than half of all the people in Catalunya.

Montjuïc: The large hill overlooking the city to the southwest is Montjuïc (mohn-jew-EEK), home to a variety of attractions, including some excellent museums (Catalan Art, Joan Miró) and the Olympic Stadium. At the base of Montjuïc, stretching toward Plaça d'Espanya, are the former **1929 World Expo Fairgrounds,** with additional fine attractions (including the CaixaForum art gallery and the bullring-turned-mall, Las Arenas).

Apart from your geographical orientation, it's smart to orient yourself linguistically to a language distinct from Spanish. Although Spanish ("Castilian"/*castellano*) is widely spoken, the native tongue in this region is Catalan—nearly as different from Spanish as Italian (see the sidebar on page 6).

PLANNING YOUR TIME

Barcelona is easily worth two days, and no one would regret having a third day (or more). If you can spare only one full day for the city, it will be a scramble, but a day you'll never forget.

When planning your time, be aware that many top sights are closed on Monday—making them especially crowded on Tuesday and Sunday (for itinerary considerations on a day-by-day basis, see the "Daily Reminder," later). Some of Barcelona's major sights can have long lines, such as the Picasso Museum, Sagrada Família, and La Pedrera; it's smart to get advance tickets (see page 25). If you're here on a weekend, dance—or watch—the *sardana* (see page 45).

Barcelona In 1 Day

For a relaxing day, stroll the Ramblas, see the Sagrada Família, add the Picasso Museum if you're a fan, and have dinner in the trendy El Born district.

To fit in much more, try the following ambitious but doable plan. You'll have to rush through the big sights (cathedral, Picasso Museum, Sagrada Família), having just enough time to visit each one but not to linger.

9:00	From Plaça de Catalunya (with its handy TI), follow my Barri Gòtic Walk and Cathedral of Barcelona Tour.
11:00	Circle back to Plaça de Catalunya and follow my self-guided Ramblas Ramble to the harborfront.
12:30	Walk along the harborfront to El Born, grabbing a quick lunch.
14:00	Take my Picasso Museum Tour.
16:00	Hop a taxi or the Metro to the Sagrada Família.
18:00	Taxi, bus, or walk to Passeig de Gràcia in the Eixample to see the exteriors of Gaudí's La Pedrera (a.k.a. Casa Milà) and the Block of Discord. Stroll back down toward Plaça de Catalunya.

ORIENTATION

19:00   If your energy is holding out, wander back into the Barri Gòtic at prime paseo time. Enjoy an early tapas dinner along the way, or a restaurant dinner later in the Old City.

Barcelona in 2, 3, or More Days

To better sample the city's ample charm, spread your visit over several days. With at least two days, divide and conquer the town geographically: Spend one day in the Old City (Ramblas, Barri Gòtic/cathedral area, Picasso Museum/El Born) and another on the Eixample and Gaudí sights (La Pedrera, Sagrada Família, Park Güell). Do Montjuïc on whichever day you're not exhausted (if any)—or, better yet, on a third day.

With extra time on any day, consider taking a hop-on, hop-off bus tour for a sightseeing overview (for instance, the Tourist Bus blue route links most Gaudí sights and could work well on Day 2).

Day 1—Old City

9:00   Follow my Barri Gòtic Walk and Cathedral of Barcelona Tour.

11:00   Head to the Ramblas using the route described in my "Barri Gòtic Shopping Walk," then follow my Ramblas Ramble (touring Palau Güell if you're a Gaudí fan) down to the harborfront.

13:00   Grab lunch in El Born or the Barri Gòtic.

14:00   Tour the Palace of Catalan Music in El Born (advance reservation required).

15:00   Follow my El Born Walk, and en route, do the Picasso Museum Tour. Afterwards complete the El Born Walk and shop to your heart's content.

Evening   Take your pick of activities: Assemble an early tapas dinner by hopping from bar to bar in El Born, and take "A Short, Sweet Walk" (page 207) for dessert. (Other good neighborhoods for tapas are the classy Eixample or touristy Barri Gòtic.) Or wait to dine at a restaurant when locals do, around 21:00. Visit a sight that's open late (for a list, see page 232). Take in a performance of Spanish guitar, flamenco or jazz, or a concert in a fancy setting (such as La Pedrera or the Palace of Catalan Music). Zip up to Montjuïc for the sunset and a drink on the Catalan Art Museum's terrace, then head down to the illuminated Magic Fountains (Fri-Sat, plus Sun and Thu in summer). Head to Barceloneta and choose your favorite *chiringuito* beach bar. For more ideas, see the Nightlife in Barcelona chapter.

Day 2—Modernisme

9:00   Take my Eixample Walk, touring La Pedrera, Casa Lleó Morera (reservation required), and/or Casa Batlló.

12:00   Eat an early lunch in the Eixample, then take a taxi or bus to the Sagrada Família.

14:00   Choose among these options: Taxi or bus to Park Güell for more Gaudí. Or take the bus to Montjuïc (if you're not going to Montjuïc on Day 3) to enjoy the city view and your pick of sights. Or explore the harborfront La Rambla de Mar and Old Port (unless you already did this on Day 1, at the end of the Ramblas Ramble).

Evening   Choose among the evening activities listed earlier.

Day 3—Montjuïc and Barceloneta

Tour Montjuïc from top to bottom, stopping at sights of interest. The top priorities are the Catalan Art Museum, CaixaForum, and Fundació Joan Miró. If the weather is good, take the scenic cable-car ride down from Montjuïc to the port, and spend the rest of the day at Barceloneta—stroll the promenade, hit the beach, and find your favorite *chiringuito* (beach bar) for dinner.

Day 4

Consider these options: Visit the markets (La Boqueria and Santa Caterina—both closed Sun). Tour more sights (Palau Güell's Modernista interior, Barcelona History Museum, Frederic Marès Museum, Chocolate Museum, and more). Take a walking or bike tour. Relax or rent a rowboat in Citadel Park.

Days 5-7

With more time, choose among several tempting day trips, including the mountaintop monastery of Montserrat, the beach resort town of Sitges, and the Salvador Dalí sights at Figueres and Cadaqués (see the Day Trips from Barcelona chapter).

Connecting with the Rest of Spain

Located in the far northeast corner of Spain, Barcelona makes a good first or last stop for your trip. With the high-speed AVE train, Barcelona is three hours away from Madrid—faster and more comfortable than flying. Or you could sandwich Barcelona between flights. From the US, it's as easy to fly into Barcelona as it is to land in Madrid, Lisbon, or Paris. Those who plan on renting a car at some point during their trip can start here first, take the train or fly to Madrid, and sightsee Madrid and Toledo, all before picking up their car—cleverly saving on several days' worth of rental fees. For more on train travel and car rentals in Spain, see the Practicalities chapter.

Daily Reminder

Sunday: Most sights are open, but Casa Lleó Morera and the Boqueria and Santa Caterina markets are closed. Some sights close early today, including the Fundació Joan Miró, Olympic and Sports Museum, and Camp Nou Stadium (all close at 14:30), along with the Chocolate Museum and Catalan Art Museum (close at 15:00). Informal performances of the *sardana* national dance take place in front of the cathedral at noon (none in Aug). Some museums are free at certain times: Catalan Art Museum and Palau Güell (free on first Sun of month); Picasso Museum, Barcelona History Museum, and the Frederic Marès Museum (free on first Sun of month plus other Sun from 15:00). The Magic Fountains come alive on summer evenings (May-Sept).

Monday: Many sights are closed, including the Picasso Museum, Catalan Art Museum, Palau Güell, Barcelona History Museum, *Santa Eulàlia* schooner (part of the Maritime Museum), Fundació Joan Miró, Frederic Marès Museum, Shoe Museum, El Born Cultural Center, and Olympic and Sports Museum. But most major Modernista sights are open today, including the Sagrada Família, La Pedrera, Park Güell, Casa Batlló, and Casa Lleó Morera.

Tuesday: All major sights are open.

Wednesday: All major sights are open.

Thursday: All major sights are open. Fundació Joan Miró and the Picasso Museum are open until 21:30 year-round, and the Magic Fountains spout on summer evenings (May-Sept).

Friday: All major sights are open. The Magic Fountains light up Montjuïc year-round.

Saturday: All major sights are open. Barcelonans occasionally dance the *sardana* on Saturdays at 18:00 in front of the cathedral, and in summer you're likely to see traditional folk activities there at 19:30. The Magic Fountains dance all year. The Catalan Art Museum is free after 15:00.

Late-Hours Sightseeing: Sights with **year-round** evening hours (19:30 or later) include the Boqueria Market, Maritime Museum, CaixaForum, Cathedral of Barcelona, Casa Batlló, Columbus Monument, Mies van der Rohe Pavilion, Las Arenas, and Church of Santa Maria del Mar.

Sights offering later hours only in **peak season** (roughly April-Sept) include the Sagrada Família, La Pedrera, Palau Güell, *Santa Eulàlia* schooner, Chocolate Museum, Park Güell, Camp Nou, Fundació Joan Miró, Olympic and Sports Museum, Catalan Art Museum, Castle of Montjuïc, Spanish Village, and Gaudí House Museum (for a rundown on specific times, see the sidebar on page 232).

Overview

TOURIST INFORMATION

Barcelona's TI has several branches (central tel. 932-853-834, www.barcelonaturisme.cat). The primary one is beneath the main square, **Plaça de Catalunya** (daily 8:30-20:30, entrance just across from El Corte Inglés department store—look for red sign and take stairs down, tel. 932-853-832).

Several other convenient branches include a kiosk near the top of the **Ramblas** (daily 8:30-20:30, at #115); on **Plaça de Sant Jaume,** just south of the cathedral (Mon-Fri 8:30-20:00, Sat 9:00-19:00, Sun 9:00-14:00, in the Barcelona City Hall at Ciutat 2); near the **cathedral,** in the Catalan College of Architects building (daily 9:00-19:00); inside the base of the **Columbus Monument** at the harbor (daily 8:30-19:30); at the **airport** in terminals 1 and 2B (both open daily 8:30-20:30); and at the **Sants train station** (daily 8:00-20:00).

You'll also find smaller info kiosks in other touristy locales: on **Plaça d'Espanya,** in the park across from the **Sagrada Família** entrance, near the **Columbus Monument** (where the shuttle bus from the cruise port arrives), at the **Nord bus station,** at the various **cruise terminals** along the port, and two on **Plaça de Catalunya.** In addition, throughout the summer, young red-jacketed tourist-info helpers appear in the most touristy parts of town; although they work for the hop-on, hop-off Tourist Bus, they are happy to answer questions.

At any TI, pick up the free city map (although the free El Corte Inglés map provided by most hotels is better), the small Metro map, the monthly *Barcelona Planning.com* guidebook (with basic tips on sightseeing, shopping, events, and restaurants), and the quarterly *See Barcelona* guide (with more in-depth practical information on museums and a neighborhood-by-neighborhood sightseeing rundown). The monthly *Time Out BCN Guide* offers a concise but thorough day-by-day list of events. And the monthly *Barcelona Metropolitan* magazine has timely and substantial coverage of local topics and events. All of these are free.

TIs are handy places to buy tickets for the Tourist Bus (described later, under "Getting Around Barcelona") or for the TI-run walking tours (described later, under "Tours in Barcelona"). They also sell tickets to FC Barcelona soccer games. All of the TIs (except the kiosks) provide a room-booking service.

Modernisme Route: Inside the Plaça de Catalunya TI is the privately run **Ruta del Modernisme** desk, which gives out a handy route map showing all 116 Modernista buildings and offers a sightseeing discount package (€12 for a great guidebook and 20-50-percent discounts to many Modernista sights—worthwhile

ORIENTATION

Central Barcelona

To Sagrada Família

AVINGUDA DIAGONAL

PALAU BARÓ DE QUADRAS

LA CONCEPCIÓ MARKET

Ⓜ Diagonal

LA PEDRERA

CHURCH OF THE HOLY CONCEPTION

Ⓜ Diagonal (to Sagrada Família)

Girona

EIX

Provença Ⓑ Ⓜ

Ⓡ Provença Train Station

QUADRAT D'OR

Water Tower Gardens

CATALANES

Ⓡ Passeig de Gràcia Train Station

CASA BATLLÓ

Ⓡ

Ⓜ Passeig de Gràcia

CASA AMATLLER

BLOCK OF DISCORD

CASA LLEÓ MORERA

CORTS

Plaça del Doctor Letamendi

Ⓜ Passeig de Gràcia

EL CORTE INGLÉS DEP'T STORE

VIA LAIETANA

Urquinaona

Bus to Airport (& Taxis) Ⓑ

Ⓜ Catalunya

Plaça de Catalunya

S. ANNA

Universitat Ⓜ

Bergara

Ⓡ FNAC

Catalunya

PORTAL DE L'ANGEL

200 Meters
200 Yards

C. DELS TALLERS

FOUNTAIN

MACBA CONTEMPORARY ART MUSEUM

Ⓜ Urgell

Plaça dels Angels

LAS RAMBLAS

ROMAN NECRÓPOLIS

BETLEM CHURCH

Plaça del Pi

Ⓜ Liceu

To Plaça d'Espanya

Plaça del Pedró

OLD

LA BOQUERIA MARKET

S. MARIA DEL PI

MIRÓ MOSAIC

Ⓜ Liceu

EL RAVAL

LICEU OPERA HOUSE

SANT ANTONI MARKET

PALAU GÜELL

Ⓜ Sant Antoni

RAMBLA DEL RAVAL

To Plaça d'Espanya & Sants Station

AVINGUDA DE MISTRAL

Poble Sec Ⓜ

Ⓜ Paral-lel

AVINGUDA DEL PARAL-LEL

Plaça d'El Molino

Plaça de Santa Madrona

FUNICULAR

MARE DE DÉU DEL REMEI

Plaça del Sortidor

To Montjuïc

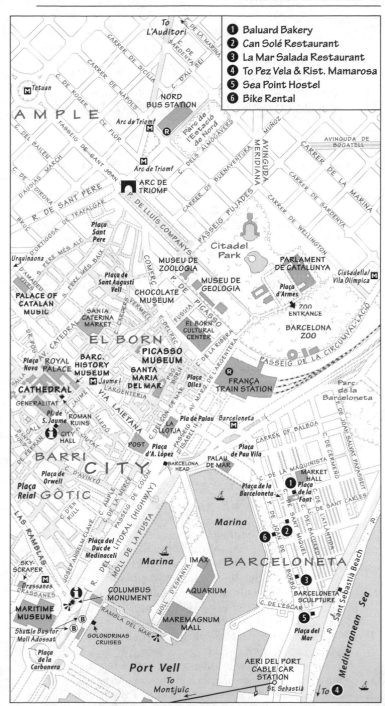

1. Baluard Bakery
2. Can Solé Restaurant
3. La Mar Salada Restaurant
4. To Pez Vela & Rist. Mamarosa
5. Sea Point Hostel
6. Bike Rental

ORIENTATION

if going beyond the biggies I cover in depth; for €18 you'll also get a guidebook to Modernista bars and restaurants; www.rutadelmodernisme.com).

Regional Catalunya TI: The all-Catalunya TI can help with travel and sightseeing tips for the entire region, and even Madrid (Mon-Sat 10:00-19:00, Sun 10:00-14:00, in Palau Robert building near the intersection of Passeig de Gràcia and Diagonal at Passeig de Gràcia 107, tel. 932-388-091, www.catalunya.com).

Sightseeing Passes: The **Articket BCN** ticket covers admission to six art museums and their temporary exhibits, letting you skip the ticket-buying lines. Sights include the recommended Picasso Museum, Catalan Art Museum, and Fundació Joan Miró (€30, valid for three months; sold at participating museums and the TIs at Plaça de Catalunya, Plaça de Sant Jaume, and Sants Station; www.articketbcn.org). If you're planning to go to three or more of the museums, this ticket will save you money and time, especially at sights prone to long lines, such as the Picasso Museum. Just show your Articket BCN (to the ticket taker, at the info desk, or at the group entrance), and you'll get your entrance ticket pronto.

On the other hand, I'd skip the **Barcelona Card,** which covers public transportation (buses, Metro, Montjuïc funicular, and *golondrinas* harbor tour) and includes free admission to mostly minor sights and small discounts on many major sights (€34/2 days, €44/3 days, €52/4 days, €58/5 days, sold at TIs and El Corte Inglés department stores, www.barcelonaturisme.com).

ARRIVAL IN BARCELONA

For more information on getting to or from Barcelona by train, plane, bus, or cruise ship, see the Barcelona Connections chapter.

HELPFUL HINTS

Theft and Scam Alert: You're more likely to be pickpocketed here—especially on the Ramblas—than about anywhere else in Europe. Most crime is nonviolent, but muggings do occur. Leave valuables in your hotel and wear a money belt.

Street scams are easy to avoid if you recognize them. Most common is the too-friendly local who tries to engage you in conversation by asking for the time or whether you speak English. If a super-friendly man acts drunk and wants to dance because his soccer team just won, he's a pickpocket. Beware of thieves posing as lost tourists who ask for your help. Don't fall for any street-gambling shell games. Beware of groups of women aggressively selling carnations, people offering to clean off a stain from your shirt, and so on. If you stop for any commotion or show on the Ramblas, put your hands in your pockets before someone else does. Assume any scuffle is simply

Sight Reservations and Advance Tickets

In busy Barcelona, you'll minimize your time in lines by getting advance tickets. For the last two sights, reservations are required.

Picasso Museum	Buy a ticket online (www.museupicasso.bcn.cat) or an Articket BCN on site (see page 24).
Sagrada Família	Timed-entry advance tickets sold online for entry and towers (www.sagradafamilia.cat, see page 151).
Casa Batlló	Advance tickets online (www.casabatllo.cat, see page 54).
La Pedrera & Casa Milà	Timed-entry advance tickets online (www.lapedrera.com, see page 56).
Palau Güell	Timed-entry advance tickets on site or online (www.palauguell.cat, see page 37).
Park Güell	Timed-entry tickets for Monumental Zone online (www.parkguell.cat, see page 163).
Palace of Catalan Music	Tour tickets sold online, by phone, or at on site box office (tel. 902-475-485, www.palaumusica.cat, see page 40).
Casa Lleó Morera	Tour tickets sold online (www.casalleomorera.com) or at culture center Palau de la Virreina, Ramblas 99 (see page 55).

a distraction by a team of thieves. Don't be intimidated...just be smart.

Personal Safety: Some areas feel seedy and can be unsafe after dark; I'd avoid the southern part of the Barri Gòtic (basically the two or three blocks directly south and east of Plaça Reial—though the strip near the Carrer de la Mercè tapas bars is better), and I wouldn't venture too deep into the Raval (just west of the Ramblas). One block can separate a comfy tourist zone from the junkies and prostitutes.

Avoiding Lines: To avoid standing in long lines at sights, it's smart to book ahead for tickets (and in some cases, it's required). For details, see the sidebar on page 25.

Festivals: Barcelona erupts with festivals all year long. For a list of the major ones, see the sidebar.

Language Barrier: In posted information throughout the city (such as museum descriptions), English plays third fiddle. You'll see Catalan first, Spanish *(castellano)* second, and English a distant third...or often not at all. Fortunately, many locals speak English.

Web Addresses: If a website doesn't work, try replacing the ".com" or ".es" with ".cat"—the web suffix for Catalunya. Many businesses are switching to this.

Internet Access: The free city network, Barcelona WiFi, has hundreds of hotspots around town; just look for the blue diamond-shaped sign with a big "W" (for details, see www.bcn.cat/barcelonawifi). And every hotel I recommend offers Wi-Fi.

Baggage Storage: Locker Barcelona is located near the recommended Hotel Denit. You can pay for the day and access your locker as many times as you want (daily 9:00-21:00, €3.50-9.50 depending on locker size, Carrer Estruc 36, tel. 933-028-796, www.lockerbarcelona.com).

Pharmacy: A 24-hour pharmacy is across from La Boqueria Market at #98 on the Ramblas. Another is on the corner of Passeig de Gràcia #90 and Provença, just opposite the entrance to La Pedrera.

Laundry: Several self-service launderettes are located around the Old City. The clean-as-a-whistle LavaXpres is centrally located near recommended Plaça de Catalunya and Ramblas hotels (self-service-€8/load, instructions in English, daily 8:00-22:00, Passatge d'Elisabets 3—see map on page 178, www.lavaxpres.com). Wash 'n Dry, just off the Ramblas, is in a seedier neighborhood just down the street past Palau Güell (self-service-€6.50/load, full service-€14.50/load, daily 9:00-23:00, Carrer Nou de la Rambla 19—see map on page 178, tel. 934-121-953).

Bike Rental: Biking is a joy in Citadel Park, the Eixample, and along the beach (suggested route described on page 72), but it's stressful in the city center, where pedestrians and cars rule. There are bike-rental places popping up in just about every part of the city; I've listed just a few. The handy **Un Cotxe Menys** ("One Car Less"), near the Church of Santa Maria del Mar (50 yards behind the flame memorial), rents bikes and gives out maps and suggested biking routes (€5/hour, €10/4 hours, €15/24 hours, daily 10:00-19:00, leave €150 or photo ID for deposit, Carrer de l'Esparteria 3—see map on page 178, tel. 932-682-105, www.bicicletabarcelona.com); they also lead bike tours (see "Tours in Barcelona," later).

To rent a bike on the Barceloneta beach, consider **Biciclot** (€5/hour, €10/3 hours, €17/24 hours, daily in summer

ORIENTATION

City of Festivals

Barcelona celebrates more festivals, markets, and street fairs than your average city. They dance the *sardana* (a circle dance), build human pyramids, parade colorful *gegants* (giant puppets), and light up the night with fireworks displays called *correfoc* (fire run). Here's a rundown of Barcelona's most lively festivals, listed roughly in chronological order.

Les Festes de Santa Eulàlia: Celebrating the patron saint of the city, this four-day festival features parades, dancing, *correfocs,* and many kid-friendly activities (mid-Feb, www.bcn.cat/santaeulalia).

El Día de Sant Jordi: This celebration of St. George, the patron saint of Catalunya, is also Barcelona's version of Valentine's Day, when lovers exchange books and flowers, and the streets are draped with the red-and-gold Catalan flag (April 23).

Corpus Christi: Barcelona's oldest festival, dating to 1320, contains traditional elements such as processions, music, and "dancing" eggs. The eggs, placed in decorated fountains, spin ("dance") atop jets of water (early June, go to http://barcelonacultura.bcn.cat and click on "Festivals and Traditions").

Grec Festival de Barcelona: The city's premier summer arts festival has dance, theater, and music, with several events at Teatre Grec—a Greek-style amphitheater (usually July, http://grec.bcn.cat).

Música als Parcs: Jazz and classical music fill the air in this popular series of evening concerts at city parks (June-Aug).

La Festa Catalana: The city hosts a little spectacle of local folk traditions—human towers *(castells),* giant puppets *(gegants),* folk music and dancing—in spring and summer on the square in front of the cathedral (Saturdays at 19:30, May through Sept, ask at TI or your hotel for more details).

Montjuïc de Nit: During this dusk-to-dawn celebration of music, cinema, art, theater, and dance, many museums stay open until at least 3:00 in the morning (mid-July, www.bcn.cat/cultura/montjuicnit).

Festes de Sant Roc: Barcelona's oldest festival is also the Barri Gòtic's biggest street party, filled with *gegants, sardana* dancing, street games, and fireworks (mid-Aug, go to http://barcelonacultura.bcn.cat and click on "Festivals and Traditions").

Festa Major de Gràcia: For eight days and nights, this festival features live music, *sardana* dancing, human pyramids, and traditional food and drinks (mid-Aug, www.festamajordegracia.cat).

La Mercè: Running five days, Barcelona's main street festival has fireworks, music, an air show, human pyramids, a parade, and much more (late Sept, www.bnc.cat/merce).

10:00-20:00, shorter hours off-season, on the sand 300 yards from Olympic Village towers at Passeig Maritime 33, tel. 932-219-778, www.bikinginbarcelona.net). Another beach option is **Barcelona Rent-A-Bike,** about four blocks from the Barceloneta Metro stop (€6/2 hours, €10/4 hours, €15/24 hours, includes helmet, daily 10:00-20:00, Passeig de Joan de Borbó 35, tel. 932-212-790, www.barcelonarentabike.com); they also have a city-center location three blocks from Plaça de Catalunya (daily 9:30-20:00, inside the courtyard at Carrer dels Tallers 45—see map on page 178, tel. 933-171-970).

You'll see racks of government-subsidized "Bicing" **borrow-a-bikes** around town, but these are only for locals, not tourists.

Updates to This Book: For any changes to this book's coverage since it was published, see www.ricksteves.com/update.

GETTING AROUND BARCELONA

Barcelona's Metro and bus system is run by **TMB**—Transports Metropolitans de Barcelona (tel. 902-075-027, www.tmb.cat). It's worth asking for TMB's excellent Metro/bus map at the TI, larger stations, or the TMB information counter in the Sants train station (not always available).

By Metro

The city's Metro, among Europe's best, connects just about every place you'll visit. A single-ride ticket *(bitllet senzill)* costs €2.15. The T10 Card is a great deal—€10.30 gives you 10 rides (cutting the per-ride cost more than in half). The card is shareable, even by companions traveling with you (insert the card in the machine per passenger). The back of your T10 card will show how many trips were taken, with the time and date of each ride. One "ride" covers you for 1.25 hours of unlimited use on all Metro and local bus lines, as well as local rides on the RENFE and Rodalies de Catalunya train lines (including rides to the airport and train station) and the suburban FGC trains. Transfers made within your 1.25-hour limit are not counted as a new ride, but you still must revalidate your T10 Card whenever you transfer.

Multiday "Hola BCN!" passes are also available (€14/2 days, €20/3 days, €25.50/4 days, €30.50/5 days). Machines at the Metro entrance have English instructions and sell all types of tickets (most machines accept credit/debit cards as well as cash).

Whatever type of ticket you use, keep it until you have exited the subway. You don't need the ticket to go through the exit, but inspectors occasionally ask riders to show it.

Barcelona has several color-coded lines, but most useful for tourists is the **L3 (green)** line. Handy city-center stops on this line include (in order):

Sants Estació—Main train station

Espanya—Plaça d'Espanya, with access to the lower part of Montjuïc and trains to Montserrat

Paral-lel—Funicular to the top of Montjuïc

Drassanes—Bottom of the Ramblas, near Maritime Museum and Maremagnum mall

Liceu—Middle of the Ramblas, near the heart of the Barri Gòtic and cathedral

Plaça de Catalunya—Top of the Ramblas and main square with TI, airport bus, and lots of transportation connections

Passeig de Gràcia—Classy Eixample street at the Block of Discord; also connection to L2 (purple) line to Sagrada Família and L4 (yellow) line (described below)

Diagonal—Gaudí's La Pedrera

The **L4 (yellow)** line, which crosses the L3 (green) line at Passeig de Gràcia, is also useful. Helpful stops include **Joanic** (bus #116 to Park Güell), **Jaume I** (between the Barri Gòtic/cathedral and El Born/Picasso Museum), and **Barceloneta** (at the south end of El Born, near the harbor action).

Before riding the Metro, study a map (available at TIs and posted at entrances) to get familiar with the system. Look for your line number and color, and find the end stop for your direction of travel. Enter the Metro by inserting your ticket into the turnstile (with the arrow pointing in), then reclaim it. Follow signs for your line and direction. On board, most trains have handy lighted displays that indicate upcoming stops. Because the lines cross one another multiple times, there can be several ways to make any one journey. (It's a good idea to keep a general map with you—especially if you're transferring.)

Watch your valuables. If I were a pickpocket, I'd set up shop along the made-for-tourists L3 (green) line.

By Bus

Given the excellent Metro service, it's unlikely you'll spend much time on **local buses** (also €2.15, covered by T10 Card, insert ticket in machine behind driver). However, buses are useful for reaching Park Güell, connecting the sights on Montjuïc, and getting to the beach.

The handy **hop-on, hop-off Tourist Bus** (Bus Turístic) offers three multistop circuits in colorful double-decker buses that go topless in sunny weather. The two-hour blue route covers north Barcelona (most Gaudí sights); the two-hour red route covers south

Barcelona's Public Transportation

To Zona Universitària

To Cornella

To Trinitat Nova

Park Güell #24, #92

#116 Lesseps M B

#116 B

#116 B

Joanic M

CAMP NOU STADIUM B #50

Maria Cristina

Les Corts

GRÀCIA

Fontana M

Verdaguer

LA PEDRERA

Diagonal M Girona

Collblanc

Plaça del Centre

EIXAMPLE

PASSEIG DE GRÀCIA STATION

Passeig de Gràcia #50

Metro Line #4 (Yellow)

SANTS MAIN TRAIN STATION
Trains to Airport, Sitges, Figueres, Madrid & other destinations

CASA BATLLÓ

Hospital Clinic

Plaça de Catalunya

To Montserrat

Metro Line #5 (Blue)

Entença M

Universitat M

Catalunya M

#24, #55

LAS

Tarragona M

AeroBus

Metro Line #1 (Red)

AeroBus

Liceu M

EL RAVAL

R M #150 B Espanya

B #55 M Paral·lel M

Poble Sec

AeroBus

CAIXA-FORUM

Plaça d'Espanya

FUNICULAR

To Airport

FUNDACIÓ JOAN MIRÓ

#55, #150 B

MIRAMAR

#150 B

MONTJUÏC

CABLE CAR

Note: Many long-distance trains use França, Passeig de Gràcia, and Catalunya stations in addition to Sants station.

MONTJUÏC CASTLE B #150

Barcelona (Barri Gòtic and Montjuïc); and the shorter, 40-minute green route covers the beaches and modern Fòrum complex (this route runs April-Oct only). All have headphone commentary (daily 9:00-20:00 in summer, until 19:00 in winter, buses run every 10-25 minutes, most frequent in summer, www.barcelonabusturistic.cat). Ask for a brochure (includes city map) at the TI or at a pickup point. One-day (€27) and two-day (€35) tickets, which you can buy on the

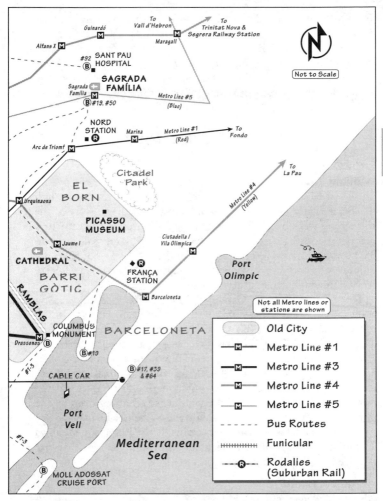

bus, at the TI, or online, offer 10 to 20 percent discounts on the city's major sights and walking tours, which will likely save you about the equivalent of half the cost of the Tourist Bus. From Plaça de Catalunya, the blue northern route leaves from El Corte Inglés; the red southern route leaves from the west—Ramblas—side of the square. A different company, **Barcelona City Tour,** offers a nearly identical service (same price and discounts, two loops instead of three, www.barcelonacitytour.cat).

By Taxi

Barcelona is one of Europe's best taxi towns. Taxis are plentiful (there are more than 11,000) and honest, whether they like it or not. The light on top shows which tariff they're charging; a green light on the roof indicates that a taxi is available. Cab rates are reasonable (€2.05 drop charge, €1/kilometer, these "*Tarif 2*" rates are in effect 8:00-20:00, pay higher "*Tarif 1*" rates off-hours, €2.10 surcharge to/from train station, €4.20 surcharge for airport or cruise port, other fees posted in window). Save time by hopping a cab (figure €10 from Ramblas to Sants Station).

Tours in Barcelona

ON FOOT
Walking Tours

The TI at Plaça de Sant Jaume offers great guided walks through the **Barri Gòtic** in English. You'll learn the medieval story of the city as you walk from Plaça de Sant Jaume through the cathedral neighborhood (€15.50, daily at 9:30, 2 hours, groups limited to 35, buy your ticket 15 minutes early at the TI desk—not from the guide, in summer stop by the office a day ahead to reserve, tel. 932-853-832, www.barcelonaturisme.cat).

The TI at Plaça de Catalunya offers a **Picasso** walk, taking you through the streets of his youth and early career and finishing in the Picasso Museum (€21.50, includes museum admission; Tue, Thu, and Sat at 15:00; 2 hours including museum visit). There are also walks for **gourmets** (€21.50, Fri and Sat at 10:30, 2 hours) and fans of **Modernisme** (€15.50, Fri and Sat 16:00, June-Sept at 18:00, 2 hours). Other themes include literary Barcelona, the Spanish Civil War, and a medieval tour for children (drop by the office for a full list). It's always smart to reserve in advance.

The Ruta del Modernisme desk inside the Plaça de Catalunya TI does tours of specific **Modernista buildings** that are otherwise not open to the public (see page 21).

"Free" Walking Tours

About a dozen companies offer "free" walks that rely on—and expect—tips to stay in business. Though led by young people who've basically memorized a clever script (rather than trained historians), these walks can be a fun, casual way to get your bearings.

Runner Bean Tours, run by Gorka, Ann-Marie, and a handful of local guides, is reliable and well-established. They offer 2.5-hour, English-only walks covering the Old City and Gaudí (both tours depart from Plaça Reial daily at 11:00 year-round, plus daily at 16:30 in April-mid-Oct, mobile 636-108-776, www.runnerbeantours.com). They also do night tours, family walks, and more. Groups can range from just a couple of people up to 30.

Discover Walks does similar daily tours in summer (Fri-Mon only off-season), with three different two-hour itineraries: Gaudí

(10:30, meet in front of Casa Batlló); Ramblas and Barri Gòtic (15:00, meet in front of Liceu Opera House on the Ramblas); and Picasso's Barcelona, covering the El Born neighborhood (17:00, meet at Plaça de l'Angel next to Jaume I Metro stop). This company distinguishes itself by using exclusively native-born guides—no expats (suggested tips: €5/person for a bad guide, €10 for a good one, €15 for a great one, www.discoverwalks.com, tel. 931-816-810).

Local Guides

The **Barcelona Guide Bureau** is a co-op with about 20 local guides who give themed tours as well as private, customized tours (check website for prices of themed walks; customized tours-€102/person for 2, €53/person for 4, Via Laietana 54, tel. 932-682-422 or 933-107-778, www.barcelonaguidebureau.com).

José Soler is a great and fun-to-be-with local guide who enjoys tailoring a walk through his hometown to your interests (€225/half-day per group, mobile 615-059-326, www.pepitotours.com, info@pepitotours.com). He and his driver can take small groups by car or van on a four-hour Barcelona Highlights tour (€425) and can meet you at your hotel, the cruise port, or airport.

Cristina Sanjuán of Live Barcelona is another good, professional guide who leads walking tours and can also arrange cruise excursions (€155/2 hours, €20/each additional hour; €195 extra for a car for up to 2 people, €220 extra for up to 6; tel. 936-327-259, mobile 609-205-844, www.livebarcelona.com, info@livebarcelona.com).

ON WHEELS

Guided Bus Tours

The **Barcelona Guide Bureau** offers several sightseeing tours leaving from Plaça de Catalunya. Tours include most sight admissions and are designed to end at a major sight in case you'd like to spend more time there. The Gaudí tour visits Casa Batlló and Sagrada Família, as well as the facade of La Pedrera (€62, daily at 9:00, 3.5 hours). Other tours offered year-round include Montjuïc (€33, daily at 12:30, 2.5 hours); All Barcelona Highlights (€59, daily at 10:00, also mid-April-Oct at 12:30, 5 hours); and Montserrat (€47, Mon-Sat at 15:00, 4 hours—a convenient way to get to this mountaintop monastery if you don't want to deal with public transportation; see Near Barcelona chapter). During the high season, there are additional Gaudí-focused tours, Ramblas walks, shopping tours, and a Fundació Joan Miró tour. You can get details and book tickets at a TI, on their website, or simply by showing up at their departure point on Plaça de Catalunya in front of the Deutsche Bank (next to Hard Rock Café—look for the guides holding orange umbrellas; tel. 933-152-261, www.barcelonaguidebureau.com).

Catalunya Tourist Bus also runs excursions to nearby destinations, including some that are difficult to reach by public transportation. Trips include **Montserrat** (€61, 8 hours, includes Gaudí's unfinished Colònia Güell development) and **Salvador Dalí sights** in Figueres and Girona (€73, 11 hours). Both itineraries depart Tuesday through Sunday at 8:30 from Plaça de Catalunya in front of El Corte Inglés (live trilingual commentary in Catalan, Spanish, and English; €5 extra for a more in-depth English audioguide; book at TIs, by phone, or online—10 percent Web discount; tel. 932-853-832, www.catalunyabusturistic.com).

For information on **hop-on, hop-off bus tours,** see "Getting Around Barcelona," earlier.

Bike Tours

Several companies run bike tours around Barcelona.

Un Cotxe Menys ("One Car Less") offers three-hour English-only bike tours daily at 11:00 year-round (April-mid-Sept also Fri-Mon at 16:30; rents bikes, too—see "Helpful Hints," earlier). Your guide leads you from sight to sight, mostly on bike paths and through parks, with a stop-and-go commentary (€22, no reservations needed, tours meet just outside TI on Plaça Sant Jaume in Barri Gòtic—or, 10 minutes later, at their bike shop in El Born near the Church of Santa Maria del Mar; Carrer de l'Esparteria 3—see map on page 178, tel. 932-682-105, www.catalunyabusturistic. com).

Barcelona CicloTour runs a similar itinerary (€22, 3 hours, departs from Hard Rock Café on Plaça de Catalunya daily at 11:00, also at 16:30 daily mid-April-Oct and Sat-Sun in Nov; 19:30 night tour departs Fri-Sun June-Sept and Fri-Sat in Oct; tel. 933-171-970, www.barcelonaciclotour.com).

OTHER TOURS AND ACTIVITIES
Spanish Civil War Tours

Nick Lloyd, who is a passionate teacher, takes small groups on walks through the old town to explain the social context and significance of the Spanish Civil War (1936-1939) in Barcelona. History buffs absolutely love this tour (€20/person, 3 hours, English only, Sun, Tue, Fri 10:00, other times according to demand, www. iberianature.com, nick.iberianature@gmail.com).

Cooking Classes and Food Tours

Cook & Taste offers private and group cooking classes in which you'll make and eat four traditional dishes paired with local wines (group classes daily at 11:00 and 17:00, €65/person, €13 extra for guided La Boquería visit offered Tue-Sat morning or Fri afternoon; private class—2 people-€215/person, 3-4 people-€150/person, includes La Boquería visit, meal, wine and recipes to take home;

Carrer Paradís 3, tel. 933-021-320, www.cookandtaste.net, info@ cookandtaste.net). They also offer a gastronomic tour guided by a chef who shows you gourmet food and wine shops, La Boquería Market, and includes some tastings (2 people-€240 per tour, 3-4 people-€265 per tour).

At **The Barcelona Taste,** Joe Littenberg and Jo Marvel, American ex-pat foodie guides and long-time Barcelona residents, take a small group of two to eight on a guided walk, making three or four stops in roughly three hours. They enthusiastically introduce you to lots of local taste treats and drinks. You can choose from a tour of the Barri Gòtic or the Gràcia neighborhood on the far side of the Eixample (€75/person, Tue-Sat at 19:00, www.thebarcelonataste. com, contact@thebarcelonataste.com).

Weekend Tour Packages for Students
Andy Steves (my son) runs **WSA Europe,** offering three-day and longer guided and unguided packages—including accommodations, sightseeing, and unique local experiences—for budget travelers across 11 top European cities, including Barcelona (from €99, see www.wsaeurope.com for details).

ORIENTATION

SIGHTS IN BARCELONA

The sights listed in this chapter are primarily arranged by neighborhood for handy sightseeing. When you see a ✪ in a listing, it means the sight is covered in much more depth in one of my walks or self-guided tours.

For tips on sightseeing, see page 282 in the Practicalities chapter. For some sights, it's either required or highly recommended that you make advance reservations (see "Sight Reservations and Advance Tickets" sidebar, page 25). Also, remember to check www.ricksteves.com/update for any significant changes that may have occurred since this book was printed.

ON OR NEAR THE RAMBLAS
▲▲▲The Ramblas

Meandering through the heart of the Old City is the Ramblas, Barcelona's most famous boulevard. Named for the long-gone

stream *(rambla)* whose course it followed, the Ramblas flows from Plaça de Catalunya, past the core of the Barri Gòtic, to the harborfront Columbus Monument. Boasting a generous pedestrian strip down the middle, the Ramblas features vibrant flower vendors, exuberantly costumed "human statues" that spring to life for a coin, and the booming **La Boqueria Market,** rife with fine people-watching opportunities.

For a self-guided tour of this pedestrian boulevard, see ✪ The Ramblas Ramble chapter.

▲La Boqueria Market

Barcelona has many characteristic market halls, but this is the most central—and the most crowded. Housed in a cool glass-and-steel structure, La Boqueria features a wide variety of produce and Catalan edibles that you'll pay a premium for. For less touristy markets, consider Santa Caterina in El Born (with avant-garde architecture; see page 117) or La Concepció in the Eixample (with a neighborhood vibe; see page 142). Still, La Boqueria's handy location right in the heart of the Old City makes it well worth a visit.

Cost and Hours: Free, Mon-Sat 8:00-20:00, best on mornings after 9:00, closed Sun, Rambla 91, tel. 933-192-584, www.boqueria.info.

For a self-guided walk through the market, see page 83 in ❂ The Ramblas Ramble chapter.

▲Palau Güell

Just as the Picasso Museum reveals a young genius on the verge of a breakthrough, this early building by Antoni Gaudí (completed in 1890) shows the architect taking his first tentative steps toward what would become his trademark curvy style. Dark and masculine, with its castle-like rooms, Palau Güell (pronounced "gway") was custom-built to house the Güell clan and gives an insight into Gaudí's artistic genius. Despite the eye-catching roof (visible from the street if you crane your neck), I'd skip Palau Güell if you plan to see the more interesting La Pedrera (see page 55).

Cost and Hours: €12, includes audioguide, free first Sun of the month, open April-Oct Tue-Sun 10:00-20:00, Nov-March Tue-Sun 10:00-17:30, closed Mon year-round, last entry one hour before closing, a half-block off the Ramblas at Carrer Nou de la Rambla 3-5, Metro: Liceu or Drassanes, tel. 934-725-775, www.palauguell.cat.

Buying Tickets: As with any Gaudí sight, you may encounter lines. Each ticket has an entry time, so at busy times you may have to wait to enter. A better option is to buy advance tickets for a set day and time of your choice, either on-site or online (but the predominantly Catalan website is tricky).

Visiting the House: The parabolic-arch **entryways,** viewable from the outside, are the first clue that this is not a typical townhouse.

For inspiration, Gaudí hung a chain to create a U-shape, then flipped it upside-down. The wrought-iron doors were cleverly designed so that those inside could see out, and light from the outside could get in—but not vice versa.

Once inside, an engaging 24-stop

Barcelona at a Glance

▲▲▲**Ramblas** Barcelona's colorful, gritty, tourist-filled pedestrian thoroughfare. **Hours:** Always open. See page 36.

▲▲▲**Picasso Museum** Extensive collection offering insight into the brilliant Spanish artist's early years. **Hours:** Tue-Sun 9:00-19:00, Thu until 21:30, closed Mon. See page 48.

▲▲▲**Sagrada Família** Gaudí's remarkable, unfinished church—a masterpiece in progress. **Hours:** Daily April-Sept 9:00-20:00, Oct-March 9:00-18:00. See page 57.

▲▲**Palace of Catalan Music** Best Modernista interior in Barcelona. **Hours:** Fifty-minute English tours daily every hour 10:00-15:00, plus frequent concerts. See page 49.

▲▲ **La Pedrera (Casa Milà)** Barcelona's quintessential Modernista building and Gaudí creation. **Hours:** Daily March-Oct 9:00-20:00, Nov-Feb 9:00-18:30. See page 55.

▲▲**Park Güell** Colorful Gaudí-designed park overlooking the city. **Hours:** Daily April-Oct 8:00-21:30, Nov-March 8:30-18:00. See page 57.

▲▲**Catalan Art Museum** World-class showcase of this region's art, including a substantial Romanesque collection. **Hours:** May-Sept Tue-Sat 10:00-20:00 (until 18:00 Oct-April), Sun 10:00-15:00, closed Mon. See page 68.

▲▲**CaixaForum** Modernista brick factory now occupied by cutting-edge cultural center featuring excellent temporary art exhibits. **Hours:** daily 10:00-20:00. See page 70.

▲**La Boqueria Market** Colorful but touristy produce market, just off the Ramblas. **Hours:** Mon-Sat 8:00-20:00, best mornings after 9:00, closed Sun. See page 37.

▲**Palau Güell** Exquisitely curvy Gaudí interior and fantasy rooftop. **Hours:** April-Oct Tue-Sun 10:00-20:00, Nov-March Tue-Sun 10:00-17:30, closed Mon year-round. See page 37.

▲**Plaça Reial** Stately square near the Ramblas, with palm trees, Gaudí-designed lampposts, and a fine slice-of-life look at Barcelona. **Hours:** Always open. See page 40.

▲**Maritime Museum** A sailor's delight, housed in a medieval shipyard (but permanent collection not likely on display until late 2015). **Hours:** Temporary exhibits daily 10:00-20:00. See page 41.

▲**Cathedral of Barcelona** Colossal Gothic cathedral ringed by distinctive chapels. **Hours:** Generally open to visitors Mon-Fri 8:00-19:30, Sat-Sun 8:00-20:00. See page 44.

▲*Sardana* **Dances** Patriotic dance in which proud Catalans join hands in a circle, often held outdoors. **Hours:** Every Sun at 12:00, sometimes also Sat at 18:00, no dances in Aug. See page 46.

▲**Barcelona History Museum** One-stop trip through town history, from Roman times to today. **Hours:** Tue-Sat 10:00-19:00, Sun 10:00-20:00, closed Mon. See page 47.

▲**Santa Caterina Market** Fine market hall built on the site of an old monastery and updated with a wavy Gaudí-inspired roof. **Hours:** Mon 7:30-14:00, Tue-Wed and Sat 7:30-15:30, Thu-Fri 7:30-20:30, closed Sun. See page 51.

▲**Church of Santa Maria del Mar** Catalan Gothic church in El Born, built by wealthy medieval shippers. **Hours:** Daily 9:00-13:30 & 16:30-20:00. See page 51.

▲**Casa Batlló** Gaudí-designed home topped with fanciful dragon-inspired roof. **Hours:** Daily 9:00-20:00. See page 54.

▲**Casa Lleó Morera** One of the best-preserved Modernista interiors in the city. **Hours:** Mandatory 70-minute guided tours Mon-Sat at 11:00 and Thu-Sat at 15:30; shorter tours also available. See page 55.

▲**Fundació Joan Miró** World's best collection of works by Catalan modern artist Joan Miró and his contemporaries. **Hours:** July-Sept Tue-Sat 10:00-20:00 (until 19:00 Oct-June), Thu until 21:30, Sun 10:00-14:30; closed Mon year-round. See page 64.

▲**1929 World Expo Fairgrounds** Expo site at the base of Montjuïc, featuring playful Magic Fountains, the impressive CaixaForum art gallery, and a cheesy Spanish Village (Las Arenas, a mall converted from a bullring, is nearby). **Hours:** Grounds always open. See page 69.

▲**Magic Fountains** Lively fountain spectacle. **Hours:** May-Sept Thu-Sun 21:00-23:00, Oct-April Fri-Sat 19:00-20:30. See page 70.

▲**Barcelona's Beaches** Fun-filled, man-made beaches reaching from the harbor to the Fòrum. **Hours:** Always open. See page 72.

audioguide, included with your admission, fills in the details. The Neo-Gothic **cellar,** with its mushroom pillars, was used as a stable—notice the big carriage doors in the back and the rings on some of the posts used to tie up the horses.

A grand staircase leads to the **living space,** including a family room, dining room, and so on. Photos show how the Güell fam-

ily—with their textile wealth—originally furnished the place. The intricacy of Gaudí's design work evokes the impossibly complex patterns that decorate great Moorish palaces. Step onto the terrace out back, and take a look at the elaborately decorated (and unmistakably organic-looking) bay window.

The tall, skinny, atrium-like **central hall** fills several floors under a parabolic dome. Behind the grand, gilded doors is a personal chapel, which made it easy to instantly convert the hall from a secular space to a religious one.

Upstairs are the Güells' his-and-hers bedrooms, along with a **film** telling the story of the two men behind this building: Gaudí and his patron, the building's resident and namesake, Eusebi Güell. At a time when most wealthy urbanites were moving to the Eixample, Güell decided to stay in the Old City.

The most dramatic space is the **rooftop;** Gaudí slathered the 20 chimneys and ventilation towers with bits of stained glass, ceramic tile, and marble to create a forest of giant upside-down ice-cream cones.

▲Plaça Reial

This genteel-feeling square, with palm trees and a pair of Gaudí-designed lampposts, is a welcoming open space in the otherwise claustrophobic Old City. You can sit down for a drink at one of the touristy bars, or just lean up against the fountain and take it all in.

For more details on Plaça Reial, see page 86 in ❷ The Ramblas Ramble chapter. For food and drink recommendations nearby, see page 205.

THE LOWER RAMBLAS AND HARBORFRONT
▲Maritime Museum (Museu Marítim)

Barcelona's medieval shipyard, the best preserved in the entire Mediterranean, is home to an excellent museum near the bottom of the Ramblas. Its permanent collection is closed for renovation (until further notice), but the museum hosts a series of worthwhile temporary exhibits.

The building's cavernous halls evoke the 14th-century days when Catalunya was a naval and shipbuilding power, cranking out 30 huge galleys a winter. As in the US today, military and commercial ventures mixed and mingled as Catalunya built its trading empire. When the permanent collection reopens, it'll cover the salty history of ships and navigation from the 13th to the 20th century. In the meantime, an impressively huge and richly decorated replica of the royal galley Juan de Austria, which fought in the 1571 Battle of Lepanto, remains on display.

Cost and Hours: €5, daily 10:00-20:00, last entry 30 minutes before closing, nice café with seating inside or out on the museum courtyard (free to enter), Avinguda de la Drassanes, Metro: Drassanes, tel. 933-429-920, www.mmb.cat.

Nearby: Your ticket also includes entrance to the *Santa Eulàlia*, an early 20th-century schooner docked just a short walk from the Columbus Monument (€1.50 for entry without museum visit, April-Oct Tue-Fri and Sun 10:00-20:30, Sat 14:00-20:30, closes at 17:30 in Nov-March, closed Mon year-round). On Saturday mornings, the schooner sets sail around the harbor for three hours—reserve well in advance (Sat 10:00-13:00, adult-€12, children 6-14-€6, tel. 933-429-920, reserves.mmaritim@diba.cat).

Columbus Monument (Monument a Colóm)

Located where the Ramblas hits the harbor, this 200-foot-tall monument was built for the 1888 world's fair and commemorates Columbus' visit to Barcelona following his first trip to America. A tight four-person elevator takes you to a glassed-in observation area at the top for congested

SIGHTS

Barcelona's Old City

EIXAMPLE

PASSEIG DE GRACIA

To Casa Batlló & La Pedrera

VIA LAIETANA

Urquinaona

Urquinaona

DE LES JONQUERES

EL CORTE INGLÉS DEP'T STORE

C. DE LES MOLES

C. DE FONTANELLA

Catalunya

Bus to Airport (& Taxis) B

GRAN VIA DE LES CORTS CATALANES

RONDA DE LA UNIVERSITAT

Plaça de Catalunya

C. D'ESTRUC

CARRER COMTAL

PORTAL DE L'ANGEL

S. ANNA

ELS 4 GATS

C. MONTSIÓ

DURAN I BAS

C. DE BERGARA

FNAC R

Universitat

CARRER DE PELAI

Catalunya

C. DE SANTA ANNA

CARRER DE LA CANUDA

FOUNTAIN

C. CUCU

CARRER DELS TALLERS

ZARA STORE

R. DE SANT ANTONI

C. MONTALEGRE

C. DE VALLDONZELLA

C. BONSUCCÉS

Plaça de la Vila de Madrid

ROMAN NECROPOLIS

C. DEL DUC

LAS RAMBLAS

C. DE LA PORTAFERRISSA

C. DEL PI

C. PALLA

MACBA CONTEMPORARY ART MUSEUM

C. D'ELISABETS

C. D'EN

BETLEM CHURCH

C. EN BOT

C. PETRITXOL

Plaça del Pi

Plaça S. Josep Oriol

Plaça dels Àngels

C. NOTARIAT

XUCLÀ

C. D'EN ROCA

DOCTOR DOU

DEL PINTOR FORTUNY

CULTURAL INFO PALAU DE LA VIRREINA

Liceu

S. MARIA DEL PI

C. DEL TIGRE

CARRER JOAQUÍN COSTA

C. DELS ÀNGELS

DEL CARME

LA BOQUERIA MARKET

CARDENAL

C. DE LA PALOMA

C. DE FERLANDINA

C. DEL PEU DE LA CREU

C. FLORISTES RAMBLA

C. DE JERUSALEM

MIRÓ MOSAIC

Liceu

CAFÉ DE L'OPERA

C. D'ARDLES

C. DE LA LLUNA

OLD

Plaça S. Agustí

LICEU OPERA HOUSE

C. DE SANT GIL

Plaça del Pedró

CARRER L'HOSPITAL

C. D'EN ROBADOR

C. JUNTA DEL COMERC

S. AGUSTÍ

C. DEL PENEDÈS

C. RIERA ALTA

C. DE SANT VICENÇ

CARRER DE SANT ANTONI ABAT

C. DE SANT RAFAEL

EL RAVAL

PALAU GÜELL

C. DE LA CENDRA

C. VISTALEGRE

CARRER DE L'AURORA

RAMBLA DEL RAVAL

CARRER DE SANT PAU

CARRER MARQUÈS DE BARBERÀ

C. DE LA CERA

CARRER DE SANT PACIÀ

C. DE LA RIERETA

C. ST. OLEGUER

DE LA RAMBLA

AVINGUDA DE LES

RONDA DE SANT PAU

CARRETES

C. SANT PAU

C. NOU

C. DE L'ARC PEL

DEL DECAMPO SAGRADO

CARRER DE LA REINA AMÀLIA

C. DE LES TÀPIES

C. NOU

AVINGUDA DE LES

C. DEL CID

C. DEL PORTAL DE SANTA MADRONA

MARQUÈS COMTE BORRELL

C. DE LES FLORS

C. DE SANT

CARRER DE L'OM

C. SANTA MADRONA

To Plaça d'Espanya & Sants Station

C. DE TAPIOLES

C. DEL POETA CABANYES

C. DE SALVÀ

Plaça d'El Molino

AVINGUDA

Paral·lel

DEL PARAL·LEL

Paral·lel

C. NOU DE LA RAMBLA

Funicular To Montjuïc

PSG DE LA CAMPAMENGA

PG DE LA

C. DE PUIG THURIGUER

C. DE RIGER PALAUDARIES

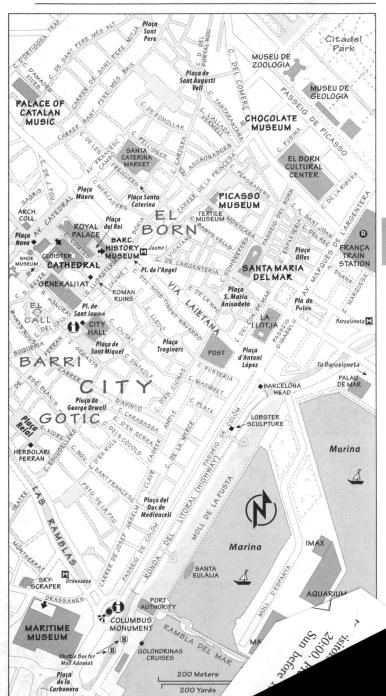

Citadel Park

MUSEU DE ZOOLOGIA

MUSEU DE GEOLOGIA

PASSEIG DE PICASSO

CHOCOLATE MUSEUM

EL BORN CULTURAL CENTER

C. D'ORTIGOSA TRAF.
C. C. D'AMADEU VIVES
C. DE SANT PERE MES ALT
C. DE SANT PERE MITJA
C. DE SANT PERE MES BAIX
C. DR. J. POU
CARRER SANT PERE MES BAIX
SAGRIS

Plaça Sant Pere
Plaça de Sant Augustí Vell

C. D. DEL FORTAL NOU
C. DEL COMERÇ
C. DE FONOLLAR
C. TANTARANTANA
L'ALLADA VERMELL
C. FUSINA

PALACE OF CATALAN MUSIC

AV. CATEDRAL
ARCH. COLL.
Plaça Nova

SANTA CATERINA MARKET

Plaça Maura
Plaça Santa Caterina

EL BORN

PICASSO MUSEUM

TEXTILE MUSEUM

C. PELLISSER
C. DE LES CAMP
AV. FRANCESC CAMPO
C. MERCADERS
C. CARDERS
C. ASSAONADORS
C. FREIXURES
BORIA
C. DE LA PRINCESA
CARRER DE LA PRINCESA
C. FLASSADERS

PASSEIG DEL BORN

C. DE LA RIBERA
C. DE LA RIBERA

ROYAL PALACE
Plaça del Rei
BARC. HISTORY MUSEUM
CATHEDRAL
SHOE MUSEUM
CLOISTER
GENERALITAT

C. COMTES
Jaume I
C. DE VIGATANS
BANYS VELLS
C. MONTCADA
C. A. SANT JOAN
C. ESPARTERIA
C. DEL SEC

FRANÇA TRAIN STATION

DUANA

SANTA MARIA DEL MAR

Plaça Olles

Plaça S. Maria Anisadeta

Plaça de Pulou

ROMAN RUINS
Pl. de l'Angel
Jaume I
C. DE L'ARGENTERIA
C. SOMBRERERS
VIA LAIETANA
C. DE LA NAU

EL CALL
C. S. SEVER
S. HONORATA
C. LLORENS
C. DEL CALL
C. JAUME I
DEL SOTS-TINENT NAVARRO

Pl. de Sant Jaume
CITY HALL

Plaça de Sant Miquel
Plaça Traginers

LA LLOTJA

Barceloneta

Pla de Pulou

Plaça d'Antoni López

BARRI

CITY

GÒTIC

C. GEGANTS
C. DATAÜF
C. DEN GIGNAS
C. MARQUET
C. PLATA
C. CUTAT
C. LLEDÍ
POST

To Barceloneta

PALAU DE MAR

Plaça de George Orwell

Plaça Reial

HERBOLARI FERRAN

D'AVINYÓ
C. CARABASSA
C. D'EN SERRA
C. DEL S CÒDOLS
C. DE LA MERCE
BARCELONA HEAD

LOBSTER SCULPTURE

Marina

LAS RAMBLAS

MONTSERRAT

C. DE VIDRE
C. ESCUDELLERS
C. NOU
C. D'EN RULI
C. SANT FRANCESC
CLAVE
PSTG. DE LA PAU

Plaça del Duc de Medinaceli

RONDA DEL LITORAL (HIGHWAY)

MOLL DE LA FUSTA

Marina

IMAX

SKY-SCRAPER
Drassanes

DRASSANES

TEATRE

CARRER DE JOSEP ANSELM
PASSEIG DE COLÓM

SANTA EULÀLIA

MOLL D'ESPANYA

AQUARIUM

MARITIME MUSEUM

PORT AUTHORITY
COLUMBUS MONUMENT

Shuttle Bus for Moll Adossat

GOLONDRINAS CRUISES

RAMBLA DEL MAR

Plaça de la Carbonera

200 Meters

200 Yards

20:00, befor...
Sun before...
istory...

but sweeping views. There is a small and usually uncrowded TI inside the base of the monument.

Cost and Hours: Monument—free and always open; elevator ride-€4.50, daily 8:30-20:30.

For more details on the monument, see page 88 of ✪ The Ramblas Ramble chapter.

Golondrinas Cruises

At the harbor near the Columbus Monument, tourist boats called *golondrinas* offer two different unguided trips. As Barcelona's skyline isn't all that striking from the water, these trips are pretty pointless unless you'd just like to go for a boat ride. The shorter version goes around the harbor in 35 minutes (€7, daily on the hour 11:30-19:00, more in summer, fewer in winter, tel. 934-423-106, www.lasgolondrinas.com). The longer 1.5-hour trip goes up the coast to the Fòrum complex and back (€14.80, can disembark at Fòrum in summer only, daily 11:30-19:30, shorter hours off-season).

THE BARRI GÒTIC

For more details on this area and several of the following sights, see my ✪ Barri Gòtic Walk.

Avinguda del Portal de l'Angel

This broad, traffic-free boulevard, which connects the modern Plaça de Catalunya to its historic cathedral district, is Barcelona's most well-trodden street. Although lined with just about every type of Spanish and international chain store you can imagine, its circa-1888 remodel has left it with a certain dignified air. Just off this drag, you'll discover humble old churches and the famous bar called Els Quatre Gats, where a young Picasso got his start. For tips on shopping along this street, see page 228.

▲Cathedral of Barcelona

The city's 14th-century, Gothic-style cathedral (with a Neo-Gothic facade) has played a significant role in Barcelona's history—but as far as grand cathedrals go, this one is relatively unexciting. Still, it's worth a visit to see its richly decorated chapels, finely carved choir, tomb of St. Eulàlia, and restful cloister with gurgling fountains and resident geese.

Cost and Hours: Generally open Mon-Fri 8:00-19:30, Sat-Sun free to enter Mon-Sat before 13:45, and daily after

Circle Dances in Squares and Castles in the Air

From group circle dancing to human towers, Catalans have some interesting and unique traditions. A memorable Barce-

lona experience is watching (or participating in) the patriotic **sardana** dances. Locals of all ages seem to spontaneously appear. For some it's a highly symbolic, politically charged action representing Catalan unity—but for most it's just a fun chance to kick up their heels. Participants gather in circles after putting their things in the center—symbolic of community and sharing (and the ever-present risk of theft). All are welcome, even tourists cursed with two left feet. The dances are held in the square in front of the cathedral on Sundays at noon (and occasionally on Saturdays at 18:00).

Holding hands, dancers raise their arms—slow-motion, *Zorba the Greek*-style—as they hop and sway gracefully to the music. The band *(cobla)* consists of a long flute, tenor and soprano oboes, strange-looking brass instruments, and a tiny bongo-like drum *(tambori)*. The rest of Spain mocks this lazy circle dance, but considering what it takes for a culture to survive within another culture's country, it is a stirring display of local pride and patriotism. During 36 years of Franco dictatorship, the *sardana* was forbidden.

Another Catalan tradition is the **castell,** a tower erected solely of people. *Castells* pop up on special occasions, such as the Festa Major de Gràcia in mid-August and La Mercè festival in late September. Towers can be up to 10 humans high. Imagine balancing 50 or 60 feet in the air, with nothing but a pile of flesh and bone between you and the ground. The base is formed by burly supports called *baixos;* above them are the *manilles* ("handles"), which help haul up the people to the top. The *castell* is capped with a human steeple—usually a child—who extends four fingers into the air, representing the four red stripes of the Catalan flag. A scrum of spotters (called *pinyas*) cluster around the base in case anyone falls. *Castelleres* are judged both on how quickly they erect their human towers and how fast they can take them down. Besides during festivals, you can usually see this spectacle in front of the cathedral on spring and summer Saturdays at 19:30 (as part of the Festa Catalana; see page 27).

One thing that these two traditions have in common is their communal nature. Perhaps it's no coincidence, as Catalunya is known for its community spirit, team building, and socialistic bent.

SIGHTS

17:15, but during free times you must pay to enter the cathedral's three minor sights (museum-€2, terrace-€3, choir-€3). The church is officially "closed" for a few hours each afternoon (Mon-Sat 13:00-17:00, Sun 14:00-17:00), but you can get in to see the interior sights by paying €7.80. Tel. 933-151-554, www.catedralbcn. org.

○ See the Cathedral of Barcelona Tour chapter.

▲Sardana Dances

If you're in town on a weekend, you can see the *sardana*, a patriotic dance in which Barcelonans link hands and dance in a circle (see sidebar on the previous page).

Cost and Hours: Free, Sun at 12:00, sometimes also Sat at 18:00, no dances in Aug, event lasts 1-2 hours, in the square in front of the cathedral.

Frederic Marès Museum (Museu Frederic Marès)

This museum, with the eclectic collection of local sculptor and packrat Frederic Marès (1893-1991), sprawls around a peaceful courtyard through several old Barri Gòtic buildings. The biggest part of the collection, on the ground and first floors, consists of sculpture—from ancient works to beautiful, evocative Gothic pieces to items from the early 20th century. Even more interesting is the extensive "Collector's Cabinet," consisting of items Marès found representative of everyday life in the 19th century. Lovingly displayed on the second and third floors are rooms upon rooms of scissors, keys, irons, fans, nutcrackers, stamps, pipes, snuffboxes, opera glasses, pocket watches, bicycles, toy soldiers, dolls, and other bric-a-brac. And in Marès' study are several sculptures by the artist himself. The tranquil courtyard café offers a pleasant break, even when the museum is closed (café open in summer only, until 22:00).

Cost and Hours: €4, free first Sun of the month and Sun from 15:00, 1.5-hour audioguide-€1; open Tue-Sat 10:00-19:00, Sun 11:00-20:00, closed Mon; Plaça de Sant Iu 5-6, Metro: Jaume I, tel. 932-563-500, www.museumares.bcn.net.

Shoe Museum (Museu del Calçat)

Shoe lovers enjoy this small museum of footwear in glass display cases, watched over by an earnest attendant. While nothing is described in English, you'll see shoes from the 1700s to today: fancy ladies' boots, Tibetan moccasins, big clown shoes, expeditionary boots that have been to Mount Everest, and shoes of the minor celebrities and politicians of Catalunya. The huge shoes at the entry are designed to fit the feet of the statue atop the Columbus Monument.

Cost and Hours: €2.50, Tue-Sun 11:00-14:00, closed Mon, Plaça Sant Felip Neri 5, Metro: Jaume I, tel. 933-014-533.

Plaça de Sant Jaume

This open-feeling square (a rarity in the tight Barri Gòtic) is flanked by the two most important administrative buildings in Catalunya: the Palau de la Generalitat (home of the autonomous Catalan government) and the Barcelona City Hall.

For more details, see page 102 of the ✪ Barri Gòtic Walk chapter.

Roman Temple of Augustus (Temple Roma d'August)

Tucked inside a small medieval courtyard, four columns from an ancient temple of Augustus are a reminder of Barcelona's Roman origins. The temple, dating from the late first century B.C., stood at one corner of the ancient forum quarter.

Cost and Hours: Free; Mon 10:00-14:00, Tue-Sat 10:00-19:00, Sun 10:00-20:00; Carrer del Paradís 10, tel. 933-152-311.

For more on the temple, see page 103 of the ✪ Barri Gòtic Walk chapter.

Plaça del Rei

Perhaps the best place in town to get a feel for Barcelona's faint connection to Old World royalty, this "Square of the Monarch" offers a good view of the Royal Palace, where both Spanish kings and Catalan counts once resided. Although the palace complex is mostly closed to tourists, parts of the building are used for exhibits for the Barcelona History Museum.

▲Barcelona History Museum
(Museu d'Història de Barcelona: Plaça del Rei)

At this main branch of the city history museum (MUHBA for short), you can literally walk through the history of Barcelona, including an underground labyrinth of excavated Roman ruins.

Cost and Hours: €7; ticket includes English audioguide and other MUHBA branches; free all day first Sun of month and other Sun from 15:00—but no audioguide during free times; open Tue-Sat 10:00-19:00, Sun 10:00-20:00, closed Mon; Plaça del Rei, enter on Vagueur street, Metro: Jaume I, tel. 932-562-122.

Visiting the Museum: Though the museum is housed in part of the former Royal Palace complex, you'll see only a bit of that grand space. Instead, the focus is on the exhibits in the cellar. Posted information is in Catalan, Spanish, and English, and you'll also find abundant English handouts; the included English audioguide provides informative, if dry, descriptions of the exhibits.

Start by watching the ten-minute introductory video in the small theater (at the end of the first floor to the left); it plays alternately in Catalan, Spanish, and English, but it's worth viewing in any language. Then take an elevator down 65 feet (and 2,000 years—see the date spin back while you descend) to stroll the streets of Roman Barcino—founded by Emperor Augustus around 10 B.C.

The history is so strong here, you can smell it. This was a working-class part of town. The archaeological route leads you through areas used for laundering clothes and dyeing garments, the remains of a factory that salted fish and produced garum (a fish-derived sauce used extensively in ancient Roman cooking), and facilities for winemaking. Next, you'll wander through bits of a seventh-century early Christian church and an exhibit in the 11th-century count's palace that shows you Barcelona through its glory days in the Middle Ages.

Finally, head upstairs (or ride the elevator to floor 0) to see a model of the city from the early 16th century. From here, you can also enter **Tinell Hall** (part of the Royal Palace), with its long, graceful, rounded vaults. Nearby, step into the 14th-century **Chapel of St. Agatha** if it's hosting a free temporary exhibit.

EL BORN

Despite being home to the top-notch Picasso Museum, El Born (also known as "La Ribera") feels wonderfully local, with a higher ratio of Barcelonans to tourists than most other city-center zones (Metro: Jaume I). Narrow lanes sprout from the neighborhood's main artery, Passeig del Born—the perfect springboard for exploring artsy boutiques, inviting cafés and restaurants, funky shops, and rollicking nightlife. For a tour of this neighborhood with more information on its sights, see the ✪ El Born Walk. For tips on shopping, see page 224 of the Shopping in Barcelona chapter.

▲▲▲Picasso Museum (Museu Picasso)

Pablo Picasso may have made his career in Paris, but the years he spent in Barcelona—from age 14 through 23—were among the most formative of his life. It was here that young Pablo mastered the realistic painting style of his artistic forebears—and it was also here that he first felt the freedom that allowed him to leave that all behind and give in to his creative, experimental urges. When he left Barcelona, Picasso headed for Paris...and revolutionized art forever.

The pieces in this excellent museum capture that priceless moment just before this bold young thinker changed the world. While you won't find Picasso's famous later Cubist works here, you will enjoy a representative sweep of his early years, from the careful crafting of art-school pieces to the gloomy hues of his Blue Period to the revitalized cheer of his Rose Period. You'll also see works from his twilight years, including dozens of wild improvisations inspired by Diego Velázquez's seminal *Las Meninas,* as well as a roomful of works that reflect the childlike exuberance of an old man playing like a young kid on the French Riviera. It's undoubtedly the top collection of Picassos here in his native country and the best anywhere of his early years.

Cost and Hours: €14, family pass-€15, free all day first Sun of month and other Sun from 15:00, audioguide-€5; Tue-Sun 9:00-19:00, Thu until 21:30, closed Mon; Carrer de Montcada 15-23, ticket office at #21, Metro: Jaume I, tel. 932-563-000, www. museupicasso.bcn.cat.

Avoiding Lines: You can skip the line either with an Articket BCN (which you can purchase on-site) or with a ticket bought in advance from the museum's website. If you just show up, expect to wait in line, sometimes for more than an hour. For more information and other crowd-beating tips, see page 124.

○ See the Picasso Museum Tour chapter.

▲▲Palace of Catalan Music (Palau de la Música Catalana)

This concert hall, built in just three years and finished in 1908, features an unexceptional exterior but boasts my favorite Modernista interior in town (by Lluís Domènech i Montaner). Its in-viting arches lead you into the 2,138-seat hall, which is accessible only with a tour (or by attending a concert). A kaleido scopic skylight features a choir singing around the sun, while playful carvings and mosaics celebrate music and Catalan culture. If you're interested in Modernisme, taking this tour (which starts with a relaxing 12-minute video) is one of the best experiences in town—and helps balance the hard-to-avoid focus on Gaudí as "Mr. Modernisme."

Cost and Hours: €18, 50-minute tours in English run daily every hour 10:00-15:00, tour times may change based on performance schedule, about 6 blocks northeast of cathedral, Carrer Palau de la Música 4, Metro: Urquinaona, tel. 902-442-882, www. palaumusica.cat.

Advance Tour Reservations Required: You must buy your ticket in advance to get a spot on an English guided tour (tickets available up to 4 months in advance—purchase yours at least 2 days before, though they're sometimes available the same day or day before—especially Oct-March). You can buy the ticket in per-

Barcelona's Best Views

Barcelona's delightful architecture is best seen up close, but to fully appreciate the city's scenic beauty, take advantage of one of many panoramic viewpoints scattered across town. For some viewpoints, you'll need to pay admission (usually €2-4), but many are free, including the view terrace at Park Güell and the castle at Montjuïc. When deciding between viewpoints, target the ones that are already on your sightseeing route.

Cable Car: Although it's pricey and slow to load, the Aeri del Port cable car between Montjuïc and Barceloneta (in either direction) offers a dramatic moving panorama of the city. See page 60.

Park Güell: Inviting, curvy benches along a spectacular terrace offer free, sweeping views of Barcelona from this foothills park. Climb even higher to the Calvary for a bird's-eye view of the park and city below. See the Park Güell Tour chapter.

Sagrada Família Towers: Two different elevators, one followed by dizzying stairs, take you up to the towers for a good view of the city and a unique angle on this fascinating church (fees involved). See the Sagrada Família Tour chapter.

Montjuïc: Overlooking the port, this hilltop affords free city views from its castle ramparts and Miramar viewpoint park, as well as from the Catalan Art Museum's terrace and stylish restaurant. See page 59.

El Corte Inglés: The gigantic department store on Plaça de Catalunya has a great view cafeteria on its ninth floor. See page 228.

La Pedrera: The rooftop of this Gaudí masterpiece offers up-close views of fairytale chimneys plus a vista of the Eixample and the distant spires of the Sagrada Família. See page 55.

Las Arenas: Take a pay glass elevator or escalate/elevate for free (from inside the building) to the restaurant-ringed roof terrace atop this former bull-ring—now a mall—for some of the best

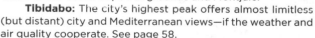

views of the World Expo Fairgrounds and Montjuïc.

Tibidabo: The city's highest peak offers almost limitless (but distant) city and Mediterranean views—if the weather and air quality cooperate. See page 58.

Cathedral of Barcelona: A pay elevator takes you up to a view terrace for an expansive city view from the heart of the Barri Gòtic.

Columbus Monument: A tiny pay elevator rides up to a glass-enclosed deck with big views of the waterfront and Ramblas. See page 41.

son at the concert hall box office (open daily 9:30-15:30, less than a 10-minute walk from the cathedral or Picasso Museum); by phone with your credit card (for no extra charge, tel. 902-475-485); or online at the concert hall website (€1 fee).

Concerts: Another way to see the hall is by attending a concert (300 per year, €20-50 tickets, see website for details and online purchases, box office tel. 902-442-882).

▲Santa Caterina Market

This eye-catching market hall was built on the ruins of an old monastery, then renovated in 2006 with a wildly colorful, swooping, Gaudí-inspired roof and shell built around its original white walls (a good exhibition at the far corner provides a view of the foundations and English explanations). The much-delayed construction took so long that locals began calling the site the "Hole of Shame." Come for the outlandish architecture, but stay for a chance to shop for a picnic without the tourist logjam of La Boqueria market on the Ramblas.

Cost and Hours: Free, Mon 7:30-14:00, Tue-Wed and Sat 7:30-15:30, Thu-Fri 7:30-20:30, closed Sun, Avinguda de Francesc Cambó 16, www.mercatsantacaterina.cat.

For more on the market, see page 117 of the ❷ El Born Walk chapter.

▲Church of Santa Maria del Mar

This so-called "Cathedral of the Sea" was built entirely with local funds and labor, in the heart of the wealthy merchant El Born quarter. Proudly independent, the church features a purely Catalan Gothic interior that was forcibly uncluttered of its Baroque decor by civil war belligerents.

Cost and Hours: Free admission daily 9:00-13:30 & 16:30-20:00, also open 13:30-16:30 with €4 ticket; €8 guided rooftop tours in summer, English tours on the hour Mon-Fri 13:00-19:00, Sat-Sun at 11:00 and 12:00; Plaça Santa Maria, Metro: Jaume I, tel. 933-102-390.

For more information on the church, see page 121 of the ❷ El Born Walk chapter.

El Born Cultural Center (El Born Centre Cultural)

Occupying the cast-iron structure of a 19th-century market, El Born Cultural Center is a multipurpose space. It hosts an exhibition devoted to Barcelona in the 18th century, an active medieval archaeological site, temporary exhibits, and a café.

Cost and Hours: Center is free and open Tue-Sun 10:00-20:00, closed Mon; €6 covers all exhibits (including audioguide for entire center), exhibits free all day first Sun of month and other

Sun from 15:00, open Tue-Sun 10:00-20:00, closed Mon; Plaça Comercial 12, www.elborncentrecultural.bcn.cat.

For more information on the center, see page 119 of the ✪ El Born Walk chapter.

Chocolate Museum (Museu de la Xocolata)

Fun for chocolate lovers, this museum—operated by the local confectioners' guild—tells the story of chocolate from Aztecs to Europeans via the port of Barcelona, where it was first unloaded and processed. But the history lesson is just an excuse to show off a series of remarkably ornate candy sculptures. These works of edible art—which change every year but often include such themes as Don Quixote or the roofs of Barcelona—begin as store-window displays for Easter or Christmas. Once the holiday passes, the confectioners bring the sculptures here to be enjoyed. The museum is only a couple of blocks from the Picasso Museum (and near Citadel Park—see next listing).

Cost and Hours: €5, Mon-Sat 10:00-19:00 (until 20:00 mid-June-mid-Sept), Sun 10:00-15:00, Carrer del Comerç 36, Metro: Jaume I, tel. 932-687-878, www.museuxocolata.cat.

THE EIXAMPLE

For many visitors, Modernista architecture is Barcelona's main draw. And one name tops them all: Antoni Gaudí (1852-1926). Barcelona is an architectural scrapbook of Gaudí's galloping gables and organic curves. A devoted Catalan and Catholic, he immersed himself in each project, often living on-site. At various times, he called Park Güell, La Pedrera (Casa Milà), and the Sagrada Família home. For more on Gaudí and some of his contemporaries, see the sidebar on page 144. For details on Modernisme, see page 139.

At the heart of the Modernista movement was the Eixample, a carefully planned "new town," just beyond the Old City, with wide sidewalks, hardy shade trees, and a rigid grid plan cropped at the corners to create space and lightness at each intersection. Conveniently, all of this new construction provided a generation of Modernista architects with a blank canvas for creating boldly experimental designs. At the edge of the Eixample is Gaudí's greatest piece of work, the yet-to-be-finished Sagrada Família.

In this section, I've focused on the big Modernista sights in the Eixample, starting at the center of this neighborhood with the **Block of Discord,** where three colorful Modernista facades compete for your attention: Casa Batlló, Casa Amatller, and Casa Lleó Morera (all on Pas-

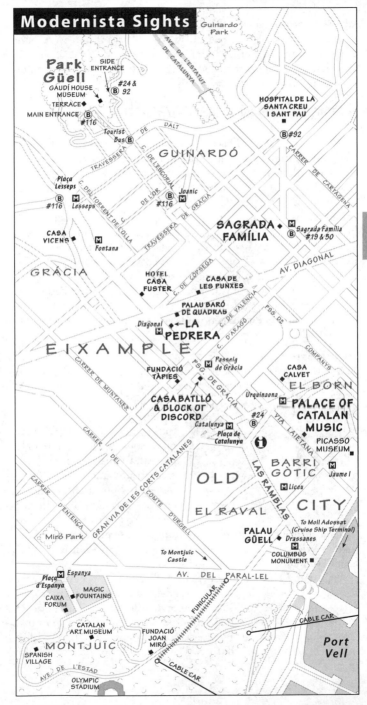

Modernista Sights

SIGHTS

seig de Gràcia—near the Metro stop of the same name—between Carrer del Consell de Cent and Carrer d'Aragó). All were built by well-known Modernista architects at the end of the 19th century. Because the mansions look as though they are trying to outdo each other in creative twists, locals nicknamed the noisy block the "Block of Discord." By the way, if you're tempted to snap photos from the middle of the street, be careful—Gaudí died after being struck by a streetcar.

From the Block of Discord, you're just four blocks from Gaudí's La Pedrera, and a quick subway ride from his Sagrada Família.

Even though Modernisme revolved around the Eixample, traces of this style can also be found elsewhere. Other Modernista highlights include Gaudí's Park Güell, where he put his colorful stamp on 30 acres of greenery (see page 57), and his Palau Güell, just off the Ramblas (see page 37); Lluís Domènech i Montaner's **Palace of Catalan Music** in El Born (see page 49); and Josep Puig i Cadafalch's **CaixaForum,** at the base of Montjuïc (page 70). For information on more Modernista sights, you can visit the Plaça de Catalunya TI, where you'll find a special desk set aside just for Modernisme seekers (see page 21). For a tour of the Eixample, including a route that connects some of these sights, see my ✪ Eixample Walk.

▲Casa Batlló

While the highlight is the roof, the interior of this Gaudí house is also interesting—and even more over-the-top than La Pedrera's.

Paid for with textile industry money, the house features a funky mushroom-shaped fireplace nook on the main floor, a blue-and-white-ceramic-slathered atrium, and an attic (with more parabolic arches). There's barely a straight line in the house. You can also get a close-up look at the dragon-inspired rooftop. Because preservation of the place is privately funded, the entrance fee is steep—but it includes a good (if long-winded) audioguide.

Cost and Hours: €21.50, daily 9:00-20:00, may close early for special events—closings posted in advance at entrance, Passeig de Gràcia 43, tel. 932-160-306, www.casabatllo.cat. Purchase a ticket online to avoid lines, which are especially fierce in the morning. Your eticket isn't a timed reservation (it's good any time within 3 months of purchase), but it will let you skip to the front of the queue.

Casa Amatller

The middle residence of the Block of Discord, Casa Amatller was designed by Josep Puig I Cadafalch. It isn't routinely open to the public, but you can admire its tiled Neo-Gothic façade and step inside the foyer to look around.

Cost and Hours: Occasional Saturday tours of the interior (under restoration) are offered—it's best to check the website for details; Passeig de Gràcia 41, tel. 670-466-260, www.amatller.org.

▲Casa Lleó Morera

This house, designed by Lluís Domènech i Montaner and finished in 1906, has one of the finest Modernista interiors in town—and it only recently opened to the public. Access is by guided tour only, which begins with the history of the Lleó Morera family and a look at the detailing on the building's exterior. Inside, you'll marvel at finely crafted mosaics, ceramic work, wooden ceilings and doors, stone sculptures, and stained glass—all which paint a picture of the life of a Catalan bourgeoisie family in the early 20th century.

Cost and Hours: €15 for 70-minute English tour Mon-Sat at 11:00 and Thu-Sat at 15:30; €12 for express 45-minute tour (in a mix of English, Spanish, and Catalan) Mon-Sat at 11:30, 12:30, 16:30, and 17:30; check website for off-season times, as some slots are dropped if it's slow; note there is no on-site box office—you must reserve and purchase your ticket online at www.casalleomorera.com, or in person at the cultural center Palau de la Virreina (Ramblas 99, tel. 933-161-000, www.lavirreina.bcn.cat). The house itself is at Passeig de Gràcia 35, tel. 936-762-733.

▲▲La Pedrera (Casa Milà)

One of Gaudí's trademark works, this house—built between 1906 and 1912—is an icon of Modernisme. The wealthy industrialist Pere Milà i Camps commissioned it, and while some still call it

Casa Milà, most call it La Pedrera (The Quarry) because of its jagged, rocky facade. While it's fun to ogle from the outside, it's also worth going inside, as it's arguably the purest Gaudí interior in town—executed at the height of his abilities (unlike his earlier Palau Güell)—and still contains original furnishings. While Casa Batlló has a Gaudí facade and rooftop, these were appended to an existing building; La Pedrera, on the other hand, was built from the ground up according to Gaudí's plans. Besides entry to the interior, a ticket also gets you access to the delightful rooftop, with its forest of colorfully tiled chimneys.

Cost and Hours: €16.50, good audioguide-€4, daily March-Oct 9:00-20:00, Nov-Feb 9:00-18:30, last entry 30 minutes before closing, at the corner of Passeig de Gràcia and Provença (visitor entrance at Provença 261-265), Metro: Diagonal, info tel. 902-400-973, www.lapedrera.com.

Avoiding Lines: As lines can be long (up to a 1.5-hour wait to get in), it's best to reserve ahead at www.lapedrera.com (tickets come with an assigned entry time). If you come without a ticket, the best time to arrive is right when it opens.

Free Entrance to Atrium: For a peek at the interior without paying for a ticket, find the door directly on the corner, which leads to the main atrium. Upstairs on the first floor are temporary exhibits (generally free, daily 10:00-20:00, closed between exhibitions).

Nighttime Visits: The building hosts guided after-hour visits dubbed "The Secret Pedrera." On this pricey visit, you'll get a guided tour of the building with the lights turned down low and a glass of *cava* (€30; English tour offered daily March-Oct at 21:15, but check changeable schedule and offerings online).

Concerts: On summer weekends, La Pedrera has an evening rooftop concert series, "Summer Nights at La Pedrera," featuring live jazz. In addition to the music, it gives you the chance to see the rooftop illuminated (€27, late June-early Sept Thu-Sat at 22:30, book advance tickets online or by phone, tel. 902-101-212, www.lapedrera.com).

Visiting the House: A visit covers three sections—the apartment, the attic, and the rooftop. Enter and head upstairs to the apartment. If it's near closing time, continue up to see the attic and rooftop first, to make sure you have enough time to enjoy Gaudí's works and the views (note that the roof may close when it rains).

The typical bourgeois **apartment** is decorated as it might have been when the building was first occupied by middle-class urbanites (a seven-minute video explains Barcelona society at the time).

Notice Gaudí's clever use of the atrium to maximize daylight in all of the apartments.

The **attic** houses a sprawling multimedia exhibit tracing the history of the architect's career, with models, photos, and videos of his work. It's all displayed under distinctive parabola-shaped arches. While evocative of Gaudí's style in themselves, the arches are formed this way partly to support the multilevel roof above. This area was also used for ventilation, helping to keep

SIGHTS

things cool in summer and warm in winter. Tenants had storage spaces and did their laundry up here.

From the attic, a stairway leads to the undulating, jaw-dropping **rooftop,** where 30 chimneys and ventilation towers play volleyball with the clouds.

Back at the **ground level** of La Pedrera, poke into the dreamily painted original entrance courtyard.

▲▲▲Sagrada Família (Holy Family Church)

Antoni Gaudí's grand masterpiece sits unfinished in a residential Eixample neighborhood 1.5 miles north of Plaça de Catalunya.

An icon of the city, the Sagrada Família boasts bold, wildly creative, unmistakably organic architecture and decor inside and out—from its melting Glory Facade to its skull-like Passion Facade to its rainforest-esque interior. Begun under Gaudí's careful watch in 1883, the project saw some setbacks in the mid-20th century, but lately the progress has been remarkable. The city has set a goal of finishing by 2026, the centennial of Gaudí's death. For now, visitors get a close-up view of the dramatic exterior flourishes, the chance to walk through the otherworldly interior, and access to a fine museum detailing the design and engineering behind this one-of-a-kind architectural marvel.

Cost and Hours: Church-€14.80, tower elevators-€4.50 each, €18.30 combo-ticket includes Gaudí House Museum at Park Güell (described next); daily April-Sept 9:00-20:00, Oct-March 9:00-18:00, last entry 15 minutes before closing; guided tours and audioguides available, Metro: Sagrada Família, exit toward Plaça de la Sagrada Família, tel. 932-073-031, www.sagradafamilia.cat.

Avoiding Lines: Lines of up to 45 minutes—and occasionally much longer—are possible at peak times. To walk right in, buy tickets online in advance for a specific entry time to the church and towers. For details on this option and more, see page 151.

Connecting with Park Güell: For information on getting to Park Güell from the Sagrada Família, see page 161.

✪ See the Sagrada Família Tour chapter.

BEYOND THE EIXAMPLE

▲▲Park Güell

Gaudí fans enjoy the artist's magic in this colorful park, located on the outskirts of town. While it takes a bit of effort to get here, Park Güell (Catalans pronounce it "gway") offers a unique look

SIGHTS

at Gaudí's style in a natural rather than urban context. Designed as an upscale housing development for early-20th-century urbanites, the park is home to some of Barcelona's most famous symbols, including a dragon guarding a whimsical staircase, and a wavy bench bordering a panoramic view terrace supported by a forest of columns. Gaudí used vivid tile fragments to decorate much of his work, creating a playful, pleasing effect. Much of the park is free, but the part visitors want to see, the **Monumental Zone**—with all the iconic Gaudí features—has an entry fee and time-limited admission. Also in the park is the **Gaudí House Museum,** where Gaudí lived for a time. Although he did not design the house, you can see a few examples of his furniture here (the house is within the free portion of the park, but charges admission). Even without its Gaudí connection, Park Güell is simply a fine place to enjoy a break from a busy city, where green space is relatively rare.

Cost and Hours: Monumental Zone—€8 at the gate or €7 online, smart to reserve tickets in advance, daily April-Oct 8:00-21:30, Nov-March 8:30-18:00, www.parkguell.cat. Gaudí House Museum—€5.50, €18.30 combo-ticket also includes Sagrada Família, daily April-Sept 10:00-20:00, Oct-March 10:00-18:00, www.casamuseugaudi.org.

Getting There: To reach Park Güell—about 2.5 miles from Plaça de Catalunya—it's easiest to take a **taxi** from downtown, though you can also get there by **bus.** For details, see page 163. For instructions on linking the Sagrada Família to Park Güell, check page 161.

● See the Park Güell Tour chapter.

Tibidabo

Tibidabo comes from the Latin for "to thee I shall give," the words the devil used when he was tempting Christ. It's still an enticing offer: At the top of Barcelona's highest peak, you're offered the city's oldest fun-fair, a great spot for kids, and—if the weather and air quality are good—an almost limitless view of the city and the Mediterranean.

Cost and Hours: €28.50, hours depend on season—generally Wed-Sun from 12:00 in July-Aug, weekends only off-season, tel. 932-117-942, www.tibidabo.cat.

Getting There: From the Plaça de Catalunya Metro station (under Café Zürich), take the L7 (brown) line to the Tibidabo stop (the blue Tourist Bus also goes to the Tibidabo stop). Then take Barcelona's only remaining tram—Tramvía Blau—from Plaça John F. Kennedy to Plaça Dr. Andreu (€4 one-way, buy tickets on board, 2-4/hour). From there, take the funicular to the top (€7.70, €4.10 if you're also paying park admission, tel. 906-427-017). A special "Tibibus" (#T2A) runs at 10:30 from Plaça de Catalunya to the park every day that it's open (€2.95, board in front of Caja Madrid bank).

Camp Nou Stadium

The home turf of FC Barcelona is a mecca for soccer fans. A tour takes you into the press room, by the box seats, through the trophy room, and past the warm-up bench, ending in a ground-level view of the field and, of course, a big shop to buy all of your official "Barça" gear. You'll also get to tour a museum tracing the highlights of Barça history, with lots of interactive touch screens and the six championship cups that the team won in a single season ("the sextuple," 2009-2010)—a feat, they say, that will never be repeated. For more on this team and its significance to Barcelona and Catalunya, see page 80.

Cost and Hours: €23 for Camp Nou Experience (includes tour and museum); mid-April-early Oct Mon-Sat 10:00-20:00 (until 18:30 rest of year), Sun 10:00-14:30; shorter hours on game days, Metro: Maria Cristina or Collblanc, tel. 902-189-900, www.fcbarcelona.cat.

MONTJUÏC

Montjuïc (mohn-jew-EEK, "Mount of the Jews"), overlooking Barcelona's hazy port, has always been a show-off. Ages ago, it was capped by an impressive castle. When the Spanish enforced their rule, they built the imposing fortress that you'll see the shell of today. The hill has also played an integral role in the construction of Barcelona's great structures—significant parts of the historic city, the cathedral, the Sagrada Família, and much more were all built with stones quarried from Montjuïc.

Montjuïc has also been prominent during the last century. In 1929, it hosted an international fair, from which many of today's sights originated. And in 1992, the Summer Olympics directed the world's attention to this pincushion of attractions once again. While Montjuïc lacks any single knockout, must-see sight, it is home to a variety of very good ones, and most visitors should find one or two attractions here to suit their interests. For art lovers, the most worthwhile sights are the Fundació Joan Miró, Catalan Art Museum, and CaixaForum.

Sightseeing Strategies: I've listed these sights by altitude, from highest to lowest—from the hill-topping castle down to the 1929 World Expo Fairgrounds at the base of Montjuïc (described in the next section). If you're visiting all of my listed sights, ride to the top by bus, funicular, or taxi, then visit them in this order so that most of your walking is downhill. However, if you want to visit only the Catalan Art Museum and/or CaixaForum, you can just take the Metro to Plaça d'Espanya and ride the escalators up (with some stair-climbing as well) to those sights.

Getting to Montjuïc: You have several choices. The simplest is to take a **taxi** directly to your destination (about €7-8 from downtown).

Buses also take you up to Montjuïc. From Plaça de Catalunya, **bus #55** rides as far as Montjuïc's cable-car station/funicular. If you want to get higher (to the castle), ride the Metro or bus #9 or #50 from Plaça de Catalunya to Plaça d'Espanya, then make the easy transfer to **bus #150** to ride all the way up the hill. Alternatively, the red Tourist Bus will get you to the Montjuïc sights.

Another option is by **funicular** (covered by Metro ticket, every 10 minutes, 7:30-22:00, from 9:00 on Sat-Sun). To reach it, take the Metro to the Paral-lel stop, then follow signs for *Parc Montjuïc* and the little funicular icon—you can enter the funicular without using another ticket. From the top of the funicular, turn left and walk gently downhill four minutes to the Miró museum, eight minutes to the Olympic Stadium, or twelve minutes to the Catalan

Art Museum. If you're heading all the way up to the castle, you can catch a bus or cable car from the top of the funicular (see castle listing, later).

For a scenic (if slow) approach to Montjuïc, you could ride the fun circa-1929 Aeri del Port **cable car** *(telefèric)* from the tip of the Barceloneta peninsula (across the harbor, near the beach) to the Miramar viewpoint park in Montjuïc. (Another station, right along the port near the Columbus Monument, is currently closed.) Since the cable car is expensive, loads excruciatingly slowly, and goes between two relatively remote parts of town, it's really not an efficient connection. It's only worthwhile for its sweeping views over town or if you'd like to, say, cap off your Montjuïc day with some beach time near Barceloneta (€11 one-way, €16.50 round-trip, 3/hour, daily 11:00-17:30, until 20:00 June-Sept, closed in high wind, tel. 934-414-820, www.telefericodebarcelona.com).

Getting Around Montjuïc: Up top, it's easy and fun to walk between the sights—especially downhill. You can also connect the sights using the red Tourist Bus or one of the public buses: Bus

#150 does a loop around the hilltop and is the only bus that goes to the castle; on the way up, it stops at or passes near the Caixa-Forum, Mies van der Rohe Pavilion, Spanish Village, Catalan Art Museum, Olympic Stadium, Fundació Joan Miró, the lower castle cable-car station/top of the funicular, and finally, the castle. On the downhill run, it loops by Miramar, the cable-car station for Barceloneta. **Bus #55** connects only the funicular/cable-car stations, Fundació Joan Miró, and the Catalan Art Museum.

Castle of Montjuïc (Castell de Montjuïc)

The castle, while just an empty brick-and-concrete shell today, offers great city views from its ramparts...and some poignant history. It was built in the 18th century with a Vauban-type star fortress design by the central Spanish government to keep an eye on Barcelona and stifle citizen revolt. Until the late 20th century, the place functioned more to repress the people of Barcelona than to defend them. Being "taken to Montjuïc" meant you likely wouldn't be seen again. When the 20th-century dictator Franco was in power, the castle was the site of hundreds of political executions. But in 2010, Spain's Prime Minister José Luis Rodríguez Zapatero, keeping a campaign promise, turned over control of the castle from Spain's national government to the city of Barcelona. These days it serves as a park, jogging destination, and host to a popular summer open-air cinema.

Beefy Civil War-vintage cannons point visitors to grand Mediterranean vistas. Survey the boats in the harbor: Ships belonging to Grimaldi Lines, an Italian company, sail off to Genoa, Rome, and Sardinia; Mallorca ferries make the eight-hour trip to Barcelonans' big party escape; and the cruise-ship terminal busily hosts 800 ships a year (Barcelona is one of the main ports of embarkation for Mediterranean cruises). The seafront stretching far to the left was part of an Olympics project that turned a derelict industrial zone into a swanky stretch of promenades, beaches, and fancy condos. At the far right is Spain's leading port; you'll see containers stretching all the way to the airport.

Cost and Hours: €5, daily April-Sept 10:00-20:00, Oct-March 10:00-18:00; €7 gets you an English tour Mon-Fri at 12:30 and 17:00, Sat-Sun at 11:30, 13:00, 16:30, and 18:00, www.bcn.cat/castelldemontjuic.

Getting There: To spare yourself the hike up to the castle and to see some great views of the city, you can ride bus #150 to the

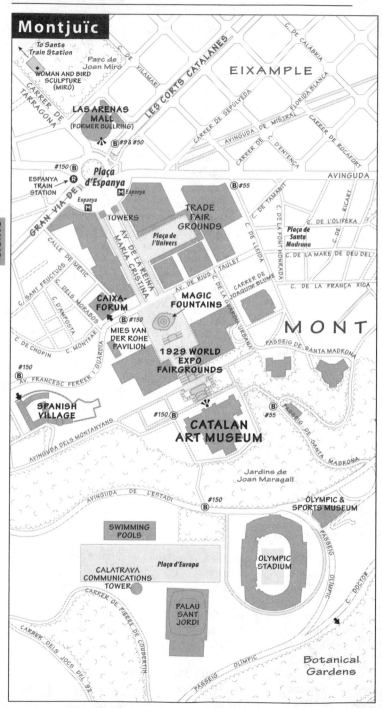

Montjuïc

To Sants Train Station

Parc de Joan Miró

WOMAN AND BIRD SCULPTURE (MIRÓ)

EIXAMPLE

C. DE CALABRIA

C. DE VILAMAR

LES CORTS CATALANES

CARRER DE SEPULVEDA

CARRER DE MISTRAL

C. D'ENTENÇA

AVINGUDA DE MISTRAL

FLORIDA BLANCA

CARRER DE ROCAFORT

LAS ARENAS MALL (FORMER BULLRING)

CARRER DE TARRAGONA

B #9 & #50

#150 B

Plaça d'Espanya

ESPANYA TRAIN STATION R

Espanya M

M Espanya

GRAN VIA DE

TOWERS

AV. DE LA REINA MARIA CRISTINA

Plaça de l'Univers

B #55

AVINGUDA

C. DE TAMARIT

C. DE L'OLIVERA

C. DE LA FONT HONRADA

C. DE LLEIDA

Plaça de Santa Madrona

TRADE FAIR GROUNDS

C. DE RICART

C. DE LA MARE DE DÉU DEL

CALLE DE MEXIC

C. SANT FRUCTUOS

C. DELS MORABOS

C. D'AMPOSTA

C. DE CHOPIN

C. MONTFAR

CAIXA-FORUM

B #150

MIES VAN DER ROHE PAVILION

AV. DE RIUS I TAULET

MAGIC FOUNTAINS

CARRER DE JOAQUIM BLUME

C. DE LA GUARDIA URBANA

C. DE LA FRANÇA XICA

1929 WORLD EXPO FAIRGROUNDS

M O N T

PASSEIG DE SANTA MADRONA

#150 B

AV. FRANCESC FERRER I GUARDIA

SPANISH VILLAGE

AVINGUDA DELS MONTANYANS

#150 B

CATALAN ART MUSEUM

B #55

PASSEIG DE SANTA MADRONA

Jardins de Joan Maragall

AVINGUDA DE L'ESTADI

#150 B

OLYMPIC & SPORTS MUSEUM

SWIMMING POOLS

CALATRAVA COMMUNICATIONS TOWER

Plaça d'Europa

PALAU SANT JORDI

OLYMPIC STADIUM

PASSEIG OLIMPIC

C. DOCTOR

CARRER DE PIERRE DE COUBERTIN

CARRER DELS JOCS DEL 92

PASSEIG OLIMPIC

Botanical Gardens

SIGHTS

base of the castle, catching it from Plaça d'Espanya, the top of the Montjuïc funicular, or various other points on Montjuïc. Or you can spring for the much pricier **cable car** (Telefèric de Montjuïc), which departs from near the upper station of the Montjuïc funicular (€7.50 one-way, €10.80 round-trip, daily June-Sept 10:00-21:00, March-May and Oct 10:00-19:00, Nov-Feb 10:00-18:00).

▲Fundació Joan Miró

Showcasing the talents of yet another Catalan artist, this museum has the best collection anywhere of art by Joan Miró (ZHOO-ahn

mee-ROH, 1893-1983). Born in Barcelona, Miró divided his time between Paris and Catalunya (including Barcelona and his favorite village, Mont-roig del Camp). This building—designed in 1975 by Josep Lluís Sert, a friend of Miró and a student of Le Corbusier—was

purpose-built to show off Miró's art.

The museum displays an always-changing, loosely chronological overview of Miró's oeuvre (as well as generally excellent temporary exhibits of 20th- and 21st-century artists). Consider renting the wonderful audioguide, well worth the extra charge.

If you don't like abstract art, you'll leave here scratching your head. But those who love this place are not faking it...they understand the genius of Miró and the fun of abstraction. Children probably understand it the best. Eavesdrop on what they say about the art; you may learn something.

Cost and Hours: €11, great audioguide-€5; July-Sept Tue-Sat 10:00-20:00 (until 19:00 Oct-June), Thu until 21:30, Sun 10:00-14:30; closed Mon year-round, 200 yards from top of funicular, Parc de Montjuïc, tel. 934-439-470, www.fundaciomiro-bcn.org. The museum has a restaurant, café, and bookshop.

◑ Self-Guided Tour: From the entrance, pass through the temporary exhibits or walk through the outdoor courtyard to reach the permanent collection, starting on the main floor.

Room 11: The massive 400-square-foot *Tapestry of the Foundation*, which Miró designed for this space in 1979, has real texture—like a painting with thick brushstrokes. Notice Miró's trademark star and moon high above. (A different tapestry, which Miró custom-made for New York City's World Trade Center around this same period, was lost in the 9/11 terrorist attacks.)

In the hallway to the next room, look through the window to find the *Mercury Fountain*, by American sculptor Alexander Calder. This piece was created for the same 1937 exhibition at

Joan Miró: The Freedom of Simplicity

Miró believed that everything in the cosmos is linked—colors, sky, stars, love, time, music, dogs, men, women, dirt, and the void. He mixed simple symbols of these things creatively, as a poet uses words. It's as liberating for the visual artist to be abstract as it is for the poet: Both can use metaphors rather than being confined to concrete explanations. Miró would listen to music and paint. It's interactive, free interpretation. He said, "For me, simplicity is freedom."

COPA DEL MUNDO DE FUTBOL ESPAÑA 82

Here are some tips to help you enjoy and appreciate Miró's art: First meditate on it, then read the title (for example, *The Smile of a Tear*), then meditate on it again. Repeat the process until you have an epiphany. There's no correct answer—it's pure poetry. Devotees of Miró say they fly with him and don't even need drugs. Psychoanalysts liken Miró's free-for-all canvases to Rorschach tests. Is that a cigar in that star's mouth?

SIGHTS

which Picasso premiered his seminal *Guernica*. Like Picasso's canvas, Calder's fountain was created to honor victims of the Spanish Civil War—in this case, the residents of Almadén, a mercury-mining town. Watch the liquid do its unpredictable thing as it drips and drops.

• *Now drift into...*

Room 12 (Sculpture Gallery): This gallery features several small bronze pieces by Miró. Ascend the ramp for a different angle. Nearby, find the stairs down to the Espai 13 installation space. Or continue to the end of the hall and downstairs to a room filled with pieces by other artists paying homage to Miró, plus a 15-minute film about Miró.

• *Make your way back to the main floor, where you'll find...*

Room 16 (Sala Joan Prats): The collection in this room loosely traces Miró's artistic development. Young Miró is a sponge of different styles—Fauvism, Cubism, Catalan folk art, Impressionism (see the canvases of beaches and countryside), Orientalism *(Portrait of a Young Girl)*—and whatever else he is exposed to. In 1920, he goes to Paris, dabbles in Dada, and socializes with Surrealists. Is Miró himself a Surrealist? Sort of. They share the same goal: circumventing the viewer's preconceptions about art and reality by juxtaposing unlikely items in order to short-circuit the brain.

Miró's early work does resemble Dalí's. But as his own idio-syncratic style evolves, Miró adds more and more abstraction to the mix. In his Green Paintings series (1925-1927), instead of placing photorealistic items against an otherworldly background (as Dalí would have), Miró arranges highly abstract symbols against a flat background. By 1925, Miró has left the figurative world behind and leaps wholeheartedly into the abyss—pushing the boundaries of abstraction. He paints a completely uninterpretable canvas...and then, just to be cheeky, titles it *Painting*.

• *Head upstairs to the...*

Second Floor: With the 1930s and the advent of the Civil War, Miró temporarily becomes more figurative with his Wind Paintings. Recognizable monsters lurk threateningly. In the early 1940s, Miró flees the Nazi takeover of France and retreats to Spain. He becomes fixated on the heavens and produces his Constellations series—23 paintings of stars, moons, and other brightly colorful items cast against bright backgrounds.

By the late 1940s, Miró is becoming internationally appreci-ated and within a few years, begins to do more public commissions. But corporatization doesn't tame Miró, as the Sixties Gallery dem-onstrates. If anything, he continues to refine his trademark style and strip everything down to basics. Star. Moon. Bird. Woman. Increasingly, Miró's works are intended as something to meditate on. Some of his best-known and most appreciated works date from this period and can't be found in any museum, but are scattered around the streets of Barcelona—in the middle of the Ramblas (see page 85), in the park behind the nearby Las Arenas bullring mall (see page 72), and elsewhere.

• *With extra time, enjoy...*

The Rest of the Museum: Gallery K contains works from the 1960s and 1970s. Return to earth with a visit to the terrace, where you'll find a modern sculpture gallery and views of the surrounding area.

Olympic and Sports Museum
(Museu Olímpic i de l'Esport)

This museum rides the coattails of the stadium across the street. You'll twist down a timeline-ramp that traces the history of the Olympic Games, interspersed with random exhibits about various sports. Downstairs you'll find exhibits designed to test your ath-leticism, a play-by-play rehash of the '92 Barcelona Olympiad, a commemoration of Juan Antonio Samaranch (the influential Cata-lan president of the IOC for two decades), a sports media exhibit, and a schmaltzy movie collage. High-tech but hokey, the museum is worth the time and money only for those nostalgic for the '92 Games.

Cost and Hours: €5.10, April-Sept Tue-Sat 10:00-20:00 (until 18:00 Oct-March), Sun 10:00-14:30, closed Mon year-round, Avinguda de l'Estadi 60, tel. 932-925-379, www.museuolimpicbcn.cat.

Olympic Stadium (Estadi Olímpic)

Aside from the memories of the medals, Barcelona's Olympic Stadium offers little to see today. But if the doors are open, you're

welcome to step inside. History panels along the railings overlooking the playing field tell the stadium's dynamic story and show the place in happier times—filled with fans as Bon Jovi, the Rolling Stones, and Madonna pack the place.

The stadium was originally built for the 1929 World Expo, but soon thereafter, played a big part in Barcelona's plan to host the "People's Olympiad." These were to take place in July of 1936 as an alternative to Hitler's Fascist Olympics, which were scheduled for that same summer in Berlin (and which Spain had planned to boycott). But just days before the Barcelona games were to begin, civil war broke out in Spain, and the event was cancelled.

Fifty-something years later, the stadium was updated and expanded in preparation for the 1992 Summer Olympics. It was officially named for Catalan patriot Lluís Companys i Jover, the left-wing leader who was president when Spain's Civil War began. Companys had pushed for the democratic alternative to Hitler's games; he was later arrested and executed by Franco.

The XXV Olympiad, which kicked off here on July 25, 1992, was memorable for several reasons. At the opening ceremonies, an archer dramatically lit the Olympic torch—which still stands high at the end of the stadium overlooking the city skyline—with a flaming arrow. Over the next two weeks, Barcelona played host to the thrill of victory—most notably at the hands of Michael Jordan, Magic Johnson, Larry Bird, and the rest of the US basketball "Dream Team"—and the agony of defeat (i.e., the nightmares of the Dream Team's opponents). These Olympics also coincided with several turning points in global geopolitics. It was the first Olympiad after the fall of the Soviet Union (and the first since 1972 without boycotts). Twelve newly independent states sent their athletes as one big Unified Team. These were also the first Games in which the post-Apartheid South African team was invited to participate; the first Games after the breakup of Yugoslavia (with four teams from that region instead of one); and the first to feature a reunified German team.

Nearby: Hovering over the stadium is the futuristic **Montjuïc Communications Tower** (designed by prominent Spanish architect Santiago Calatrava), originally used to transmit Olympic highlights and lowlights around the world.

▲▲Catalan Art Museum
(Museu Nacional d'Art de Catalunya)

The big vision for this wonderful museum is to showcase Catalan art from the 10th century through about the mid-20th century. Often called "the Prado of Romanesque art" (and "MNAC" for short), it holds Europe's best collection of Romanesque frescoes. It also offers a particularly good sweep of modern Catalan art—fitting, given Catalunya's astonishing contribution to the Modern. Art aficionados are sure to find something in this diverse collection to tickle their fancy. It's all housed in the grand Palau Nacional, an emblematic building from the 1929 World Expo, with magnificent views over Barcelona, especially from the building's rooftop terrace (see below).

Cost and Hours: €12, includes temporary exhibits and rooftop terrace, ticket valid for two days within one month, free Sat from 15:00 and first Sun of month; audioguide-€3.10; rooftop access only-€3; open May-Sept Tue-Sat 10:00-20:00 (until 18:00 Oct-April), Sun 10:00-15:00, closed Mon, last entry 30 minutes before closing; in massive National Palace building above Magic Fountains, near Plaça d'Espanya—take escalators up; tel. 936-220-376, www.mnac.cat.

Getting to the Rooftop Terrace: To reach the terrace from the main entrance, walk past the bathrooms to the left and show your ticket to get on the elevator. You'll ride up nearly to the viewpoint, but then must hike up a couple of flights of stairs to the terrace.

Visiting the Museum: As you enter, pick up a map. The left wing is Romanesque, and the right wing is Gothic, exquisite Renaissance, and Baroque. Upstairs is more Baroque, plus modern art, photography, coins, and more.

The MNAC's rare, world-class collection of **Romanesque** (Romànic) art came mostly from remote Catalan village churches (most of the pieces were moved to the museum in the early 1920s to save them from scavenging art dealers). A series of videos shows the process of extracting the frescoes from the churches to move them to the museum. The Romanesque wing features a remarkable array of 11th- to 13th-century frescoes, painted wooden altar fronts, and ornate statuary. This classic Romanesque art—with flat

SIGHTS

2-D scenes, each saint holding his symbol, and Jesus (easy to identify by the cross in his halo)—is impressively displayed on replicas of the original church ceilings and apses.

Across the way, in the **Gothic** wing, fresco murals give way to vivid 14th-century wood-panel paintings of Bible stories. A roomful of paintings (Room 26) by the Catalan master Jaume Huguet (1412-1492) deserves a look, particularly his *Consecration of St. Agusti Vell*.

For a break, go to the right from the Gothic exit to glide under the huge **dome,** which once housed an ice-skating rink. This was the prime ceremony room and dance hall for the 1929 World Expo.

From the big ballroom, you can ride the glass elevator upstairs to the **Renaissance and Modern Art** section, covering Spain's Golden Age (Zurbarán, heavy religious scenes, Spanish royals with their endearing underbites) and Romanticism (dewy-eyed Catalan landscapes). Down on the ground floor are minor works by major—if not necessarily Catalan—names (Velázquez, El Greco, Tintoretto, Rubens, and so on).

Another museum highlight is the **Modern** section, which takes you on an enjoyable walk from the late 1800s to about 1950. It's kind of a Catalan Musée d'Orsay, offering a big chronological clockwise circle covering Symbolism, Modernisme, *fin de siècle* fun, Art Deco, and more. Find the early 20th-century paintings by Catalan artists Santiago Rusiñol and Ramon Casas, both of whom had a profound impact on a young Picasso (and, through him, on all of modern art). Casas was also one of the financiers of Els Quatre Gats, the hangout of Modernista artists (see page 204); his fun Toulouse-Lautrec-esque works, including a whimsical self-portrait on a tandem bicycle, are crowd-pleasers. Crossing over to the "Modern 2" section, you'll find furniture (pieces that complement the empty spaces you likely saw in Gaudí's buildings—including a Gaudí wooden sofa), Impressionism, the shimmering landscapes of Joaquim Mir, and several distinctly Picasso portraits of women.

The museum also has a coin collection, seductive sofas scattered about, the chic and pricey Oleum restaurant (with vast city views), and a comfy outdoor terrace café (serving snacks with more city views).

▲1929 World Expo Fairgrounds

With the World Expo in 1929, Montjuïc morphed into an extravagant center for fairs, museums, and festivals. Nearly everything you see here dates from 1929 (the exceptions are

CaixaForum and Las Arenas mall). The expo's theme was to demonstrate how electricity was about more than lightbulbs: Electricity powered the funicular, the glorious expo fountains, the many pavilion displays, and even the flame atop the fountain marking the center of Plaça d'Espanya (and celebrating the electric company that sponsored the show). If Barcelona is known for growing through big events, this certainly is a good example.

Standing at Plaça d'Espanya (or, better yet, on the rooftop terrace of the bullring mall—described later), look through the double-brick-tower gate, down the grand esplanade, and imagine it alive with fountains and lined by proud national pavilions showing off all that was modern in 1929. Today the site is home to the Fira de Barcelona convention center. The Neo-Baroque fountain provides a brilliant centerpiece for Plaça d'Espanya.

Getting There: The fairgrounds sprawl at the base of Montjuïc, from the Catalan Art Museum's doorstep to Plaça d'Espanya. The easiest option is to see these sights on your way down from Montjuïc. Otherwise, ride the Metro to Espanya, then use the series of stairs and escalators to climb up through the heart of the fairgrounds (eventually reaching the Catalan Art Museum).

▲Magic Fountains (Font Màgica)

Music, colored lights, and huge amounts of water make an artistic and coordinated splash in the evening near Plaça d'Espanya.

Cost and Hours: Free, 20-minute shows start on the half-hour; almost always May-Sept Thu-Sun 21:00-23:00, no shows Mon-Wed; Oct-April Fri-Sat 19:00-20:30, no shows Sun-Thu; from the Espanya Metro stop, walk toward the towering National Palace.

▲▲CaixaForum

The CaixaForum Social and Cultural Center (sponsored by the leading Catalan bank) is housed in one of Barcelona's most important Art Nouveau buildings. In 1911, Josep Puig i Cadafalch (a top architect often overshadowed by Gaudí) designed the Casaramona textile factory, which showed off Modernista design in an industrial rather than a residential context. It functioned as a factory for less than a decade, then later served a long stint as a police station under Franco. Beautifully refurbished in 2002, the facility reopened as a great center for bringing culture and art to the people of Barcelona.

Cost and Hours: Free entrance to building, exhibits-€4, daily 10:00-20:00, Avinguda de Francesc Ferrer i Guàrdia 6-8, tel. 934-768-600, http://obrasocial.lacaixa.es—click on "Culture."

Visiting the Center: From the lobby, signs point to *Sala 2, 3, 4,* and *5*; each hosts different (and typically outstanding) temporary exhibitions. Ride the escalator to the first floor, which features a modest but interesting exhibit about the history and renovation of the building, including a model and photos. Then head into the appealing red-brick courtyard, from which you can access the various exhibition halls. (The sight features generally limited English descriptions.)

Take the stairs or elevator up to the Modernista Terrace, boasting a wavy floor, bristling with fanciful brick towers, and offering views over the complex and to Montjuïc. Enjoy the genius of Puig i Cadafalch's Modernista design, which provided state-of-the-art working conditions—natural light, good ventilation, and even two trademark towers filled with water (which could be broken to put out any factory fires). The various buildings (designed to be separate from each other to reduce the risk of fire) were built on terraces to level out the Montjuïc slope. Notice that there's no smokestack. This was one of the first electric-powered factories in town.

Mies van der Rohe Pavilion (Pabellón Mies van der Rohe)

Architecture pilgrims flock to the pavilion that Ludwig Mies van der Rohe designed for the German exhibits at the 1929 expo. Although it was dismantled at the end of the fair, the building was heralded as a seminal example of modern architecture, and in the 1980s, the city of Barcelona reconstructed it on the original site. It's small and stripped-down—a strictly functional "Modernist" (i.e., decidedly *not* Modernista) structure. Inside are examples of the Barcelona Chair, the tubular steel and leather-cushioned chair that's become an icon of 20th-century furniture design. This building—staring down the CaixaForum from across the street—is a reminder that even just a couple of decades later, architecture highbrows already considered the over-the-top flourishes of Modernisme passé and overdone, or even embarrassing; Gaudí, Puig i Cadafalch, and company would fall out of fashion until the late 20th century.

Cost and Hours: €5, daily 10:00-20:00, Avinguda de Francesc Ferrer i Guàrdia 7, tel. 934-234-016, www.miesbcn.com.

Spanish Village (Poble Espanyol)

This five-acre model village (a long hike up from the main World Expo esplanade; best to take bus #150 up) was built as part of the expo to show off the cultural and architectural diversity in Spain.

Replicating traditional architecture from all over the country, the village was mostly a shell to contain gift shops—and today it still serves the same purpose. Craftspeople do their clichéd thing (mostly in the morning), and friendly shopkeepers offer plenty of tasty samples of traditional and local edibles. I think it's tacky and overpriced, but if you never expect to visit an authentic Spanish village (this place is popular with cruise groups), here's a pale substitute.

Cost and Hours: €11, €3.50 audioguide explains all the buildings, daily 10:00-20:00 or later, closes earlier off-season, www.poble-espanyol.com.

▲Las Arenas (Bullring Mall)

What do you do with a big bullfighting arena that's been sitting empty for decades? Make a mall. The grand Neo-Moorish Modernista *plaça de toros* functioned as an arena for bullfights from around 1900 to 1977, and then reopened in 2011 as a mall. It now hosts everything you'd expect in a modern shopping center: lots of brand-name shops, a food-court basement, a 12-screen cinema complex, and a rock-and-roll museum.

The **rooftop terrace,** with stupendous views of Plaça d'Espanya and Montjuïc, is ringed with eateries (reachable by external glass elevator for €1 or from inside escalators/elevators for free). Besides getting a bird's-eye perspective of the fairgrounds, you can gaze down at Parc de Joan Miró, which includes the giant sculpture *Woman and Bird (Dona i Ocell).* This was one of the works (including the mosaic on the Ramblas—see page 85) that the city commissioned from the artist to welcome visitors. Miró's sense of humor is evident—if the sculpture seems phallic, keep in mind that the Catalan word for "bird" is also slang for "penis."

Cost and Hours: Free, daily 10:00-22:00, restaurants serve until 24:00 and later, Gran Via de les Corts Catalanes 373-385, Metro: Espanya, www.arenasdebarcelona.com.

THE BEACHES AND NEARBY

▲Barcelona's Beaches

Barcelona has created a summer tourist trade by building a huge stretch of beaches east of the town center. From Barceloneta, an uninterrupted band of sand tumbles three miles northeast to the Fòrum. Before the 1992 Olympics, this area was an industrial wasteland nicknamed the "Catalan Manchester." Not anymore. The industrial zone was demolished and dumped into the sea, while sand was dredged from the seabed to make the pristine beaches locals enjoy today. Looking out to sea, you can't miss the W Hotel, shaped like a windblown sail, dominating a small peninsula.

The overall scene is great for sunbathing and for an evening paseo before dinner. It's like a resort island—complete with lounge chairs, volleyball, showers, WCs, bike paths, and inviting beach bars called *chiringuitos*. Each beach segment has its own vibe: Sant Sebastià (closest, popular with older beachgoers and families), Barceloneta (with many seafood restaurants), Nova Icària (pleasant family beach), and Mar Bella (attracts a younger crowd, clothing-optional).

Getting There: The Barceloneta Metro stop leaves you blocks from the sand. To get to the beaches without a hike, take the bus. From the Ramblas, bus #59 will get you as far as Barceloneta Park; bus #D20 leaves from the Columbus Monument and follows a similar route. Bus #V15 runs from Plaça de Catalunya to the tip of Barceloneta (near the W Hotel).

Biking the Beach: For a break from the city, rent a bike (in El Born, Citadel Park, or Barceloneta—for details, see page 26) and take the following little ride: Explore Citadel Park, filled with families enjoying a day out (described above). Then roll through Barceloneta. This artificial peninsula was once the home of working-class sailors and shippers. From the Barceloneta beach, head up to the Olympic Village, where the former apartments for 13,000 visiting athletes now house permanent residents. The village's symbol, Frank Gehry's striking "fish," shines brightly in the sun. A bustling night scene keeps this stretch of harborfront busy until the wee hours. From here you'll come to a series of man-made crescent-shaped beaches, each with trendy bars and cafés. If you're careless or curious (down by Platja de la Mar Bella), you might find yourself pedaling past people working on an all-over tan. In the distance is the huge solar panel marking the site of the Fòrum shopping and convention center.

Citadel Park (Parc de la Ciutadella)

In 1888, Barcelona's biggest, greenest park, originally the site of a much-hated military citadel, was transformed for a Universal Exhibition (world's fair). The stately Triumphal Arch at the top of the park, celebrating the removal of the citadel, was built as the main entrance. Inside you'll find wide pathways, plenty of trees and grass, a zoo, and museums of geology and zoology. Barcelona, one of Europe's most densely populated cities, suffers from a lack of real green space. This park is a haven and is especially enjoyable on weekends, when it teems with happy families (for more on the zoo and on kids' activities in Citadel Park, see the Barcelona with Children chapter). Enjoy the ornamental fountain that the young Antoni Gaudí helped design, and consider a jaunt in a rental rowboat on the lake in the center of the park. Check out the tropical Umbracle greenhouse and the Hivernacle winter garden, which has a pleasant café-bar (Mon-Sat 10:00-14:00 & 17:00-20:30, Sun 10:30-14:00, shorter hours off-season).

Cost and Hours: Park—free, daily 10:00 until dusk, north of França train station, Metro: Arc de Triomf, Barceloneta, or Ciutadella-Vila Olímpica.

The Fòrum

The original 1860 vision for Barcelona's enlargement would have extended the boulevard called Diagonal right to the sea. Developers finally realized this goal nearly a century and a half later, with the opening of the Fòrum neighborhood. Go here for a taste of today's Barcelona: nothing Gothic, nothing quaint, just big and modern—a mall, waterfront esplanade, and a convention center.

Among the modern structures here, you can't miss the triangular **Edifici Fòrum.** Built for a 2004 Universal Forum of Cultures conference and exhibition, the eccentric building was initially controversial, but it's since become a well-regarded landmark. Among other things, the Fòrum tries to be an inspiration for environmental engineering. Waste is burned to produce heat, and a giant solar panel creates perfectly clean and sustainable energy.

Getting There: You can get out to the Fòrum by bike, bus, or taxi via the long and impressive beach. Or the Metro zips you there in just a few minutes from the center (Metro: Fòrum).

THE RAMBLAS RAMBLE

*From Plaça de Catalunya
to the Waterfront*

For more than a century, this walk down Barcelona's main boule-vard has drawn locals and visitors alike. While its former elegance has been tackified somewhat by tourist shops and fast-food joints, this still has the best people watching in town. Walk the Ramblas at least once to get the lay of the land, then venture farther afield. It's a one-hour, level stroll, with an easy return by Metro.

The word "Ramblas" is plural; the street is actually a succession of five separately named segments. But street signs and addresses treat it as a single long street—"La Rambla," singular. On this pedestrian-only Champs-Elysées, you'll raft the river of Barcelo-nese life, passing a grand opera house, elegant cafés, flower stands, retread prostitutes, brazen pickpockets, power-dressing con men, artists, street mimes, and people looking to charge more for a shoe-shine than what you paid for the shoes.

Orientation

Length of This Walk: Allow an hour. If you have less time, focus on the stretch between the Fountain of Canaletes and the Miró mosaic at Liceu. With more time, dip into La Boqueria Market.

When to Go: The Ramblas is two different streets by day and by night. To fully experience its yin and yang, walk it once in the evening and again in the morning, grabbing breakfast on a stool in a market café.

Getting There: This walk begins at the Plaça de Catalunya end of the Ramblas, across the square from El Corte Inglés depart-ment store (Metro: Plaça de Catalunya).

La Boqueria Market: Free, Mon-Sat 8:00-20:00, best mornings after 9:00, closed Sun, Rambla 91.

RAMBLAS RAMBLE

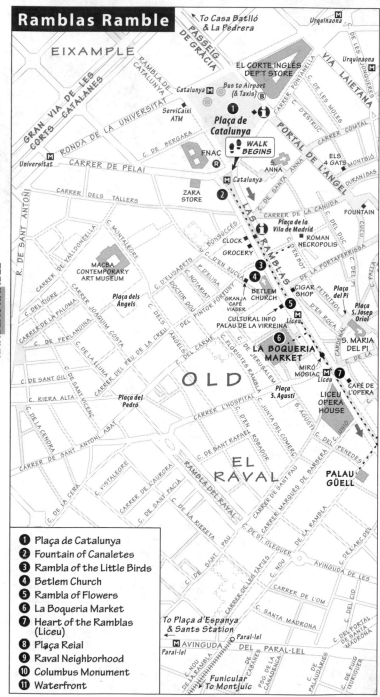

Ramblas Ramble

EIXAMPLE

To Casa Batlló
& La Pedrera

PASSEIG DE GRÀCIA

Urquinaona

VIA LAIETANA

Urquinaona

EL CORTE INGLÉS
DEP'T STORE

Bus to Airport
(& Taxis)

Catalunya

ServiCaixi
ATM

❶ Plaça de
Catalunya

WALK
BEGINS

ELS
4 GATS

FNAC

Universitat

RONDA DE LA UNIVERSITAT

C. DE BERGARA

Catalunya

S.
ANNA

CARRER DE PELAI

ZARA
STORE

❷

Catalunya

CARRER DE LA CANUDA

FOUNTAIN

CARRER DELS TALLERS

BONSUCCÉS

Plaça de la
Vila de Madrid

ROMAN
NECROPOLIS

CLOCK

MACBA
CONTEMPORARY
ART MUSEUM

GROCERY

❸

❹

Plaça dels
Àngels

GRANJA
CAFÉ VIADER

BETLEM
CHURCH

CIGAR
SHOP

Plaça
del Pi

CULTURAL INFO
PALAU DE LA VIRREINA

❺

Liceu

Plaça
S. Josep
Oriol

S. MARIA
DEL PI

❻
LA BOQUERIA
MARKET

OLD

Plaça
S. Agustí

MIRÓ
MOSAIC

Liceu

❼

CAFÉ DE
L'OPERA

Plaça del
Pedró

LICEU
OPERA
HOUSE

EL
RAVAL

RAMBLA DEL RAVAL

PALAU
GÜELL

To Plaça d'Espanya
& Sants Station

Paral·lel

AVINGUDA   DEL   PARAL·LEL

Paral·lel

Funicular
To Montjuïc

❶ Plaça de Catalunya
❷ Fountain of Canaletes
❸ Rambla of the Little Birds
❹ Betlem Church
❺ Rambla of Flowers
❻ La Boqueria Market
❼ Heart of the Ramblas
   (Liceu)
❽ Plaça Reial
❾ Raval Neighborhood
❿ Columbus Monument
⓫ Waterfront

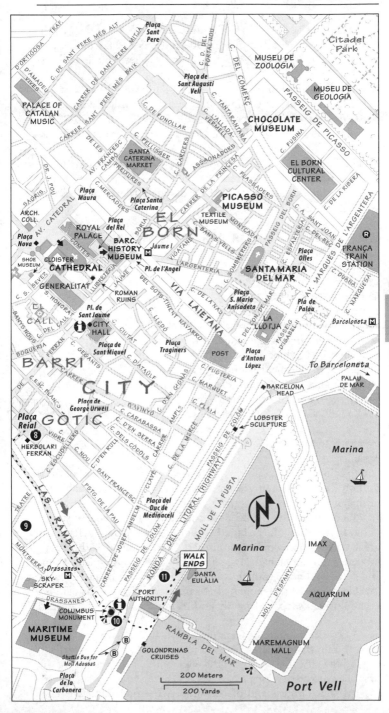

Palau Güell: €12, includes audioguide, free first Sun of the month, open April-Oct Tue-Sun 10:00-20:00, Nov-March Tue-Sun 10:00-17:30, closed Mon year-round, Carrer Nou de la Rambla 3-5.

Columbus Monument: Elevator-€4.50, daily 8:30-20:30, last ride 30 minutes before closing, Plaça del Portal de la Pau.

Santa Eulália: €1, Tue-Fri and Sun 10:00-20:30, Sat 14:00-20:30, closes at 17:30 Nov-March, closed Mon year-round, Moll de la Fusta quay.

Eating: The eateries here are tourist traps: Do not eat or drink on the Ramblas. But just off the street you'll find a few handy lunch spots, and the stalls of La Boqueria Market invite grazing. For details, see page 198.

The Walk Begins

• *Start your ramble on Plaça de Catalunya, at the top of the Ramblas.*

❶ Plaça de Catalunya

Dotted with fountains, statues, and pigeons, and ringed by grand Art Deco buildings, this plaza is Barcelona's center. The square's
stern, straight lines are a reaction to the curves of Modernisme (which predominates in the Eixample district, just above the square). Plaça de Catalunya is the hub for the Metro, bus, airport shuttle, and Tourist Bus. It's where Barcelona congregates to watch soccer matches on the big screen, to demonstrate, to celebrate,
and to enjoy outdoor concerts and festivals. More than half of the 8 million Catalans live in greater Barcelona, and for the inhabitants of this proud nation, this is their Times Square.

Geographically, the 12-acre square links the narrow streets of old Barcelona with the broad boulevards of the newer city. Four great thoroughfares radiate from here. The Ramblas is the popular pedestrian promenade. Passeig de Gràcia has fashionable shops and cafés (and noisy traffic). Rambla de Catalunya is equally fashionable but cozier and more pedestrian-friendly. Avinguda del Portal de l'Angel (shopper-friendly and traffic-free) leads to the Barri Gòtic.

Historically, Plaça de Catalunya links the modern city with its past. In the 1850s, when Barcelona tore down its medieval walls to expand the city, this square on the edge of the walls was one of the first places to be developed.

At the Ramblas end of the square, the odd, inverted-staircase **monument** represents the shape of Catalunya and honors one of its former presidents, Francesc Macià i Llussà, who declared independence for the breakaway region in 1931. (It didn't quite stick.) Sculptor Josep Maria Subirachs, whose work you'll see at the Sagrada Família (see page 156), designed it.

The venerable Café Zürich, just across the street from the monument, is a popular downtown rendezvous spot for locals. Homesick Americans might prefer the nearby Hard Rock Café. And the giant El Corte Inglés department store towering above the square (on the northeast side) has just about anything you might need.

• *Cross the street and start heading down the Ramblas. To get oriented, pause 20 yards down, at the ornate lamppost with a fountain as its base (on the right, near #129).*

❷ Fountain of Canaletes

The black-and-gold **fountain** has been a local favorite for more than a century. When Barcelona tore down its medieval wall and transformed the Ramblas from a drainage ditch into an elegant promenade, this fountain was one of its early attractions. Legend says that a drink from the fountain ensures that you'll come back to Barcelona one day. Watch the tourists—eager to guarantee a return trip—struggle with the awkwardly high water pressure. It's still a popular let's-meet-at-the-fountain rendezvous spot and a gathering place for celebrations and demonstrations. Fans of the Barcelona soccer team rally here before a big match—some touch their hand to their lips, then "kiss" the fountain with their hand for good luck. It's also a good spot to fill up your water bottle.

As you survey the Ramblas action, get your bearings for our upcoming stroll. You'll see the following features here and all along the way:

The wavy **tile work** of the pavers underfoot represents the stream that once flowed here. *Rambla* means "stream" in Arabic, and this used to be a drainage ditch along the medieval wall of the Barri Gòtic. Many Catalan towns, established where rivers approach the sea, have streets called "Ramblas." Today Barcelona's "stream" has become a river of humanity.

Look up to see the city's characteristic shallow **balconies.** They're functional as well as decorative, with windows opening

from floor to ceiling to allow more light and air into the tight, dark spaces of these cramped old buildings. The **plane trees** lining the boulevard are known for their peeling bark and hardiness in urban settings. These deciduous trees are ideal for the climate, letting in maximum sun in the winter and providing maximum shade in the summer. Nowadays, fewer residents live around here—they've been supplanted by businesses and tourism. This shapes what's sold along the Ramblas: There are fewer flower shops and more market stalls catering to tourists.

Nearby, notice the **chairs** fixed to the sidewalk at jaunty angles. It used to be that you'd pay to rent a chair here to look at the constant parade of passersby. Seats are now free, and it's still the best people-watching in town. Enjoy these chairs while you can—you'll find virtually no public benches or other seating farther down the Ramblas, only cafés that serve beer and sangria in just one (expensive) size: *gigante.*

Across from the fountain and a few steps down, notice the first of many **ONCE booths** along this walk (pronounced OHN-thay, the Spanish "11"). These sell lottery tickets that support Spain's organization of the blind, a powerful advocate for the needs of people with disabilities.

• *Continue strolling.*

All along the Ramblas are **newsstands** (open 24 hours). Among their souvenirs, you'll see soccer paraphernalia, especially the scarlet-and-blue of FC Barcelona (known as "Barça"). The team is owned by its more than 170,000 "members"—fans who buy season tickets, which come with a share of ownership (the team's healthy payroll guarantees that they're always in contention). Their motto, "More than a club" *(Mes que un club),* suggests that Barça represents not only athletic prowess but also Catalan cultural identity. This comes to a head during a match nicknamed "El Clásico," in which they face their bitter rivals, Real Madrid (whom many Barça fans view as stand-ins for Castilian cultural chauvinism).

Walk 100 yards farther to #115 and the venerable **Royal Academy of Science and Arts building** (it's now home to a performing-arts theater). Look up: The clock high on the facade marks official Barcelona time—synchronize. Notice the **TI** kiosk right on the Ramblas—a handy stop for any questions. The **Carrefour** supermarket just behind it has cheap groceries (at #113, Mon-Sat 10:00-22:00, closed Sun).

• *You're now standing at the...*

❸ Rambla of the Little Birds

Traditionally, kids brought their parents here to buy pets, especially on Sundays. But animal-rights groups lobbied to cut back on the stalls because so many families were making impulse buys with no serious interest in taking care of these cute little critters—and many ended up being flushed. Today, only one of the traditional pet kiosks survives—and there's not a bird in sight; you'll find mostly bird-related pet supplies and recorded chirping.

• *At #122 (the big, modern Citadines Hotel on the left, just behind the pet kiosk), take a 100-yard detour through a passageway marked* Passatge de la Ramblas *to a restored...*

Roman Necropolis: Look down and imagine a 2,000-year-old tomb-lined road. In Roman cities, tombs (outside the walls)

typically lined the roads leading into town. Emperor Augustus spent a lot of time in modern-day Spain conquering new land, so the Romans were sure to incorporate Hispania into the empire's infrastructure. This road, Via Augusta, led into the Roman port of Barcino (today's highway to France still follows the route laid out by this Roman thoroughfare). Looking down at these ruins, you can see how Roman Barcino was about 10 feet lower than today's street level. For more on this city's Roman chapter, follow my Barri Gòtic Walk, later.

• *Return to the Ramblas and continue 100 yards or so to the next street, Carrer de la Portaferrissa (across from the big church). Turn left a few steps and look right to see the* **decorative tile** *over a fountain still in use by locals. The scene shows the original city wall with the gate that once stood here and the action on what is today's Ramblas. Now cross the boulevard to the front of the big church.*

❹ Betlem Church

This imposing church is dedicated to Bethlehem, and for centuries locals have flocked here at Christmastime to see Nativity scenes.

The church is 17th-century Baroque: Check out the

sloping roofline, ball-topped pinnacles, corkscrew columns, and scrolls above the entrance. The Baroque and also Renaissance styles are relatively unusual in Barcelona because it missed out on several centuries of architectural development. Barcelona enjoyed two heydays: during the medieval period (before the Renaissance) and during the turn of the 20th century (after Baroque). In between those periods, from about 1500 until 1850, the city's importance dropped—first, New World discoveries shifted lucrative trade to ports on the Atlantic, and then the Spanish crown kept unruly Catalunya on a short leash.

For a sweet treat, head around to the narrow lane on the far side of the church (running parallel to the Ramblas) to the recommended **Café Granja Viader,** which has specialized in baked and dairy delights since 1870. Step inside to see Viader family photos and early posters advertising Cacaolat—the local chocolate milk Barcelonans love. (For other sugary treats nearby, follow "A Short, Sweet Walk" on page 207.)

• *Continue down the boulevard, through the stretch called the...*

❺ Rambla of Flowers

This colorful block, lined with flower stands, is the Rambla of Flowers. Besides admiring the blossoms on display, gardeners will covet

the seeds sold here for varieties of radishes, greens, peppers, and beans seldom seen in the US—including the iconic green Padrón pepper of tapas fame (if you buy seeds, you're obligated to declare them at US customs when returning home). On the left, at #100, **Gimeno** sells cigars. Step inside and appreciate the dying art of cigar boxes. Go ahead, do something forbidden in America but perfectly legal here...buy a Cuban (little singles for €1). Tobacco shops sell stamps and phone cards, plus bongs and marijuana gear—the Spanish approach to pot is very casual. While people can't legally sell marijuana, they're allowed to grow it for personal use and consume it.

• *Continue to the Metro stop marked by the red M. At #91 (on the right) is the arcaded entrance to Barcelona's great covered market, La Boqueria. If this main entry is choked with visitors (as it often is), you can skirt around to a side entrance, one block in either direction (look for the round arches that mark passages into the market colonnade).*

❻ La Boqueria Market

This lively market hall is an explosion of chicken legs, bags of live snails, stiff fish, delicious oranges, odd odors, and sleeping dogs.

The best day for a visit is Saturday, when the market is thriving. It's closed on Sundays, and locals avoid it on Mondays, when it's open but (they believe) vendors are selling items that aren't necessarily fresh—especially seafood, since fishermen stay home on Sundays.

Since as far back as 1200, Barcelonans have bought their animal parts here. The market was originally located by the walled city's entrance, as many medieval markets were (since it was more expensive to trade within the walls). It later expanded into the colonnaded courtyard of a now-gone monastery before being topped with a colorful arcade in 1850.

While tourists are drawn like moths to a flame to the area around the main entry (below the colorful stained-glass sign), locals know that the stalls up front pay the highest rent—and therefore have to inflate their prices and cater to out-of-towners. For example, the juices along the main drag just inside the entrance are tempting, but if you venture to the right a couple of aisles, the clientele gets more local and the prices drop dramatically.

Stop by the recommended **Pinotxo Bar**—it's just inside the market, under the sign—and snap a photo of Juan. Animated Juan and his family are always busy feeding shoppers. Getting Juan to crack a huge smile and a thumbs-up for your camera makes a great shot...and he loves it. The stools nearby are a fine perch for enjoying both your coffee and the people-watching.

The market and lanes nearby are busy with tempting little eateries (several are listed on page 202). Drop by a café for an *espresso con leche* or breakfast *tortilla española* (potato omelet). Once you get past the initial gauntlet, do some exploring. The small square on the north side of the market hosts a farmers market in the mornings. Wander around—as local architect Antoni Gaudí used to—and gain inspiration. Go on a scavenger hunt for some of these items:

Produce stands show off seasonal fruits and vegetables that you'll see on local menus. ("Market cuisine" is big at Barcelona restaurants—chefs come to markets like this each morning to rustle up ingredients.) The tubs of little green peppers that look like jalapeños are lightly fried for the dish called *pimientos de Padrón*. In a culinary form of Russian roulette, a few of these mild peppers sometimes turn out to be hot—greeting the eater with a fiery jolt. In the fall, you'll see lots of mushrooms; in the winter, artichokes.

Full legs of *jamón* (ham) abound. The many varieties of *jamón serrano* are distinguished by the type of pig it comes from and what that pig ate. Top quality are *ibérico* (Iberian type) and *bellota* (acorn eaters)—even by the slice these are very expensive, but gourmets pay €200 or more to go whole hock.

You'll see many types of *chorizo*, the red Spanish sausage that's sometimes spicy (a rare bit of heat in an otherwise tame cuisine). Also keep an eye out for a few meats that are uncommon in American dishes—rabbit and suckling pig. Beware: *Huevos de toro* means bull testicles—surprisingly inexpensive...and oh so good.

The **fishmonger** stalls could double as a marine biology lab; in this Mediterranean city, people have come up with endless ways to harvest the sea. Notice that fish is sold whole, not filleted—local shoppers like to look their dinner in the eye to be sure it's fresh. Count the many different types of shrimp (*gamba, scampi, langostino*, clawed *cigala*). One of the weirdest Spanish edibles is the tubular razor clam *(navaja de almeja)*, with something oozing out of each end.

Some stalls specialize in dried **salt cod** *(bacalao)*. Historically, codfish—preserved in salt and dried—provided desperately needed protein on long sea voyages and was critical in allowing seafaring cultures like that of Catalunya to venture farther from their home ports. Before it can be eaten, salt cod must be rehydrated. Fish stalls sell it either covered in salt or submerged in water, to hasten the time between market and plate.

Certain food items are associated with a particular town—for example, anchovies from L'Escala, shrimp from Palamos, and so on. Among Catalans, this is a sort of code designating quality (like "Idaho potatoes" or "Washington apples" in the US).

Olives are a keystone of the Spanish diet. Take a look at the 25 kinds offered at Graus Olives i Conserves shop (straight in, near the back).

• *Head back out to the street and continue down the Ramblas.*

You're skirting the western boundary of the old Barri Gòtic neighborhood. As you walk, glance to the left through a modern cutaway arch for a glimpse of the medieval church tower of **Santa Maria del Pi,** a popular venue for guitar concerts (see the Nightlife in Barcelona chapter). This also marks Plaça del Pi and a great shopping street, Carrer Petritxol, which runs parallel to the Ramblas (see the Shopping in Barcelona chapter).

Now look across to the other side of the Ramblas. At the corner, find the highly regarded **Escribà** bakery, with its fine Modernista facade and interior (look for the *Antigua Casa Figueras* sign arching over the doorway). Notice the beautiful mosaics of twining plants, the stained-glass peacock displaying his tail feathers, and the undulating woodwork. In the sidewalk in front of the door, a plaque dates the building to 1902 (plaques like this identify historic shops all over town).

• *After another block, you reach the Liceu Metro station, marking the...*

➐ Heart of the Ramblas

At the Liceu Metro station's elevators, the Ramblas widens a bit into a small, lively square (Plaça de la Boqueria). Liceu marks the

midpoint of the Ramblas, halfway between Plaça de Catalunya and the waterfront.

Underfoot in the center of the Ramblas, find the much-trod-upon red-white-yellow-and-blue **mosaic** by homegrown abstract artist Joan Miró. The mosaic's black arrow represents an anchor, a reminder of the city's attachment to the sea. Miró's simple, colorful designs are found all over the city, from murals to mobiles to the La Caixa bank logo. The best place in Barcelona to see his work is in the Fundació Joan Miró at Montjuïc (see page 64).

The surrounding buildings have playful ornamentation typical of the city. The **Chinese dragon** holding a lantern (at #82) decorates a former umbrella shop (notice the fun umbrella mosaics high up). While the dragon may seem purely decorative, it's actually an important symbol of Catalan pride for its connection to the local patron saint, St. George (Jordi).

Hungry? Swing around the back of the umbrella shop to the recommended **Taverna Basca Irati** tapas bar (a block up Carrer del

Cardenal Casanyes). This is one of many user-friendly, Basque-style tapas bars in town; instead of ordering, you can just grab or point to what looks good on the display platters, then pay per piece.

Back on the Ramblas, a few steps down (on the right) is the **Liceu Opera House** (Gran Teatre del Liceu), which hosts world-class opera, dance, and theater (box office around the right side, open Mon-Fri 13:30-20:00). Opposite the opera house is Café de l'Opera (#74), an elegant stop for an expensive beverage. This bustling café, with Modernista decor and a historic atmosphere, boasts that it's been open since 1929, even during the Spanish Civil War.

• *We've seen the best stretch of the Ramblas; to cut this walk short, you could catch the Metro back to Plaça de Catalunya. Otherwise, let's continue to the port. The wide, straight street that crosses the Ramblas in another 30 yards (Carrer de Ferran) leads left to Plaça de Sant Jaume, the government center.*

Head down the Ramblas another 50 yards (to #46), and turn left down an arcaded lane (Carrer de Colom) to the square called...

❽ Plaça Reial

Dotted with palm trees, surrounded by an arcade, and ringed by yellow buildings with white Neoclassical trim, this elegant square has a colonial ambience. It comes complete with old-fashioned taverns, modern bars with patio seating, and a Sunday coin-and-stamp market (10:00-14:00). Completing the picture are Gaudí's first public works (the two colorful helmeted lampposts). While this used to be a seedy and dangerous part of town, recent gentrification efforts have given it new life, making it inviting and accessible. (The small streets stretching toward the water from the square remain a bit sketchier.) It's a lively hangout by day or by night (for nightlife options, see page 234). Big spaces like this (as well as the site of La Boqueria Market) often originated as monasteries. When these were dissolved in the 19th century, their fine colonnaded squares were incorporated into useful public spaces. To just relax over a drink and enjoy the scene, the **Ocaña cocktail bar** is a good bet.

• *Head back out to the Ramblas.*

Across the boulevard, a half-block

detour down Carrer Nou de la Rambla brings you to **Palau Güell,** designed by Antoni Gaudí (on the left, at #3-5). Even from the outside, you get a sense of this innovative apartment, the first of Gaudí's Modernista buildings. As this is early Gaudí (built 1886-1890), it's darker and more Neo-Gothic than his more famous later work. The two parabolic-arch doorways and elaborate wrought-iron work signal his emerging nonlinear style. Recently renovated, Palau Güell offers an informative look at a Gaudí interior (see listing on page 37). Pablo Picasso had a studio at #10 (though there's nothing to see there today).

• *Proceed along the Ramblas.*

❾ Raval Neighborhood

The neighborhood on the right-hand side of this stretch of the Ramblas is El Raval. Its nickname was Barri Xines—the world's only Chinatown with nothing even remotely Chinese in or near it. Named for the prejudiced notion that Chinese immigrants went hand-in-hand with poverty, prostitution, and drug dealing, the neighborhood's actual inhabitants were poor Spanish, North African, and Roma (Gypsy) people. At night, the Barri Xines was frequented by prostitutes, many of them transvestites, who catered to sailors wandering up from the port. Today, it's becoming gentrified, but it's still a pretty rough neighborhood.

At about this part of the Ramblas, you'll see the first of the drag's surreal and goofy **human statues.** These performers—with creative and elaborate costumes—must audition and register with the city government; to avoid overcrowding, only 15 can work along the Ramblas at any one time. To enliven your Ramblas ramble, stroll with a pocketful of small change. As you wander downhill, drop coins into their cans (the money often kicks the statues into entertaining gear). Warning: Wherever people stop to gawk, pickpockets are at work.

You're also likely to see some old-fashioned **shell games** in this part of town. Stand back and observe these nervous no-necks at work. They swish around their little boxes, making sure to show you the pea. Their shills play and win. Then, in hopes of making easy money, fools lose big time.

Near the bottom of the Ramblas, take note of the Drassanes Metro stop, which can take you back to Plaça de Catalunya when this walk is over. The skyscraper to the right of the Ramblas is the

Edificio Colón. When it was built in 1970, the 28-story structure was Barcelona's first high-rise. Near the skyscraper is the Maritime Museum, housed in what were the city's giant medieval shipyards (permanent collection most likely not on display in 2015; see listing on page 41).

• *Up ahead is the...*

❿ Columbus Monument

The 200-foot **column** honors Christopher Columbus, who came to Barcelona in 1493 after journeying to America. This Catalan

answer to Nelson's Column on London's Trafalgar Square (right down to the lions perfect for posing with at the base) was erected for the 1888 Universal Exposition, an international fair that helped vault a surging Barcelona onto the world stage.

The base of the monument, ringed with four winged victories (taking flight to the four corners of the earth), is loaded with symbolism: statues and reliefs of mapmakers, navigators, early explorers preaching to subservient Native Americans, and (enthroned just below the winged victories) the four regions of Spain. The reliefs near the bottom illustrate scenes from Columbus' fateful voyage. It's ironic that Barcelona celebrates this explorer; the discoveries of Columbus started 300 years of decline for the city, as Europe began to face West (the Atlantic and the New World) rather than East (the Mediterranean and the Orient). Within a few decades of Columbus, Barcelona had become a depressed backwater, and didn't rebound until events like the 1888 Expo cemented its status as a comeback city. A tiny elevator ascends to the top of the monument, lifting visitors to an observation area for fine panoramas over the city (entrance/ticket desk in TI inside the base of the monument).

• *Scoot across the busy traffic circle to survey the...*

⓫ Waterfront

Stand on the boardwalk (between the modern bridge and the kiosks selling harbor cruises), and survey Barcelona's bustling maritime zone. Although the city is one of Europe's top 10 ports, with many busy industrial harbors and several cruise terminals, this low-impact stretch of seafront is clean, fresh, and people-friendly.

As you face the water, the frilly yellow building to your left is the fanciful Modernista-style port-authority building. The wooden pedestrian **bridge** jutting straight out into the harbor is a modern extension of the Ramblas. Called La Rambla de Mar ("Rambla of the Sea"), the bridge swings out to allow boat traffic into the marina; when closed, the footpath leads to an entertainment and shopping complex. Just to your right are the *golondrinas* **harbor cruise** boats, which can be fun if you'd love to get out on the water (though the views from the harbor aren't great; for details, see page 44).

• *Turn left and walk 100 yards along the promenade between the port authority and the harbor.*

This delightful promenade is part of Barcelona's **Old Port** (Port Vell), stretching from the Columbus Monument to the Barceloneta neighborhood. The port's pleasant sailboat marina is completely enclosed by La Rambla del Mar's shopping and entertainment zone (notice that La Rambla del Mar connects back around to the mainland at the far end of the port, creating a handy pedestrian loop). Its attractions include the Maremagnum shopping mall, an IMAX cinema, a huge aquarium, restaurants, and piles of people. Late at night, it's a rollicking youth hangout. Along the promenade is a permanently moored historic schooner, the *Santa Eulàlia* (part of the Maritime Museum—see page 41)

Imagine: A little more than two decades ago, this was a gloomy, depressed warehouse zone. But to spiff up its front door for the 1992 Olympics, city leaders refurbished the port area, routing a busy highway underground to create this fine walkway sprinkled with palm trees and eye-pleasing public art. On a sunny day, it's fun to walk the length of the promenade to the iconic *Barcelona Head* sculpture (by American Pop artist Roy Lichtenstein, not quite visible from here), which puts you right at the edge of El Born, one of the city's most enjoyable shopping and restaurant areas. (For details, ○ see the El Born Walk chapter.)

From here, you can also pick out some of Barcelona's more distant charms. The triangular spit of land across the harbor is **Barceloneta.** This densely populated community was custom-built to house fishermen and sailors whose traditional neighborhood in El Born was razed so Philip V could build a military citadel there in the 18th century. Today's Barceloneta is a little gritty but charming, popular for its relatively low real-estate prices (given its handy proximity to the town center) and its easy access to a gorgeous and inviting stretch of broad, sandy beaches (on the other side of the Barceloneta peninsula). From Barceloneta, beaches and boardwalks lead all the way to the modern Fòrum development (see page 74).

Looking back toward the Columbus Monument, you'll see in the distance the majestic, 570-foot bluff of **Montjuïc,** a park-like setting dotted with a number of sights and museums (see page 59; to get there, ride the Metro from Drassanes one stop to the Parallel stop, then take the funicular up).

• *Your ramble is over. If it's a nice day, consider strolling the promenade and looping back around on La Rambla del Mar. Or maybe dip into El Born. If you're truly on vacation, walk through Barceloneta to the beach.*

To get to other points in town, your best bet is to backtrack to the Drassanes Metro stop, at the bottom of the Ramblas. Alternatively, you can catch buses #14 or #59 from along the top of the promenade back to Plaça de Catalunya.

BARRI GÒTIC WALK

From Plaça de Catalunya to Plaça del Rei

Barcelona's Barri Gòtic (Gothic Quarter) is a bustling world of shops, bars, and nightlife packed into narrow, winding lanes and undiscovered courtyards. This is Barcelona's birthplace—where the ancient Romans built a city, where medieval Christians built their cathedral, where Jews gathered together, and where Barcelonans lived within a ring of protective walls until the 1850s, when the city expanded.

Today, this area of atmospheric tight lanes—nicknamed simply "El Gòtic"—is Barcelona's most historic neighborhood. It's a tangled-yet-inviting grab bag of grand squares, schoolyards, Art Nouveau storefronts, baby flea markets (on Thursdays), musty junk shops, classy antique shops (on Carrer de la Palla), street musicians strumming Catalan folk songs, and balconies with domestic jungles behind wrought-iron bars.

Treat this self-guided walk as a historical scavenger hunt. You'll focus on the earliest chunk of Roman Barcelona, right around the cathedral, and explore some legacy sights from the city's medieval era. For a more contemporary flavor, explore the shopping streets nearby (see page 223) or head to El Born (see the El Born Walk chapter).

Orientation

Length of This Walk: Figure 1.5 hours, not including entering sights such as the cathedral.

When to Go: If you want to visit the cathedral when admission is free, take this walk in the morning or late afternoon. If you'd like to enter the museums mentioned on this walk, avoid Monday, when some sights are closed.

Getting There: Start at the southeast corner of the Plaça de Catalunya (Metro: Plaça de Catalunya).

Church of Santa Anna: Free, suggested €2 donation, hours usually Mon-Sat 11:00-19:00, Sun 11:00-13:00, Plazoleta de Santa
Anna.

Cathedral of Barcelona: Generally free except in afternoon, open
Mon-Fri 8:00-19:30, Sat-Sun 8:00-20:00, €7.50 to enter
Mon-Sat 12:45-17:15 and Sun 13:45-17:15, Plaça de la Seu.
(For more details, see the Cathedral Tour chapter.)

Old Main Synagogue: €2.50, April-Oct Mon-Fri 10:30-18:00,
Sat-Sun 10:30-15:00, shorter hours off-season, Carrer Marlet
5, tel. 933-170-790, www.calldebarcelona.org.

Roman Temple of Augustus: Free; good English info, Mon
10:00-14:00, Tue-Sun 10:00-19:00; Carrer del Paradís 10.

Barcelona History Museum: €7, Tue-Sat 10:00-19:00, Sun 10:00-
20:00, closed Mon, off Plaça del Rei.

Eating: For restaurants and tapas bars along the way, see page 203.

The Walk Begins

• *Start on Barcelona's grand main square,* **Plaça de Catalunya** *(described on page 78 of The Ramblas Ramble chapter). From the northeast corner (between the giant El Corte Inglés department store and the
Banco de España), head down the broad pedestrian boulevard called...*

❶ Avinguda del Portal de l'Angel

For much of Barcelona's history, this was a major city gate. A medieval wall enclosed the city, and there was an entrance here—the
"Gate of the Angel" that gives the street its name. An angel statue
atop the gate purportedly kept the city safe from plagues and bid
voyagers safe journey as they left the security of the city. Imagine
the fascinating scene here at the Gate of the Angel, where Barcelona stopped and the Iberian wilds began.

Much later, this same boulevard (and much of the city) got
a facelift in preparation for the 1888 Universal Exposition, the
first international fair held in Spain. (The same event prompted
the construction of the Columbus Monument at the bottom of the
Ramblas.) The improvements to the Gate of the Angel are a good
example of Barcelona's habit of spiffing itself up for big events. The
city dressed up for another exposition in 1929 (Plaça d'Espanya
fairgrounds) and again for the 1992 Olympic Games (sports facilities on Montjuïc and rejuvenated waterfront).

Picture the traffic congestion here in the 1980s, before this
street was closed to most motorized vehicles. Today, you're elbow
to elbow with shoppers cruising through some of the most expensive retail space in town. It's pretty globalized and sanitized, with

lots of high-end Spanish and international chains. You'll notice branches of Zara, Oysho, Bershka, and Massimo Dutti, all owned by the same man (Amancio Ortega Gaona, the third-richest person in the world, according to locals). He gets the best locations for his shops, each tailored to target a different market segment (for a rundown, see page 228 in the Shopping in Barcelona chapter).

But a handful of businesses with local roots survive. For example, on the right at the first corner (at #21), a green sign marks **Planelles Donat**—long appreciated for its ice cream, sweet *turró* (or *turrón*, almond-and-honey candy), refreshing *orxata* (or *horchata*, almond-flavored drink), and *granissat* (or *granizado*, ice slush). Imagine how historic shops like this one started, with artisans from villages camping out here in a vestibule of some big building, selling baskets of their homemade goodies—and eventually evolving into real shops. Planelles Donat is from the town of Xixona (shee-shoh-nah).

• *A block farther down, pause at Carrer de Santa Anna to admire the Art Nouveau awning at another El Corte Inglés department store. From here, take a half-block detour to the right on Carrer de Santa Anna. At #32 go through a large entryway into to a pleasant, flower-fragrant courtyard with the...*

❼ Church of Santa Anna

This 12th-century gem was an *extra muro* ("outside the walls") church; look for its marker cross still standing outside. Because it was part of a convent, the church has a fine cloister—an arcaded walkway around a leafy courtyard (viewable to the left of the church). Climb the modern stairs for views of the bell tower. If the church is open, you'll see a bare Romanesque interior and Greek-cross floor plan, topped with an octagonal wooden roof. The recumbent-knight tomb is of Miguel de Boera, renowned admiral of Charles V. The door at the far end of the nave leads to the cloister (€2 donation requested, church hours usually daily 11:00-19:00).

As you head back to the main drag, you'll pass—a few doors down—a **condom shop** on your left. It advertises (to men with ample self-esteem): *Para los pequeños*

Barri Gòtic Walk

EL CORTE INGLÉS
DEP'T STORE
Ⓑ Bus to Airport
(& Taxis)

To Casa Batlló
& La Pedrera
ⓘ

C. FONTANELLA

CARRER DE LES MOLES

CARRER D'ESTRUC

100 Meters

100 Yards

👣 WALK
BEGINS

❶

PLANELLES
DONAT

AVINGUDA

CARRER COMTAL

SANTA
ANNA

SOM
NATURALS

CONDOM
SHOP

❷

DEL PORTAL DE L'ANGEL

ELS
QUATRE
GATS

CARRER DE MONTSIÓ

❸

CARRER DE SANTA ANNA

BARRI

DURAN I BAS

LOANER
BIKES

C. DELS

❹ ⊚

ATM

CARRER DE LA CANUDA

CARRER DEL DUC

CARRER CUCURULLA

REIAL
CERCLE
ARTISTIC
MUSEUM

Plaça de la
Vila de Madrid

ROMAN
NECROPOLIS

CARRER D'EN BOT

GÒTIC

FARGAS
CHOCOLATES

CARRER DE LA PORTAFERRISSA

LAS

BETLEM
CHURCH

RAMBLAS

CARRER DEL PI

CARRER DE LA PALLA

LIBRERÍA
ANGEL
BATLLE
POSTERS

CASA COLOMINA
SWEETS

KOKUA
SHOE SHOP

ORO
LÍQUIDO
OLIVE OILS

C. DELS

CARRER

VICENS
SWEETS

GRANJA
LA PALLARESA
(CHURROS CON
CHOCOLATE)

CAELUM
CAFÉ

CULTURAL INFO
PALAU DE LA VIRREINA

CARRER D'EN ROCA

PETRITXOL

Ⓜ Liceu

JOSEP
ROCA
CUTLERY

Plaça
del Pi

Plaça
S. Josep
Oriol

CUSTO ◆ VAHO SHOP

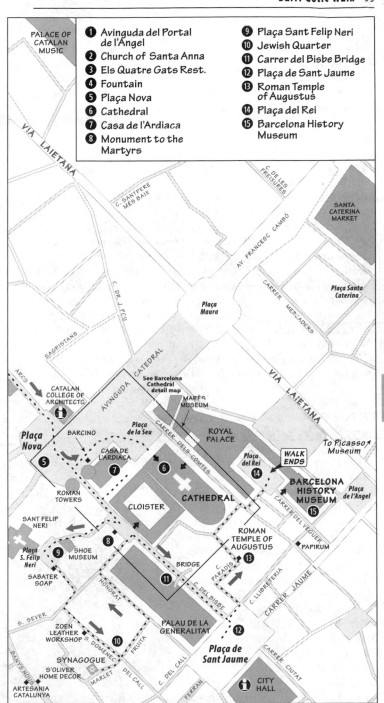

PALACE OF CATALAN MUSIC

1. Avinguda del Portal de l'Angel
2. Church of Santa Anna
3. Els Quatre Gats Rest.
4. Fountain
5. Plaça Nova
6. Cathedral
7. Casa de l'Ardiaca
8. Monument to the Martyrs
9. Plaça Sant Felip Neri
10. Jewish Quarter
11. Carrer del Bisbe Bridge
12. Plaça de Sant Jaume
13. Roman Temple of Augustus
14. Plaça del Rei
15. Barcelona History Museum

VIA LAIETANA

C. DE LES FREIXURES

C. SANTPERE MÉS BAIX

AV. FRANCESC CAMBÓ

SANTA CATERINA MARKET

CARRER MERCADERS

Plaça Santa Caterina

C. DR. J. PCU

SAGRISTANS

Plaça Maura

VIA LAIETANA

BARRI GÒTIC WALK

ARCS

CATALAN COLLEGE OF ARCHITECTS

AVINGUDA CATEDRAL

See Barcelona Cathedral detail map

MARÈS MUSEUM

ROYAL PALACE

Plaça Nova

BARCINO

Plaça de la Seu

CASA DE L'ARDIACA
7

6

CARRER DELS COMTES

Plaça del Rei
14

WALK ENDS

To Picasso Museum

ROMAN TOWERS

CLOISTER

CATHEDRAL

BARCELONA HISTORY MUSEUM
15

Plaça de l'Angel

SANT FELIP NERI

8

ROMAN TEMPLE OF AUGUSTUS

CARRER DEL VEGUER

Plaça S. Felip Neri
9

SHOE MUSEUM

PAPIRUM

BRIDGE
11

C. PARADIS

13

SABATER SOAP

HONORAT

C. DEL BISBE

C. LLIBRETERIA

CARRER JAUME I

S. SEVER

ZOEN LEATHER WORKSHOP

S. DOMENEC

10

PALAU DE LA GENERALITAT

12

FRUITA

CARRER CIUTAT

SYNAGOGUE

S'OLIVER HOME DECOR

MARLET

DEL CALL

C. DEL CALL

Plaça de Sant Jaume

BANYS NOUS

ARTESANIA CATALUNYA

FERRAN

CITY HALL

placeres de la vida ("For the little pleasures in life"). This sign is in Spanish, because the letter *ñ* doesn't exist in Catalan. Instead, Catalans write "ny" for this sound (as in "Catalunya"—which elsewhere in Spain is written "Cataluña").

• *Backtrack to Avinguda Portal de l'Angel. At Carrer de Montsió (on the left), opposite the Zara store, side-trip half a block to...*

❸ Els Quatre Gats

This restaurant (at #3) is a historic monument, tourist attraction, nightspot, and recommended eatery. It's famous for being the circa-1900 bohemian-artist hangout where Picasso nursed drinks with friends and had his first one-man show (in 1900). The building itself, by prominent architect Josep Puig i Cadafalch, represents Neo-Gothic Modernisme. Stepping inside, you feel the turn-of-the-century vibe. Rich Barcelona elites and would-be avant-garde artists looked to Paris, not Madrid, for cultural inspiration. Consequently, this place was clearly inspired by the Paris scene (especially Le Chat Noir cabaret/café, the hangout of Montmartre intellectuals). Like Le Chat Noir, Els Quatre Gats even published its own artsy magazine for a while. The story of the name? When the proprietor told his friends that he'd stay open 24 hours a day, they said, "No one will come. It'll just be you and four cats" (Catalan slang for "just a few people"). While you can have a snack, meal, or drink here, you're welcome to just admire the menu cover art—originally painted by Picasso—and take a quick look around (ask *"Solo mirar, por favor?"*).

• *Return to and continue down Avinguda del Portal de l'Angel. In a square on the left, notice the rack of **city loaner bikes**, part of the popular and successful "Bicing" program designed to reduce car traffic (available only to Barcelona residents). You'll soon reach a fork in the road and a building with a...*

❹ Fountain

The blue-and-yellow tilework, a circa-1918 addition to this even-older fountain, depicts ladies carrying jugs of water. In the 17th century, this was the last watering stop for horses before leaving town. As recently as 1940, about 10 percent of Barcelonans still got their water from fountains like this.

• *Shoppers will feel the pull of wonderful little shops down the street to the right. But be strong and take the left fork, down Carrer dels Arcs.*

Pause after a few steps at the yellow La Caixa ATM (on the right, under the terrace). Touch the screen to see various international languages pop up—in addition to English, French, and German, you'll see the **four languages of Spain** and their flags: Català (Catalan; thin red-and-gold stripes), Galego (Galicia, in northwest Spain; white with a diagonal blue slash), Castellano (Español or Spanish; broad red, yellow, and red bands), and Euskara (Basque; red, green, and white). As a would-be breakaway nation fiercely proud of its own customs and language, Catalunya is in solidarity with other small ethnic groups. Catalans are sure to include Basque here, for instance, just as they'd expect to see Catalan on ATMs in Basque Country.

Just past the ATM, you'll pass the *Reial Cercle Artístic Museum,* a private collection of Dalí's work—sculptures, prints, and several hundred lithographs—fun for fans of Surrealism (€10, daily 10:00-22:00).

• *Enter the large square called...*

❺ Plaça Nova

Two bold **Roman towers** flank the main street. These once guarded the entrance gate of the ancient Roman city of Barcino. The big stones that make up the base of the (reconstructed) towers are actually Roman. Near the base of the left tower, **modern bronze letters** spell out "BARCINO." The city's name may have come from Barca, one of Hannibal's generals, who is said to have passed through during Hannibal's roundabout invasion of Italy. At Barcino's peak, the **Roman wall** (see the section stretching to the left of the towers) was 25 feet high and a mile around, with 74 towers. It enclosed a population of 4,000.

One of the towers has a bit of reconstructed **Roman aqueduct** (notice the streambed on top). In ancient times, bridges of stone carried fresh water from the distant hillsides into the walled city.

Opposite the towers is the modern **Catalan College of Architects** building (Collegi d'Arquitectes de Barcelona, TI inside),

which is, ironically for a city with so much great architecture, quite ugly. The frieze was designed by Picasso (1962) in his distinctive simplified style, showing (on three sides) Catalan traditions: shipping, music, the *sardana* dance, bullfighting, and branch-waving kings and children celebrating a local festival. Picasso spent his formative years (1895-1904, ages 14-23) here in the old town. He drank with fellow bohemians at Els Quatre Gats (which we just passed) and frequented brothels a few blocks from here on Carrer d'Avinyó ("Avignon")—which inspired his influential Cubist painting *Les Demoiselles d'Avignon*. Picasso's hunger to be on the cutting edge propelled him from the Barri Gòtic to Paris, where he eventually remade modern art.

• *Immediately to the left as you face the Picasso frieze,* **Carrer de la Palla** *is an inviting shopping street (and the starting point of my "Barri Gòtic Shopping Walk"; see page 223). But let's head left through Plaça Nova and take in the mighty facade of the...*

❻ Cathedral of Barcelona

While this location has been a center of Christian worship since the fourth century, what you see today dates (mainly) from the 14th century, with a 19th-century Neo-Gothic facade. The facade is a virtual catalog of Gothic motifs: a pointed arch over the entrance, robed statues, tracery in windows, gargoyles, and bell towers with winged angels. This Gothic variation is called French Flamboyant (meaning "flame-like"), and the roofline sports the prickly spires meant to give the impression of a church flickering with spiritual fires. The

area in front of the cathedral is where Barcelonans dance the *sardana* (see page 45).

The cathedral's interior—with its vast size, peaceful cloister, and many ornate chapels—is worth a visit. ❂ See the Cathedral of Barcelona Tour chapter. (If you interrupt this tour and visit the cathedral now, you'll exit from the cloister a block down Carrer del Bisbe. From there you can circle back to the right to visit stop #7—or skip #7 and step directly into stop #8.)

• *As you stand in the square facing the cathedral, look far to your left to see the multicolored, wavy canopy marking the roofline of the* **Santa Caterina Market.** *The busy street between here and the market—called Via Laietana—is the boundary between the Barri Gòtic and the funkier, edgier* **El Born** *neighborhood. (My self-guided El Born Walk starts at the Santa Caterina Market; see page 117.)*

For now, return to the Roman towers. Pass between the towers to head up Carrer del Bisbe, and take an immediate left, up the ramp to the entrance of...

❼ Casa de l'Ardiaca

It's free to enter this mansion, which was once the archdeacon's resi-

dence and now functions as the
city archives. The elaborately
carved doorway is Renaissance.
To the right of the doorway
is a carved mail slot by 19th-
century Modernista architect
Lluís Domènech i Montaner.
Enter a small courtyard with a

fountain. Notice how the century-old palm tree seems to be held
captive by urban man. Next, step inside the lobby of the city archives, where there are often free temporary exhibits. At the left
end of the lobby, go through the archway and look down into the
stairwell—this is the back side of the ancient Roman wall. Back
in the courtyard, climb to the balcony for views of the cathedral
steeple and gargoyles. From this vantage point, note the small Romanesque chapel on the right (the only surviving 13th-century bit
of the cathedral) and how it's dwarfed by the towering cathedral.

• *Return to Carrer del Bisbe and turn left. After a few steps, you reach a
small square with a bronze statue ensemble.*

❽ Monument to the Martyrs of Independence

Five Barcelona patriots—including two priests—calmly receive
their last rites before being garroted (strangled) for resisting Na-

poleon's occupation of Spain in the
early 19th century. They'd been out-
raged by French atrocities in Madrid
(depicted in Goya's famous *Third
of May* painting in Madrid's Prado
Museum). According to the plaque
marking their mortal remains, these
martyrs to independence gave their
lives in 1809 *"por Dios, por la Patria, y por el Rey"*—for God, country, and king.

Tiles flanking the monument tell the story: On the far left, the
patriots receive their last communion in prison. On the near left,
they're escorted out of the citadel—that hated symbol of foreign
occupation. On the near right is the execution scene. Priests, considered privileged, were strangled, while the common people were
hung; see ropes and a ladder on the right above the three doomed
men huddled with their priests. (The French last used the guil-
lotine in 1977, and Spain last used the garrote in 1974. Europe is
generally appalled that the US still executes people.) All the martyrs are buried across the way in the cathedral cloister.

The plaza offers interesting views of the cathedral's towers.
Opposite the square is the "back door" entrance to the cathedral
(through the cloister; relatively uncrowded and open sporadically).

On this square (and throughout the Barri Gòtic), you're likely to see immigrants selling knickknacks on the street, along with groups of hippies—nicknamed the "dog-and-flute people."

• *Exit the square down tiny Carrer de Montjuïc del Bisbe (to the right as you face the martyrs). This leads to the cute...*

❾ Plaça Sant Felip Neri

This shaded square serves as the playground of an elementary school and is often bursting with energetic kids speaking Catalan (just a generation ago, this would have been illegal and they would be speaking Spanish). The Church of Sant Felip Neri, which Gaudí attended, is still pocked with bomb damage from the Spanish Civil War. As a stronghold of democratic, anti-Franco forces, Barcelona saw a lot of fighting. The shrapnel that damaged this church was meant for the nearby Catalan government building (Palau de la Generalitat, which we'll see later on this walk).

Just as the Germans practiced their new air force technology in Guernica in the years leading up to World War II, the fascist friends of Franco (both German and Italian) also helped bomb Barcelona from the air. As was the fascist tactic, a second bombing followed the first as survivors combed the rubble for lost loved ones. A plaque on the wall (left of church door) honors the 42 killed—mostly children—in that 1938 aerial bombardment.

In the medieval tangle of the Barri Gòtic, there originally were very few open spaces—except for cemeteries clustering around churches. Many squares today, like this one, started out as cemeteries. They later became open spaces when, with the Enlightenment (c. 1800) and modern concern for hygiene, graveyards were moved outside of town.

The buildings here were paid for by the guilds that powered the local economy (notice the carved reliefs high above). On the corner where you entered the square is the former home of the shoemakers' guild; today it's the fun little **Shoe Museum** (described on page 46). Also fronting the square is the fun **Sabater Hermanos** artisanal soap shop (see page 226).

• *Exit the square down Carrer de Sant Felip Neri. At the T-intersection, turn right onto Carrer de Sant Sever, then immediately left on Carrer de Sant Domènec del Call (look for the blue El Call sign). You've entered the...*

⑩ Jewish Quarter (El Call)

In Catalan, a Jewish quarter goes by the name El Call—literally "narrow passage," for the tight lanes where medieval Jews were forced to live, under the watchful eye of the nearby cathedral. (Or some believe El Call comes from the Hebrew *kahal*, which means congregation.) At the peak of Barcelona's El Call, some 4,000 Jews were crammed into just a few alleys in this neighborhood.

Walk down Carrer de Sant Domènec del Call, passing the **Zoen leather workshop and showroom,** where everything is made on the spot (on the right, at #15). Pass though the charming little square (a gap in the dense tangle of medieval buildings cleared by another civil war bomb) where you will find a rust-colored sign displaying a map of the Jewish Quarter. Take the next lane to the right (Carrer de Marlet). On the right is the low-profile entrance to what was likely Barcelona's **main synagogue** during the Middle Ages (Antigua Sinagoga Mayor, €2.50 admission includes a little tour by the attendant if you ask). The structure dates from the third century, but it was destroyed in a brutal pogrom in 1391. The city's remaining Jews were expelled in 1492, and artifacts of their culture—including this synagogue—were forgotten for centuries. In the 1980s, a historian tracked down the synagogue using old tax-collection records. Another clue that this was the main synagogue: In accordance with Jewish traditions, it stubbornly faces east (toward Jerusalem), putting it at an angle at odds with surrounding structures. The sparse interior includes access to two small subterranean rooms with Roman walls topped by a medieval Catalan vault. Look through the glass floor to see dyeing vats used for a later shop on this site (run by former Jews who had been forcibly converted to Christianity).

• *From the synagogue, start back the way you came but continue straight ahead, onto Carrer de la Fruita. At the T-intersection, turn left, then right, to find your way back to the Martyrs Statue. From here, turn right down Carrer del Bisbe, likely passing a street musician (the city gives permits for quality buskers to perform at set points like this one) to the...*

⑪ Carrer del Bisbe Bridge

This structure—reminiscent of Venice's Bridge of Sighs—connects the Catalan government building (on the right) with what was the Catalan president's ceremonial residence (on the left). Though the bridge looks medieval, it was constructed in the 1920s by Catalan architect Joan Rubió (a follower of Gaudí), who also did the carved ornamentation on the buildings.

Check out the jutting angels on the bridge, the basket-carrying maidens on the president's house, the gargoyle-like faces on the government building. Find monsters, skulls, goddesses, old men with beards, climbing vines, and coats of arms.

The delicate façade a few steps farther down on the right marks the 15th-century entry to the government palace.

• *Continue along Carrer del Bisbe to...*

ⓘ Plaça de Sant Jaume

This stately central square of the Barri Gòtic takes its name from the Church of St. James (in Catalan: Jaume, JOW-mah) that once stood here. After the church was torn down in 1823, the square was fixed up and rechristened "Plaça de la Constitució" in honor of the then-decade-old Spanish constitution. But the plucky Catalans never embraced the name, and after Franco, they went back to the original title—even though the namesake church is long gone.

Set at the intersection of ancient Barcino's main thoroughfares, this square was once a Roman forum. In that sense, it's been the seat of city government for 2,000 years. Today it's home to the two top governmental buildings in Catalunya: Palau de la Generalitat and, across from it, the Barcelona City Hall.

For more than six centuries, the **Palau de la Generalitat** (to your immediate right as you enter the square) has housed the offices of the autonomous government of Catalunya. It always flies the Catalan flag next to the obligatory Spanish one. Above the building's doorway is Catalunya's patron saint—St. George (Jordi), slaying the dragon. The dragon (which you'll see all over town) is an important Catalan symbol. From these balconies, the nation's leaders (and soccer heroes) greet the people on momentous days. The square is often the site of demonstrations, from a single aggrieved citizen with a megaphone (the phone company billed me twice!) to riotous thousands (demanding independence from Spain, for instance).

Facing the Generalitat across the square is the **Barcelona City Hall** (Casa de la Ciutat). It sports a statue (in the niche to the left of the door) of a different James— "Jaume el Conqueridor." The 13th-century King Jaume I is credited with freeing Barcelona from French control, granting self-government, and setting it on a course to become a major city. He was the driving force behind construction of the Royal Palace (which we'll see shortly).

(side margin) **BARRI GÒTIC WALK**

Locals treasure the independence these two government buildings represent. In the 20th century, Barcelona opposed the dictator Francisco Franco (who ruled from 1939 to 1975), and Franco retaliated. He abolished the regional government and (effectively) outlawed the Catalan language and customs. Two years after Franco's death, joyous citizens packed this square to celebrate the return of self-rule.

Look left and right down the main streets branching off the square; they're lined with ironwork streetlamps and balconies draped with plants. Carrer de Ferran, which leads to the Ramblas, is classic Barcelona.

In ancient Roman days, when Plaça de Sant Jaume was the town's central square, two main streets converged here—the Decumanus (Carrer del Bisbe—bishop's street) and the Cardus (Carrer de la Llibreteria/Carrer del Call). The forum's biggest building was a massive temple of Augustus, which we'll see next.

• *Facing the Generalitat, exit the square going up the second street to the right of the building, on tiny Carrer del Paradís. Follow this street as it turns right. When it swings left, pause at #10, the entrance to the...*

⑩ Roman Temple of Augustus

You're standing at the summit of Mont Tàber, the Barri Gòtic's highest spot. A plaque on the wall reads: "Mont Tàber, 16.9 meters" (elevation 55 feet). A millstone inlaid in the pavement at the doorstep of #10 also marks the spot. It was here that the ancient Romans founded the town of Barcino around 15 B.C. They built a *castrum* (fort) on the hilltop, protecting the harbor.

Go inside for a peek at the last vestiges of an imposing Roman temple (Temple Roma d'August). All that's left now are four col

umns and some fragments of the transept and its plinth (good English info on-site). The huge columns, dating from the late first century B.C., are as old as Barcelona itself. They were part of the ancient town's biggest structure, a temple dedicated to the Emperor Augustus, who was worshipped as a god. These Corinthian columns (with deep fluting and topped with leafy capitals) were the back corner of a 120-foot-long temple that extended from here to Barcino's forum.

• *Continue down Carrer del Paridís one block. When you bump into the back end of the cathedral, take a right, and go downhill a block (down*

BARRI GÒTIC WALK

Carrer de la Pietat/Baixada de Santa Clara) until you emerge into a square called...

⓮ Plaça del Rei

The buildings enclosing this square exemplify Barcelona's medieval past. The central section (topped by a five-story addition) was the core of the **Royal Palace** (Palau Reial Major). A vast hall on its ground floor once served as the throne room and reception room. From the 13th to the 15th century, the Royal Palace housed Barcelona's counts as well as the resident kings of Aragon. In 1493, a triumphant Christopher Columbus, accompanied by six New World natives (whom he called "*indios*") and several pure-gold statues, entered the Royal Palace. King Ferdinand and Queen Isabella rose to welcome him home and honored him with the title "Admiral of the Oceans."

To the right is the palace's church, the 14th-century **Chapel of Saint Agatha,** which sits atop the foundations of a Roman wall

(entrance included in Barcelona History Museum admission; see page 47.)

To the left is the **Viceroy's Palace** (Palau del Lloctinent, for the ruler's right-hand man). This 16th-century building currently serves as the archives of the Crown of Aragon. After Catalunya became part of Spain in the 15th century, the Royal Palace became a small regional residence, and the Viceroy's Palace became the headquarters of the local Inquisition. Step inside to see the delightful Renaissance courtyard, a staircase with coffered wood ceilings, and a temporary exhibit space. Among the archive's treasures (though it's rarely on display) is the 1492 Santa Fe Capitulations, a contract between Columbus and the monarchs about his upcoming sea voyage. (See the poster of the yellowed document on the wall outside, with an English explanation.)

Ironically, Columbus' discovery of new trade routes (abandoning the Mediterranean for the Atlantic) made Barcelona's port less important, and soon the royals moved elsewhere.

• *From the square, go downhill onto Carrer del Veguer, where you'll find the entrance to the...*

⓯ Barcelona History Museum

This museum contains primarily objects from archaeological digs around Barcelona. But the real highlight is

BARRI GÒTIC WALK

underground, where you can examine excavated Roman ruins. For a peek at the Roman streets without going in, look through the low windows lining the street. For details on visiting the museum, see page 47.

• *Your walk is over. It's easy to get your bearings by backtracking to either Plaça de Sant Jaume or the cathedral (where you can follow my "Barri Gòtic Shopping Walk," described on page 223). The Jaume I Metro stop is two blocks away (leave the square on Carrer del Veguer and turn left). From here, you could head over to the Santa Caterina Market to browse for lunch before tackling my* ○ *El Born Walk from there or visiting the Picasso Museum (* ○ *see the Picasso Museum Tour chapter). Or simply wander through more of this area, enjoying Barcelona at its Gothic best.*

CATHEDRAL OF BARCELONA TOUR

Although Barcelona's cathedral doesn't rank among Europe's finest (and frankly, barely cracks the Top 20), it's important, easy to visit, and—most of the time—free to see. This quick tour introduces you to the cathedral's highlights: its vast nave, rich chapels, tomb of St. Eulàlia, and the oasis-like setting of the cloister. Other sights inside (which you'll pay separately for) are the elaborately carved choir, the elevator up to the view terrace, and the altarpiece museum.

Orientation

Cost: Free in the morning (Mon-Sat before 12:45, Sun before 13:45) and late afternoon (after 17:15), but you have to pay for the cathedral's three minor sights—choir-€2.80, elevator to terrace-€3, and museum-€2. Even though the church claims to be "closed" for several hours in the afternoon (Mon-Sat 13:00-17:00, Sun 14:00-17:00), you can still get in by paying €7.80 (which covers admission to the three interior sights). In other words, one way or another you'll pay around €8 to thoroughly tour the place; however, if you're skipping the three extras inside, aim to visit the church when it's free.

Hours: Cathedral generally open Mon-Fri 8:00-19:30, Sat-Sun 8:00-20:00. Choir open Mon-Sat 9:00-19:00, closed Sun afternoons. Terrace open Mon-Sat 9:00-18:00, closed Sun. Museum open daily 10:00-19:00, closed Sun. Choir, terrace, and museum may close earlier on slow days.

Dress Code: The dress code is strictly enforced; don't wear tank tops, shorts, or skirts above the knee.

Getting There: The huge, can't-miss-it cathedral is in the center of the Barri Gòtic on Plaça de la Seu (Metro: Jaume I). For an in-

Cathedral of Barcelona

To
Plaça de Catalunya
via Avinguda del
Portal de l'Angel

To Paça Maura, →
Santa Caterina Market
& El Born

Plaça Nova

BARCINO
SCULPTURE

ROMAN
TOWERS

DIOCESÀ
MUSEUM

CASA
D'ADRIACO

**Plaça
de la Seu**

CARRER DEL BISBE

**CATHEDRAL MAIN
ENTRANCE** STAIRS

SANTA
LUCIA

FONT

8

MUSEUM

SIDE
CHAPELS

1

N
A
V
E

CHRIST OF
LEPANTO

2

2

CLOISTER
ENTRANCE

GEESE

WC

3

CHOIR

7

ST.
RITA

ST
JORDI

CATHEDRAL

CARRER DELS COMTES

POND

CLOISTER
ENTRANCE

CLOISTER

TRANSEPT

5

CARRER DEL BISBE

CARRER DE LA PIETAT

CLOISTER
ENTRANCE

CATALAN
COAT OF
ARMS

4

**HIGH
ALTAR**

6

To
Plaça de
Sant Jaume

1 Nave
2 Side Chapels
3 Choir
4 High Altar
5 To Crypt & Tomb
 of Eulàlia
6 Elevator to Terrace
7 Cloister
8 Altarpiece Museum

To
Roman Temple
of Augustus

To
Plaça del Rei

20 Meters

20 Yards

C. PARIDIS

N

teresting way to reach the cathedral from Plaça de Catalunya, and some commentary on the surrounding neighborhood, ✪ see the Barri Gòtic Walk chapter.

Getting In: The main, front door is open most of the time. While it can be crowded, the line generally moves fast. Sometimes you can also enter directly into the cloister (through the door facing the Martyrs Statue on the small square along Carrer del Bisbe) or through the side door (facing the Frederic Marès Museum along Carrer dels Comtes).

Information: Tel. 933-151-554, www.catedralbcn.org.

Length of This Tour: Allow 30 minutes, not counting the optional sights (choir, view terrace, museum). With limited time, zip past the many side chapels, but be sure to linger in the cloister.

Services: A tiny, semiprivate WC is in the center of the cloister.

Photography: Allowed without a flash.

BACKGROUND

This has been Barcelona's holiest spot for 2,000 years. The Romans built their Temple of Jupiter here. In A.D. 343, the pagan temple was replaced with a Christian cathedral. That building was supplanted by a Romanesque-style church (11th century). The current Gothic structure was started in 1298 and finished in 1450, during the medieval glory days of the Catalan nation. The facade was humble, so in the 19th century the proud local bourgeoisie (enjoying a second Golden Age) redid it in a more ornate, Neo-Gothic style. Construction was capped in 1913 with the central spire, 230 feet tall.

The Tour Begins

• *Enter the main door and look up, letting your eyes adjust to the low light. (If you're entering through another door, loop around to start in the nave.)*

❶ The Nave

The spacious church is 300 feet long and 130 feet wide. Tall pillars made of stone blocks support the crisscross vaults. Each round keystone where the arches cross features a different saint. Typical of many Spanish churches, there's a choir— an enclosed area of wooden seats in the middle of the nave, creating a more intimate space for worship. The Gothic church also has fine stained glass, ironwork chandeliers, a 16th-century organ (left transept), tomb- stones in the pavement, and an "ambulatory" floor plan, allowing worshippers to amble around to the chapel of their choice.

❷ Side Chapels

The nave is ringed with 28 chapels. Besides being worship spaces, these serve as interior buttresses supporting the roof (which is why the exterior walls are smooth, without the normal Gothic buttresses outside). Barcelona honors many of the homegrown saints found in these chapels with public holidays.

From the 13th to 15th century, these side chapels were simply moneymakers for the church. After the Black Death ravaged the population—and the economy— the church rented chapels to guilds to function as private offices, which came with the medieval equivalent of safety-deposit boxes and notary public (documents signed here came with the force of God). Notice how the iron gates are more than decorative—they were protective. The rich ornamentation was sponsored by local guilds. Think of it: The church was the community's most high-profile space, and these chapels were a kind of advertising to illiterate worshippers.

The Church is still fund-raising. Candles, which aren't free, power your prayers. As you visit the chapels, employ one or more electronic candles. Pop in a coin and you'll get a candle for every €0.10 you donate. Try it—€0.50 turns on five candles.

• *We'll walk past a few of these chapels, just to get a sense of them. Begin by heading to the back-left corner (over your left shoulder as you enter the main door).*

The chapel at the back corner of the nave has an old **baptismal font** that once stood in the original fourth century church. The Native Americans that Columbus brought to town were supposedly baptized here.

• *Work your way down the left aisle.*

The first chapel along the left wall is dedicated to **St. Severus,** the bishop here way back in A.D. 290.

The second chapel was by, for, and of the local **shoe guild.** Notice the two painted doors with shoes above them that lead to the back office. As the patron of shoemakers was St. Mark, there are plenty of winged lions in this chapel.

• *Backtrack a bit, to the large chapel in the back-right corner.*

This chapel (reserved for worship) features the beloved **"Christ of Lepanto"** crucifix. They say the angular wooden figure of Christ leaned to dodge a cannonball during the history-changing Battle of Lepanto (1571), which stopped the Ottomans (and Islam) from advancing into Europe.

• *Now head down the right aisle.*

The second chapel has a statue of **St. Anthony** holding the Baby Jesus. His feast day (January 17) is one of many celebrated in the city with an appearance by the *gegants* (giant puppets), a street fair, horse races, and a blessing of pets.

The third chapel honors a 20th-century bishop, **San Josep Oriol,** who survived an assassination attempt in the cathedral cloister.

The golden fourth chapel is for **St. Roch** (at the top, pointing to his leg wound, above St. Pancraç), whose feast day is celebrated joyously in the Barri Gòtic in mid-August.

The fifth chapel has a black-and-white sideways statue of **St. Ramon (Raymond) of Penyafort** (1190-1275), the Dominican Bishop of Barcelona who heard Pope Gregory IX's sins and is the patron saint of lawyers (and, therefore, extremely busy). Ramon figures into the city's biggest festival, La Mercè, since he had a miraculous vision of the Virgin of Mercy.

The eighth chapel is worth a look for its over-the-top golden altarpiece decor nearly crowding out **Bishop Pacià**—considered one of the Church fathers (c. A.D. 310-391).

• *If you want to visit the interior of the choir (described next), pay €3 or show your ticket at the choir entrance (straight ahead from the church's main doors). Otherwise, you can circle around to the far end and peer through the barrier.*

❸ Choir

The 15th-century choir *(coro)* features ornately carved stalls. During the standing parts of the Mass, the chairs were folded up, but VIPs still had those little wooden ledges to lean on. Each was creatively carved and—since you couldn't sit on sacred things—the artists were free to enjoy some secular and naughty fun here. In 1518, the stalls were painted with the coats of arms of Europe's nobility. They gathered here as members of the Knights of the Golden Fleece to honor Charles V, King of Spain, who was making his first trip to the country he ruled. Like a proto-UN, they also discussed how to work together to defend Europe from the Turkish threat. Check out the detail work on the impressive wood-carved pulpit near the altar, supported by flying angels.

• *At the front of the church stands the...*

❹ High Altar

Look behind the altar (beneath the crucifix) to find the bishop's chair, or cathedra. As a cathedral, this church is the bishop's seat—hence its Catalan nickname of *La Seu*. To the left of the altar is the organ and the elevator up to the terrace. To the right of the altar, the wall is decorated with Catalunya's yellow-and-red coat of arms. Under that, the two wooden coffins on the wall are of two powerful Counts of Barcelona (Ramon Berenguer I and his third wife, Almodis), who ordered the construction of the 11th-century Romanesque cathedral that preceded this structure.

• *Descend the steps beneath the altar, into the crypt, to see the...*

❺ Tomb of Eulàlia

The marble-and-alabaster sarcophagus (1327-1339) contains the remains of St. Eulàlia. The cathedral is dedicated to this saint.

Thirteen-year-old Eulàlia, daughter of a prominent Barcelona family, was martyred by the Romans for her faith in A.D. 304. Murky legends say she was subjected to 13 tortures. First she was stripped naked and had her head shaved, though a miraculous snowfall hid her nakedness. Then she was rolled down the street in a barrel full of sharp objects. After further torments failed to kill her, she was crucified on an X-shaped cross—a symbol you'll find carved into pews and seen throughout the church.

The relief on the coffin's side tells her story in three episodes: she preaches Christianity to the pagan Roman ruler; he orders her to die (while she pleads for mercy); and she's crucified on the X-shaped cross. As one of Barcelona's two patron saints, Eulàlia is honored with a festival (with *gegants*, fireworks, and human towers) in mid-February.

• *The ❻ elevator in the left transept takes you up to the rooftop terrace, made of sturdy scaffolding pieces, for an expansive city view (€3).*

Otherwise, head to the right transept and go through the door to enter the...

❼ Cloister

Exit through the right transept and into the circa-1450 cloister—the arcaded walkway surrounding a lush courtyard. Ahhhh. It's a tropical atmosphere of palm, orange, and magnolia trees; a fish pond; trickling fountains; and squawking geese.

From within the cloister, look back at the **arch** you just came through, an impressive mix of Romanesque (arches with chevrons, from the earlier church) and Gothic (pointy top).

The nearby **fountain** has a tiny statue of St. Jordi (George) slaying the dragon. Jordi is one of the patron saints of Catalunya and by far the most popular boy's name here. During the Corpus Christi festival in June, kids come here to watch a hollow egg dance atop the fountain's spray.

As you wander the cloister (clockwise), check out the **coats of arms** as well as the **tombs** in the pavement. These were rich merchants who paid good money to be buried as close to the altar as possible. Notice the symbols of their trades: scissors, shoes, bakers, and so on. The cloister had a practical, economic purpose. The church sold out its chapel space, and this opened up an entire new wing to donors. A second floor was planned (look up) but not finished.

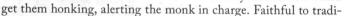

The resident **geese** have been here for at least 500 years. There are always 13, in memory of Eulàlia's 13 years and 13 torments. Other legends say they're white as a symbol of her virginity. Before modern security systems, they acted as alarms. Any commotion would get them honking, alerting the monk in charge. Faithful to tradition, they honk to this very day.

Farther along the cloister, next to the door, the **Chapel of Santa Rita** (patron saint of impossible causes) usually has the most candles. In the next corner of the cloister is the barrel-vaulted **Chapel of Santa Lucía,** a small 13th-century remnant of the earlier Romanesque cathedral. It's quite dark, as churches were before the advent of Gothic style. People hoping for good eyesight (Santa Lucía's specialty) pray here. Notice the nice eyes in the modern restoration of the altar painting.

• *At the far end of the cloister, you'll find the...*

❽ Altarpiece Museum (Museu Capitular)

The little museum (€2 entry) has the six-foot-tall 14th-century Great Monstrance, a ceremonial display case for the communion wafer. Made of gold and studded with jewels, it's really three separate parts: a church-like central section, topped with a crown canopy, standing on a golden chair. This huge monstrance with its wafer is paraded through the streets during the Corpus Christi festival. Nearby is a gold-plated silver statue of St. Eulàlia, carrying the X-shaped cross she was crucified on. An 11th-century baptismal font from the Romanesque church is also on view.

The next room, the Sala Capitular, has several altarpieces, including a *pietá* (a.k.a. *Desplà*) by Bartolomé Bermejo (1490). An anguished Mary cradles a twisted Christ against a bleak, stormy landscape. It's unique in Spanish art for its Italianesque, Renaissance 3-D. Rather than your basic gold backdrop, this has a strong foreground (the mourners), middle distance (the cross), and background (the city and distant hills). The kneeling donors who paid for the painting are photorealistic, complete with reading glasses and five o'clock shadows.

• *Our tour is over. May peace be with you.*

EL BORN WALK

From Via Laietana
to the Waterfront

The neighborhood called El Born (a.k.a. "La Ribera") is bohemian-chic, with funky shops, upscale cafés and wine bars, a colorful market hall, unique boutiques, gritty bars and nightclubs, and one of Barcelona's top museums (celebrating the early works of Picasso). Anchored by the Church of Santa Maria del Mar and just a short stroll from the waterfront, El Born is a rewarding neighborhood to explore and a welcome escape from the sightseeing grind.

Back when Barcelona was Barcino—a walled Roman town—this area was farmland. As the city sprawled beyond its walls, El Born was "born" into a neighborhood with a main square that, over the years, hosted jousting tournaments, festivals, Inquisition-era heretic-burnings, and other public spectacles. Later, during the medieval city's trading heyday, El Born housed the wealthiest shippers and merchants. Its streets are lined with their grand mansions—which, like the much-appreciated Church of Santa Maria del Mar, were built with shipping wealth. All of that came crashing down in 1714, when the Spanish crown crushed Catalan hopes and razed a big chunk of this district to erect an imposing citadel (now a delightful park). The focus of the city shifted west, to the Barri Gòtic, and El Born became a largely forgotten backwater.

But in recent years, as the Barri Gòtic has become overrun by tourism, El Born has retained its pleasantly rough-around-the-edges appeal. While it's gentrifying and becoming one of the city's most in-demand residential areas, its tight lanes are lined not with chain stores, but with innovative one-off shops that, more often than not, make what they sell. Although we'll cover some history, this walk is designed to take you past some enticing boutique streets and provide a route for you to venture off and make your own discoveries.

Orientation

Length of This Walk: About one hour, not including shopping stops.

With Limited Time: Focus on the core of El Born, where these places and sights cluster: Passeig del Born, the Monument of Catalan Independence, Church of Santa Maria del Mar, and the characteristic shopping lanes.

Getting There: This walk begins at Plaça d'Antoni Maura, where the pedestrian area in front of the Cathedral of Barcelona meets Via Laietana. The closest Metro stop is Jaume I.

Name Game: This neighborhood (between the Barri Gòtic to the west and Citadel Park to the east) goes by several names. The traditional name, **La Ribera,** generally implies the entire area. **El Born,** the name locals tend to use, technically refers to the southern half of this area (below Carrer de la Princesa—basically the zone covered by this walk), although it's sometimes also used to describe the entire neighborhood. Complicating matters, the city's official title for this district is "Sant Pere, Santa Caterina i la Ribera."

Santa Caterina Market: Free, Mon 7:30-14:00, Tue-Wed and Sat 7:30-15:30, Thu-Fri 7:30-20:30, closed Sun, Avinguda de Francesc Cambó 16.

El Born Cultural Center: Center is free and open Tue-Sun 10:00-20:00, closed Mon; café open until 24:00; €6 covers all exhibits (including audioguide for entire center), exhibits free all day first Sun of month and other Sun from 15:00, open Tue-Sun 10:00-20:00, closed Mon; Plaça Comercial 12.

Picasso Museum: €14, free all day first Sun of month and other Sun from 15:00; Tue-Sun 9:00-19:00, Thu until 21:30, closed Mon; Carrer de Montcada 15-23.

Church of Santa Maria del Mar: Free, daily 9:00-13:30 & 16:30-20:00; pay €4 to visit 13:30-16:30; Plaça Santa Maria.

The Walk Begins

• *Our walk starts in front of the Cathedral of Barcelona. As you stand facing the cathedral, head left toward the Santa Caterina Market. You'll see its undulating roof in the distance. To get there, you'll cross...*

❶ Via Laietana

This traffic-choked street slices through Barcelona's Old City. It marks the boundary between the Barri Gòtic (behind you) and El Born (in front of you). When the road was built in 1908, Barcelona was turning its back on its Gothic past and racing into its Mod-

El Born Walk

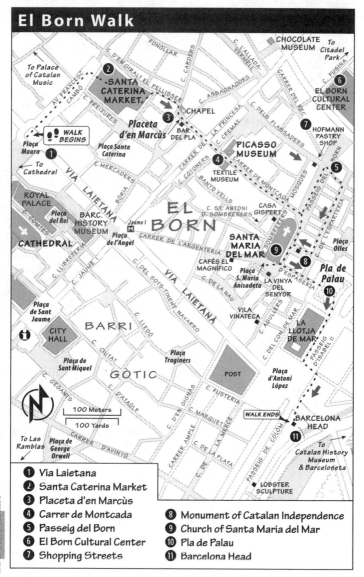

1 Via Laietana
2 Santa Caterina Market
3 Placeta d'en Marcùs
4 Carrer de Montcada
5 Passeig del Born
6 El Born Cultural Center
7 Shopping Streets
8 Monument of Catalan Independence
9 Church of Santa Maria del Mar
10 Pla de Palau
11 Barcelona Head

ernista future—and hundreds of historic buildings were torn up to create this new artery.

When you cross the street, you're in the neighborhood called Sant Pere. While less colorful and gentrified than El Born, just to the south (or right), Sant Pere is home to a thriving residential population of mostly immigrants. A few short blocks to your left is one of the city's architectural treasures—Lluís Domènech i Montaner's Modernista-style **Palace of Catalan Music** (see listing on page 49).

• *Across Via Laietana and ahead, on the right, you can't miss the...*

❷ Santa Caterina Market

While tourists swarm the more famous La Boqueria Market on the Ramblas, Santa Caterina Market is a lively dose of local color, still

primarily serving its neighborhood. This is the place to buy *jamón* and cheese without the crowds or tourist markup.

The market, built on the ruins of an old monastery (see the exhibit at the far corner for a view of the foundations with English explana-

tions), was finally renovated in 2006 with a swooping roof and shell built around its original white walls. The roof's bright colors evoke Gaudí and the colorful fruit within.

The much-delayed construction took so long that locals began calling the site the "Hole of Shame." Its Catalan architect, Enric Miralles, is best known for designing the Scottish Parliament Building in Edinburgh—an unlikely connection that's also oddly fitting, since both the Catalans and the Scots consider themselves "nations without states."

Inside are beautifully lit produce stalls with mouthwatering presentations and surprising variety (one stall displays 20 kinds of tomatoes). There are lots of tempting eateries—locals eat before shopping so as not to overbuy. For tips on exploring the market, see the description on page 37 for La Boqueria, which offers similar products.

• *Walk through the market from one end to the other—keeping an eye out for those monastery ruins. (If the market is closed, you can simply loop around the left side to the far end.) Exiting through the back of the market, angle left to the corner of the square and find the tiny Carrer d'en Giralt el Pellisser. Going down this lane, you'll pop out facing a chapel and, on the right, the tiny square that seems more like a street called...*

❸ Placeta d'en Marcùs

On this square is a humble Romanesque chapel, Capella d'en Marcùs, from the 1100s, supposedly the oldest church in town. In medieval times, this is where locals would pause to share the news. Across the street from the chapel's front door, above the plaque for #1, notice the sign with the horse and the word *entrada* (entrance). This is an old-fashioned way of marking the direction of one-way streets in this tight tangle of lanes. Across the tiny square past the chapel, find the sign's twin, *salida* (exit), above the street sign for Carrer dels Assaonadors. You'll spot signs like these all over El Born and the Barri Gòtic.

• *Passing between the chapel and the recommended Bar del Pla, continue straight down the lane called...*

❹ Carrer de Montcada

Follow this street one block until you reach the busy, bar-lined **Carrer de la Princesa.** If you turned right here, you'd go to the Jaume I Metro stop, Barri Gòtic, and cathedral area. Instead, cross Princesa and continue straight, noticing that Carrer de Montcada has suddenly become the most touristy street in El Born—thanks to the Picasso Museum, which lies just ahead. The street is named for the Montcada family, who owned the buildings that now house the museum (which consists of five mansions laced together). Because it connected the wealthy merchant district right near the waterfront with the tradesmen's quarter farther north, this drag attracted an elite class of homeowner during its 15th-century heyday and is lined to this day with many noble palaces.

A block down is the **Picasso Museum,** focused on the artist's early, formative works. You could visit the museum now if the line's not too long (❂ see the Picasso Museum Tour chapter), or you could come back after finishing this walk. In addition to the museum, Carrer de Montcada is lined with other art galleries, cafés, shops, and restaurants. While some are good (such as the recommended El Xampanyet bar, just down the street and on the right), most cater decidedly to tourist tastes. Browse the entire length of Carrer de Montcada.

• *At the end of the street, you'll pop out onto...*

❺ Passeig del Born

This long boulevard is the neighborhood center. Formerly a jousting square (as its Roman circus-esque shape indicates), it got its name, "El Born," from an old Catalan word for "tournament" (the name was eventually given to the entire neighborhood).

These days, Passeig del Born is a popular springboard for exploring tapas bars, fun restaurants, and nightspots in the narrow streets all around. Wandering around here at night, you'll find piles of inviting and intriguing little restaurants (I've listed my favorites on page 206).

• *At the far end of Passeig del Born is the...*

❻ El Born Cultural Center
(El Born Centre Cultural)

This vast, steel-frame, 19th-century construction was inspired by similar French market halls, which were the rage in the mid-19th century. Built in 1871 and the first such structure in town, **El Born Market** served as the city's main produce market hall until 1971, when it was relocated to the suburbs. The loss of the market led to the neighborhood's steep decline; only in the last decade or so has El Born become rejuvenated.

Today the market hall is open as the El Born Cultural Center, home to a permanent Barcelona 1700 exhibit as well as temporary displays. Enter for free to peruse the airy public space, look down at the medieval excavations, and read plaques about the history. You can also enjoy a drink in its modern café or pay to see the exhibits.

The excavation below the market hall comes with a story poignant for locals. Before 1714, this neighborhood lost an uprising against the Spanish. Residents were forced to destroy their homes and use those very stones to build the citadel for their Spanish overlords—a fortress symbolic to this day of foreign control over Catalunya. The citadel came with a one-kilometer wide-open zone, so no buildings were allowed where the market stands today. Then, in 19th century, a big marketplace was established here, thriving for a hundred years (1871-1971). The large hall had stood vacant since the market closed, but recent construction work revealed the medieval foundations of those pre-1714 buildings. From the railing you can look down at the pre-1714 street pavement stones and brick footprints of homes (well-described in English). The Barcelona 1700 exhibit brings that age to life with paintings, artifacts, and videos.

• *From the cultural center, return a block or so back into Passeig del Born and turn left on the arcaded Carrer del Rec. This part of El Born has a high concentration of...*

❼ Shopping Streets

Fashion boutiques populate the area around **Carrer del Rec.** And on the side streets, you can see local "fashions" flapping in the breeze from characteristic wrought-iron balconies. While strict building codes prohibit people from drying laundry outside their homes in most of the city, an exception is made for El Born—since this medieval quarter lacks interior courtyards.

Feel free to browse around now (or come back later), but eventually you'll want to take the first right turn, down **Carrer de l'Esparteria**—another great shopping street. As elsewhere in El Born, most street names are tied to a particular craft or product; for example, the third street on the right, Carrer de la Formatgeria, was home to the cheesemakers—and still today, it faces a fondue shop.

Stick with the street as it jogs slightly left and becomes Carrer dels Ases, pausing at **Carrer del Malcuinat** (on the right), literally "Badly Cooked Street." Looking left, you'll notice you're just a block off the port. In the Middle Ages, this lane was home to unpretentious eateries serving fill-the-tank meals to undiscerning sailors who were fresh off the boat. These days, no self-respecting restaurateur has the nerve to open an eatery along here (except, strangely, an Irish pub).

· *Turn right down the short Carrer del Malcuinat, emerging at a big square with the...*

❽ Monument of Catalan Independence

The square is called Plaça del Fossar de les Moreres ("The Burial Place of the Mulberry Trees"). The lone mulberry tree and mod-

ern monument honor a 300-year-old massacre that's still fresh in the Catalan consciousness. On September 11, 1714, the Bourbon King Philip V, ruling from Madrid, completed a successful 14-month siege of Barcelona (the "Catalan Alamo"). In retaliation for the local resistance to Bourbon rule, he massacred Catalan patriots. From that day on, the king outlawed Catalan language, culture, and institutions, kicking off more than two centuries of cultural suppression. For example, no university was allowed in Barcelona from 1720 to 1850. To establish his hold, the king demolished 20 percent of the homes in the nearby fishermen's quarter in order to build a gigantic citadel. These suddenly homeless seafarers were moved to the tightly grid-planned Barceloneta quarter, designed by a military architect, jutting out into the harbor just east of here. Meanwhile, the loss of a huge chunk of El Born contributed to this neighborhood's decline, as shipping shifted farther west, to the Barri Gòtic's harbor at Port Vell.

This square marks the site of a mass grave of the massacred Catalan patriots. The **eternal flame** burns atop this monument, and 9/11 remains a sobering anniversary for the Catalans, who still harbor a grudge. They say when heading to the toilet, "I'm going to Philip's house."

Here or elsewhere in El Born (which is a particularly feisty

EL BORN WALK

neighborhood), you may see displayed the ***estelada* flag,** the symbol of Catalan separatists: It features the typical red-and-gold horizontal stripes of the Catalunya flag, but with a blue triangle and white star on the hoist side. This design comes from the flag of a former Spanish colony that fought hard for its independence—Cuba. It's a provocative image to Spaniards who want to keep Catalunya in their country.

• *The hulking building dominating this square is the Church of Santa Maria del Mar. To reach its entrance, turn left and walk alongside it, until you get to the small square in front of the church.*

❾ Church of Santa Maria del Mar

This 14th-century church is the proud centerpiece of El Born. "Del Mar" means "of the sea," and that's where the money came from.

This is where shipwrights and merchants came to worship. The proud shippers built this church in less than 60 years, so it has a harmonious style that is considered pure Catalan Gothic. Located outside the city walls, this was a defiantly independent symbol of neighborhood pride; to this day, it's fully supported not by the Church or the city, but by the community.

On the big **front doors,** notice the figures of workers who donated their time and sweat to build the church. The stone for the church was quarried at Montjuïc and had to be carried across town on the backs of porters called *bastaixos*. Although they've always been celebrated by residents, their work is now more widely appreciated, following the release of the 2006 novel *Cathedral of the Sea*, which tells the story of the church's construction from the perspective of an ambitious *bastaixo*.

Step inside the church. The largely unadorned **Gothic interior** used to be more highly decorated with Baroque frills, up until the Spanish Civil War (1936-1939). During the war, the Catholic Church sided with the conservative forces of Franco against leftists supporting the Spanish Republic. In retaliation, the working class took their anger out on this church, burning all of its wood furnishings and decor (carbon still blackens the ceiling). Today the church remains stripped down—naked in all its Gothic glory. The tree-like columns inspired Gaudí (their influence on the columns inside his Sagrada Família church is obvious). Sixteenth-century sailors left models of their ships at the foot of the altar for Mary's protection. Even today, a classic old Catalan ship remains at Mary's feet. As within the Cathedral of Barcelona, here you can see the characteristic Catalan Gothic buttresses flying inward, defining

Indulgences near the Church

Barcelona's most colorful bohemian quarter—this neighborhood around the Church of Santa Maria del Mar—offers plenty of inviting places to eat, drink, and shop. Explore!

The recommended La Vinya del Senyor wine bar, good for a drink or a meal, faces the front door of the church, and several other recommended eateries are nearby (see page 206 of Eating in Barcelona). For liquid and gourmet food souvenirs, try Vila Vinateca, a wine shop with (they claim) the widest selection in Barcelona (Mon-Sat 8:30-20:30, closed Sun, Carrer des Agullers 7—as you face the church it's buried in the streets over your right shoulder, tel. 902-327-777).

A caffeine jolt awaits at Cafés El Magnífico, selling what's reputed to be the city's best coffee beans (Mon-Sat 10:00-20:00, closed Sun, one block up Carrer de l'Argenteria at #64—immediately to the left as you face the church's front door, tel. 933-196-081). For a fragrant snack, head to Casa Gispert, which has been roasting nuts in the same wood-fired oven since 1851. Drop in to enjoy the aroma of fire-roasted nuts and pick up a snack (Tue-Fri 9:30-14:00 & 16:00-20:30, Sat 10:00-14:00 & 17:00-20:30, closed Sun-Mon; facing front door of church, circle around left side and walk almost all the way to the end—store is on the left at Carrer dels Sombrerers 23, tel. 933-197-535).

Near Casa Gispert is the start of an excellent shopping area. Head up the little lane just to the right of Gispert, Carrer de Sant Antoni dels Sombrerers. Follow this street as it jogs left, then (at the dead end), turn right onto Carrer dels Banys Vells. Follow this all the way up to Princesa—a bunch of great shops hide along the lanes branching off to the left. Many of them have workshops actually producing the goods for sale. The streets wedged between here and Carrer de l'Argenteria are particularly interesting and an easy place to score some cool finds, including handmade clothing, accessories, bags, and more.

the chapels that ring the nave. Brilliant stained glass—most notably the rose window over the main entry—flood the interior with soft light.

Around the right side of the church is a poignant memorial to the "Catalan Alamo" of September 11, 1714 (described earlier, under "Monument of Catalan Independence").

• If you've seen enough, you could end our walk now and give in to El Born's many buyable and edible temptations (see sidebar for ideas). To continue on to the **waterfront**, face the cathedral, and turn right up Carrer d'Espaseria. You'll pop out at the square...

⑩ Pla de Palau

The hulking building on your right, at the end of the square, is **La Llotja de Mar,** or fish exchange. Back when Barcelona was a major shipping center and El Born was its ritziest neighborhood, this was one of Europe's first stock exchanges. From the late 17th through the late 20th century, the building also housed the prestigious Barcelona Arts and Crafts School. The oldest design school in Spain (from 1715), this local institution has provided state-subsidized instruction to budding artists—including Pablo Picasso and Joan Miró.

• *Walk along the front of La Llotja de Mar, cross the wide street, and turn right to walk under the shaded arches of the big arcaded building. At the busy intersection, turn left around the corner and come face-to-face with the...*

⑪ *Barcelona Head*

This sculpture, created for the 1992 Summer Olympics by American Pop artist Roy Lichtenstein, instantly became an icon of the city. It brings together the colors of Miró, the tiles of Gaudí, the Cubism of Picasso, and the comic-newsprint trademark of Lichtenstein. The grand Main Post Office stands just behind it.

Down the promenade from the head, look for the canopy with a giant, whimsical **lobster sculpture** waving from on top. This was designed by Javier Mariscal. While the restaurant that commissioned this work is long gone, the cheery lobster survives—one more piece of invigorating public art on Barcelona's fine waterfront, a veritable open-air contemporary art museum.

• *Barcelona's inviting waterfront beckons. From here, you can walk left, past the Catalan History Museum, to reach **Barceloneta** and the beach (or consider renting a bike at the recommended Un Cotxe Menys shop for a pedal down the beach promenade to the Fòrum—described on page 26). Going right takes you along the delightful art-lined **promenade** next to the Old Port (bristling with sailboats) to the Columbus Monument at the bottom of the Ramblas. Another option is to head up busy **Via Laietana,** which we crossed at the beginning of this walk. Or you can backtrack to the **Picasso Museum** and take my self-guided tour (see next chapter). Finally, if you haven't yet explored El Born's shopping streets (see sidebar on previous page), what better time than now?*

EL BORN WALK

PICASSO MUSEUM TOUR

Museu Picasso

This is the best collection in the country of the work of Spaniard Pablo Picasso (1881-1973). And since Picasso spent his formative years (from age 14 to 23) in Barcelona, it's the best collection of his early works anywhere. The museum is sparse on later, better-known works from his time of international celebrity; visit this museum not to see famous canvases but to get an intimate portrait of the young man finding his way as an artist. By experiencing his youthful, realistic art, you can better understand his later, more challenging art and more fully appreciate his genius.

Picasso's personal secretary amassed many examples of his work and bequeathed them to Barcelona. The artist, happy to have a museum showing off his work in the city of his youth, added to the collection throughout his life. The artworks are scattered through several connected Gothic palaces.

Orientation

Cost: €14, free all day first Sun of month and other Sun from 15:00. The family pass (*carnet familiar*) available for €15 is a great deal, admitting parents and kids under 18 to the permanent and special exhibits.

Hours: Tue-Sun 9:00-19:00, Thu until 21:30, closed Mon, last entry 30 minutes before closing.

Crowd-Beating Tips: There's almost always a line, sometimes with waits of more than an hour. The busiest times are mornings before 13:00, all day Tuesday, and during the free entry times on Sundays (see above). If you have an Articket BCN or plan on buying one (see page 24), skip the line by going to the "Meeting Point" entrance (30 yards to the right of the main entrance). You can also skip the line by buying your ticket online at www.museupicasso.bcn.cat (no additional booking fee). Stuck in line without a ticket? Figure that about 25 people are admitted every 10 minutes.

Getting There: It's at Carrer de Montcada 15-23; the ticket office is at #21. From the Jaume I Metro stop, it's a quick five-minute walk. Just head down Carrer de la Princesa (across the busy Via Laietana from the Barri Gòtic), turning right on Carrer de Montcada. It's a 10-minute walk from the cathedral and many parts of the Barri Gòtic; for an interesting approach from the cathedral area, ✪ take the El Born Walk.

Information: Tel. 932-563-000, www.museupicasso.bcn.cat.

Tours: The 1.5-hour audioguide costs €5 and offers ample detail about the collection.

Length of This Tour: Allow at least an hour, or more time for lingering. If you have less time, focus on the first part of the collection (through the Blue Period), with Picasso's lesser-known but formative early works.

Services: The ground floor, which is free to enter, has a required bag check, as well as a handy array of other services (bookshop, WC, and cafeteria).

Photography: Strictly forbidden.

Cuisine Art: Outside the museum, right along Carrer de Montcada in either direction, are several great recommended tapas bars: With your back to the museum, a few steps to the left are **El Xampanyet, Taverna Tapeo,** and **Euskal Etxea** (fine places for a quick bite), while to the right (across Carrer de la Princesa and up a block) is **Bar del Pla.** For details about these and other characteristic places nearby, see the Eating in Barcelona chapter.

The Tour Begins

The Picasso Museum's collection of nearly 300 paintings is presented more or less chronologically (though specific pieces may be out for restoration or on tour, and the rooms are rearranged every few months or so). But with the help of thoughtful English descriptions for each stage (and guards who don't let you stray), it's easy to follow the evolution of Picasso's work. This tour is arranged by the stages of his life and art.

• *Begin in rooms 1 and 2.*

Boy Wonder

Pablo's earliest art (in the first room) is realistic and earnest. His work quickly advances from childish pencil drawings (such as *Hercules,* 1890), through a series of technically skilled **art-school works** (copies of plaster feet and arms), to oil paintings of impres-

Picasso Museum—First Floor

Not to Scale

ELEV.

Room 1

MAIN HALLWAY

Stairs to Ground Floor

Stairs from Ground Floor

TOUR BEGINS

Room 15

TOUR ENDS

ENTRANCE
(AT GROUND LEVEL)

CARRER DE MONTCADA

← To Santa Caterina Market
(5 min. walk)

To Church of Santa Maria del Mar →
(5 min. walk)

To Jaume 1 [M] (5 min. walk)
& Cathedral (10 min. walk)

❶ Portraits &
   Art-School Work
❷ First Communion
❸ Science and Charity
❹ Horta de San Joan
❺ Velázquez Copy
❻ Cancan Dancer
❼ Still Life
❽ The Waiting (Margot)
❾ Motherhood
❿ Rooftops of Barcelona
⓫ Portrait of Bernadetta
   Bianco
⓬ Woman with Mantilla
⓭ Gored Horse
⓮ Synthetic Cubism
⓯ Las Meninas Studies
⓰ Ceramics
⓱ French Riviera
⓲ Portraits of Jacqueline (2)

sive technique. Even at a young age, his **portraits** of grizzled peasants demonstrate surprising psychological insight. Because his dedicated father—himself a curator and artist—kept everything his son ever did, Picasso must have the best-documented youth of any great painter.

• In Room 2, you'll find more paintings relating to Pablo's...

Developing Talent

During a summer trip to Málaga in 1896, Picasso dabbles in a series of fresh, Impressionistic-style landscapes (relatively rare in Spain

PICASSO MUSEUM

at the time). As a 15-year-old, Pablo dutifully enters art-school competitions. His first big work, *First Communion*, features a prescribed religious subject, but Picasso makes it an excuse to paint his family. His sister Lola is the model for the communicant, and the features of the man beside her belong to Picasso's father. Notice his sister Lola's exquisitely painted veil. This piece is heavily influenced by the academic style of local painters.

Picasso's relatives star in a number of portraits from this time. If it's on view, find the **portrait of his mother** (this and other family portraits may be out on loan to the Picasso Museum in Málaga). The teenage Pablo is working on the fine details and gradients of white in her blouse and the expression in her cameo-like face. Notice the signature. Spaniards keep both parents' surnames, with the father's first, followed by the mother's: Pablo Ruiz Picasso.

• *Continue into Room 3.*

Early Success

Science and Charity (1897), which won second prize at a fine-arts exhibition, got Picasso the chance to study in Madrid. Now Pi-

casso conveys real feeling. The doctor (modeled on Pablo's father) represents science. The nun represents charity and religion. From her hopeless face and lifeless hand, it seems that Picasso believes nothing will save this woman from death. Pablo painted a little perspective trick: Walk back and forth across the room to see the bed stretch and shrink. Three small studies for this painting (on the right) show how this was an exploratory work. The frontier: light.

Picasso travels to Madrid for further study. Stifled by the stuffy fine-arts school there, he hangs out instead in the Prado Museum and learns by copying the masters. (An example of his impressive mimicry is coming up in a later room.) Having absorbed the wisdom of the ages, in 1898 Pablo visits **Horta de San Joan,** a rural Catalan village, and finds his artistic independence. (See the small landscapes and scenes of village life he did there.) Poor and without a love in his life, he returns to Barcelona.

• *Head to Room 4.*

Pablo Picasso (1881-1973)

Pablo Picasso was the most famous and, for me, the greatest artist of the 20th century. Always exploring, he became the master of many styles (Cubism, Surrealism, Expressionism, and so on) and of many media (painting, sculpture, prints, ceramics, and assemblages). Still, he could make anything he touched look unmistakably like "a Picasso."

Born in Málaga, Spain, Picasso was the son of an art teacher. At a very young age, he quickly advanced beyond his teachers. Picasso's teenage works are stunningly realistic and capture the inner complexities of the people he painted. As a youth in Barcelona, he fell in with a bohemian crowd that mixed wine, women, and art.

In 1900, at age 19, Picasso started making trips to Paris. Four years later, he moved to the City of Light and absorbed the styles of many painters (especially Henri de Toulouse-Lautrec) while searching for his own artist's voice. His paintings of beggars and other social outcasts show the empathy of a man who was himself a poor, homesick foreigner. When his best friend, Spanish artist Carlos Casagemas, committed suicide, Picasso plunged into a **Blue Period** (1901-1904)—so called because the dominant color in these paintings matches their melancholy mood and subject matter (emaciated beggars, hard-eyed pimps, and so on).

In 1904, Picasso got a steady girlfriend (Fernande Olivier) and suddenly saw the world through rose-colored glasses—the **Rose Period.** He was further jolted out of his Blue Period by the "flat" look of the Fauves. Not satisfied with their take on 3-D, Picasso played with the "building blocks" of line and color to find new ways to reconstruct the real world on canvas.

At his studio in Montmartre, Picasso and his neighbor Georges Braque worked together, in poverty so dire they often didn't know where their next bottle of wine was coming from. And then, at the age of 25, Picasso reinvented painting. Fascinated by the primitive power of African and Iberian tribal masks, he sketched human faces with simple outlines and almond eyes. Intrigued by the body of his girlfriend, Fernande, he sketched it from every angle, then experimented with showing several different views on the same canvas. A hundred paintings and nine months later, Picasso gave birth to a monstrous canvas of five nude, fragmented prostitutes with mask-like faces—*Les Demoiselles d'Avignon* (1907).

This bold new style was called **Cubism.** With Cubism, Picasso shattered the Old World and put it back together in a new way. The subjects are somewhat recognizable (with the help of the titles), but they're built with geometric shards (let's call them "cubes")—like viewing the world through a kaleidoscope of brown and gray. Cubism gives us several different angles of the subject at once—say, a woman seen from the front and side angles simultaneously, resulting in two eyes on the same side of the nose. This involves showing the traditional three dimensions, plus Einstein's new fourth dimension—the time it takes to walk around the subject to see other angles.

In 1918, Picasso married his first wife, Olga Kokhlova, with whom he had a son. He then traveled to Rome and entered a **Classical Period** (the 1920s) of more realistic, full-bodied women and children, inspired by the three-dimensional sturdiness of ancient statues. While he flirted with abstraction, throughout his life Picasso always kept a grip on "reality." His favorite subject was people. The anatomy might be jumbled, but it's all there.

Though he lived in France and Italy, Picasso remained a Spaniard at heart, incorporating Spanish motifs into his work. Unrepentantly macho, he loved bullfights, seeing them as a metaphor for the timeless human interaction between the genders. The horse—clad with blinders and pummeled by the bull—has nothing to do with the fight. To Picasso, the horse symbolizes the feminine, and the bull, the masculine. Spanish imagery—bulls, screaming horses, a Madonna—appears in Picasso's most famous work, *Guernica* (1937, on display in Madrid). The monumental canvas of a bombed village summed up the pain of Spain's brutal civil war (1936-1939) and foreshadowed the onslaught of World War II.

At war's end, Picasso left Paris, his wife, and all of his emotional baggage behind, finding fun in the sun in the **south of France.** Sun! Color! Water! Spacious skies! Freedom! Senior citizen Pablo Picasso was reborn, enjoying worldwide fame. He lived at first with the beautiful young painter Françoise Gilot, mother of two of his children, but soon replaced her with another young beauty, Jacqueline Roque, who became his second wife. Dressed in rolled-up white pants and a striped sailor's shirt, bursting with pent-up creativity, Picasso often cranked out a painting a day. Picasso's Riviera works set the tone for the rest of his life—sunny, lighthearted, childlike, experimenting in new media and using motifs of the sea, of Greek mythology (fauns, centaurs), and animals (birds, goats, and pregnant baboons). His simple drawing of doves became an international symbol of peace.

Picasso also made collages, built "statues" out of wood, wire, ceramics, papier-mâché, or whatever, and even turned everyday household objects into statues (like his famous bull's head made of a bicycle seat with handlebar horns). **Multimedia** works like these have become so standard today that we forget how revolutionary they were when Picasso invented them. His last works have the playfulness of someone much younger. As it is often said of Picasso, "When he was a child, he painted like a man. When he was old, he painted like a child."

Barcelona Freedom

Art Nouveau is all the rage in Barcelona when Pablo returns there in 1900. Upsetting his dad, he quits art school and falls in with

the avant-garde crowd. These bohemians congregate daily at Els Quatre Gats ("The Four Cats," a popular restaurant to this day—see page 204). Picasso even created the **menu cover** for this favorite hangout (it's sometimes on view here in Room 4). Further establishing his artistic freedom, he paints **portraits** of his new friends (including one of Jaume Sabartés, who later became his personal assistant and donated the works to establish this museum). Still a teenager, Pablo puts on his first one-man show at Els Quatre Gats in 1900.

Notice young Picasso's nearly perfect **copy** of a portrait of Philip IV by an earlier Spanish master, Diego Velázquez. (Near the end of this tour, we'll see a much older Picasso riffing on another Velázquez painting.)

• *The next few pieces are displayed in rooms 5, 6, and 7.*

Paris

In 1900 Picasso makes his first trip to Paris, a city bursting with life, light, and love. Dropping the paternal surname Ruiz, Pablo establishes his commercial brand name:

"Picasso." Here the explorer Picasso goes bohemian and befriends poets, prostitutes, and artists. He paints **cancan dancers** like Toulouse-Lautrec, **still lifes** like Paul Cézanne, brightly colored Fauvist works like Henri Matisse, and Impressionist **landscapes** like Claude Monet.

In *The Waiting (Margot),* the subject—with her bold outline and strong gaze—pops out from the vivid, mosaic-like background. It is Cézanne's technique of "building" a figure with "cubes" of paint that will inspire Picasso to invent Cubism—soon.

• *Turn right into the hall, then—farther along—right again, to find rooms 8 and 9.*

Blue Period

Picasso travels to Paris several times (he settles there permanently in 1904). The suicide of his best friend, his own poverty, and the influence of new ideas linking color and mood lead Picasso to abandon jewel-bright color for his Blue Period (1901-1904). He cranks out stacks of blue art just to stay housed and fed. With blue backgrounds (the coldest color) and depressing subjects, this period was revolutionary in art history. Now the artist is painting not what he sees, but what he feels. Just off Room 8, look for the touching portrait of a mother and child, *Motherhood* (this very fragile pastel is only displayed intermittently), which captures the period well. Painting misfits and street people, Picasso, like Velázquez and Toulouse-Lautrec, sees the beauty in ugliness.

Back home in Barcelona, Picasso paints his hometown at night from **rooftops** (in the main part of Room 8). The painting is still blue, but here we see proto-Cubism...five years before the first real Cubist painting.

• *In the left section of Room 8, we get a hint of Picasso's...*

Rose Period

Picasso is finally lifted out of his funk after meeting a new lady, Fernande Olivier. He moves out of the blue and into the happier Rose Period (1904-1907). For a fine example, see the portrait of a woman wearing a classic Spanish mantilla *(Portrait of Bernadetta Bianco)*. Its soft pink and reddish tones are the colors of flesh and sensuality. (This is the only actual Rose Period painting in the museum, but don't be surprised if it is out on loan.)

Barcelona

Picasso spent six months back in Barcelona in 1917 (his girlfriend, a Russian ballet dancer, had a gig in town). The paintings in these rooms demonstrate the artist's irrepressible versatility: He's already developed Cubism (with his friend Georges Braque; more on this below), but he also continues to play with other styles. In *Woman with Mantilla* (Room 9), we see a little Post-Impressionistic Pointillism in a portrait that is as elegant as a classical statue. Nearby, *Gored Horse* has all the anguish and power of his iconic *Guernica* (painted years later).

Cubism

Pablo's role in the invention of the revolutionary Cubist style is well-known—at least I hope so, since this museum has no true Cubist paintings. A Cubist work gives not only the basics of a subject—it shows every aspect of it simultaneously. The technique of "building" a subject with "cubes" of paint simmered in Picasso's artistic stew for years. In this museum, you'll see some so-called **Synthetic Cubist paintings**—a later variation that flattens the various angles, as opposed to the purer, original "Analytical Cubist" paintings, in which you can simultaneously see several 3-D facets of the subject.

• *Remember that this museum focuses on Picasso's early years. As a result, it has very little from the most famous and prolific "middle" part of his career—basically, from Picasso's adoption of Cubism to his sunset years on the French Riviera. (To fill in these gaps in his middle career, see the "Pablo Picasso" sidebar earlier in this chapter.) Skip ahead more than 30 years and into rooms 12-14 (at the end of the main hallway, on the right).*

Picasso and Velázquez

A series of Picasso's works relate to what many consider the greatest painting by anyone, ever: Diego Velázquez's *Las Meninas* (the 17th-century original is displayed in Madrid's Prado Museum). Heralded as the first completely realistic painting, *Las Meninas* became an obsession for Picasso centuries later.

Picasso, who had great respect for Velázquez, painted more than **40 interpretations** of this piece. Picasso seems to enjoy a relationship of equals with Velázquez. Like artistic soul mates, the two Spanish geniuses spar and tease. Picasso deconstructs Velázquez and then injects light, color, and perspective as he improvises on the earlier masterpiece. In Picasso's big black-and-white canvas, the king and queen (reflected in the mirror in the back of the room) are hardly seen, while the painter towers above everyone. The two women of the court on the right look like they're in a tomb—but they're wearing party shoes. Browse the various studies, a playground of color and perspective. See the fun Picasso had playing paddleball with Velázquez's tour de force—filtering Velázquez's realism through the kaleidoscope of Cubism.

• *Head back down the hall and turn right, through the **ceramics** area (Room 16), to find a flock of carefree white birds in Room 15.*

The French Riviera (Last Years)

Picasso spends the last 36 years of his life living simply in the south of France. He said many times that "Paintings are like windows open to the world." We see his sunny Riviera world: With simple black outlines and Crayola colors, Picasso paints sun-splashed nature, peaceful doves, and the joys of the beach. He dabbles in the timeless art of ceramics, shaping bowls and vases into fun animals decorated with simple, childlike designs. He's enjoying life with his second (and much younger) wife, Jacqueline Roque, whose portraits hang nearby.

Picasso died with brush in hand, still growing. Sadly, since Picasso vowed never to set foot in a fascist, Franco-ruled Spain, the artist never returned to his homeland...and never saw this museum (his death came in 1973—two years before Franco's). However, to the end, Picasso continued exploring and loving life through his art.

• *Our tour is finished. You're in the heart of the delightful El Born neighborhood. For a self-guided walk of this area,* ❂ *see my El Born Walk.*

EIXAMPLE WALK

From Plaça de Catalunya to
La Pedrera (and Beyond)

Literally "The Expansion," L'Eixample is where Barcelona spread when it burst at the seams in the 19th century. Rather than allowing unchecked growth, city leaders thoughtfully funneled Barcelona's newfound wealth into creating a standardized yet refreshingly open grid plan—as if attempting to achieve the opposite of the claustrophobic Gothic lanes that had contained locals for centuries.

The creation of the Eixample also coincided with a burst in architectural creativity, as great Modernista minds such as Antoni Gaudí, Lluís Domènech i Montaner, and Josep Puig i Cadafalch were given both artistic license and seemingly limitless funds to adorn the new boulevards with fanciful facades. It was a perfect storm of urban planning, unbridled architectural innovation, Industrial Age technology, ample wealth, and Catalan cultural pride.

This walk takes you through the Eixample's "Golden Quarter" (Quadrat d'Or) to see two of the city's Modernista musts—the Block of Discord and La Pedrera (Casa Milà)—as well as several other sights. The roundabout route also winds you through some pleasant, relatively untouristy residential neighborhoods that showcase modern Barcelona's unusual street plan and everyday life in this elegant quarter.

Orientation

Length of This Walk: Allow about 1.5 hours (more if you tour any of the sights). If you have less time, skip the first part of this walk and make a beeline for the Block of Discord and La Pedrera.

Planning Your Time: If you want to see the interiors, reservations are essential for Casa Lleó Morera, and advance purchase is smart for Casa Batlló and La Pedrera.

Getting There: This walk starts at Plaça de Catalunya (Metro: Plaça de Catalunya).

Church of the Holy Conception: Free, daily 7:30-13:00 & 17:00-21:00, enter at Carrer de Roger de Llúria 70, through the cloister.

La Concepció Market: Free, Mon and Sat 8:00-15:00, Tue-Fri 8:00-20:00, closed Sun, Carrer de València 317, tel. 934-575-329.

Casa Batlló: €21.50, daily 9:00-20:00; for advance ticketing, see page 54.

Casa Lleó Morera: €15, most days 10:00 English tour, for reservations, see page 55.

Fundació Antoni Tàpies: €7, covered by Articket BCN, Tue-Sun 10:00-19:00, closed Mon, Carrer d'Aragó 255, tel. 934-870-315.

La Pedrera (Casa Milà): €16.50, daily March-Oct 9:00-20:00, Nov-Feb 9:00-18:30, last entry 30 minutes before closing, for advance ticketing and crowd-beating tips, see page 55.

Palau Baró de Quadras (Institut Ramón Llul): Free, Mon-Thu 8:00-20:00, Fri until 19:00, closed Sat-Sun, www.llull.cat.

Eating: Several fine tapas bars and restaurants are on or near the course of this walk. For details, see page 211.

BACKGROUND

Barcelona boomed in the 1800s, with its population doubling (from a half-million to a million) over the course of one century. Before its roaring 19th century, Barcelona languished through centuries of stagnation: Columbus' discoveries had shifted trade from the Mediterranean to the Atlantic. Catalunya also suffered under the thumb of Madrid, which feared—perhaps rightfully—a Catalan uprising. Eventually, Queen Isabella II loosened Madrid's grip on Barcelona. This land of abundant coal deposits and many rivers flowing from the Pyrenees to the Mediterranean provided the perfect resources for powering textile mills. Industrialization brought people from all over Spain (and beyond) to find work, and Barcelona's textile magnates powered a remarkably robust economy. Barcelona was back on the map.

But the upwardly mobile city had nowhere to grow. Because of the Madrid government's centuries-old restrictions, the city was forced to stay within its medieval walls. By the mid-19th century, 200,000 residents were crammed into the Old City. It was a slum of steep and crowded tenements where disease was rampant, the air was choked with coal soot, and the quality of life was miserable. It was clear that expansion was necessary.

Throughout Europe in the Industrial Age, cities (like Paris, Vienna, and Copenhagen) were dealing with similar growing pains: dense population and squalor needlessly corralled into tight quarters by antiquated defensive city walls. The solution: Tear down those walls. Use the land once taken by walls and moats for circular boulevards, parks, and lakes—and expand.

In 1854, the Spanish Queen Isabella II allowed Barcelona to tear down the medieval wall and expand northward. Because very little existed outside the Old City, urban planners had a blank slate.

Civil engineer Ildefons Cerdà (1815-1876) proposed a carefully plotted, remarkably modern, and efficient grid of streets that would surround the convoluted tangle of Barcelona's Old City. Uptown Barcelona would be a unique variation on the common grid-plan city. By snipping off the building corners, light and spacious octagonal "squares" were created at every intersection.

Work began in 1860 on Cerdà's progressive Eixample plan, which envisioned a new town in which everything was made accessible to everyone. Each block-square district would have easy access to its own hospital, park, market, schools, and day-care centers. Restrictions on the height, width, and depth of buildings ensured that sunlight would reach every unit. The hollow space found inside each "block" of apartments would form a neighborhood park. Although parts of Cerdà's vision didn't quite pan out, the Eixample is an urban success.

The birth of the Eixample also coincided with two other important moments in the city's history: The revival of Catalan cultural pride (the Renaixença) and the emergence of Catalunya's own spin on Art Nouveau—Modernisme (see sidebar, later).

Rich-and-artsy big shots bought plots along the Eixample grid and hired some of the best and brightest architects in the business, including Antoni Gaudí, Lluís Domènech i Montaner, and Josep Puig i Cadafalch. It's no accident that Modernista mansions come with big bay windows and outlandish decoration: The people who paid for them wanted both to be seen, and to be recognized for their forward-thinking embrace of the new art. The wealthiest landowners built as close to the center as possible—that's why the most distinctive buildings are near Passeig de Gràcia.

Today's Eixample remains Barcelona's upscale and genteel uptown. It's also one center of the local gay community (especially a few blocks west of Passeig de Gràcia, around Carrer d'Aribau), earning it the nickname "Gayshample." The heart of the Eixample is the Quadrat d'Or, or "Golden Quarter," with the richest collection of Modernista facades...and the richest local residents. As you walk through the streets, peek into the big, ornate iron-and-

Eixample Walk

GRÀCIA

EIXAMPLE

QUADRAT D'OR

1. Passeig de Gràcia
2. Tapas 24 Rest.
3. Water Tower Garden
4. Church of the Holy Conception
5. La Concepció Market
6. J. Murria Queviures Grocery
7. Centre Cultural La Casa Elizalde
8. Block of Discord
9. Rambla de Catalunya
10. La Pedrera (Casa Milà)

glass doorways of almost any apartment building to see the eclectic decorative entrance halls and old-fashioned elevators. This remains one of the city's most desirable neighborhoods.

The Walk Begins

• *Begin at Plaça de Catalunya. Head up the broad boulevard (Passeig de Gràcia) at the top end of the giant El Corte Inglés department store. Walk up two blocks (on the right side of this street) to the huge intersection with Gran Via de les Corts Catalanes; there's a big fountain in the middle.*

❶ Passeig de Gràcia

In the 500 feet between here and the Barri Gòtic, you've traveled 500 years—from the medieval Gothic vibe of the Barri Gòtic to the ambitiously modern late-19th-century Eixample.

In Catalan, *passeig* means "boulevard"—and this one leads to Gràcia, once a separate town but now overwhelmed by Barcelona's growth and a neighborhood within the city. As one of the first major thoroughfares of the Eixample, this was prime real estate. To this day, the boulevard remains the top street in town. Notice the extra-wide girth of this drag, the inviting parklike median strips, and the unique Modernista lampposts anchored by Gaudí-style benches slathered with broken white tile mosaics.

Originally Barcelona's wealthy class built elaborate residences along here. But within just a few decades, as the city continued

to grow and real estate was at a premium, it became more lucrative to tear down those mansions and replace them with multistory apartment buildings. (One of the few surviving original mansions, now the Comedia theater, is kitty-corner across the intersection—just beyond the fountain.) Notice that, despite great architectural variation in their facades, most Eixample homes share an identical design: The entire building was owned by one family which lived in the middle and rented space above and below. Shops and businesses were on the ground floor; above that, a large first (our "second") floor, where the wealthy family lived; and, higher up, smaller floors for tenants. Throughout the Eixample, you'll

Modernisme and the Renaixença

Modernisme is Barcelona's unique contribution to the Europe-wide Art Nouveau movement. Meaning "a taste for what is

modern"—things like streetcars, electric lights, and big-wheeled bicycles—this free-flowing organic style lasted from 1888 to 1906.

Broadly speaking, there were two kinds of Modernisme (Catalan Art Nouveau). Early Modernisme is a kind of Neo-Gothic, clearly inspired by medieval castles and towers—logically, since architects wanted to recall the days when Barcelona was at its peak. From that same starting point, Antoni Gaudí branched off on his own, adding the color and curves we most associate with Barcelona's Modernisme look.

The aim was to create objects that were both practical and decorative. To that end, Modernista architects experimented with new construction techniques. Their most important material was concrete, which they could use to make a hard stone building that curved and rippled like a wave. Then they sprinkled it with brightly colored glass and tile. The structure was fully modern, but the decoration was a clip-art collage of nature images, exotic Moorish or Chinese themes, and fanciful Gothic crosses and knights to celebrate Catalunya's medieval glory days.

It's ironic to think that Modernisme was a response against the regimentation of the Industrial Age—and that all those organic shapes were only made possible thanks to Eiffel Tower-like iron frames. As you wander through the Eixample looking at all those fanciful facades and colorful, leafy, flowing, blooming shapes in doorways, entrances, and ceilings, remember that many of these homes were built at the same time as the first skyscrapers in Chicago and New York City.

Underpinning Modernisme was the Catalan cultural revival movement, called the Renaixença. Across Europe, it was a time of national resurgence. It was the dawn of the modern age, and downtrodden peoples—from the Basques to the Irish to the Hungarians to the Finns—were throwing off the cultural domination of other nations and celebrating what made their own culture unique. Here in Catalunya, the Renaixença encouraged everyday people to get excited about all things Catalan—from their language, patriotic dances, and inspirational art to their surprising style of architecture.

see that the first floor is usually taller and more elaborate than the other floors—often with balconies or bay windows that higher floors are lacking. (Most of these houses predate the elevator; after that convenience was invented and widely installed, penthouse living became popular.) Many houses have two doors—one for the owners and another for the upstairs tenants. Most house blocks had an interior garden courtyard for ventilation and light, although over time many of these spaces have been covered over by one-story structures or parking lots.

Because the Eixample was developed during the Renaixença, you'll spot Catalan themes, such as St. George (Jordi)—the local patron saint—slaying the dragon.

See any flags? Catalunya's flag is a simple block of narrow red-and-gold stripes. But the version with the blue triangle with a white star is a call for independence from Spain inspired by the flag of Cuba (which successfully won its independence from Spain long ago).

Speaking of Catalan pride, imagine this street (and the ones around it) clogged with an estimated one million furious Catalans. It happened on July 10, 2010, after Spanish constitutional courts overturned key provisions of a Catalan statute for home rule (which had been approved by an overwhelming 73 percent of Catalan voters). These patriots of Catalunya—which considers itself a "nation without a state"—waved flags that read, *Som una nació. Nosaltres decidim.* (We are a nation. We decide.) This peaceful demonstration was a reminder that the Catalans—like the Basques and the Scots—take home rule very seriously. As locals here grumble for more autonomy and vote on self-rule, Spain will make economic concessions to keep the industrial powerhouse of Catalunya a part of Spain.

Continue one more block up Passeig de Gràcia (to the intersection with Carrer de la Diputació) to appreciate the delightfully airy street plan you'll find throughout the Eixample. Notice that the four corners are cropped off, creating a wide-open pleasant space at the intersection (which can be filled by café tables, inviting benches, or public art).

• *From here, turn right on Carrer de la Diputació. (If you're tight on time, you can continue directly ahead to stop #8 on this walk, the Block of Discord.)*

❷ Tapas 24

A few steps down on the left, you'll see the recommended Tapas 24, a popular and trendy Eixample tapas bar (for tapas bar listings, see page 211). Continue one block down Carrer de la Diputació, noticing the distinctive paving stones (four squares with a circle in each one). This is one of a handful of distinctive patterns on mass-produced tiles that are a symbol of Barcelona.

• *At the corner, cross the street and turn left up Carrer de Pau Claris. Halfway up the block, notice the gated **passage** on the right (Passatge Permanyer, at #116). Cut through here for a peek at a fine residential strip buried in the middle of the block. Although such passageways were not a planned feature of the Eixample, here and there they've been carved out of the buildings' central courtyards, and make a pretty stroll. Popping out the other end, go right to cross the street and jog 30 yards to the left, then go down the passage at #56 (on the right, marked* Jardins de Torre de les Aigües, *€1.50 late June–early Sept when pool is open, Mon–Sat 10:00–20:00). This leads you to a...*

❸ Water Tower Garden

This tranquil (if somewhat sterile) courtyard has trees, benches, and a wading pool, all watched over by a brick water tower from

1867. In the summer, a temporary "beach" is created here for neighborhood families. Courtyards like this were part of the original vision for the Eixample. Each block was supposed to have a shared central patio, but over the last century, many of them have been converted to other purposes. More recently, as properties become available, the city of Barcelona has slowly begun restoring Cerdà's original public spaces. The *Serveis* sign indicated a public WC.

• *Exiting the garden the way you entered, turn right and head up Carrer de Roger de Llúria. Cross Carrer del Consell de Cent, passing under the pretty yellow Neo-Renaissance facade slapped onto a modern building.*

Continue another block and cross another street (Carrer d'Aragó). Go straight up Carrer de Roger de Llúria a half-block, entering the delightful cloister with orange, magnolia, and palm trees at #70, on the right of the...

❹ Church of the Holy Conception

Work your way through the cloister to the interior of the church. This purely Gothic, 14th-century church with a 15th- and 16th-century cloister once stood in the Old City. But when the wall that once surrounded the Old City came down as part of Barcelona's expansion, a few historic churches like this one were moved, brick by brick, to new locations in the 1870s. The bell tower came from a different Gothic church.

• *Exiting the church through its front door (or back through the cloister and around to the front door), turn left, go one block, and cross Carrer del Bruc. Pass the detailed iron gate and columns of the entrance to the Seu del Districte Eixample—the Eixample's own "seat," or branch office, of City Hall. Continuing straight just beyond that, you'll reach (on the left)...*

❺ La Concepció Market

While it has many of the same features as La Boqueria (on the Ramblas) and the Santa Caterina Market (in El Born), this market (with a modern supermarket in the basement and a garage below that) has virtually zero tourists. Walk through the building, from one end to the other. It's a good place to sample local cheeses, buy olives, or pick up some fruit. At the far end, you'll emerge into a delightful flower market crowding the sidewalk.

• *Turn left and stroll along...*

Carrer de València

As you walk, you'll pass many more flower stands and the turreted Municipal Conservatory of Barcelona on the corner, a city-run music academy. Ponder the fact that in just a couple of blocks, we've passed a church, a municipal building, a market, and a school (just up the street next to the market). This is very much in keeping with the original vision for the Eixample: a series of self-sufficient neighborhood zones that give residents easy access to important services. A market like this serves each neighborhood here—part of the grand original plan.

Continuing straight on Carrer de València, you'll pass (at the corner, on the right) an unfortunate brick monstrosity that breaks up the Eixample harmony, followed by its antidote, at #293, a fine Modernista building with wrought-iron railings and twin bay windows. Cross the street. On your left, step into the Navarro flower shop. It's open 24-7 so there's just no excuse to miss it. Take a fragrant stroll, looping deep into the shop, noticing if there's a seasonal theme.

At the next intersection, cross the street to peek inside the classic Modernista grocery of ❻ **J. Murria Queviures.** This old-fashioned gourmet deli is stocked with pricey ingredients for a top-end picnic that may be a bit too classy for a park bench. Breathe deep to smell the cheese aging in the cellar. The vintage ad on the corner—dubbed *La Mona y el Mono (The Classy Lady and the Monkey)*—advertised anise liquor to Modernista-era clients.

Press ahead a half-block farther to the ❼ **Centre Cultural La Casa Elizalde** (Carrer de València 302, on the left). This cultural center, a facility of the city of Barcelona, is a hive of creative and personal growth activities. Head into the passage, noticing the community bulletin board listing classes and events. Continuing down the hall, you'll pop out into an appealing courtyard in the middle of the block with benches. Look up and around the buildings for a taste of the typical inner patios for the entire block of buildings, a quiet sanctuary from the busy Eixample streets. You'll find WCs inside the building: women, first floor; men, second floor.

• *Head back out to the street and turn left (the way you were going). At the end of the block, go left down Carrer de Pau Claris. After a block, turn right on the wide Carrer d'Aragó. Walk one block, stand on the corner, and you'll find yourself kitty-corner from the...*

❽ Block of Discord (Illa de la Discòrdia)

One block, three buildings, three astonishingly creative Modernista architects. Over a short span of time, the three big names of Catalunya's bold Art Nouveau architectural movement erected innovative facades along this one short stretch of Passeig de Gràcia. Although each of these architects has better works elsewhere in town, this is the most convenient place to see their sharply contrasting visions side by side. While these three buildings were done by famous, groundbreaking architects, the whole block is a jumble of delightful architectural whimsy. Reliefs, coats of arms, ironwork, gables, and bay windows adorn otherwise ordinary buildings.

• *Work your way down the block, beginning with the unmistakably Gaudí-style facade that's one building in from the corner.*

Casa Batlló (#43)

The most famous facade on the block is that of the green-blue, ceramic-speckled Casa Batlló, designed by Antoni Gaudí (you can tour the interior—see listing on page 54). It's thought that Gaudí based the work on the popular legend of St. George

Modernista Masters: Gaudí and Beyond

Yes, you'll hear plenty about Gaudí, but he's merely one of many great minds who contributed to the architectural revolution of Modernisme. Here's a rundown of the movement's stars—great talents with names much harder to pronounce and remember than Gaudí's. For a sense of the historical context that gave rise to these talented architects, see the "Modernisme and the Renaixença" sidebar, earlier.

The Stars of Modernisme

Antoni Gaudí (1852-1926), Barcelona's most famous Modernista artist, was descended from four generations of metalworkers—a lineage of which he was quite proud. He incorporated ironwork into his architecture and came up with novel approaches to architectural structure and space. Gaudí's work strongly influenced his younger Catalan contemporary, Salvador Dalí. Notice the similarities: While Dalí was creating unlikely and shocking juxtapositions of photorealistic images, Gaudí did the same in architecture—using the spine of a reptile for a bannister or a turtle shell design on windows. Entire trips (and lives) are dedicated to seeing the works of Gaudí, but on a brief visit in Barcelona, the ones most worth considering are his great unfinished church, the Sagrada Família; several mansions in the town center, including La Pedrera, Casa Batlló, and Palau Güell; and Park Güell, his ambitious and never-completed housing development.

While Gaudí gets 90 percent of the tourists' attention, two other great Modernista architects were just as important: Lluís Domènech i Montaner and Josep Puig i Cadafalch. Gaudí was certainly a remarkable innovator, but these two were perhaps more purely representative of the Modernista style.

Lluís Domènech i Montaner (1850-1923), a professor and politician, was responsible for some major civic buildings, including his masterwork, the Palace of Catalan Music (described on page 49), and the Hospital de Sant Pau, a sprawling complex covering nine blocks (roughly between the Sagrada Família and Park Güell). Domènech i Montaner also designed Casa Lleó Morera on the Block of Discord (described later) and Casa Fuster (now a luxury hotel—see page 149), along with several works in the towns of Canet de Mar, Comillas, and others.

Josep Puig i Cadafalch (1867-1956) was a city planner who oversaw the opening up of Via Laietana (through the middle of the Old City, see page 115), the redevelopment of Montjuïc for the 1929 World Expo, and a redesign of the monastery at Santa Maria de Montserrat. Later he flourished as a Modernista architect in his own right, best known for manor houses such as Casa de les Punxes (described on page 149) and Casa Amatller on the Block of Discord (described later). He designed the brick Casaramona factory complex, which was recently converted into the cutting-edge CaixaForum exhibition space (see page 70). Perhaps most importantly, Puig i Cadafalch designed Casa Martí, a home for the Modernista hangout bar Els Quatre Gats, which became a cradle of sorts for the whole movement. The bar still welcomes visitors today (see page 204).

Supporting Cast

All architects worked with a team of people who, while not famous, made real contributions. For example, Gaudí's colleague **Josep Maria Jujol** (1879-1949) is primarily responsible for much of what Gaudí became known for—the broken-tile mosaic decorations (called *trencadís*) on Park Güell's benches and La Pedrera's chimneys.

Joan Martorell i Montells (1833-1906) was a professor, mentor, and employer of a young Antoni Gaudí. Although an accomplished architect in his own right, Martorell's most important role was as a facilitator of his prized student: He oversaw the committee that hired Gaudí to build the Sagrada Família, and introduced Gaudí to **Eusebi Güell,** who became Gaudí's most important benefactor.

Eusebi Güell (1846-1918) used his nearly $90 billion fortune to bankroll Gaudí and others, much as the Medici financed Michelangelo and Leonardo da Vinci. Güell's name still adorns two of Gaudí's most important works: Palau Güell and Park Güell (described on pages 37 and 57). The other Modernista architects also had deep-pocketed patrons who financed their works.

(Jordi) slaying the dragon: The humpback roofline suggests a cresting dragon's back, and the smallest, top balcony is shaped like a rosebud (echoing the legend that a rose grew in the place where St. George spilled the dragon's blood). The building's tibia-like pillars and skull-like balconies evoke the dragon's victims. Look at the first-floor bay window. If you squint (and perhaps smoke some pot, the consumption of which is legal here, by the way), you might see a bat with outstretched wings, relating to a Catalunyan folk legend. Notice also the random broken tiles, a Gaudí trademark that only later became appreciated. The tiled roof has a soft-ice-cream-cone turret topped with a cross. But some see instead a Mardi Gras theme, with mask-like balconies, a facade flecked with purple and gold confetti, and the ridge of a harlequin's hat up top. The inscrutable Gaudí preferred to leave his designs open to interpretation.

Before moving on, turn 180 degrees and look across the boulevard to see the straight iron-framed apartment building at #52—structurally the same as Casa Batlló. In 1904, when Gaudí was hired to renovate Casa Batlló, it looked like that.

• *Next door is...*

Casa Amatller (#41)

Josep Puig i Cadafalch completely remodeled this house for the Amatller family. The facade features a creative mix of three of Spain's historical traditions: Moorish-style pentagram-and-vine designs; Gothic-style tracery, gargoyles, and bay windows; and the step-gable roof from Spain's Habsburg connection to the Low Countries. Notice the many layers of the letter "A": The house itself (with its gable) forms an A, as does the decorative frieze over the bay window on the right side of the facade. Within that frieze, you'll see several more As sprouting from branches (*amatller* means "almond tree"). The reliefs above the smaller windows show off the hobbies of the Amatller clan: Find the cherubs holding the early box camera, the open book, and the amphora jug (which the family collected). Look through the second-floor bay window to see the corkscrew column.

For another dimension of Modernisme, peek into the ground-floor windows of the Bagues Joieria jewelry shop and notice the slinky pieces by Spanish Art Nouveau jeweler Masriera.

• *Now head left, to the end of the block. There, on the corner, you'll find...*

Casa Lleó Morera (#35)

This paella-like mix of styles is the work of the architect Lluís Domènech i Montaner, who also designed the Palace of Catalan Music. The lower floors have classical columns and a Greek-temple-like bay window. (Notice the real marble column—supporting nothing but some aristocrat's ego—placed for all to see behind the bay window.) Farther up are Gothic balconies of rosettes and tracery, while the upper part has faux Moorish stucco work. The whole thing is ornamented with fantastic griffins, angels, and fish. Flanking the third-story windows are figures holding the exciting inventions of the day—the camera, lightbulb, and gramophone— designed to demonstrate just how modern the homeowners were in this age of Modern-isme. The wonderful interior is now open to the public for limited guided tours (see listing on page 55).

• *From here, it's four long blocks to Gaudí's Modernista masterpiece, La Pedrera. While the easiest route is to simply turn around and plow back up Passeig de Gràcia—passing top-end shops—it's more interesting to detour around the block. From this corner, walk up Carrer del Consell de Cent, past galleries, high-end shops, and a Starbucks, to another splashy Eixample boulevard—Rambla de Catalunya. When you hit this delightful street, go into the park-like median strip and turn right.*

❾ Rambla de Catalunya

As you head up Rambla de Catalunya, you'll find a narrower, more manageable street lined with inviting cafés and shops—boutiques that are still upscale, but generally more local and unique than those on the main drag.

After one block, a half-block detour (to the right) on Carrer d'Aragó gets you to the **Fundació Antoni Tàpies**, dedicated to the 20th-century abstract artist from Barcelona. The Montaner-designed building sums up the Modernist credo: modern brick, iron, and glass materials; playful decorative motifs; and a spacious, functional, and light-filled interior. The tangled rooftop is called "The Cloud and the Chair." The collection itself is pricey to view, but fans of the artist's work will enjoy seeing his distinct mud-caked canvases. Tàpies (1923-2012) laid the canvas on the floor, covered it with wet varnish, and sprinkled in dust, dirt, and paint. Then he drew simple designs in the still-wet goop, capturing the primitive power of cavemen tracing the first art in mud with a stick.

• *Continue up the median of Rambla de Catalunya. As you stroll three blocks, enjoy the variety of facades, and ahead, on the mountaintop, the 19th-century Church of the Sacred Heart. When you get to Carrer de Provença, turn right and make your way to...*

⓾ La Pedrera (a.k.a. Casa Milà)

This Gaudí exterior laughs down on the crowds filling Passeig de Gràcia. La Pedrera ("The Quarry") has a much-photographed

roller coaster of melting-ice-cream eaves. This is Barcelona's quintessential Modernista building and was Gaudí's last major work (1906-1910) before he dedicated his final years to the Sagrada Família.

The building has a steel structural skeleton to support its weight (a new construction technique at the time). Gaudí's planned statues of the Virgin Mary and archangels were vetoed by the owner. If you have time—and the line's not too long—consider touring the house's interior and rooftop (see listing on page 55). Or just take a peek inside the main atrium for free.

• *From here, you can head back to Plaça de Catalunya—it's a straight shot, seven blocks down Passeig de Gràcia. The Diagonal Metro station near La Pedrera, on the L3 (green) line, has easy connections to Plaça de Catalunya and other key stops.*

But for a finale to our walk, consider heading another two blocks up Passeig de Gràcia to the boundary of the Eixample. Just after La Pe-drera, on the right, look for the fun Vinçon shop with its stylish office and home furnishings (see page 227 of the Shopping in Barcelona chapter). Then continue up Passeig de Gràcia until you run into...

Avinguda Diagonal

This aptly named boulevard slashes diagonally through the middle of the Eixample, connecting the neighborhood to the port.

Diagonal marks the end of the Eixample; just across the street begins the neighborhood of **Gràcia.** Compared to the urban, up-scale street plan of the Eixample, Gràcia feels like what it is—a onetime small town that's now part of a big city, with narrower streets and more character. Gràcia is known as an upper-middle-class, intellectual part of town, with many design schools and a youthful scene (see page 236 in the Nightlife in Barcelona chapter).

Cross over to the left side of Passeig de Gràcia and find the

Catalunya TI. Go through the gate to the left of the TI entrance to find your way to one of Barcelona's most enjoyable little parks—a tropical oasis in the heart of the city. Relax.

• *If you're a Modernista completist, it's just a short walk from here to three more fine buildings—"extra credit" for those fascinated by this era.*

Modernista Detour

Cross Diagonal, continuing two long blocks on Passeig de Grà-cia. Where the street curves around the tree-lined median, you'll find the **Hotel Casa Fuster,** a fine Modernista building by Lluís Domènech i Montaner. This top-of-the-top luxury hotel is a favorite of Woody Allen (who has an affinity for Barcelona, featuring it in his film *Vicky Cristina Barcelona*). Seeking a place to play jazz in town, Allen prodded the hotel to sponsor jazz concerts. The hotel's Café Vienés now hosts a jazz night every Thursday (for details, see page 233).

Backtrack to Diagonal to reach two works by Josep Puig i Cadafalch. Take a left (go east) down the busy Diagonal boulevard. After a block, you reach the **Palau Baró de Quadras** (Diagonal 373, on the right across the street). Puig i Cadafalch's plateresque (Spain's medieval "silverwork" style of intricate decoration) facade celebrates a time when Catalunya was powerful, and the statues flanking the door—of St. George defeating the dragon—make the building's Catalan pride even more evident. Today the building houses Institut Ramón Llul, dedicated to promoting Catalan language and culture. As a public cultural center, it's a rare Modernista interior that's free to enter and explore (closed Sat-Sun).

Continuing another block and a half down Diagonal leads to the distinctively turreted Casa Terrades (at #416, on the left)—bet-

ter known as **Casa de les Punxes** ("House of Spikes"). Here Puig i Cadafalch lassoed together what had been three separate buildings into one large complex, wrapping them in a fanciful Gothic castle cloak (no inside access). The turrets, spires, balconies, and ceramic tiles celebrate Catalan culture.

• *Back at Passeig de Gràcia (where it hits Diagonal), you have several options:*

The **Diagonal Metro stop** *(right in front of you) is on L3 (green), which zips you effortlessly to Plaça de Catalunya, Liceu (middle of the Ramblas), and Drassanes (bottom of the Ramblas).*

You can also use the Metro to reach the pièce de résistance *of Modernisme, the* **Sagrada Família:** *Head west one block on Carrer del Ros-*

selló to find the entrance to the Diagonal stop for L5 (blue); take it to the Sagrada Família stop. (See the ○ Sagrada Família Tour chapter.)

*Or, to visit another great Modernista sight, hop on bus #24 to Gaudí's **Park Güell** (catch it on Passeig de Gràcia just south of Diagonal, same side of street as La Pedrera; get off at Ctra Carmel–Parc Güell stop; ○ see the Park Güell Tour chapter).*

SAGRADA FAMÍLIA TOUR

Architect Antoni Gaudí's most famous and awe-inspiring work is this unfinished, super-sized church. With its cake-in-the-rain facade and otherworldly spires, the church is not only an icon of Barcelona and its trademark Modernista style, but also a symbol of this period's greatest practitioner. As an architect, Gaudí's foundations were classics, nature, and religion. The church represents all three.

Nearly a century after his death, people continue to toil to bring Gaudí's designs to life. There's something powerful about a community of committed people with a vision, working on a church that won't be finished in their lifetime—as was standard in the Gothic age. The progress of this remarkable building is a testament to the generations of architects, sculptors, stonecutters, fund-raisers, and donors who've been caught up in the audacity of Gaudí's astonishing vision. After paying the steep admission price (becoming a partner in this building project), you will actually feel good. If there's any building on earth I'd like to see, it's the Basílica de la Sagrada Família...finished.

Orientation

Cost: Church-€14.80, church and tower elevator-€19.30, €18.30 combo-ticket includes Gaudí House Museum at Park Güell (see page 57).

Hours: Daily April-Sept 9:00-20:00, Oct-March 9:00-18:00, last entry 15 minutes before closing.

Advance Tickets: To avoid the ticket-buying line, you can reserve an entry time and buy tickets in advance for both the church and the tower elevators. The easiest option is to book online at www.sagradafamilia.cat, which allows you to print tickets at home.

With pre-purchased tickets, head straight for the "online ticket office" window, to the right of the main ticket line, and show your ticket to the guard.

Crowd-Beating Tips: The ticket windows and entrance for individuals are on the west side of the church, at the Passion Facade. Though the line can seem long (often curving around the block), it generally moves quickly; you can ask for an estimate from the guards at the front of the line. Still, waits can be up to 45 minutes at peak times—and occasionally stretch much longer (most crowded in the morning). To minimize waiting, arrive right at 9:00 (when the church opens) or after 16:00. To skip the line, buy advance tickets, take a tour, or hire a private guide.

Getting There: The Sagrada Família Metro stop puts you right on the doorstep: Exit toward Plaça de la Sagrada Família. The church address is Carrer de Mallorca 401.

Information: Tel. 932-073-031, www.sagradafamilia.cat.

Tours: The 50-minute English tours (€4.50) run May-Oct daily at 11:00, 12:00, 13:00, and 15:00, though there's no noon tour Mon-Fri in Nov-April (choose tour time when you buy ticket). Or rent the good 1.5-hour audioguide (€4.50). Good English information is posted throughout.

Tower Elevators: Two different elevators take you (for a fee) partway up the towers for a great view of the city and a gargoyle's-eye perspective of the loopy church.

The easier option is the **Passion Facade elevator,** which takes you 215 feet up and down. You can climb higher, but expect the spiral stairs to be tight, hot, and congested.

The **Nativity Facade elevator** is more exciting and demanding. You'll get the opportunity to cross the dizzying bridge between the towers, but you'll need to take the stairs all the way down.

The elevators cost €4.50 each, and each ticket comes with an entry time. It's best to **reserve online** (see "Advance Tickets," above) to get your tower entry time in sync with your church visit. Although you can buy tower tickets at the main ticket office at any time you're at the church, the tickets can sell out quickly (particularly for the time slots during your visit), so you might end up with an inconvenient tower-entry time several hours later in the day, long after you're ready to leave the church.

Length of This Tour: Allow 1.5 hours. If you have less time, skip the museum and schoolhouse, and max out on ogling the magnificent building itself, inside and out.

Nearby: Inviting parks flank the building, facing the two completed facades.

A Dream Made Real

For over 130 years, Barcelona has labored to bring Antoni Gaudí's vision to reality. Local craftsmen often cap off their careers by spending a couple of years on this exciting construction site. The present architect has been at it since 1985. The work is funded exclusively by private donations and entry fees, which is another reason its completion has taken so long. Your admission helps pay for the ongoing construction.

Like Gothic churches of medieval times, the design has evolved over the decades. At heart, it's Gothic, a style much admired by Gaudí. He added his own Art Nouveau/Modernisme touches, guided by nature and engineering innovations. Today the site bristles with cranking cranes, rusty forests of rebar, and scaffolding. Sagrada Família offers a fun look at a living, growing bigger-than-life building.

Sagrada Família Timeline

1882	The church is begun in Gothic-revival style (by architect Francisco de Paula del Villar).
1883	Paula del Villar quits, and Antoni Gaudí is hired—and proceeds to completely re-envision the church's design.
1892	Gaudí begins the Nativity Facade.
1914	Gaudí turns his attention exclusively to the Sagrada Família.
1925	The first bell tower is completed.
1926	Gaudí dies with the project about 20 percent complete.
1936-1939	The Spanish Civil War halts all work; the crypt is burned, along with many of Gaudí's plans.
1950s	Building resumes in earnest with the start of the Passion Facade.
1976	The four Passion spires are finished, bringing the total of completed spires to eight (out of 18 planned).
1980s	Computer technology is introduced, greatly accelerating the pace of construction.
2000	The nave roof is completed.
2005	Passion statues are completed.
2010	Crossing vaults are finished (enclosing the roof), and Pope Benedict XVI dedicates the church as a basilica.
2026?	The church should be finished by the 100th anniversary of Gaudí's death. Make a date to attend the dedication with your kids...to teach them a lesson in delayed gratification.

BACKGROUND

Gaudí labored on the Sagrada Família for 43 years, from 1883 until his death in 1926 (see sidebar previous page). Since then, construction has moved forward in fits and starts, though much progress was made in recent decades, thanks to Barcelona's 1992 Olympics renaissance, the ensuing rediscovery of the genius of Gaudí, and advances in technology. In 2010, the main nave was finished enough to host a consecration Mass by the pope (as a Catholic church, it is used for services, though irregularly). As I stepped inside on my last visit, the brilliance of Gaudí's vision for the interior was apparent.

The main challenges today: Ensure that construction can withstand the vibrations caused by the speedy AVE trains rumbling underfoot, construct the tallest church spire ever built, and find a way to buy out the people who own the condos in front of the planned Glory Facade so that Gaudí's vision of a grand esplanade approaching the church can be realized. The goal, which seems overly optimistic but tantalizing nonetheless, is to finish the church by the 100th anniversary of Gaudí's death, in 2026.

The Tour Begins

• *Start at the ticket entrance (at the Passion Facade) on the western side of the church. The view is best from the park across the street. Before heading to the ticket booth, take in the...*

❶ Exterior

Stand and imagine how grand this church will be when completed. The four 330-foot spires topped with crosses are just a fraction of

this mega-church. When finished, the church will have 18 spires. Four will stand at each of the three entrances. Rising above those will be four taller towers, dedicated to the four Evangelists. A tower dedicated to Mary will rise still higher—400 feet. And in the very center of the complex will stand the grand 560-foot Jesus tower, topped with a cross that will shine like a spiritual lighthouse, visible even from out at sea.

The Passion Facade that tourists enter today is only a side entrance to the church. The grand main entrance will be around to the right. That means that the nine-story apartment building will eventually have to be torn down to accommodate it. The three facades—Nativity, Passion, and Glory—will chronicle Christ's life

Sagrada Família

Pond

To Hospital de la Santa Creu i Sant Pau & Bus #92 to Park Güell

AVINGUDA DE GAUDÍ

Plaça de Gaudí

20 Meters
20 Yards

M Sagrada Família

CARRER DE LA MARINA

FENCE

M Sagrada Família

NATIVITY FACADE

❼ ⟶ **MUSEUM**

❻

ELEV. ☒

SPIRES

CLOISTER

BRONZE DOOR

CARRER DE PROVENÇA

AMBULATORY

CHOIR

T R A N S E P T

❹

NAVE

MODEL

❺

GLORY FACADE

Ⓑ #19 & #50

SPIRES

CLOISTER

❸ ☒ELEV.

PASSION ❷ **FACADE**

FENCE

SERVI-CAIXA ATM ◆

RAMP

❽ **SCHOOL**

UNFINISHED ESPLANADE

CARRER DE MALLORCA

EXIT

M Sagrada Família

TICKETS & ENTRANCE

CARRER DE SARDENYA

Ⓣ

Plaça de Sagrada Família

❶ ⟵

👣 **TOUR BEGINS**

❶ View of the Exterior
❷ Passion Facade
❸ Atrium
❹ Interior & 4 Red Porphyry Columns

❺ Glory Facade
❻ Nativity Facade
❼ Ramp to Museum
❽ School

from birth to death to resurrection. Inside and out, a goal of the church is to bring the lessons of the Bible to the world. Despite his boldly modern architectural vision, Gaudí was fundamentally traditional and deeply religious. He designed the Sagrada Família to be a bastion of solid Christian values in the midst of what was a humble workers' colony in a fast-changing city.

When Gaudí died, only one section (on the Nativity Facade) had been completed. The rest of the church has been inspired by Gaudí's long-range vision, but designed and executed by others. This artistic freedom was amplified in 1936, when civil war shelling burned many of Gaudí's blueprints. Supporters of the ongoing work insist that Gaudí, who enjoyed saying, "My client [God] is not in a hurry," knew he wouldn't live to complete the church and recognized that later architects and artists would rely on their own muses for inspiration. Detractors maintain that the church's design is a uniquely, intensely personal one and that it's folly (if not disrespectful) for anyone to try to guess what Gaudí would have intended. Studying the various plans and models in the museum below the church, it's clear that Gaudí's plan evolved dramatically the longer he worked. Is it appropriate to keep implementing a century-old vision that can no longer be modified by its creator? Discuss.

• *Pass through the ticket entrance into the complex, approaching closer to the...*

❷ Passion Facade

Judge for yourself how well Gaudí's original vision has been carried out by later artists. The Passion Facade's four spires were designed by Gaudí and completed (quite faithfully) in 1976. But the lower part was only inspired by Gaudí's designs. The stark sculptures were interpreted freely (and controversially) by Josep Maria Subirachs (1927-2014), who completed the work in 2005.

Subirachs tells the story of Christ's torture and execution. The various scenes—Last Supper, betrayal, whipping, and so on—zig-

zag up from bottom to top, culminating in Christ's crucifixion over the doorway. The style is severe and unadorned, quite different from Gaudí's signature playfulness. But the bone-like archways are closely based on Gaudí's original designs. And Gaudí had made it clear that this facade should be grim and terrifying.

The facade is full of symbolism. A stylized Alpha-and-Omega is over the door (which faces the setting sun). Jesus, hanging on the cross, has hair made of an open book, symbolizing the word of God. To the left of the door is a grid of numbers, always adding up to 33—Jesus' age at the time of his death. The distinct face of the man below and left of Christ is a memorial to Gaudí. Now look high above: The two-ton figure suspended between the towers is the soul of Jesus, ascending to heaven.

• *Enter the church. As you pass through the* ❸ *atrium, look down at the fine porphyry floor (with scenes of Jesus' entry into Jerusalem), and* *look right to see one of the **elevators** up to the towers. For now, continue into the...*

❹ Interior

Typical of even the most traditional Catalan and Spanish churches, the floor plan is in the shape of a Latin cross, 300 feet long and 200 feet wide. Ultimately, the church will encompass 48,000 square feet, accommodating 8,000 worshippers. The nave's roof is 150 feet high. The crisscross arches of the ceiling (the vaults) show off Gaudí's distinctive engineering. The church's roof and flooring were only completed in 2010—just in time for Pope Benedict XVI to arrive and consecrate the church.

Part of Gaudí's religious vision was a love for nature. He said, "Nothing is invented; it's written in nature." Like the trunks of trees, these **columns** (56 in all) blossom with life, complete with branches, leaves, and knot-like capitals. The columns are a variety of colors—brown clay, gray granite, dark-gray basalt. The taller columns are 72 feet tall; the shorter ones are exactly half that.

The angled columns form many **arches.** You'll see both parabolas (U-shaped) and hyperbolas (flatter, elliptical shapes). Gaudí's starting point was the Gothic pointed arch used in medieval churches. But he tweaked it after meticulous study of which arches are best at bearing weight.

Little **windows** let light filter in like the canopy of a rainforest, giving both privacy and an intimate connection with God. The clear glass is temporary and will gradually be replaced by stained glass. As more and more stained glass is installed, splashes of color will breathe even more life into this amazing space. Gaudí envisioned an awe-inspiring canopy with a symphony of colored light to encourage a contemplative mood.

High up at the back half of the church, the U-shaped **choir**—suspended above the nave—can seat 1,000. The singers will eventually be backed by four organs (there's one now).

Work your way up the grand nave, walking through this forest of massive columns. At the center of the church stand four **red porphyry columns,** each marked with an Evangelist's symbol and name in Catalan: angel (Mateu), lion (Marc), bull (Luc), and eagle (Joan). These columns support a ceiling vault that's 200 feet high—and eventually will also support the central steeple, the 560-foot Jesus tower with the shining cross. The steeple will be further supported by four underground pylons, each consisting of 8,000 tons of cement. It will be the tallest church steeple in the world, though still a few feet shorter than the city's highest point at the summit of Montjuïc hill, as Gaudí believed that a creation of man should not attempt to eclipse the creation of God.

Stroll behind the altar through the **ambulatory** to reach a small chapel set aside for prayer and meditation. Look through windows down at the **crypt** (which holds the tomb of Gaudí). Peering down into that surprisingly traditional space, imagine how the church was started as a fairly conventional, 19th-century Neo-Gothic building until Gaudí was given the responsibility to finish it.

• *Head to the far end of the church, to what will eventually be the main entrance. Just inside the door, find the **bronze model** of the floor plan for the completed church. Facing the doors, look high up to see Subirachs' statue of one of Barcelona's patron saints, **George (Jordi)**. While you can't see it, imagine what outside these doors will someday be the...*

❺ Glory Façade

Study the life-size image of the **bronze door,** emblazoned with the Lord's Prayer in Catalan, surrounded by "Give us this day our

daily bread" in 50 languages. If you were able to walk through the actual door, you'd be face-to-face with...drab, doomed apartment blocks. In the 1950s, the mayor of Barcelona, figuring this day would never really come, sold the land destined for the church project. Now the city must buy back these buildings in order to complete Gaudí's vision: that of a grand esplanade leading to this main entry. Four towers will rise. The facade's sculpture will represent how the soul passes through death, faces the Last Judgment, avoids the pitfalls of hell, and finds its way to eternal glory with God. Gaudí purposely left the facade's design open for later architects—stay tuned.

• *Backtrack up the nave, and exit through the right transept. Once outside, back up as far as you can to take in the...*

❻ Nativity Facade

This is the only part of the church essentially finished in Gaudí's lifetime. The four spires decorated with his unmistakably non-linear sculpture mark this facade as part of his original design. Mixing Gothic-style symbolism, images from nature, and Modernista asymmetry, the Nativity Facade is the best example of Gaudí's original vision, and it established the template for future architects.

The theme of this facade, which faces the rising sun, is Christ's birth. A statue above the doorway shows Mary, Joseph, and Baby Jesus in the manger, while curious cows peek in. It's the Holy Family—or "Sagrada Família"—for whom this church is dedicated. Flanking the doorway are the three Magi and adoring shepherds. Other statues show Jesus as a young carpenter and angels playing musical instruments. Higher up on the facade, in the arched niche, Jesus crowns Mary triumphantly.

The facade is all about birth and new life, from the dove-covered Tree of Life on top to the turtles at the base of the columns flanking the entrance. At the bottom of the Tree of Life is a white pelican. Because it was believed that this noble bird would kill itself to feed its young, it was often used in the Middle Ages as a symbol for the self-sacrifice of Jesus. The chameleon gargoyles at the outer corners of the facade (just above door level) represent the changeability of life. It's as playful as the Passion

Facade is grim. Gaudí's plans were for this facade to be painted. Cleverly, this attractive facade was built and finished first to bring in financial support for the project.

The four **spires** are dedicated to apostles, and they repeatedly bear the word "Sanctus," or holy. Their colorful ceramic caps symbolize the miters (formal hats) of bishops. The shorter spires (to the left) symbolize the Eucharist (communion), alternating between a chalice with grapes and a communion host with wheat.

To the left of the facade is one section of the **cloister.** Whereas most medieval churches have their cloisters attached to one side of the building, the Sagrada Família's cloister will wrap around the church, more than 400 yards long.

• *Notice the second* **elevator** *up to the towers. But for now, head down the ramp to the left of the facade, where you'll find WCs and the entrance to the...*

❼ Museum

Housed in what will someday be the church's crypt, the museum displays Gaudí's original **models and drawings,** and chronicles the progress of construction over the last 130 years. Wander among the plaster models used for the church's construction, including a model of the nave so big you walk beneath it. The models make clear the influence of nature. The columns seem light, with branches springing forth and capitals that look like palm trees. You'll notice that the models don't always match the finished product—these are ideas, not blueprints set in stone. The Passion Facade model (near the entrance) shows Gaudí's original vision, with which Subirachs tinkered very freely (see "Passion Facade," earlier).

Turn up the main hallway. On the left you can peek into a busy **workshop** still used for making the same kind of plaster models Gaudí used to envision the final product in 3-D. Farther along, a small hallway on the right leads to some original Gaudí architectural **sketches** in a dimly lit room and a worthwhile 20-minute **movie** (generally shown in English at :50 past each hour).

From the end of this hall, you have another opportunity to look down into the crypt and at **Gaudí's tomb.** Gaudí lived on the site for more than a decade and is buried in the Neo-Gothic 19th-century crypt (also viewable from the apse). There's a move afoot to make Gaudí a saint. Gaudí prayer cards provide words of devotion to his beatification. Perhaps someday his tomb will be a place of pilgrimage.

Back in the main hallway, on the right is the intriguing **"Hanging Model"** for Gaudí's unfinished Church of Colònia Güell (in a suburb of Barcelona), featuring a similar design to the Sagrada Família. The model illustrates how the architect used gravity to calculate the arches that support the church. Wires dangle like suspended chains, forming perfect hyperbolic arches. Attached to these are bags, representing the weight the arches must support. Flip these arches over, and they can bear the heavy weight of the roof. The mirror above the model shows how the right-side-up church is derived from this. Across the hall is a small exhibit commemorating **Pope Benedict XVI's** 2010 consecration visit.

After passing some original sculptures from the Glory Facade (on the right) and continuing beneath a huge plaster model, turn right to find **three different visions** for this church. Notice how the arches evolved as Gaudí tinkered, from the original, pointy Neo-Gothic arches, to parabolic ones, to the hyperbolic ones he eventually settled on. Also in this hall are replicas of the **pulpit** and **confessional** that Gaudí, the micromanager, designed for his church. Before exiting at the far end of the hall, scan the photos (including one of the master himself) and timeline illustrating how construction work has progressed from Gaudí's day to now.

• *You'll exit near where you started, at the Passion Facade.*

❽ School and Rest of Visit

The small building outside the Passion Facade was a school Gaudí erected for the children of the workers building the church. Today it includes more exhibits about the design and engineering of the church, along with a classroom and a replica of Gaudí's desk as it was the day he died. Pause for a moment to pay homage to the man who made all this possible. Gaudí—a faithful Catholic whose medieval-style mysticism belied his Modernista architecture career—was certainly driven to greatness by his passion for God.

• *Our tour is over. From here, you have several options.*

> *Return to Central Barcelona: You can either hop on the Metro or take one of two handy buses (both stop on Carrer de Mallorca, directly in front of the Glory Facade). Bus #19 takes you back to the Old City in 15 minutes, stopping near the cathedral and in the El Born district (with the ❂ Picasso Museum and ❂ El Born Walk). Bus #50 goes from the Sagrada Família to the heart of the Eixample (corner of Gran Via de les Corts Catalanes and Passeig de Gràcia—near the start of the ❂ Eixample Walk), then continues on to Plaça Espanya where you can hop off for the Montjuïc sites (see "Getting to Montjuïc" on page 60).*

> *Visit Park Güell: Many visitors like to combine their visit here with a trip to Park Güell, which sits nearly two (uphill) miles to the northwest (❂ see the Park Güell Tour). By far the easiest way to get there is to spring for a taxi (around €10-12).*

> *But if you prefer public transportation and don't mind a little walking, here's a scenic way to get there that also takes you past another, often overlooked Modernista masterpiece: With the Nativity Facade at your back, walk to the near-left corner of the park across the street. Then cross the street to reach the diagonal Avinguda de Gaudí (between the Repsol gas station and the KFC). Follow the funky lampposts four blocks gradually uphill (about 10 minutes) along Avinguda de Gaudí, a pleasantly shaded, café-lined pedestrian street. Soon you reach the striking Modernista-style Hospital de la Santa Creu i Sant Pau, designed by Lluís Domènech i Montaner (for more about him, see page 144). Visit the complex to see the interior and view the courtyards (€8, €14 guided tour; April-Oct Mon-Sat 10:00-18:30, Nov-March until 16:30, Sun 10:00-14:30; English tours offered Mon-Sat at 12:00, 13:00, 16:00, and 17:00—no 17:00 tour Nov-March, Sun at 12:00 and 13:00; tel. 932-682-444, www.*

visitsantpau.com). Facing the main entrance, go right to catch bus #92 on Carrer de Sant Antoni Maria Claret, which will take you to the side entrance of Park Güell.

From the Sagrada Família, you could also get to Park Güell by taking the Metro to the Joanic stop, then hop on bus #116 (described on page 163)—but that involves two changes...and less scenery.

PARK GÜELL TOUR

Tucked in the foothills at the edge of Barcelona, this fanciful park—designed by Antoni Gaudí—combines playful design, inviting spaces, and a terrace offering sweeping views over the rooftops of the city.

When the entire park was free to enter, it became so popular that it was nearly trampled by tourists, obscuring the very sights they'd come to see. To control crowds, the part of the park with the most popular sights was declared the Monumental Zone, which requires an admission fee and a timed entry to visit. This fairly compact zone contains a pair of gingerbread-style houses, a grand staircase monitored by a colorful dragon, a forest of columns supporting a spectacular view terrace, and an undulating balcony slathered in tile shards.

Outside the zone, the rest of the park contains the Gaudí House Museum, Calvary viewpoint, picnic area, and a pleasant network of nature trails—all of which (except the museum) are free.

No matter where you visit—inside the zone or out—what you're sure to see is Barcelonans and tourists alike enjoying a day at the park.

Orientation

Cost and Hours: Much of the park is free, but you'll need a timed-entry ticket to see the iconic Gaudí features—the trademark dragon, tiled stairway, wavy benches, view terrace, and more—in the **Monumental Zone** (€8 at the gate or €7 online, www.parkguell.cat). The number of visitors admitted to the Monumental Zone at any one time is strictly limited, so it's smart to **reserve ahead online** as much as three months in advance. Once inside, you can stay in the Monumental Zone as long as you want, but when you leave the zone, you can't return. The park is open daily April-Oct 8:00-21:30, Nov-March 8:30-18:00.

The **Gaudí House Museum,** outside the Monumental Zone, costs €5.50 (€18.30 combo-ticket includes Sagrada Família church) and is open daily April-Sept 10:00-20:00, Oct-March 10:00-18:00, www.casamuseugaudi.org.

Length of this Tour: An hour is plenty to take this tour, but the park is a pleasant place to linger longer.

Getting There: Park Güell is about 2.5 miles from Plaça de Catalunya, beyond the Gràcia neighborhood in Barcelona's foothills. If asking for directions, be aware that Catalans pronounce it "Park Gway" (sounds like "parkway").

From downtown, a **taxi** will drop you off at the main entrance for about €12. From Plaça de Catalunya, the blue Tourist Bus stops about two blocks downhill from the main entrance, and **public bus** #24 travels from Plaça de Catalunya to the park's side entrance. From elsewhere in the city, follow this **Metro-plus-bus combination:** Go by Metro to the Joanic stop and look for the Carrer de l'Escorial exit. Walk up Carrer de l'Escorial to the bus stop in front of #20. Take bus #116 directly to the park's main entrance; you'll see gingerbread-gate houses and a grand stairway. To get back to the city center after your visit, catch bus #116 going in the same direction; get off at Plaça de Lesseps and take the Metro from there. (It's a 15-minute downhill walk from the park's main entrance to the Lesseps Metro: Walk straight ahead down Carrer de Larrard, turn right on busy Travessera de Dalt, and walk for several blocks to reach the Metro entrance.)

For tips on reaching Park Güell from Gaudí's Sagrada Família church, see page 161.

Eating in the Park: Options are limited. On the main view terrace (in the Monumental Zone), a **snack bar** with tables offers simple sandwiches and beverages. A few vendors hawk drinks and snacks at the side entrance. If you've packed a **picnic** (a good idea), head just above the Rosary pathway near the main terrace, where you'll find tree-shaded tables.

OVERVIEW

Funded by his frequent benefactor Eusebi Güell, Gaudí intended this 30-acre garden to be a 60-residence housing project—a kind of gated community. Work began in 1900, but progress stalled in 1914 with the outbreak of World War I and the project never resumed. Only two houses were built, neither designed by Gaudí—the structures are now home to the Gaudí House Museum and Casa Trias (not open to the public). As a high-income housing de-

PARK GÜELL

velopment, it flopped; but as a park, it's a delight, offering another peek into Gaudí's eccentric genius in a setting that's more natural than man-made—appropriate considering the naturalism that pervades Gaudí's work.

Many sculptures and surfaces in the park are covered with colorful *trencadís* mosaics—broken ceramic bits rearranged into new patterns. This Modernista invention, made of discarded tile, dishes, and even china dolls from local factories, was an easy, cheap, and aesthetically pleasing way to cover curvy surfaces like benches and columns. Although Gaudí promoted the technique, most of what you see was executed by his collaborator, Josep Maria Jujol.

The Tour Begins

• *This tour assumes you're arriving at the front/main entrance (by taxi or bus #116). If you instead arrive at the side entrance and already have your Monumental Zone ticket, walk straight ahead through the gate to find the terrace with colorful mosaic benches, then walk down to the stairway and front entrance.*

Front Entrance

Before entering the park, notice the **mosaic medallions** along the outside wall that say "park" in English—reminding folks that Park Güell was modeled on the British "garden city" concept of integrating urban communities with green space.

Entering the park, you walk through a palm-frond **gate** and pass Gaudí's gas lamps (1900-1914), both made of wrought iron. His dad was a blacksmith, and he always enjoyed this medium.

Two Hansel-and-Gretel gingerbread lodges flank the entrance, signaling to visitors that this park is a magical space. One of the buildings houses a good bookshop; the other is home to the skippable **La Casa del Guarda,** a branch of the Barcelona History Museum (MUHBA). The sparse exhibit inside features video slideshows about Gaudí's building methods and works, old black-and-white movies of the age, and no real artifacts. True Gaudí fans might want to take a close look at the structure, though, as it's one of the few built examples of his ideas for simple housing. (The Gaudí House Museum, described later, is more interesting to me.)

• *Now face the grand...*

Park Güell

Area shaded in gray is the Monumental Zone

"PATHWAY OF COLUMNS"

CASA TRIAS

SNACK BAR

WC

TERRACE

PICNIC AREA

UPPER VIADUCT

MIDDLE VIADUCT

ROSARY PATHWAY

CASA GÜELL (SCHOOL)

CURVY BENCHES

GAUDÍ HOUSE MUSEUM

SIDE ENTRANCE

#24, #92 B

Park

CALVARY

MARKET-PLACE

STAIRWAY & FOUNTAINS

Güell

BOOK-STORE

Entry Courtyard

LOWER VIADUCT

WALL

CARRETERA DEL CARMEL

CARRER D'OLOT

CASA DEL GUARDA

TAXIS

MAIN ENTRANCE

#116 B

CARRER DE MERCEDES

CARRER DE SANT JOSEP

CARRER DE LARRARD

CARRER DE MARIANAO

CARRER DE SANT JOSEP COTTOLENGO

To Blue Tourist Bus (5 min. walk) & M Lesseps (15 min. walk)

100 Meters

100 Yards

Stairway

The **cave-like enclosures** flanking the stairs were functional: One was a garage for Eusebi Güell's newfangled automobiles, while the other was a cart shelter.

Three **fountains** are stacked in the middle of the stairway. The first, at the base of the steps, is rocky and leafy, typical of Gaudí's naturalism. Next is a red-and-gold-striped Catalan shield with the head of a serpent poking out. The third is a very famous dragon—an icon of the park (and of Barcelona). While the dragon—slain by Barcelona's patron saint, George

(Jordi)—is a symbol of Catalan pride, this creature also evokes the crocodile mascot of Nîmes, France, where Eusebi Güell spent much of his youth. As for the ornamental brown tripod at the top of the stairs: Is it the Oracle of Delphi? The tail of the serpent whose head pokes out down below? Or something else entirely? Gaudí lets the viewer decide.

• At the top, dip into the...

Marketplace (Hall of 100 Columns)

This space was designed to house a **produce market** for the neighborhood's 60 mansions. The Doric columns—each lined at the base with white ceramic shards—add to the market's vitality (despite the hall's name, there are only 86 columns). White ceramic pieces also cover the multiple domes of the ceiling, which is interrupted by colorful mosaic rosettes. Look up to find four giant sun-like decorations representing the four seasons. Notice the hook in the middle of each one, where a lantern could be hung. Arranged around these are smaller rosettes, meant to suggest the lunar cycle. Street performers and musicians like the acoustics here.

• Continue up the left-hand staircase, looking left, down the playful...

"Pathway of Columns"

Gaudí drew his inspiration from nature, and this arcade is like a surfer's perfect tube. This is one of many clever double-decker **viaducts** that Gaudí designed for the grounds: vehicles up top, pedestrians in the portico down below. Gaudí intended these walk-

ways to remind visitors of the pilgrim routes that crisscross Spain (such as the famous Camino de Santiago). Eusebi Güell lived in the pink house (now a school) next to the terrace. This house predates the park project and was not designed by Gaudí.

• At the top of the stairway, you pop out on the...

Terrace

Sit on a colorful bench and enjoy one of Barcelona's best views. (Find Gaudí's Sagrada Família church in the distance.) The 360-foot-long bench is designed to fit your body ergonomically. Supposedly, Gaudí enlisted a construction worker as his guinea pig to figure out exactly where to place the lumbar support (back in a time when "ergonomics" and "lumbar support" hadn't even been invented). To Gaudí, this terrace evoked ancient Greek theaters that burrowed scenically into the sides of hills—but its primary purpose was that of the ancient Greek agora, a wide-open meeting place. Gaudí engineered a water-catchment system by which rain hitting this plaza would flow through natural filters, then through the columns of the market below to a 300,000-gallon underground cistern. The water was bottled and sold as a health cure (this location—far away from polluting city factories—had a healthy cachet); excess water powers the park's fountains. Notice the lion's-head gargoyles and the big stone droplets that cling to the outside edge of the terrace, which hint at this hidden functional purpose.

• *From here, as you face the city, the* **Gaudí House Museum** *is to your left, and the* **Calvary** *is high up on your right (both described next). These sights are outside the Monumental Zone; remember that once you leave the zone, you can't return.*

Gaudí House Museum
This pink house with a steeple, standing in the middle of the park (near the side entrance), was Gaudí's home for 20 years. Designed not by Gaudí but by a fellow architect, it was originally built as a model home to attract prospective residents. Gaudí lived here from 1906 until 1925. His humble artifacts are mostly gone, but the house is now a museum with some quirky Gaudí furniture. Though small, it offers a good taste of what could have been.

The main drag connecting this house to the terrace, called the **Rosary Pathway,** is lined with giant stone balls that represent the beads of a rosary. During the years he lived here, the reverent Gaudí would pray the rosary while walking this path.

The Calvary
High on a wooded hill beyond the pink school building is a stubby stone tower topped with three crosses, representative of the Hill of Calvary where Jesus was crucified. Gaudí envisioned the topography of Park Güell as a metaphor for the soul's progress: starting at the low end and toiling uphill to reach spiritual enlightenment (a chapel was originally intended to occupy this spot). And indeed, the park's higher paths seem to converge to lead pilgrims to this summit. The tower rewards those who huff up here with grand views over Barcelona and its bay.

The Rest of the Park
Like any park, this one is made for aimless rambling. As you wander, imagine living here a century ago—if this gated community had succeeded and was filled with Barcelona's wealthy. When con-

sidering the failure of Park Güell as a community development, also consider that it was an idea a hundred years ahead of its time. Back then, high-society ladies didn't want to live so far from the cultural action. Today, the surrounding neighborhoods are some of the wealthiest in town, and a gated community here could be a big hit.

SLEEPING IN BARCELONA

For hassle-free efficiency, I favor hotels and restaurants that are handy to your sightseeing activities. Rather than list hotels scattered throughout Barcelona, I describe several favorite neighborhoods and recommend the best accommodations values in each, from dorm beds to fancy doubles with all the comforts.

A major feature of this book is its extensive listing of good-value rooms. I like places that are clean, central, relatively quiet at night, reasonably priced, friendly, small enough to have a hands-on owner and stable staff, run with a respect for Spanish traditions, and not listed in other guidebooks. (In Barcelona, for me, meeting six out of these eight criteria means it's a keeper.) I'm more impressed by a convenient location and a fun-loving philosophy than flat-screen TVs and a pricey laundry service.

Barcelona is Spain's most expensive city. Still, it has reasonably priced rooms. Book your accommodations well in advance, especially if you'll be traveling during busy times. Cheap places are more crowded in summer; fancier business-class hotels fill up in winter and offer discounts on weekends and in summer. When considering relative hotel values, in summer and on weekends you can often get modern comfort in centrally located business-class hotels for about the same price (€100) as you'll pay for ramshackle charm. See page 314 for a list of major holidays and festivals in Spain; for tips on making reservations, see page 174.

RATES AND DEALS

I've described my recommended accommodations using a Sleep Code (see sidebar). Prices listed are for one-night stays in peak season, and assume you're booking directly with the hotel (not through an online hotel-booking engine or TI). Booking services extract a commission from the hotel, which logically closes the door on special deals. Book direct.

Some hotels include the 10 percent IVA tax in the room price; others tack it onto your bill. Additionally, the city levies a tourist tax (ranging from €0.65-2.25/person per night).

My recommended hotels each have a website (often with a built-in booking form) and an email address; you can expect a response in English within a day (and often sooner).

If you're on a budget, it's smart to email several hotels to ask for their best price. Comparison-shop and make your choice. This is especially helpful when dealing with the larger hotels that use "dynamic pricing," a computer-generated system that predicts the demand for particular days and sets prices accordingly: High-demand days will often be more than double the price of low-demand days. This makes it impossible for a guidebook to list anything more accurate than a wide range of prices. I regret this trend. While you can assume that hotels listed in this book are good, it's very difficult to say which ones are the better value unless you email to confirm the price.

As you look over the listings, you'll notice that some accommodations promise special prices to Rick Steves readers. To get these rates, you must book direct (that is, not through a booking site like TripAdvisor or Booking.com), mention this book when you reserve, and then show the book upon arrival. Rick Steves discounts apply to readers with ebooks as well as printed books. Because I trust hotels to honor this, please let me know if you don't receive a listed discount. Note, though, that discounts understandably may not be applied to promotional rates.

In general, prices can soften if you do any of the following: offer to pay cash, stay at least three nights, or mention this book. You can also try asking for a cheaper room or a discount, or offer to skip breakfast.

TYPES OF ACCOMMODATIONS
Hotels
Spain offers some of the best accommodations values in Western Europe. Most places are government-regulated, with posted prices.

Spain has stringent restrictions on smoking in public places. Smoking is not permitted in common areas, but hotels can designate 10 percent of their rooms for smokers.

Some hotels don't use central heat before November 1 and after April 1 (unless it's unusually cold); prepare for cool evenings if you travel in spring and fall. Summer can be extremely hot. Many rooms come with mini-refrigerators; stock yours with cold drinks. Consider air-conditioning, fans, and noise (since you'll want your window open).

Be aware that some hotels have centrally controlled air-conditioning—and the manager may choose the temperature (with an eye on his bottom line). In some hotel rooms, air-conditioning units are mounted high on the wall. These come with control sticks (like a TV remote, sometimes requiring a deposit) that generally have similar symbols: fan icon (toggle through wind power); louver icon (choose steady air flow or waves); snowflake and sunshine icons (heat or cold); clock ("O" setting: run *x* hours before turning off; "I" setting: wait *x* hours to start); and the temperature control (20 degrees Celsius is comfortable).

If you're arriving early in the morning, your room probably won't be ready. You can drop your bag safely at the hotel and dive right into sightseeing.

Hotel elevators, while becoming more common, are often very small—pack light, or you may need to take your bags up one at a time. Many Barcelona hotels now have a scale (costs about €1) you can use to check the weight of your bags before heading to the airport.

While many of my recommended hotels are on pedestrian streets, night noise can be a problem (especially in cheap places, which have single-pane windows). Always ask to see your room first. If you suspect night noise will be a problem, request a quiet *(tranquilo)* room in the back or on an upper floor *(piso alto)*. In most cases, view rooms *(con vista)* come with street noise. You'll often sleep better and for less money in a room without a view.

Hoteliers can be a great help and source of advice. Most know their city well, and can assist you with everything from public transit and airport connections to finding a good restaurant, the nearest launderette, or a Wi-Fi hotspot.

Even at the best places, mechanical breakdowns occur: Air-conditioning malfunctions, sinks leak, hot water turns cold, and toilets gurgle and smell. Report your concerns clearly and calmly at the front desk. For more complicated problems, don't expect instant results. Any legitimate place is legally required to have a complaint book *(libro de reclamaciones)*. A request for this book will generally prompt the hotelier to solve your problem to keep you from writing a complaint.

To guard against theft in your room, keep valuables out of sight. Some rooms come with a safe, and other hotels have safes at the front desk. I've never bothered using one.

Checkout can pose problems if surprise charges pop up on your bill. If you settle your bill the afternoon before you leave, you'll have time to discuss and address any points of contention (before 19:00, when the night shift usually arrives).

Above all, keep a positive attitude. Remember, you're on vaca-

Sleep Code

(€1 = about $1.40, country code: 34)

Price Rankings

To help you sort easily through my listings, I've divided the accommodations into three categories, based on the highest price for a standard double room with bath during high season:

$$$ **Higher Priced**—Most rooms €150 or more.
  $$ **Moderately Priced**—Most rooms between €100-150.
    $ **Lower Priced**—Most rooms €100 or less.

Prices can change without notice; verify the hotel's current rates online or by email. For the best prices, always book directly with the hotel.

Abbreviations

To pack maximum information into minimum space, I use the following code to describe accommodations in this book. Prices listed are per room, not per person. When a price range is given for a type of room (such as double rooms listed for €100-150), it means the price fluctuates with the season, size of room, or length of stay; expect to pay the upper end for peak-season stays. In Spain, high season *(temporada alta)* is from July to September; shoulder season *(temporada media)* is roughly April through June and October; and low season *(temporada baja)* runs from November through March.

  S = Single room (or price for one person in a double).
  D = Double or twin room. "Double beds" are often two twins sheeted together and are usually big enough for nonromantic couples.
  T = Triple (generally a double bed with a single).
  Q = Quad (usually two double beds; adding an extra child's bed to a T is usually cheaper).
  b = Private bathroom with toilet and shower or tub.
  s = Private shower or tub only (the toilet is down the hall).

According to this code, a couple staying at a "Db-€140" hotel would pay a total of €140 (about $196) for a double room with a private bathroom. Unless otherwise noted, breakfast is included, hotel staff speak basic English, and credit cards are accepted. There's almost always Wi-Fi and/or a guest computer available, either free or for a fee.

Making Hotel Reservations

Reserve your rooms several weeks in advance—or as soon as you've pinned down your travel dates. Note that some national holidays merit your making reservations far in advance (see page 314). Also, trade fairs crop up throughout the year and can send rates soaring—search online for trade fair dates (see the trade show calendar at www.firabarcelona.com/en/home).

Requesting a Reservation: It's easiest to book your room through the hotel's website. (For the best rates, always use the hotel's official site and not a booking agency's site.) If there's no reservation form, or for complicated requests, send an email (see below for a sample request). Most recommended hotels take reservations in English.

The hotelier wants to know:
- the number and type of rooms you need
- the number of nights you'll stay
- your date of arrival (use the European style for writing dates: day/month/year)
- your date of departure
- any special needs (such as bathroom in the room or down the hall, cheapest room, twin beds vs. double bed, and so on)

Mention any discounts—for Rick Steves readers or otherwise—when you make the reservation.

Confirming a Reservation: Most places will request a credit-card number to hold your room. If they don't have a secure online reservation form—look for the *https*—you can email it (I do), but it's safer to share that confidential info via a phone call or two emails (splitting your number between them).

Canceling a Reservation: If you must cancel, it's courteous—

tion. If your hotel is a disappointment, spend more time out enjoying the city you came to see.

Hostales *and* Pensiones

Budget hotels—called *hostales* and *pensiones*—are easy to find, inexpensive, and, when chosen properly, a fun part of the Spanish cultural experience. These places are often family-owned, and may or may not have amenities like private bathrooms and air-conditioning. Don't confuse a *hostal* with a hostel—a Spanish *hostal* is an inexpensive hotel, not a hostel with bunks in dorms.

Hostels

You'll pay about €15-18 per bed to stay at a hostel *(albergue juvenil)*. Travelers of any age are welcome if they don't mind dorm-style accommodations and meeting other travelers. Most hostels offer kitchen facilities, guest computers, Wi-Fi, and a self-service laun-

From: rick@ricksteves.com
Sent: Today
To: info@hotelcentral.com
Subject: Reservation request for 19-22 July

Dear Hotel Central,

I would like to reserve a room for 2 people for 3 nights, arriving 19 July and departing 22 July. If possible, I would like a quiet room with a double bed and a bathroom inside the room.

Please let me know if you have a room available and the price.

Thank you!
Rick Steves

and smart—to do so with as much notice as possible, especially for smaller family-run places. Be warned that cancellation policies can be strict; read the fine print or ask about these before you book. Internet deals may require prepayment, with no refunds for cancellations.

Reconfirming a Reservation: Always call to reconfirm your room reservation a few days in advance. For smaller hotels and *pensiones,* I call again on my day of arrival to tell my host what time I expect to get there (especially important if arriving late—after 17:00).

Phoning: For tips on how to call hotels overseas, see page 204.

dry. Nowadays, concerned about bedbugs, hostels are likely to provide all bedding, including sheets. Family and private rooms may be available on request.

Independent hostels tend to be easygoing, colorful, and informal (no membership required); www.hostelworld.com is the standard way backpackers search and book hostels, but also try www.hostelz.com and www.hostels.com. **Official hostels** are part of Hostelling International (HI) and share an online booking site (www.hihostels.com). HI hostels typically require that you either have a membership card or pay extra per night.

Apartments

It's easy, though not necessarily cheaper than a hotel room, to rent a furnished apartment in Barcelona. Consider this option if you're traveling as a family or with friends, staying a week or longer, and planning to cook many of your own meals. For more information on apartment rentals, see the end of this chapter.

OTHER ACCOMMODATION OPTIONS

Whether you're in a city or the countryside, renting an apartment, house, or villa can be a fun and cost-effective way to delve into Europe. Websites such as HomeAway and its sister sites VRBO and GreatRentals let you correspond directly with European property owners or managers.

Airbnb and Roomorama make it reasonably easy to find a place to sleep in someone's home. Beds range from air-mattress-in-living-room basic to plush-B&B-suite posh. If you want a place to sleep that's free, Couchsurfing.org is a vagabond's alternative to Airbnb. It lists millions of outgoing members, who host fellow "surfers" in their homes.

Accommodations

NEAR PLAÇA DE CATALUNYA

These hotels have sliding-glass doors leading to shiny reception areas, air-conditioning, and modern bedrooms. Most are on big streets within two blocks of Barcelona's exuberant central square, where the Old City meets the Eixample. As business-class hotels, they have hard-to-pin-down prices that fluctuate with demand. I've listed the average rate you'll pay. But in summer and on weekends, supply often far exceeds the demand, and many of these places cut prices to around €100—always check websites for a deal. Most of these are located between two Metro stops: Catalunya and Universitat; if arriving by Aerobus, note that the bus also stops at both places. Some of my recommended hotels are on Carrer Pelai, a busy street; for these, request a quieter room in back.

$$$ Hotel Catalonia Plaça Catalunya has four stars, an elegant old entryway with a modern reception area, splashy public spaces, slick marble and hardwood floors, 140 comfortable but simple rooms, and a garden courtyard with a pool a world away from the big-city noise. It's a bit pricey for the quality of the rooms—you're paying for the posh lobby (Db-€200 but can swing much higher or lower with demand, extra bed-€39, breakfast-€19, air-con, elevator, guest computer, Wi-Fi, a half-block off Plaça de Catalunya at Carrer de Bergara 11, Metro: Catalunya, tel. 933-015-151, www.hoteles-catalonia.com, catalunya@hoteles-catalonia.es).

$$ Hotel Denit is a small, stylish, 36-room hotel on a pedestrian street two blocks off Plaça de Catalunya. It's chic, minimalist, and fun: Guidebook tips decorate the halls, and the rooms are sized like T-shirts ("small" Sb-€79-109, "medium" Db-€99-119, "large"

The Good and Bad of Online Reviews

User-generated travel review websites—such as TripAdvisor, Booking.com, and Yelp—have quickly become a huge player in the travel industry. These sites give you access to actual reports—good and bad—from travelers who have experienced the hotel, restaurant, tour, or attraction.

My hotelier friends in Europe are in awe of these sites' influence. Small hoteliers who want to stay in business have no choice but to work with review sites—which often charge fees for good placement or photos, and tack on commissions if users book through the site instead of directly with the hotel.

While these sites work hard to weed out bogus users, my hunch is that a significant percentage of reviews are posted by friends or enemies of the business being reviewed. I've even seen hotels "bribe" guests (for example, offer a free breakfast) in exchange for a positive review. Also, review sites can become an echo chamber, with one or two flashy businesses camped out atop the ratings, while better, more affordable, and more authentic alternatives sit ignored further down the list. (For example, I find review sites' restaurant recommendations skew to very touristy, obvious options.)

Remember that a user-generated review is based on the experience of one person. That person likely stayed at one hotel and ate at a few restaurants, and doesn't have much of a basis for comparison. A guidebook is the work of a trained researcher who has exhaustively visited many alternatives to assess their relative value. I recently checked out some top-rated TripAdvisor listings in various towns; when stacked up against their competitors, some are gems, while just as many are duds.

Both types of information have their place, and in many ways, they're complementary. If a hotel or restaurant is well-reviewed in a guidebook or two, and also gets good ratings on one of these sites, it's likely a winner.

Db-€119-144, "XL" Db-€149-164, includes breakfast, air-con, elevator, guest computer, Wi-Fi, Carrer d'Estruc 24, Metro: Catalunya, tel. 935-454-000, www.denit.com, info@denit.com).

$$ Hotel Inglaterra is owned by the same people as Hotel Denit (listed above) but on the other side of Plaça de Catalunya. It has 60 rooms, a more traditional style, a rooftop terrace, and small swimming pool (Sb-€119, Db-€139, €30 more for bigger "deluxe" rooms, includes breakfast if you book through their website—otherwise it's €15, air-con, elevator, guest computer, Wi-Fi, Carrer de Pelai 14, Metro: Universitat, tel. 935-051-100, www.hotel-inglaterra.com, reservas@hotel-inglaterra.com).

$$ Hotel Reding, on a quiet street a 10-minute walk west

Barcelona's Old City Hotels

EIXAMPLE

PASSEIG DE GRÀCIA

To Casa Batlló
& La Pedrera

URQUINAONA 🄼

VIA LAIETANA

EL CORTE INGLÉS
DEP'T STORE

Urquinaona 🄼

GRAN VIA DE LES CORTS CATALANES

Catalunya 🄼

Bus to Airport
(& Taxis) 🅑

C. FONTANELLA

C. DE LES MOLES

❷

C. D'ESTRUC

DE LES JONQUERES

RONDA DE LA UNIVERSITAT

❻

Plaça de
Catalunya

PORTAL DE L'ÀNGEL

C. COMTAL

❶

C. DE BERGARA

❶

ELS
4 GATS

C. MONTSIÓ

Universitat 🄼

CARRER DE PELAI

FNAC 🅁

S.
ANNA

DURAN I BAS

CARRER DELS TALLERS

❹ ❸ ❺

C. DE SANTA ANNA

Catalunya 🄼

❼ ❶❷

CARRER DE LA CANUDA

FOUNTAIN

R. DE SANT ANTONI

C. VALLDONZELLA

C. MONTALEGRE

❶❾

❽

C. BONSUCCÉS

Plaça de la
Vila de Madrid

❶❸

C. DEL DUC

C. CUCUR

LAS RAMBLAS

MACBA
CONTEMPORARY
ART MUSEUM

C. D'ELISABETS

D'ELISABETS

C. D'EN

❶❽

ROMAN
NECROPOLIS

C. D'EN BOT

C. DE LA PORTAFERRISSA

C. DEL PI

C. PALLA

❶❺

C. DEL TIGRE

C. DE LA PALOMA

C. JOAQUIM COSTA

C. DE LA LLUNA

Plaça dels
Àngels

C. DOCTOR DOU

C. NOTARIAT

C. DEL PINTOR FORTUNY

XUCLÀ

BETLEM
CHURCH

C. PETRITXOL

Plaça
del Pi

❾

Plaça
S. Josep
Oriol

C. DE FERLANDINA

C. DELS ÀNGELS

C. DEL PEU DE LA CREU

C. DEL CARME

C. FLORISTES RAMBLA

CULTURAL INFO
PALAU DE LA VIRREINA

Liceu 🄼

C. D'EN ROCA

S. MARIA
DEL PI

C. D'AROLES

C. DE SANT GIL

DE SANT VICENÇ

RIERA ALTA

Plaça del
Pedró

C. DE JERUSALEM

LA BOQUERIA
MARKET

MIRÓ
MOSAIC

Liceu 🄼

CAFÉ DE
L'ÒPERA

OLD

Plaça
S. Agustí

❿

LICEU
OPERA HOUSE

CARRER L'HOSPITAL

C. JUNTA DEL COMERÇ

C. DE L'UNIÓ

C. D'EN ROBADOR

DE SANT RAFAEL

EL
RAVAL

C. DEL PENEDÈS

C. DE SANT PAU

RAMBLA DEL RAVAL

C. MARQUÈS DE BARBERÀ

DE LA RAMBLA

PALAU
GÜELL

❶❽

C. DE SANT PAU

C. DE LA RIERETA

C. DE ST. OLEGUER

C. NOU
DE LA RAMBLA

C. DE LES TÀPIES

C. DE L'ARC DEL

AVINGUDA DE LES

C. DEL CID

To Plaça d'Espanya
& Sants Station

Paral·lel 🄼
Paral·lel

CARRER DE L'OM

C. DE LES CABANES

C. SANTA MADRONA

AVINGUDA   DEL

PARAL·LEL

C. NOU DE LA RAMBLA

PSG. DE LA CANADENCA

Funicular
To Montjuïc

C. DE
PALAUDÀRIES

C. DE SANTA MADRONA

C. DE PUIG I XURIGUER

❶ Hotel Catalonia Plaça
     Catalunya
❷ Hotel Denit
❸ Hotel Inglaterra
❹ Hotel Reding
❺ Hotels Lleó & Atlantis
❻ Hotel Ginebra
❼ Hotel Continental Barcelona
❽ Hostería Grau
❾ Hostal el Jardí
❿ Hostal Operaramblas
⓫ Hotel Neri
⓬ Hotel Nouvel
⓭ NH Hotel Barcelona Centro
⓮ Hotel Banys Orientals
⓯ Hotel Racó del Pi
⓰ Hotel Regencia Colón
⓱ Gothic Point Hostel
⓲ Launderettes (2)
⓳ Bike Rentals (2)

SLEEPING

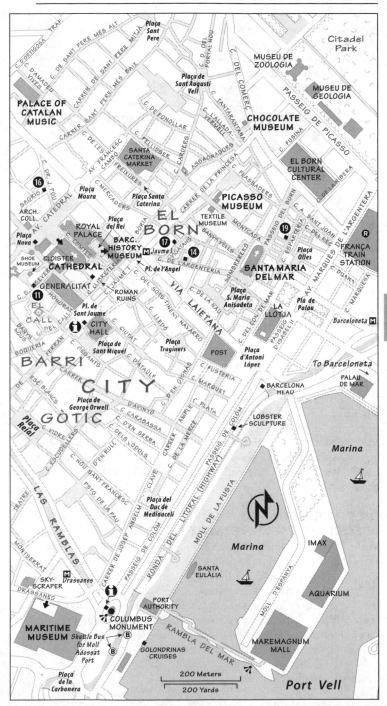

Plaça Sant Pere

C. PORTIGOSA · C. TRAF.

C. C. DE SANT PERE MÉS ALT

C. D'AMADEU VIVES

C. DEL PORTAL NOU

C. DEL COMERÇ

Citadel Park

MUSEU DE ZOOLOGIA

MUSEU DE GEOLOGIA

PALACE OF CATALAN MUSIC

CARRER DE SANT PERE MÉS BAIX

C. DE FONOLLAR

Plaça de Sant Augustí Vell

C. TANTARANTANA

L'ILLADA VERMELL

PASSEIG DE PICASSO

CHOCOLATE MUSEUM

CARRER DE LES DE SANT PERE

AV. FRANCESC CAMBO

C. PELLISSER

C. CARDERS

C. ASSAONADORS

C. FUSINA

EL BORN CULTURAL CENTER

C. DE LA RIBERA

SANTA CATERINA MARKET

C. FREIXURES

C. MERCADERS

Plaça Santa Caterina

CARRER DE LA PRINCESA

C. FLASSADERS

● 16

Plaça Maura

EL BORN

PICASSO MUSEUM

PASSEIG DEL BORN

C. A. SANT JOAN

C. DEL REC

SAGRIS

ARCH. COLL.

AV. CATEDRAL

ROYAL PALACE

Plaça del Rei

BARC. HISTORY MUSEUM

TEXTILE MUSEUM

MONTCADA

C. ESPARTERIA

● 19

Plaça Olles

C. DE LARGENTERA

FRANÇA TRAIN STATION

Plaça Nova

C. COMTES

● 17

Ⓜ Jaume I

● 14

C. DE LARGENTERIA

SANTA MARIA DEL MAR

C. DE LES MARQUES DE L'ARGENTERA

Ⓡ

SHOE MUSEUM

CLOISTER

CATHEDRAL

C. S. SEVERE

C. JAUME I

Pl. de l'Angel

SOMBRERERS

BANYS VELLS

C. DUANA

C. MARQUESA

● 11

GENERALITAT

C. HONORAT

ROMAN RUINS

C. DEL SOTS-TINENT NAVARRO

VIA LAIETANA

C. DE LA NAU

Plaça S. Maria Anisadeta

LA LLOTJA

Pla de Palau

Barceloneta Ⓜ

EL CALL

BANYS NOUS

C. DEL CALL

Pl. de Sant Jaume

Ⓘ CITY HALL

C. CIUTAT

C. LLEDÓ

C. DEL CON. DE MAR

PASSEIG D'ISABEL II

BARRI

BOQUERIA

C. FERRAN

C. GEGANTS

Plaça de Sant Miquel

C. D'ATAULF

Plaça Traginers

POST

Plaça d'Antoni López

To Barceloneta

CITY

C. D'ESC BLANCS

Plaça de George Orwell

D'AVINYO

C. FUSTERIA

C. MARQUET

BARCELONA HEAD

PALAU DE MAR

GÒTIC

C. VIDRES

C. CARABASSA

C. D'EN SERRA

C. D'EN GIGNAS

C. PLATA

LOBSTER SCULPTURE

Plaça Reial

C. ESCUDELLERS

C. DELS CODOLS

C. DE LA MERCE

PASSEIG DE COLOM

Marina

C. NOU SANT FRANCESC

C. D'EN RUIC

CLAVE

PSTG. DE LA PAU

Plaça del Duc de Medinaceli

MOLL DE LA FUSTA

RONDA DEL LITORAL (HIGHWAY)

Marina

IMAX

LAS RAMBLAS

MONTSERRAT

CARRER DE JOSEP ANSELM

PASSEIG DE COLOM

SANTA EULÀLIA

MOLL D'ESPANYA

AQUARIUM

SKY-SCRAPER

Ⓜ Drassanes

DRASSANEG

Ⓘ

PORT AUTHORITY

MAREMAGNUM MALL

MARITIME MUSEUM

Ⓘ ● ● COLUMBUS MONUMENT

Shuttle Bus for Moll Adossat Port Ⓑ

Ⓑ

GOLONDRINAS CRUISES

RAMBLA DEL MAR

Plaça de la Carbonera

200 Meters

200 Yards

Port Vell

SLEEPING

of the Ramblas and Plaça de Catalunya action, is a slick and sleek place renting 44 mod rooms at a reasonable price (Db-€125—this rate includes breakfast with this book in 2015, but only if you book directly with the hotel—otherwise pay €15 for breakfast, prices go up during trade fairs, extra bed-€33, air-con, elevator, guest computer, Wi-Fi, Carrer de Gravina 5, Metro: Universitat, tel. 934-121-097, www.hotelreding.com, recepcion@hotelreding.com).

$$ Hotel Lleó (YAH-oh) is well-run, with 92 big, bright, and comfortable rooms; a great breakfast room; and a generous lounge (Db-€140-170 but flexes way up with demand, extra bed-about €30, breakfast-€13, air-con, elevator, guest computer, Wi-Fi, small rooftop pool, Carrer de Pelai 22, midway between Metros: Universitat and Catalunya, tel. 933-181-312, www.hotel-lleo.com, info@hotel-lleo.com).

$$ Hotel Atlantis is solid, with 50 big, nondescript, modern rooms and fair prices for the location (Sb-€92, Db-€120, Tb-€138, check for deals on website, includes breakfast, air-con, elevator, guest computer, Wi-Fi, Carrer de Pelai 20, midway between Metros: Universitat and Catalunya, tel. 933-189-012, www.hotelatlantis-bcn.com, inf@hotelatlantis-bcn.com).

$ Hotel Ginebra is a renovated, modern, and fresh version of the old-school *pension* in a classic, well-located building at the corner of Plaça Catalunya (Sb-€70-100, Db-€100-150, Tb-€120-180, Qb-€140-180, rates drop dramatically Nov-March, breakfast-€8, laundry, air-con, elevator, guest computer, Wi-Fi, Rambla de Catalunya 1, Metro: Catalunya, tel. 932-502-017, www.barcelonahotelginebra.com, info@barcelonahotelginebra.com). To receive a free breakfast and 5 percent discount, first book direct through their standard website, then visit www.barcelonahotelginebra.com/voucher/, fill in your details and the code "HGinebra-RickSteves," and print a voucher to present at check-in.

ON OR NEAR THE RAMBLAS: AFFORDABLE HOTELS WITH "PERSONALITY"

These places are generally family-run, with ad-lib furnishings, more character, and lower prices.

$$ Hotel Continental Barcelona, in a building overlooking the top of the Ramblas, offers classic, tiny view-balcony opportunities if you don't mind the noise. Its 39 comfortable but faded rooms come with clashing carpets and wallpaper, and perhaps one too many clever ideas. Choose between your own little Ramblas-view balcony (where you can eat your breakfast) or a quieter back room. J. M.'s (José María's) free breakfast and all-day snack-and-drink bar are a plus (Sb-€98, Db-€108, twin Db-€118, Db with Ramblas balcony-€128, extra bed-€40/adult or €20/child, 5 percent discount off these rates with this book in 2015 when you book directly with the hotel, air-con, elevator, quiet terrace, guest computer, Wi-Fi, Ramblas 138, Metro: Catalunya, tel. 933-012-570, www. hotelcontinental.com, barcelona@hotelcontinental.com).

$$ Hostería Grau is a homey, family-run, and renovated, eco-conscious hotel. Its 24 cheery rooms are a few blocks off the Ramblas in the colorful university district—but double-glazed windows keep it quiet (Db-€110-125, "superior" Db-€120-135, Tb-€135-155, Qb-€160-180, 5 percent discount off these rates when you book directly with the hotel, breakfast extra, strict cancellation policy, air-con, elevator, some rooms with terrace, guest computer, Wi-Fi, 200 yards up Carrer dels Tallers from the Ramblas at Ramelleres 27, Metro: Catalunya, tel. 933-018-135, www. hostalgrau.com, reservas@hostalgrau.com, Monica).

$ Hostal el Jardí offers 40 clean, remodeled rooms on a breezy square in the Barri Gòtic. Many of the tight, plain, comfy rooms come with petite balconies (for an extra charge) and enjoy an almost Parisian ambience. It's a good deal only if you value the quaint-square-with Barri-Gòtic ambience—you're definitely paying for the location. Book well in advance, as this family-run place has an avid following (small basic interior Db-€75, nicer interior Db-€90, outer Db with balcony or twin with window-€95, large outer Db with balcony or square-view terrace-€110, no charge for extra bed, breakfast-€6, air-con, elevator, some stairs, guest computer, Wi-Fi, halfway between Ramblas and cathedral at Plaça Sant Josep Oriol 1, Metro: Liceu, tel. 933-015-900, www.eljardi-barcelona.com, reservations@eljardi-barcelona.com).

$ Hostal Operaramblas, with 68 simple rooms 20 yards off the Ramblas, is clean, institutional, modern, and a great value. The street can feel a bit seedy at night, but it's safe, and the hotel is very secure (Sb-€46, Db-€66, book through website and use code "operaramblas" for 10 percent discount, no breakfast but coffee and snack machines in lobby, air-con only in summer, elevator, pay guest computer, Wi-Fi, Carrer de Sant Pau 20, Metro: Liceu, tel. 933-188-201, www.operaramblas.com, info@operaramblas.com).

IN THE OLD CITY

These accommodations are buried in Barcelona's Old City, mostly in the Barri Gòtic. The Catalunya, Liceu, and Jaume I Metro stops flank this tight tangle of lanes; I've noted which stop(s) are best for each.

$$$ Hotel Neri is posh, pretentious, and sophisticated, with 22 rooms spliced into the ancient stones of the Barri Gòtic, overlooking an overlooked square (Plaça Sant Felip Neri) a block from the cathedral. It has big flat-screen TVs, pricey modern art on the bedroom walls, dressed-up people in its gourmet restaurant, and high-class service (Db-€260-300, suites-€320-400, generally cheaper on weekdays; breakfast-€22 weekdays, €25 weekends, beverage not included; air-con, elevator, Wi-Fi, rooftop tanning deck, Carrer de Sant Sever 5, Metro: Liceu or Jaume I, tel. 933-040-655, www.hotelneri.com, info@hotelneri.com).

$$$ Hotel Nouvel, in an elegant, Victorian-style building on a handy pedestrian street, is less business-oriented and offers more character than the others listed here. It boasts royal lounges and 78 comfy rooms (Sb-€75-100, Db-€110-165, online deals can be far cheaper, 10 percent discount off these prices with this book when you reserve directly by email, extra bed-€35, includes breakfast, €20 deposit for TV remote, air-con, elevator, guest computer, pay Wi-Fi, Carrer de Santa Anna 20, Metro: Catalunya, tel. 933-018-274, www.hotelnouvel.com, info@hotelnouvel.com).

$$$ NH Hotel Barcelona Centro, with 156 rooms and tasteful chain-hotel predictability, is professional yet friendly, buried in the Barri Gòtic just three blocks off the Ramblas (Db-€160, but rates fluctuate with demand, bigger "superior" rooms on a corner with windows on 2 sides-€25 extra, breakfast-€16, air-con, elevator, pay guest computer, Wi-Fi, Carrer del Duc 15, Metro: Catalunya or Liceu, tel. 932-703-410, www.nh-hotels.com, barcelonacentro@nh-hotels.com).

$$ Hotel Banys Orientals, a modern, boutique-type place, has a people-to-people ethic and refreshingly straight prices. Its 43 restful rooms are located in the El Born district on a pedestrianized street between the cathedral and Church of Santa Maria del Mar (Sb-€87, Db-€105, breakfast-€10, air-con, guest computer, Wi-Fi, Carrer de l'Argenteria 37, 50 yards from Metro: Jaume I, tel. 932-688-460, www.hotelbanysorientals.com, reservas@hotelbanysorientals.com). They also run the adjacent, recommended El Senyor Parellada restaurant.

$$ Hotel Racó del Pi, part of the H10 hotel chain, is a quality, professional place with generous public spaces and 37 modern, bright, quiet rooms. It's located on a wonderful pedestrian street immersed in the Barri Gòtic (Db-often around €130-145, can be as low as €80, cheaper if you book "nonrefundable" room online, breakfast-€16, air-con, guest computer, Wi-Fi, around the corner from Plaça del Pi at Carrer del Pi 7, 3-minute walk from Metro: Liceu, tel. 933-426-190, www.h10hotels.com, h10.raco.delpi@h10.es).

$$ Hotel Regencia Colón, in a handy location one block in front of the cathedral, offers 50 slightly older but solid, classy, and well-priced rooms (Db-€120-155 but fluctuate with demand—check website for best rates, extra bed-€37, breakfast-€13, air-con, elevator, slow Wi-Fi, Carrer dels Sagristans 13, Metro: Jaume I, tel. 933-189-858, www.hotelregenciacolon.com, info@ hotelregenciacolon.com).

IN THE EIXAMPLE

For an uptown, boulevard-like neighborhood, sleep in the Eixample, a 10-minute walk from the Ramblas action (see map on page 184). Most of these places use the Passeig de Gràcia or Catalunya Metro stops. Because these stations are so huge—especially Passeig de Gràcia, which sprawls underground for a few blocks—study the maps posted in the station to establish which exit you want before surfacing.

$$ Hotel Granvía, filling a palatial brightly renovated 1870s mansion, offers a large, peaceful sun patio, several comfortable common areas, and 58 spacious modern rooms (Sb-€75-185, Db-€90-150, superior Db-€105-225, family room-€120-245, mention Rick Steves to include breakfast, otherwise it's €14, air-con, elevator, Wi-Fi, Gran Via de les Corts Catalanes 642, Metro: Passeig de Gràcia, tel. 933-181-900, www.hotelgranvia.com, hgranvia@ nnhotels.com).

$$ Hotel Continental Palacete, with 19 small rooms, fills a 100-year-old chandeliered mansion. With flowery wallpaper and ornately gilded stucco, it's gaudy in the city of Gaudí, but it's also friendly, quiet, and well-located. Guests have unlimited access to the outdoor terrace and the "cruise inspired" fruit, veggie, and drink buffet (Sb-€108, Db-€145, €35-45 more for bigger and brighter view rooms, 5 percent discount with this book in 2015 when you book directly with the hotel, extra bed-€55/adult or €40/ child, includes breakfast, air-con, guest computer, Wi-Fi, 2 blocks northwest of Plaça de Catalunya at corner of Rambla de Catalunya and Carrer de la Diputació, Rambla de Catalunya 30, Metro: Passeig de Gràcia, tel. 934-457-657, www.hotelcontinental.com, palacete@hotelcontinental.com).

$ Hostal Oliva, family-run with care, is a spartan, old-school place with 15 basic, bright, high-ceilinged rooms and no breakfast or public spaces. It's on the fourth floor of a classic old Eixample building in a perfect location, just a couple of blocks above Plaça de Catalunya (S-€41, Sb-€51, D-€71, Db-€91, elevator, Wi-Fi, corner of Passeig de Gràcia and Carrer de la Diputació, Passeig de Gràcia 32, Metro: Passeig de Gràcia, tel. 934-880-162, www. hostaloliva.com, hostaloliva@lasguias.com).

$ BCN Fashion House B&B is a meditative place with 10 basic rooms, a peaceful lounge, and a leafy backyard terrace on the first floor of a nondescript old building (S-€36-56, D-€56-83,

SLEEPING

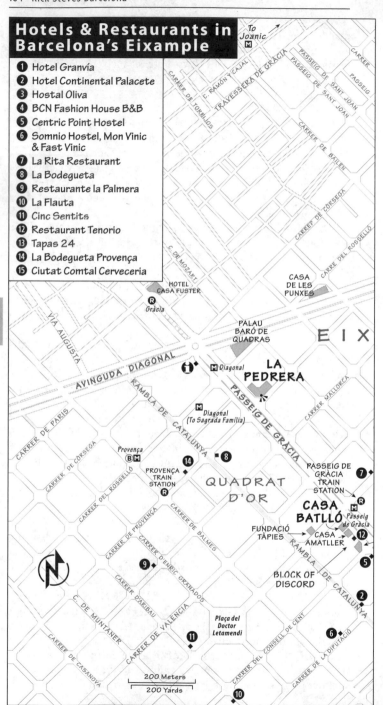

Hotels & Restaurants in Barcelona's Eixample

To Joanic

1. Hotel Granvía
2. Hotel Continental Palacete
3. Hostal Oliva
4. BCN Fashion House B&B
5. Centric Point Hostel
6. Somnio Hostel, Mon Vinic & Fast Vinic
7. La Rita Restaurant
8. La Bodegueta
9. Restaurante la Palmera
10. La Flauta
11. Cinc Sentits
12. Restaurant Tenorio
13. Tapas 24
14. La Bodegueta Provença
15. Ciutat Comtal Cerveceria

HOTEL CASA FUSTER

Gràcia

CASA DE LES PUNXES

PALAU BARÓ DE QUADRAS

E I X

AVINGUDA DIAGONAL

Diagonal

LA PEDRERA

VIA AUGUSTA

RAMBLA DE CATALUNYA

Diagonal (To Sagrada Família)

PASSEIG DE GRÀCIA

CARRER DE PARIS

Provença

PROVENÇA TRAIN STATION

QUADRAT D'OR

PASSEIG DE GRÀCIA TRAIN STATION

CASA BATLLÓ

Passeig de Gràcia

FUNDACIÓ TÀPIES

CASA AMATLLER

BLOCK OF DISCORD

RAMBLA DE CATALUNYA

C. DE MUNTANER

Plaça del Doctor Letamendi

200 Meters
200 Yards

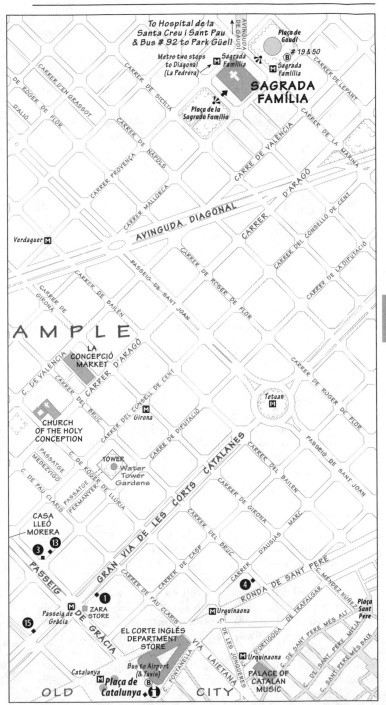

To Hospital de la
Santa Creu i Sant Pau
& Bus # 92 to Park Güell

AVINGUDA DE GAUDÍ

Plaça de
Gaudí

19 & 50

Metro two stops
to Diagonal
(La Pedrera)

Sagrada
Família

Sagrada
Família

CARRER DE SICÍLIA

CARRER DE LEPANT

SAGRADA
FAMÍLIA

CARRER DEN GRASSOT

CARRER DE NÀPOLS

Plaça de la
Sagrada Família

DALIÓ

DE ROGER DE FLOR

CARRER PROVENÇA

CARRER DE VALÈNCIA

CARRER DE LA MARINA

CARRER MALLORCA

CARRER
D'ARAGÓ

AVINGUDA DIAGONAL

CARRER

Verdaguer M

CARRER DE ROSER DE FLOR

CARRER DEL CONSELLO DE CENT

CARRER DE LA DIPUTACIÓ

CARRER DE
GIRONA

CARRER DE BAILÈN

PASSEIG DE SANT JOAN

A M P L E

LA
CONCEPCIÓ
MARKET

CARRER D'ARAGÓ

CARRER DE ROGER DE FLOR

C. DE VALÈNCIA

CARRER DEL BRUC

CARRER DEL CONSELL DE CENT

Girona M

CHURCH
OF THE HOLY
CONCEPTION

CARRER DE DIPUTACIÓ

PASSATGE
MEDEZVIGO

C. DE ROGER DE LLÚRIA

TOWER
Water
Tower
Gardens

CARRER DEL BAILÈN

PASSEIG DE SANT JOAN

PASSATGE
PERMANYER

C. DE PAU CLARIS

PASSATGE
PERMANYER

CARRER DE GIRONA

Tetuan
M

CARRER DE ROGER DE FLOR

CASA
LLEÓ
MORERA

❸ ⓭

GRAN VIA DE LES CORTS CATALANES

CARRER DE CASP

CARRER DEL BRUC

CARRER D'AUSIAS MARC

PASSEIG

CARRER DE PAU CLARIS

RONDA DE SANT PERE

❹

C. MENDEZ NÚÑEZ

Plaça
Sant
Pere

DE GRÀCIA

❶ ZARA
STORE

M

Urquinaona M

C. D'ORTIGOSA DE TRAFALGAR

C. DE SANT PERE MÉS ALT

Passeig de
Gràcia M

⓯

EL CORTE INGLÉS
DEPARTMENT
STORE

Urquinaona M

C. DE LES JONQUERES

C. FONTANELLA

VIA LAIETANA

PALACE OF
CATALAN
MUSIC

C. DE SANT PERE MÉS BAIX

Catalunya

Bus to Airport
(& Taxis)

M Plaça de
Catalunya ❶

B

OLD   CITY

SLEEPING

bigger "veranda" D-€73-93, Db-€90-125, 2-night minimum stay, includes breakfast, Wi-Fi, between Carrer d'Ausiàs Marc and Ronda de Sant Pere at Carrer del Bruc 13, just steps from Metro: Urquinaona, mobile 637-904-044, www.bcnfashionhouse.com, info@bcnfashionhouse.com).

HOSTELS

Equity Point Hostels: Barcelona has a terrific chain of well-run and centrally located hostels (tel. 932-312-045, www.equity-point. com), providing €25-32 dorm beds (prices lower off-season) in 4- to 14-bed coed and female rooms with €2 sheets and towels, guest computers, Wi-Fi, included breakfast, lockers (B.Y.O. lock, or buy one there), and plenty of opportunities to meet other backpackers. They're open 24 hours but aren't party hostels, so they enforce quiet after 23:00. There are three locations to choose from: the Eixample, Barri Gòtic, or near the beach. **$ Centric Point Hostel** is a huge place renting 400 cheap beds at what must be the best address in Barcelona (bar, kitchen, Passeig de Gràcia 33—see map on page 184, Metro: Passeig de Gràcia, tel. 932-151-796, www. centricpointhostel.com). **$ Gothic Point Hostel** rents 130 beds a block from the Picasso Museum (roof terrace, Carrer Vigatans 5— see map on page 178, Metro: Jaume I, reception tel. 932-687-808, www.gothicpoint.com). **$ Sea Point Hostel** has 70 beds on the beach nearby, but is closed roughly November through February (Plaça del Mar 4—see map on page 22, Metro: Barceloneta, reception tel. 932-247-075, www.equity-point.com/our-hostels/).

$ Somnio Hostel, an innovative smaller place run by a pair of American expats, has 10 simple, clean rooms (S-€50, D-€87, Db-€95; air-con, self-service laundry, guest computer, Wi-Fi, Carrer de la Diputació 251, second floor, Metro: Passeig de Gràcia, tel. 932-725-308, www.somniohostels.com, info@somniohostels. com). They have a second location that's five blocks farther out.

APARTMENTS

I recommend these two apartment-booking companies in Barcelona. Unlike huge aggregator websites like HomeAway or VRBO, these companies handpick their listings. Search their websites for a listing you like, then submit your reservation online.

$$ Cross-Pollinate is a reputable online booking agency representing B&Bs and apartments in a handful of European cities, including Barcelona. Choose a place online and submit a reservation; if the place is available, you'll be charged a small deposit and emailed the location and check-in details. Policies vary from owner to owner, but in most cases you'll pay the balance on arrival in cash. Barcelona listings range from a B&B double room near Sagrada

Família for €70 per night to a three-bedroom Eixample apartment sleeping eight for €295 per night. Minimum stays vary from one to three nights (US tel. 800-270-1190, www.cross-pollinate.com, info@cross-pollinate.com).

$$ Tournights Barcelona, run by American Frederick, rents 55 renovated apartments with kitchens. Most are near the beach in the lively Barceloneta neighborhood; others are in the Barri Gòtic or Eixample (2 people-€105 April-Oct, €85 Nov-March; prices vary with size—see photos and videos on website, €50 cleaning fee, 2- to 3-night minimum stay, discount for 7-night stay, 20 percent deposit required to reserve online, pay balance in cash when you arrive, no breakfast, arrange meeting to check in when you reserve, mobile 620-585-594, www.tournights.com, info@tournights.com).

EATING IN BARCELONA

Contents

Barcelona, the capital of Catalan cuisine, offers a tremendous variety of colorful places to eat, ranging from workaday eateries to homey Catalan bistros *(cans)* to crowded tapas bars to avant-garde restaurants. In general, Barcelona's restaurants rise to a higher level than elsewhere in Spain, propelled by a contingent of talented chefs who aren't afraid to experiment, the relative affluence, and the availability of good fresh ingredients—especially fish and seafood.

Dining Out

Barcelona's restaurants can be divided into two types: sit-down restaurants and tapa bars. At the restaurants, meal times are late and portions are generous if not quite American-sized. Tapas bars serve small plates (some in a sit-down setting, while others are more stand-up) throughout the afternoon and evening. While finer tapas bars can provide a serious dining option with a small-plates-style menu, formal restaurants don't offer tapas—and they start their service much later than the American norm.

As in the rest of Spain, the people of Catalunya eat late—lunch from 14:00 to 16:00, dinner after 21:00. When dining out, take your schedule into consideration. If you want to eat early (American time), go to a tapas bar. Because the big meal is lunch (from the siesta heritage), people work a little later and have a smaller supper. That's one reason tapas are such a hit for locals in the evening.

If you're holding out for a restaurant, the earliest you can go is about 20:30, when the place is empty or filled with tourists interested in eating a bit earlier. Going after 21:00 is better, but if you wait until 22:00, it can be hard to get into popular restaurants.

In basic restaurants and bars, you'll often find daily lunch specials *(menú del día)* for €10 to €12. And you can always graze cheaply in bars offering an array of affordable tapas and individual bites called *pintxos* (or *pinchos*).

When restaurant hunting, find places away from the tourist crowds on low-rent streets that are filled with locals. A good general rule of thumb: Don't eat (or drink) on the Ramblas or Passeig de Gràcia. And avoid any restaurant that posts big photographs of its food.

Sometimes the distinction between a bar and a restaurant blurs. Formal restaurants have a standard à la carte menu. Many tapas bars are a combination of restaurant and bar—with some tables in the back or outside on the *terraza*. And though tourists are often hot on tapas, these combo places are likely to serve larger *raciones* (dinner plate-sized serving) rather than bite-size tapas.

In any tapas bar, couples or small groups typically order a few *raciones* and share the plates family-style. This can be very economical if you don't over-order. Remember this is informal, social eating and there is nothing wrong with ordering a tapa or two to start before deciding whether to continue in the same bar or at all.

Don't expect "My name is Carlos and I'll be your waiter tonight" cheery service. Service is often *serio*—it's not friendly or unfriendly...just proficient. Ask for the bill in Catalan by saying "*El compte?*" Tipping is not a big concern here. Locals round it up 5 percent or so if the service was exceptional.

If ordering mineral water in a restaurant, it's economical to request a *botella grande de agua* (big bottle). They push the more profitable small bottles. For a glass of tap water, specify *un vaso de agua del grifo.* The waiter may counter with "*Embotellada?*" ("Bottled?"), hoping to sell you something. Be strong and insist on tap water *(del grifo)* and you'll get it. That being said, the tap water in Barcelona, while perfectly safe, does not taste particularly good; some bar owners are rather insistent on not serving it to their clientele.

Whether you go to a restaurant or bar, you won't be bothered by indoor smoke. Smoking is banned in closed public spaces in Spain.

While the menu is usually in Spanish and Catalan, these days—with the feisty spirit of Catalan independence stoked— you'll often find menus in Catalan and English without Spanish. In any Catalan bar or restaurant, an occasional *si us plau* (please) or *moltes gràcies* (thank you very much) will go a long way with the locals, who are extremely proud of their language, history, and culture. An *adéu* (good-bye), *que vagi bé* (have a good one!) or, in the evening, *bona nit* (good evening/night) on your way out the door will certainly earn you a smile. For more Catalan restaurant phrases, see page 194.

A Note on Food Terms: Catalan and Spanish (in that order) are the official languages of Barcelona. Throughout this book, I've given most food terms in Spanish, but have added Catalan where helpful. For tapas and bar terms in Spanish and Catalan, consult the "General Tapas Terms," "Tapas Menu Decoder," and "Drinking Words" charts later in this chapter. To make this primer on eating in Barcelona appropriately Catalan—as opposed to just Spanish with a Barcelona accent, Joe Littenberg of the recommended Barcelona Taste food tour (see page 35) helped me write this section.

Catalan Cuisine

Cod, hake, tuna, squid, and anchovies appear on many menus, and you'll see Catalan favorites such as *fideuà*, a thin, flavor-infused noodle served with seafood—a kind of Catalan paella—and *arròs negre*, black rice cooked in squid ink. *Pa amb tomàquet* is the classic Catalan way to eat your bread—toasted white bread with olive oil, tomato, and a pinch of salt. It's often served with tapas and used to make sandwiches. As everywhere in Spain, Catalan cooks love garlic and olive oil—many dishes are soaked in both.

The Catalan cuisine can be a bit heavy for Americans more accustomed to salads, fruits, and grains. A few perfectly good vegetarian and lighter options exist, but you'll have to seek them out. The secret to getting your veggies at restaurants is to order two courses, because the first course generally has a green option. Resist the cheese-and-ham appetizers and instead choose first-course menu items such as creamed vegetable soup, *parrillada de verduras* (sautéed vegetables), or *ensalada mixta*. (Spaniards rarely eat only a salad, so salads tend to be small and simple—just iceberg lettuce, tomatoes, and maybe olives and tuna.)

While the famous cured *jamón* (ham) is not as typically Catalan as it is Spanish, you'll still find lots of it in Catalunya. Another popular Spanish dish is the empanada—a pastry turnover filled with seasoned meat and vegetables. The cheapest meal is a simple *bocadillo de jamón* (ham sandwich on a baguette), sold virtually everywhere.

BREAKFAST

Hotel breakfasts are generally handy, optional, and pricey. You can save €5 or so by skipping your hotel breakfast and starting your day with the locals at a corner bar or at a colorful café in or near one of Barcelona's public markets. Ask for the *desayunos* (breakfast special, usually available until noon), which can include coffee, a pastry (or small sandwich), and juice for one price—cheaper than ordering them separately. Sandwiches can either be on white bread (*sandwich*) or on a baguette *(bocadillo)*.

A basic and standard savory breakfast item is the *tostada (torrada* in Catalan)—toasted white bread with some olive oil and cured ham, *fuet* (a typical Catalan cured sausage), or cheese. Another option is the *bikini*, a grilled ham-and-cheese sandwich named after a local bar, Sala Bikini. For something more substantial, look for a *tortilla española*—an inexpensive potato omelet cooked fresh each morning, served in slices, and often accompanied by *pa amb tomàquet*.

Those with a sweet tooth will find various sweet rolls (*bollos* or *bollería*). The familiar croissant, called a *palmera* (palm-shaped), is often coated in chocolate. A *caracol* ("snail"-shaped) is sometimes similar to a cinnamon roll. A *napolitana* is a rolled pastry, usually filled with chocolate (like a French *pain au chocolat*) or with a custard-like cream. A cream puff is a *bamba de nata*, and a doughnut is a *rosquilla* (doughnut).

If you like a doughnut and coffee in American greasy-spoon joints, you must try the Spanish equivalent: greasy cigar-shaped fritters called *churros (xurros* in Catalan) or the thicker *porras*. Dip them in warm chocolate pudding or your *café con leche*.

Here are some key words for breakfast with some Catalan variations:

café solo	shot of espresso
café con leche (café amb llet)	espresso with hot milk
café Americano	espresso with lots of water
cortado (tallat)	espresso with a little milk
té or *infusión*	tea
zumo	juice
zumo de naranja natural	freshly squeezed orange juice
pan (pa)	bread
pa amb tomàquet	toasted white bread with olive oil, tomato, and salt
tostada con aceite	toasted bread with olive oil
sandwich	white bread sandwich

EATING

bocadillo (bocata)	baguette sandwich
...*con jamón/queso*	...with ham/cheese
tortilla española	potato omelet
bollos, bollera (pastisseria)	sweet pastry
croissant	croissant

TAPAS BARS

You can eat well any time of day in tapas bars. Tapas are small portions of seafood, salads, meat-filled pastries, deep-fried tasties, and on and on.

There are several kinds of tapas bars: Traditional Spanish-style bars serve dishes in portions called *raciones,* or the smaller half-servings, *media-raciones,* that allow you to better sample a variety of the regional cuisine. Two people can fill up on four *media-raciones.* Basque-style tapas bars lay the food out on the countertop. These tapas are called *pintxos* (or *pinchos*) and are wildly popular in Barcelona. (Remember to save the toothpicks so they know how many *pintxos* you've had when it's time to pay.) There are also traditional Catalan tapas bars and *bodegas* (originally a name denoting wine cellars but preserved as many *bodegas* evolved into restaurants). Catalan tapas menus typically include more seafood, delicious local olives, and a traditional sausage called *butifarra.* All this food is accompanied by local beers, wines, and, of course, the beloved sweet vermouth. Part of the joy of eating at tapas bars is that you make it a mobile feast, visiting two or three bars during a single meal.

Tapas typically cost from €2 apiece and up. Some bars push larger portions—*raciones*—rather than smaller tapas. Barcelona tapas bars generally do not provide a free, small tapa with the purchase of a drink as may be found elsewhere in Spain.

Some bars charge less if you stand or grab a stool at the bar and around 20 percent more if you sit at a table or on the terrace. While tapas prices are generally posted, I look for a small official-looking menu (generally posted somewhere near the cashier) to see the drink options and the price difference between the *barra* (bar), the *mesa* or *salón* (indoor tables), and the *terraza* (outdoor tables).

If you're standing and a table opens up, it's OK to move as long as you signal to the waiter; anything else you order will be charged at the higher *mesa/salón* price. In the right place, a quiet snack and drink on a terrace on the town square is well worth the small extra charge. But the cheapest seats sometimes get the best show. Sit at the bar and study your bartender—he's an artist.

I'll be blunt. The authentic tapas experience can be intimidating: elbowing up to a bar crowded with pushy locals, squinting at a hand-scrawled monolingual chalkboard menu, and trying to communicate with the brusque bartender. Your bartender isn't a "waiter" in any sense. He's not there to patiently help you sort through your options—he wants to take your order, period. Hang back and observe before ordering. Read the posted or printed menu.

When you're ready to order, be assertive or you'll never be served. *Si us plau* (please) or *perdó* (excuse me) grabs the server's attention. Then quickly rattle off what you'd like (pointing to other people's food if necessary). Don't worry about paying until you're ready to leave (he's keeping track of your tab). To get the bill, ask: *El compte?*

Although tapas are served throughout the day, the real action begins late—21:00 at the earliest. But for beginners, an earlier start is easier and comes with less commotion. For less competition at the bar, go early or on Monday and Tuesday (but always check to see if a bar or restaurant is open on Sundays and Mondays, as many close at least on one of those days).

Chasing down a particular bar for tapas nearly defeats the purpose and spirit of tapas—they are impromptu. Just drop in at any lively place

TYPICAL DESSERTS

In Catalunya, as in Spain, desserts are sometimes an afterthought. Here are a few items you may see on menus in Barcelona:

mel i mató	a light Catalan cheese with honey
músic de fruits secs	a selection of nuts and dried fruits
crema catalana	a Catalan take on crème brulèe
arroz con leche	rice pudding
brazo de gitano	sponge cake filled with butter cream; literally gypsy's arm
flan de huevo	flan (crème caramel)
fruta de temporada	fruit in season
queso	cheese
helados (variados)	ice cream (various flavors)
torrijas	sweet French toast-like fritters

SPANISH AND CATALAN BEVERAGES

Spain is one of the world's leading producers of grapes, and that means lots of excellent wine: both red *(tinto)* and white *(blanco)*. Major wine regions include Valdepeñas and Penedès (cabernet-style wines from near Barcelona); Rioja (spicy, lighter reds from the tempranillo grape, from the high plains of northern Spain); and Ribera del Duero (northwest of Madrid). For a basic glass of

Tapas Menu Decoder

You can often just point to what you want on the menu or in the display case, say *si us plau*, and get your food, but the words in these charts will help you learn the options and fine-tune your request. Many of Barcelona's tapas bars use Catalan terms, so I've given both Spanish (first column) and Catalan (second column). When you see the same word in both columns, it's not a mistake—in some instances, a particular word (either Spanish or Catalan) is preferred.

Spanish	Catalan
pincho	pintxo
tapa	tapa
media-ración	mitja ració
ración	ració
surtido	assortit
frito	fregit
a la plancha	a la planxa
a la parrilla	a la graella
brocheta	broqueta
¿Cuánto cuesta...	Quant costa...
...una tapa?	...una tapa?

Sandwich Terms

Many tapas come in sandwich form—tasty bites on a baguette.

Spanish	Catalan
bocadillo	entrepà/bocata
canapé	canapè
flauta	flauta
montadito	montadito
sandwich	sandvitx

Typical Tapas

Spanish	Catalan	English
aceitunas	olives	olives
albóndigas	mandonguilles	spiced meatballs with sauce
almejas	cloïsses	clams
almendras	ametlles	almonds
anchoas	anxoves	cured anchovies
atún	tonyina	tuna
bacalao	bacallà	cod
bombas	bombes	fried meat-and-potato ball

EATING

Spanish	Catalan	English
boquerones	*seitons*	anchovies cured in vinegar
calamares fritos	*calamars fregits*	fried squid rings
caracoles	*cargols*	tree snails (May-Sept)
champiñones	*xampinyons*	mushrooms
charcutería	*xarcuteria*	cured meats
chorizo	*xoriço*	spicy sausage
croquetas	*croquetes*	croquettes—breaded and fried béchamel with fillings (often jamón)
empanadillas	*crestes*	pastries stuffed with meat or seafood
ensaladilla rusa	*ensalada russa*	potato salad with lots of mayo, peas, and carrots
espinacas...	*espinacs...*	spinach
...con garbanzos	*...amb cigrons*	...with garbanzo beans
fuet	*fuet*	Catalan salami-like sausage
gambas...	*gambes...*	shrimp...
...a la plancha	*...a la planxa*	...grilled
...al ajillo	*...al ajillo*	...with garlic
...cáscara	*...closca*	...shell
gazpacho	*gaspatxo*	cold tomato soup
jamón	*pernil*	cured ham (like prosciutto)
mejillones	*musclos*	mussels
morcilla	*botifarró*	blood sausage
patatas bravas	*patates braves*	fried potatoes with spicy tomato sauce
pescaditos fritos	*peixet fregit*	assortment of fried little fish
pimiento (relleno)	*pebrot(farcit)*	pepper (stuffed)
pimientos de Padrón	*pebrots de Padró*	lightly fried small green peppers
pinchos morunos	*pintxos morunos*	skewer of spicy lamb or pork
pulpo	*pop*	octopus
queso manchego	*formatge manxec*	classic Spanish sheep-milk cheese
revuelto...	*remenat...*	scrambled eggs...
...de setas	*...de bolets*	...with wild mushrooms
sardinas	*sardines*	sardines
tortilla española	*truita de patata*	potato omelet

Drinking Words

Here are some words to help you quench your thirst—in Spanish (first column) and Catalan (second column). ¡*Salud*! (*Salut*! in Catalan)—Cheers!

Wine and Spirits

Spanish	Catalan	English
vino	*vi*	wine
rojo	*negre*	red
blanco	*blanc*	white
cava	*cava*	sparkling wine
un tinto	*un vi negre*	small glass of house red wine
un blanco	*un vi blanc*	small glass of house white wine
un crianza	*un criança*	a glass of nicely aged, quality wine
un reserva	*un reserva*	much higher quality (and pricier) wine
gran reserva	*gran reserva*	oldest, highest quality wine
chato	*gotet*	small glass of house wine
tinto de verano	*tinto de verano*	red wine with sweetened soda (similar to sangria)
seco	*sec*	dry
dulce	*dolç*	sweet
mucho cuerpo	*molt cos*	full-bodied
afrutado	*afruitat*	fruity
vermú	*vermut*	vermouth (sweet, generally)
jerez	*xerès*	sherry (fortified wine from Jerez)

red wine, you can order *un tinto* (*un vi negre* in Catalan). But for quality wine, ask for *un crianza* (old), *un reserva* (older), or *un gran reserva* (oldest). The single most important tip for good, economical wine drinking is to ask for *un crianza*—for little or no more money than a basic *tinto*, you'll get a quality, aged wine.

Cava is the local answer to champagne: same process but with Catalan grapes. Sangria (a punch of red wine mixed with fruit slices and often loads of sugar) is refreshing and popular with tourists—but it's not served in authentic bars, where locals generally prefer *tinto de verano* (wine with sweetened soda).

Beer

Spanish	Catalan	English
cerveza	*cervesa*	beer
caña	*canya*	small glass of draft beer
mediana	*mediana*	bottle of beer (33cl)
quinto	*quinto*	small bottle of beer (20cl)
clara	*clara*	shandy—beer with lemon soda
sidra	*sidra*	dry cider, a bit more alcoholic than beer

Nonalcoholic Beverages

Spanish	Catalan	English
agua con gas	*aigua amb gas*	sparkling mineral water
agua sense gas	*aigua sin gas*	plain mineral water
un vaso de agua del grifo	*un got d'aigua de l'aixeta*	glass of tap water
refresco	*refresc*	soft drink
mosto	*most*	nonalcoholic grape juice, red or white, served wherever wine is served
una cerveza sin alcohol	*una cervesa sense alcohol*	nonalcoholic beer

EATING

Most places just have the standard local beer—a light lager—on tap. To get a small draft beer, ask for a *caña*. In Barcelona, local options include Estrella Damm, the slightly newer and trendier Moritz, and various craft beers. One of the most appreciated Spanish lagers, however, comes from Galicia and is called Estrella Galicia (no relation to Estrella Damm).

Bars often serve fresh-squeezed orange juice *(zumo de naranja natural)*. For something completely different, try *horchata* (*orxata* in Catalan), a sweet, milky beverage extracted from *chufa* tubers (a.k.a. tiger nuts or earth almonds).

One challenge for tapas bar-hoppers is that you'll generally order a drink in each place. If you're visiting several different bars (as you should), this can add up. If you'd like to drink a lot without getting drunk, remember a few key terms: *caña* (small beer), *clara* (small beer with lemonade), *tinto de verano* (red wine with sweetened soda), and *una sin* (nonalcoholic beer, pronounced "seen"). The *mosto* (*most* in Catalan) is also a great way to enjoy excellent Spanish grape juice that hasn't been fermented into its alcoholic cousin.

And, as they say in Catalan, *Bon profit* (Bon appétit)!

Restaurants

Most of my listings are lively spots with a busy tapas scene at the bar, along with restaurant tables where larger plates are typically

enjoyed family-style. I've listed mostly practical, characteristic, colorful, and affordable restaurants. My recommendations are grouped by neighborhood and handy to the sights. I've distinguished the tapas places from the more formal restaurants serving sit-down meals. Note that many restaurants

close in August (or July), when the owners take a vacation.

Catalans seem to have an affinity for Basque culture, so you'll find a lot of **Basque-style tapas places** here (look for *basca* or *euskal taberna*; *euskal* means "Basque"—or just look for lots of toothpicks). Enticing buffets of bite-size tapas invite you to simply take what you want. These places are particularly user-friendly, since you don't have to look at a menu or wait to be served—just grab what looks good, order a drink, and save your toothpicks (they'll count them up at the end to tally your bill). I've listed several of these bars (including Taverna Basca Irati, Xaloc, and Sagardi Euskal Taberna), though there are many others.

NEAR THE RAMBLAS

The entire length of the Ramblas itself is a tourist trap. Simply put: Do not eat or drink on the Ramblas (to make the rip-off prices even worse, when it comes time to pay, you may find that your bag has been stolen). However, within a few steps of the Ramblas, you'll find handy lunch places, an inviting market hall, and some good vegetarian options. For locations, see the map on page 200.

Lunching Simply yet Memorably near the Ramblas

Although these places are enjoyable for a lunch break during your Ramblas sightseeing, many are also open for dinner.

Taverna Basca Irati serves 40 kinds of hot and cold Basque *pintxos* for €2 each. These are small open-faced sandwiches—like sushi on bread. Muscle in through the hungry local crowd, get an empty plate from the waiter, and then help yourself. Every few minutes, waiters circulate with platters of new, still-warm munchies. Grab one as they pass by...it's addictive (you'll be charged by the number of toothpicks left on your plate when you're done). For drink options, look for the printed menu on the wall in the back. Wash down your food with €3 glasses of Rioja (full-bodied red wine), Txakolí (sprightly Basque white wine) or *sidra* (apple wine) poured from on high to add oxygen and bring out the flavor (daily 11:00-24:00, a block off the Ramblas, behind arcade at Carrer del Cardenal Casanyes 17, Metro: Liceu, tel. 933-023-084).

Restaurant Elisabets is a rough little neighborhood eatery packed with antique radios. It's popular with locals for its €12 "home-cooked" three-course lunch special; even cheaper *menú rapid* options are also available (13:00-16:00 only). Stop by for lunch, survey what those around you are enjoying, and order what looks best. Apparently, locals put up with the service for the tasty food (€3 tapas, Mon-Sat 7:30-23:00, closed Sun and Aug, 2 blocks west of Ramblas on far corner of Plaça del Bonsuccés at Carrer d'Elisabets 2, Metro: Catalunya, tel. 933-175-826).

Café Granja Viader is a quaint time capsule, family-run since 1870. They boast about being the first dairy business to bottle and distribute milk in Spain. This feminine-feeling place—specializing in baked and dairy treats, toasted sandwiches, and light meals—is ideal for a traditional breakfast. Or indulge your sweet tooth: Try a glass of *orxata* (or *horchata*—*chufa*-nut milk, summer only), *llet mallorquina* (Majorca-style milk with cinnamon, lemon, and sugar), *crema catalana* (crème brûlée, their specialty), or *suis* ("Swiss"—hot chocolate with a snowcap of whipped cream). *Mel i mató* is fresh cheese with honey...very Catalan (Mon-Sat 9:00-13:00 & 17:00-21:00, closed Sun, a block off the Ramblas behind Betlem Church at Xuclà 4, Metro: Liceu, tel. 933-183-486).

Cafeteria: For a quick, affordable lunch with a view, the ninth-floor cafeteria at **El Corte Inglés** can't be beat (€10 salads and sandwiches, also café with €1.50 coffee and sit-down restaurant with €20 fixed-price meals, Mon-Sat 10:00-22:00, closed Sun, Plaça de Catalunya, Metro: Catalunya, tel. 933-063-800).

Picnics: Shoestring tourists buy groceries at **El Corte Inglés** (described above, supermarket in basement), **Carrefour Market** (Mon-Sat 10:00-22:00, closed Sun, Ramblas 113, Metro: Liceu), and **La Boqueria** market (closed Sun, described next).

Barcelona's Old City Restaurants

EATING

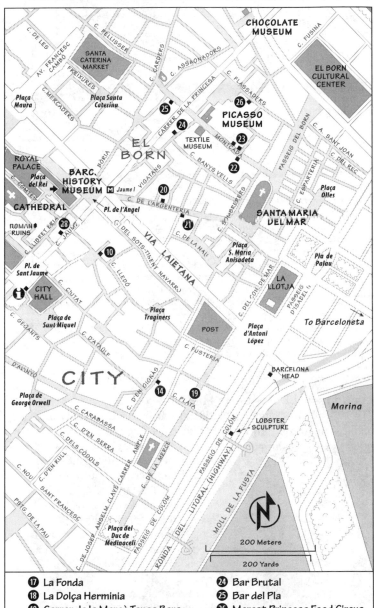

EATING

17 La Fonda
18 La Dolça Herminia
19 Carrer de la Mercè Tapas Bars
20 El Senyor Parellada
21 Sagardi Euskal Taberna & Sagardi Restaurant
22 El Xampanyet
23 Taverna Tapeo & Euskal Etxea Basque Tavern
24 Bar Brutal
25 Bar del Pla
26 Mercat Princesa Food Circus
27 Mucci's Pizza
28 Wok to Walk (3)
29 Casa Colomina
30 Granja La Pallaresa
31 Fargas Chocolate Shop

Budget Meals Around Town

Bright, clean, and inexpensive **sandwich shops** proudly hold the cultural line against the fast-food invasion that has hamburgerized the rest of Europe. Catalan sandwiches are made to order with the classic tomato-spread bread, *pa amb tomàquet*. You'll see two big local chains (Bocatta and Pans & Company) everywhere, but these serve mass-produced McBaguettes ordered from a multilingual menu. I've had better luck with hole-in-the-wall sandwich shops—virtually as numerous as the chains—where you can see exactly what you're getting.

For other options, try **Mucci's Pizza** for good, fresh €2 pizza slices and empanadas (two locations just off the Ramblas, at Bonsuccés 10 and Tallers 75, www. muccis.com). **Wok to Walk** makes tasty food on the run, serving up noodles and rice in takeaway containers with your choice of meat and/or veggies and finished with a savory sauce (€6-9, three locations—by the main door of the Boqueria Market, two steps from the Liceu Opera House, and near Plaça de Sant Jaume, www.woktowalk.com). Kebab places are another good, super-cheap standby; you'll see them all over town, offering a quick and tasty meal for about €3-4.

EATING

In and near La Boqueria Market

Try eating at La Boqueria Market at least once. Like all farmers markets in Europe, this place is ringed by colorful, good-value eateries.

Lots of stalls sell fun takeaway food—especially fruit salads and fresh-squeezed juices—ideal for picnickers.

There are several good bars—many with enticing plates of seafood—around the market busy with shoppers munching at the counter (breakfast, tapas all day, coffee). The market, and most of the eateries listed here (unless noted), are open Monday through Saturday from 8:00 until 20:00 (though things get very quiet after about 16:00) and are closed on Sunday (nearest Metro: Liceu). For a more complete description of the market itself, see page 83 of my Ramblas Ramble chapter.

Pinotxo Bar is just to the right as you enter the market. It's a fun—if touristy—spot for coffee, breakfast (spinach *tortillas,* or whatever's cooking, with toast), or tapas. Fun-loving Juan and his family are La Boqueria fixtures. Grab a stool across the way to sip your drink with people-watching views. Be careful—this place can get expensive (Mercat de la Boqueria 466, tel. 933-171-731, www. pinotxobar.com).

Kiosko Universal is popular for its great prices on wonderful fish dishes. As you enter the market from the Ramblas, it's all the way to the left. If you see people waiting, ask who's last in line *("¿El último?")* or go to the cashier to put your name on a list. You'll eat immersed in the spirit of the market (€7-14 *menú del día* with different fresh-fish options, €7 mixed veggies, €10 mushroom stir-fries, always packed but better before 12:30, tel. 933-178-286).

Casa Guinart is fairly expensive, but it's one of the few old-time places surviving around La Boqueria. Today it's bohemian-chic with elegance and a great scene both inside and out; the tables are seemingly designed to help you enjoy the market action. Look for it in the far right corner as you enter the market (Ramblas 95, tel. 933-178-887, www.casaguinart.com).

Vegetarian Eateries near the Ramblas

Biocenter, a Catalan soup-and-salad restaurant busy with local vegetarians, takes its cooking very seriously and feels a bit more like a real restaurant than most (€8-10 weekday lunch specials include soup or salad and plate of the day, €15 dinner specials, otherwise €7-9 salads and €11-13 main dishes, Mon-Sat 13:00-23:00, Sun 13:00-16:00, 2 blocks off the Ramblas at Carrer del Pintor Fortuny 25, Metro: Liceu, tel. 933-014-583).

Teresa Carles, a classy and casual restaurant near Plaça de Catalunya, offers vegetarian soups, salads, pastas, risotto, and dishes made with seitan (wheat meat). You can wash it down with fresh juices or a small selection of wines (€6-13.50 main dishes, €3.50 juices, breakfast available, daily 9:00-23:30, Carrer Jovellanos 2, Metro: Universitat or Catalunya, tel. 933-171-829, www. teresacarles.com).

IN THE BARRI GÒTIC

These eateries populate Barcelona's atmospheric Gothic Quarter, near the cathedral. Choose between a sit-down meal at a restaurant or a string of tapas bars. For locations, see the map on page 200.

Restaurants in the Barri Gòtic

La Vinateria del Call, buried deep in the Jewish Quarter, is one of the oldest wine bars in town. It offers a romantic restaurant-style meal of tapas with fine local wines. While you can eat at the bar, I'd settle in at a candlelit table. They have more than 100 well-priced wines, including a decent selection of Catalan wines at €2.50 a glass. Three or four plates of their classic tapas will fill two people (daily 19:30-24:00; with back to church, leave Plaça de Sant Felip Neri and walk two short blocks to Sant Domènec del Call 9; Metro: Jaume I, tel. 933-026-092, www.lavinateriadelcall.com).

Café de l'Academia is a delightful place on a pretty square tucked away in the heart of the Barri Gòtic—but patronized mainly by the neighbors. They serve refined cuisine with Catalan roots, using what's fresh from the market. The candlelit, air-conditioned interior is rustic yet elegant, with soft jazz, flowers, and modern art. And if you want to eat outdoors on a convivial, mellow square...this is the place. Reservations can be smart (€10-15 first courses, €13-20 second courses, fixed-price lunch for €11.50 at the bar or €15 at a table, Mon-Fri 13:30-16:00 & 20:30-23:30, closed Sat-Sun, near the City Hall square, off Carrer de Jaume I up Carrer de la Dagueria at Carrer dels Lledó 1, Metro: Jaume I, tel. 933-198-253).

Els Quatre Gats ("The Four Cats") was once the haunt of the Modernista greats—including a teenaged Picasso, who first publicly displayed his art here, and architect Josep Puig i Cadafalch, who designed the building. Inspired by Paris' famous Le Chat Noir café/cabaret, Els Quatre Gats celebrated all that was modern at the turn of the 20th century (for more on the illustrious history of the place, see page 96 in the Barri Gòtic Walk). You can snack or drink at the bar, or go into the back for a sit-down meal. While touristy (less so later), the food and service are good, and the prices aren't as high as you might guess (€17 three-course lunch special Mon-Fri 13:00-16:00, €12-28 plates, daily 10:00-24:00, just steps off Avinguda del Portal de l'Angel at Carrer de Montsió 3, Metro: Catalunya, tel. 933-024-140).

Xaloc is a fine place in the old center for nicely presented gourmet tapas. It's a woody, modern, and spacious dining room with a fun energy, good service, and reasonable prices. The walls are covered with *Ibérica* hamhocks and wine bottles. They focus on home-style Catalan classics and serve only one quality of ham—and it's tops. A gazpacho, plank of ham, *pa amb tomàquet*, and nice glass of wine make a terrific light meal (€2-7.50 tapas, €6-14 main dishes, open daily, drinks and cold tapas 11:00-23:00, kitchen open 13:00-17:00 & 19:00-23:00, a block toward the cathedral from Plaça de Sant Josep Oriol at Carrer de la Palla 13, Metro: Catalunya, tel. 933-011-990).

Bar del Pi is a simple, hardworking bar serving good salads, sandwiches, and tapas. It has just a handful of tables on the most inviting little square in the Barri Gòtic (daily 9:00-23:00, Plaça de Sant Josep Oriol 1, Metro: Liceu, tel. 933-022-123).

Restaurant Agut, around since 1924, features a comfortable, wood-paneled dining room that's modern and sophisticated, but still retains a slight bohemian air. The pictures lining the walls are by Catalan artists who are said to have exchanged their canvases for a meal. The menu includes very tasty traditional Catalan food, with some seasonal specialties (€14 three-course weekday lunch special, €10-15 starters, €13-29 main dishes, Tue-Sat 13:30-16:00 & 20:30-23:30, Sun 13:30-16:00 only, closed Mon, just up from Carrer de la Mercè and the harbor at Carrer d'En Gignàs 16, Metro: Jaume I, tel. 933-151-709).

Andilana Restaurants: A local chain called Andilana has several bright, modern eateries that are wildly popular for their artfully presented Spanish and Mediterranean cuisine, crisp ambience, and unbeatable prices (www.grupandilana.com). Because of their three-course €10 lunches and €16-21 dinners (both with wine), all are crowded with locals and in-the-know tourists (à la carte: €7-9 starters, €8-11 main dishes; the first three are near Metro: Liceu). Warning: These places are notoriously busy. **Les Quinze Nits** has great seating right on atmospheric Plaça Reial (daily 12:30-23:30, at #6—you'll see the line around 20:30 right before they open their large upstairs dining room, tel. 933-173-075). Two others are within a block: **La Crema Canela,** a few steps above Plaça Reial, feels cozier than the others and is the only one that takes reservations (Mon-Thu 13:00-23:00, Fri-Sun until 23:30, Passatge de Madoz 6, tel. 933-182-744). **La Fonda** is a block below Plaça Reial (daily 13:00-23:30, Carrer dels Escudellers 10, tel. 933-017-515). Another location, **La Dolça Herminia,** is near the Palace of Catalan Music in El Born (daily 13:00-15:45 & 20:30-23:30, 2 blocks toward Ramblas from Palace of Catalan Music at Carrer de les Magdalenes 27, Metro: Jaume I, tel. 933-170-676); another restaurant in the chain, **La Rita,** is described later, under "Restaurants in the Eixample."

Tapas on Carrer de la Mercè in the Barri Gòtic

This area lets you experience a rare, unvarnished bit of old Barcelona with great *tascas*—colorful local tapas bars. Get small plates (for maximum sampling) by asking for "tapas," not the bigger "*raciones.*" Glasses of *vino tinto* go for about €1. And though trendy uptown restaurants are safer, better-lit, and come with English menus and less grease, these places will stain your journal. The neighborhood's dark, the regulars are rough-edged, and you'll get a glimpse of a crusty Barcelona from before the affluence hit. Nowadays many new, mod restaurants are popping up in

EATING

the city, but don't be seduced—you came here for something different. Try Galician *pimientos de Padrón*—Russian roulette with little green peppers that are lightly fried in oil and salted...only a few are jalapeño-spicy. At the cider bars, it's traditional to order *queso de cabrales* (a very moldy blue cheese) and spicy chorizo (sausage), ideally prepared *al diablo* ("devil-style")—soaked in wine, then flambéed at your table. Several places serve *leche de pantera* (panther milk)—liquor mixed with milk.

From the bottom of the Ramblas (near the Columbus Monument, Metro: Drassanes), hike east along Carrer de Josep Anselm Clavé. When you reach Plaça de la Mercè, follow the small street (Carrer de la Mercè) that runs along the right side of the square's church. For a montage of edible memories, wander the next three or four blocks and consider these spots, stopping wherever looks most inviting. Most of these places close down around 23:00. If you want more refined bar-hopping possibilities, skip over to Carrer Ample and Carrer d'En Gignàs, inland streets parallel to Carrer de la Mercè.

Bar Celta (marked *la pulpería*, at #16) has a bit less character than the others, but eases you into the scene with fried fish, octopus, and *patatas bravas*, all with Galician Ribeiro wine. Farther down at the corner (#28), **La Plata** keeps things wonderfully simple, serving extremely cheap plates of sardines (€2.70), little salads, and small glasses of keg wine (€1). **Tasca el Corral** (#17) serves mountain favorites from northern Spain by the half-*ración* (see their list), such as *queso de cabrales*, chorizo *al diablo*, and *cecina* (cured meat, like *jamón* but made from beef)—drink them with *sidra* (hard cider sold by the bottle-€6). **Sidrería Tasca La Socarrena** (#21) offers hard cider from Asturias in €6.50 bottles with *queso de cabrales* and chorizo. At the end of Carrer de la Mercè, **Cervecería Vendimia** slings tasty clams and mussels (hearty *raciones* for €4-6 a plate—they don't do smaller portions, so order sparingly). Sit at the bar and point to what looks good. Their *pulpo* (octopus) is more expensive and is the house specialty.

IN EL BORN

El Born (a.k.a. La Ribera), the hottest neighborhood in town, sparkles with eclectic and trendy as well as subdued and classy little restaurants hidden in the small lanes surrounding the Church of Santa Maria del Mar. While I've listed a few well-established tapas bars that are great for light meals, to really dine, simply wander around for 15 minutes and pick the place that tickles your gastronomic fancy. I think those who say they know what's best in this area are kidding themselves—it's changing too fast and the choices are too personal. One thing's for sure: There are a lot of talented and hardworking restaurateurs with plenty to offer. Consider start-

A Short, Sweet Walk

Let me propose this three-stop dessert (or, since these places close well before the traditional Barcelona dinnertime, a late-afternoon snack). Start with a chunk of *torró* or a glass of *orxata,* then munch some *churros con chocolate,* and end with a visit to a fine *xocolateria*—all within a three-minute walk of one another in the Barri Gòtic just off the Ramblas (Metro: Liceu). Start at the corner of Carrer de la Portaferrissa midway down the Ramblas. For the best atmosphere, begin your walk at about 18:00. For locations, see the map on page 200.

Torró at Casa Colomina: Walk down Carrer de la Portaferrissa to #8 (on the right). Casa Colomina, founded in 1908, specializes in homemade *torró* (or *turrón* in Spanish)—a variation of nougat made with almond, honey, and sugar, brought to Spain by the Moors 1,200 years ago. Three different kinds are sold in €9-15 slabs: *blando, duro,* and *yema* (€2.20 pre-wrapped chunks on the counter). In the summer, the shop also sells ice cream and the refreshing *orxata* (or *horchata,* a drink made from *chufa* nuts). Order a glass and ask to see and eat a *chufa* nut (daily 10:00-20:30, tel. 933-122-511).

Churros con Chocolate at Granja La Pallaresa: Continue down Carrer de la Portaferrissa, taking a right at Carrer Petritxol to this fun-loving *xocolateria.* Elegant, older ladies gather here for the Spanish equivalent of tea time—dipping their greasy *churros* into pudding-thick cups of hot chocolate (€4.50 for five *churros con chocolate*). Or, for a more local treat, try an *ensaïmada* (a Mallorca-style croissant with powdered sugar) or the *crema catalana,* like a crème brûlée (Mon-Fri 9:00-13:00 & 16:00-21:00, Sat-Sun 9:00-13:00 & 17:00-21:00, Carrer Petritxol 11, tel. 933-022-036).

Homemade Chocolate at Fargas: For your last stop, head for the ornate Fargas chocolate shop. Continue down Carrer Petritxol to the square, hook left through the two-part square, and then left up Carrer del Pi to the corner of Carrer de la Portaferrissa. Since the 19th century, gentlemen with walking canes have dropped by here for their chocolate fix. Founded in 1827, this is one of the oldest and most traditional chocolate shops in Barcelona. If they're not too busy, ask to see the old chocolate mill *("¿Puedo ver el molino?")* to the right of the counter. (It's still used, but nowadays it's powered by a machine rather than a donkey in the basement.) They sell even tiny quantities (one little morsel) by weight, so don't be shy. A delicious chunk of the crumbly semi-sweet house specialty costs €0.50 (glass bowl on the counter). The tempting bonbons in the window cost about €1-2 each (Mon-Sat 9:30-13:30 & 16:00-20:00, closed Sun).

EATING

ing off your evening with a glass of fine wine at one of the *enotecas* on the square facing the Church of Santa Maria del Mar (such as La Vinya del Senyor). Sit back and admire the pure Catalan Gothic architecture. Most of my listings are either on Carrer de l'Argenteria (stretching from the church to the cathedral area) or on or near Carrer de Montcada (near the Picasso Museum). Many restaurants and shops in this area are, like the Picasso Museum, closed on Mondays.

For all of these eateries, use Metro: Jaume I. For locations, see the map on page 200.

Near the Church of Santa Maria del Mar

El Senyor Parellada, filling a former cloister, is an elegant restaurant (not a tapas bar) with a smart, tourist-friendly waitstaff. It serves a fun menu of Mediterranean and Catalan cuisine with a modern twist, all in a classy chandeliers-and-white-tablecloths setting (€10-18 plates, daily 13:00-15:45 & 20:30-23:30, Carrer de l'Argenteria 37, 100 yards from the Jaume I Metro stop, tel. 933-105-094).

Sagardi Euskal Taberna offers a wonderful array of Basque goodies—tempting *pintxos* and *montaditos* (small open-faced sandwiches) at €2 each—along its huge bar. Ask for a plate and graze (just take whatever looks good). You can sit on the square with your plunder for about 20 percent extra. Wash it down with Txakolí, a Basque white wine poured from the spout of a huge wooden barrel into a glass as you watch. When you're done, they'll count your toothpicks to tally your bill. Study the two price lists—bar and terrace—posted at the bar (daily 12:00-24:00, Carrer de l'Argenteria 62-64, tel. 933-199-993).

Sagardi, hiding behind the thriving tapas bar described above, is a mod, rustic, and minimalist restaurant committed to serving Basque T-bone steaks and grilled specialties with only the

best ingredients. A big open kitchen with sizzling grills contributes to the ambience. Reservations are smart (€12-24 first courses for two, €20-28 second courses, plan on €50 for dinner; daily 13:00-16:00 & 20:00-24:00, Carrer de l'Argenteria 62, tel. 933-199-993, www.sagardi.com).

Near the Picasso Museum

El Xampanyet ("The Little Champagne Bar"), a colorful family-run bar with a fun-loving staff (Juan Carlos, his mom, and the man who may be his father), specializes in tapas and anchovies. Don't be put off by the seafood from a tin: Catalans like it this way. A *sortido* (assorted plate) of *carne* (meat) or *pescado* (fish) with *pa amb tomàquet* makes for a fun meal. It's filled with tourists during the sightseeing day, but this is a local favorite after dark. The scene is great but—especially during busy times—it's tough without Spanish skills. When I asked about the price, Juan Carlos said, "Who cares? The ATM is just across the street." Plan on spending €25 for a meal with wine (same price at bar or table, Tue-Sat 12:00-15:30 & 19:00-23:00, Sun 12:00-16:00, closed Mon, a half-block beyond the Picasso Museum at Carrer de Montcada 22, tel. 933-197-003).

Taverna Tapeo is a mod, classy alternative to the funky Xampanyet across the street with a long bar and tiny tables serving near-gourmet tapas (€6-10 plates, 12:00-16:00, 19:00-24:00, closed Mon, Carrer de Montcada 29, tel. 933-101-607).

Euskal Etxea Basque Tavern is another bar with an enticing array of small bites and open-face Basque-style sandwiches, all for €2 each. It's self-service and you pay by the number of toothpicks when done. For drink options, find the menu posted by the bar (daily 10:00-24:00, Placeta Montcada 1, tel. 933-102-185).

Bar Brutal is a creative, fun-loving, and edgy bohemian-chic place with a young local following. It serves a mix of Spanish and Italian dishes with an emphasis on wines (€10-15 plates, Tue-Sun 13:00-24:00, closed Mon, Carrer de la Barra de Ferro 1, tel. 932-951-797).

Bar del Pla is a local favorite—near the Picasso Museum but far enough away from the tourist crowds. This brightly lit, classic diner/bar—overlooking a tiny crossroads next to Barcelona's oldest church—serves traditional Catalan dishes, *raciones*, and tapas. Their crispy beef with foie gras (€6) is a highlight. Prices listed on the fun and accessible menu are the same at the bar or at a table. Eating at the bar puts you in the middle of a great scene (€6-12 tapas, Mon-Sat 12:00-23:00, closed Sun; with your back to the Picasso Museum, head right two blocks past Carrer de la Princesa to Carrer de Montcada 2; tel. 932-683-003, www.bardelpla.cat).

Mercat Princesa Food Circus fills an old palace with a hive of trendy new bars and eateries sharing a central zone of tables; it's a big corporate venture. The energy is great as is the variety: oysters, sushi, paella, and pizza. If nothing else, it's fun to simply explore. If eating here at a busy time, you may be frustrated by waiting in successive slow-moving lines to get all the elements of your meal (daily 9:00-24:00, behind the Picasso Museum, Carrer dels Flassaders 21, tel. 932-681-518, www.mercatprincesa.com).

EATING

IN THE EIXAMPLE

The people-packed boulevards of the Eixample are lined with appetizing eateries featuring breezy outdoor seating. Choose between a real restaurant or an upscale tapas bar (for the best variety, I prefer Rambla de Catalunya). For locations, see the map on page 184.

Restaurants in the Eixample

La Rita is a fresh and dressy little restaurant serving Catalan cuisine near the Block of Discord. Their lunches (three courses with wine for €10.30, daily 13:00-15:45) and dinners (€10 plates, €21 fixed-price dinners, Sun-Thu 20:30-23:30, Fri-Sat 21:00-23:00) are a great value. Like most of its sister Andilana restaurants—described on page 205—it takes no reservations and its prices attract a loyal following, so arrive just before the doors open...or wait (near corner of Carrer de Pau Claris and Carrer d'Aragó at d'Aragó 279, a block from Metro: Passeig de Gràcia, tel. 934-872-376).

La Bodegueta is an atmospheric below-street-level bodega serving hearty wines, homemade vermouth, *anchoas* (anchovies), tapas, and *flautas*—sandwiches made with flute-thin baguettes. On a nice day, it's great to eat outside, sitting in the median of the boulevard under shady trees. Its daily €13 three-course lunch special with wine is a deal (Mon-Fri only, 13:00-16:00). A long block from Gaudí's La Pedrera, this makes a fine sightseeing break (Mon-Sat 7:00-24:00, Sun 18:30-24:00, at intersection with Carrer de Provença, Rambla de Catalunya 100, Metro: Provença, tel. 932-154-894).

Restaurante la Palmera serves a mix of Catalan, Mediterranean, and French cuisine in an elegant room with bottle-lined walls. This untouristy place offers great food, service, and value—for me, a very special meal in Barcelona. They have three zones: the classic main room, a more forgettable adjacent room, and a few outdoor tables. I like the classic room. Reservations are smart (€12-19 plates, creative €21 six-plate *degustation* lunch—also available during dinner Mon-Thu, open Mon-Sat 13:00-15:45 & 20:00-23:15, closed Sun, Carrer d'Enric Granados 57, at the corner with Carrer Mallorca, Metro: Provença, tel. 934-532-338, www.lapalmera.cat).

La Flauta fills two floors with enthusiastic eaters (I prefer the ground floor). It's fresh and modern, with a fun, no-stress menu featuring €5 small plates, creative €5 *flauta* sandwiches, and a €13 three-course lunch deal including a drink. Consider the list of *tapas del día*. Good €2.60 wines by the glass are listed on the blackboard. This is a place to order high on the menu for a satisfying, moderately priced meal (Mon-Sat 7:00-24:00, closed Sun, upbeat and helpful staff, no reservations, just off Carrer de la Diputació at Carrer d'Aribau 23, Metro: Universitat, tel. 933-237-038).

Cinc Sentits ("Five Senses"), with only about 30 seats, is my gourmet recommendation. At this chic, minimalist, slightly snooty place, all the attention goes to the fine service and beautifully presented dishes. The €59 *essència menú* and the €79 *sensacions menú* are unforgettable extravaganzas. Expect *menús* only—no à la carte. It's run by Catalans who lived in Canada (so there's absolutely no language barrier) and serve avant-garde cuisine inspired by Catalan traditions and ingredients. Reservations are essential (Tue-Sat 13:30-15:00 & 20:30-22:00, closed Sun-Mon, near Carrer d'Aragó at Carrer d'Aribau 58, between Metros: Universitat and Provença, tel. 933-239-490, www.cincsentits.com, maître d' Eric).

Restaurant Tenorio hides between the famous buildings and clamoring tourists in the Block of Discord. It's an actual restaurant (no tapas, eat late). This modern, dressy, and spacious place serves a mix of international and Catalan dishes, concocted in the bustling open kitchen at the back (€10 salads, €15 plates, Passeig de Gràcia 37, Metro: Passeig de Gràcia, tel. 932-720-592).

Mon Vinic, a sleek, trendy wine bar that's evangelical about local wine culture, offers an amazing eating experience. Considered one of top wine bar/restaurants in town, their renowned chef creates made-to-order Mediterranean dishes for enjoying with the wine (€10-15 starters—designed to share, €8 creative tapas, €25 main dishes with vegetables and potatoes, €22 lunch *menú*, Diputació 249, Metro: Passeig de Gràcia, tel. 932-726-187, www. monvinic.com).

Fast Vinic is like a gourmet fast-food and sandwich bar with fine Catalan wines ready by the glass. It's owned by the fancy Mon Vinic wine bar/restaurant next door (12:00-24:00, closed Sun, Diputació 251, tel. 934-873-241).

Tapas Bars in the Eixample

Many trendy and touristic tapas bars in the Eixample offer a cheery welcome and slam out the appetizers. These three are particularly handy to Plaça de Catalunya and the Passeig de Gràcia artery (closest Metro stops: Catalunya and Passeig de Gràcia).

Tapas 24 makes eating fun. This local favorite, with a few street tables, fills a spot a few steps below street level with happy energy, friendly service, funky decor (white counters and mirrors), and good yet pricey tapas. Along with daily specials, the menu has all the typical standbys and quirky inventions (such as the tiny McFoie burger—order it well-done if you don't want it to moo on your plate). The owner, Carles Abellan, is one of Barcelona's hot chefs; although his famous fare is pricey, you can enjoy it without going broke. Prices are the same whether you dine at the bar, a table, or outside. Figure about €50 for lunch for two with wine. Come early or wait; no reservations are taken (€4-14 tapas, €12-16 plates, Mon-Sat 9:00-24:00, closed Sun, just off Passeig de Gràcia at Carrer de la Diputació 269, tel. 934-880-977, www.carlesabellan.es/restaurantes-tapas-24).

La Bodegueta Provença, a lively tapas bar/café, has a multigenerational clientele and a pleasant buzz. Sit at a stool at the marble counter or grab a table, indoors or out. If you and your partner are hungry, order the half-kilo grilled steak piled high with Padrón peppers—wow! (€5-10 tapas, daily 7:00-24:00, Carrer de Provença 233, tel. 932-151-725).

Ciutat Comtal Cerveceria brags that it serves the best *montaditos* (€2-4 little open-faced sandwiches) and beers in Barcelona. It's an Eixample favorite, with an elegant bar and tables plus good seating out on the Rambla de Catalunya for all that people-watching action. It's packed 21:00-23:00, when you'll likely need to put your name on a list and wait. While it has no restaurant-type menu, the list of tapas and *montaditos* is easy, fun, and comes with a great variety (including daily specials, most tapas around €4-10, daily 8:00-24:00, facing the intersection of Gran Via de les Corts Catalanes and Rambla de Catalunya at Rambla de Catalunya 18, tel. 933-181-997).

IN BARCELONETA

Barceloneta is the historic, grid-plan district jutting into the harbor (Metro stop: Barceloneta). It's surrounded by big harbor action and popular waterfront zones—about a 10-minute walk from the Barri Gótic or the bottom of the Ramblas (and a fun destination on a rental bike). Barceloneta has three personalities: its workaday interior—historically home to dock workers and fishermen—gathered around its central square; its harborfront with a line of fish restaurants facing the marina; and its trendy and newly created beach zone stretching north from the towering Hotel W. For locations, see the map on page 22.

In or near the Main Square

The main square in the middle of Barceloneta (Plaça del Poeta Boscà) is homey with a 19th-century iron-and-glass market, families at play in the park, and lots of hole-in-the-wall eateries and bars.

In the market and spilling onto the square, **El Guindilla Taverna del Mercat** is a good value for a basic local meal in a memorable setting (daily, Plaça del Poeta Boscà 2, tel. 932-215-458).

Baluard, one of Barcelona's most highly regarded artisan bakeries, faces one side of the big market hall. Line up with the locals to get a loaf of heavenly bread, a pastry, or a slice of pizza (Mon-Sat 8:00-21:00, closed Sun, Carrer del Baluard 38, tel. 932-211-208).

Restaurante Can Solé, serving seafood since 1903, is a splurge. Hiding on a nondescript lane between the square and the marina, this venerable yet homey restaurant draws a celebrity crowd, judging by the autographed pictures of the famous and not-so-famous that line the walls (Tue-Sat 13:30-16:00 & 20:30-23:00, Sun 13:30-16:00, closed Mon, Carrer de Sant Carles 4, one block off the harborfront promenade, tel. 932-215-012, www.restaurantcansole.com).

On the Waterfront

The main drag—Passeig de Joan de Borbó—faces the city and is lined with multiple, interchangeable seafood restaurants and cafés. Consider **La Mar Salada,** a traditional seafood restaurant with a slightly modern twist (€35-40 meals, €16 weekday lunch *menú*, Wed-Mon 13:00-16:00 & 20:00-23:00, closed Tue, indoor and outdoor seating, Passeig de Joan de Borbó 59, tel. 932-212-127, www.lamarsalada.cat).

On the Beach

The *chiringuito* tradition of funky eateries lining Barcelona's beach now has serious competition from trendy bars and restaurants. A piece of modern art in the sand—a bunch of cubical shacks piled high—stands like a memorial to these beloved-but-seasonal beach joints. Now the spendy places have moved in, and all along the beach you have restaurants offering both indoor and terrace tables with a sea view. My favorites are at the far south end near the towering Hotel W.

Pez Vela is the top-end option with a fashionable local crowd and its own disk jockey (€35 dinners, Passeig del Mare Nostrum 19, tel. 932-216-317, www.grupotragaluz.com/eventos/pez-vela). Cheaper—and with far less pretense—is the next-door **Ristorante Mamarosa,** a family-friendly Italian place (€20 pastas, sharable €15 pizza, Passeig del Mare Nostrum 21, tel. 933-123-586, www.mamarosabeach.com).

EATING

BARCELONA WITH CHILDREN

Barcelona is a great place to travel with kids; it's bubbling with inexpensive, quirky sights and an infectious human spirit. Sure, there's an amusement park, a zoo, and a science museum, but your kids will have an adventure simply wandering down the city's tangled streets. And when it's time for a break, Barcelona has one of Europe's best urban beach scenes.

Trip Tips

EATING

Your kids may be surprised to find out that Catalan food is nothing like Mexican food back home. Picky eaters may have a hard time with *jamón*, deep-fried dishes, and strange seafood. Try these tips to keep your kids content throughout the day.

- Start the day with a good breakfast (at hotels, kids sometimes eat free).
- Picnic lunches or dinners work well. Try large grocery stores such as Carrefour Market, El Corte Inglés, or Bonpreu. Or drop by a *panadería* (bakery) which often have baguette sandwiches, pizza by the slice, and empanadas (meat pies). Near the beach? Head to the market—El Mercat de la Barceloneta—near the Barceloneta Metro stop (Mon-Thu and Sat 7:00-15:00, Fri 7:00-20:00, closed Sun; Plaça de la Font 1, tel. 932-216-471). Having snacks on hand can avoid meltdowns (and can help your kids avoid them, too).
- Choose easy eateries. A good, safe (though not exotic) bet is the cafeteria/restaurant at the **El Corte Inglés** department store on Plaça de Catalunya (service all day, €7 kids menu). Quick chain restaurants such as Bocatta or Pans & Company serve reasonably priced *bocadillos* and fries—and grownups can

order a beer. **Tapa Tapa** has booth seating just right for kids, and the pictograph menus make ordering fun (just north of Plaça de Catalunya at Passeig de Gràcia 44, tel. 934-883-369). For a sweet break for both you and the kids, try the **Pudding** café. You can snack or have a light meal sitting next to a giant mushroom or in the kids' play area (not many toys or games, but the kids don't mind). It's in the El Born neighborhood near the Church of Santa Maria del Mar; look for it on Plaza Foso de las Moreras right behind the eternal flame (cupcakes-€3.50, sandwiches/quiche-€4.50, daily 11:00-21:00, Carrer de Pau Claris 90, tel. 936-678-748, www.wepudding.com).

- Catalans eat late—usually about 21:00 or 22:00—and dinner can take two hours. If you're eating late with your kids at a restaurant, bring something to occupy them and seek out places on squares where kids can run free while you dine. Catalan children go out and stay out late, so don't worry about your kids disturbing others as they gambol around the plaza.

SIGHTSEEING

The key to a successful Barcelona family vacation is to slow down. Tackle one or two key sights each day, mix in a healthy dose of pure fun at a park or beach, and take extended breaks when needed.

- Incorporate your child's interests into each day's plans. Let your kids make some decisions: choosing lunch spots or deciding which stores to visit. Turn your kid into your personal tour guide and navigator of the Metro system. Deputize your child to lead you on my self-guided walks and museum tours.

- Since a trip is a splurge for parents, the kids should enjoy a larger allowance, too. Provide ample money and ask your kids to buy their own treats, postcards, and trinkets within that daily budget.

- Seek out kid-friendly museums, such as CosmoCaixa or the Maritime Museum. If you're visiting art museums with younger children, hit the gift shop first so you can buy postcards; then hold a scavenger hunt to find the pictured artwork.

- Even if you have the most well-behaved kids in the world, mix-ups happen. It's good to have a "what if" procedure in place in case something goes wrong, such as getting separated in the Metro. Be sure to give each child a business card from your hotel so they have local contact information.

- If your kids love playing in the sand, consider staying in an apartment (see page 186) near one of Barcelona's many beaches. Easy access to the beach offers a convenient daily activity for children, and the sights and attractions of the city are easily accessible by Metro or bus.

Top Sights and Activities

KID-CENTRIC ATTRACTIONS
Tibidabo

This 100-year-old amusement park (the city's oldest) sits atop the Tibidabo foothills above town; visiting it could easily fill an entire day. The fun starts even before you arrive, as a funicular (€7.70, €4.10 with park admission) can take you right to the park entrance. At the top, kids will find a mixture of 25 Disneyland-like rides and some vintage attractions appealing to younger children, teens, and adults alike; older kids might like modern attractions such as a 4-D cinema show and the Tibidabo Express roller-coaster. Many enjoy the maze of mirrors—you have to wear gloves so the mirrors stay fingerprint-free.

Cost and Hours: Kids under 3 feet tall are free, kids under 4 feet are charged €10.30, adults pay €28.50; hours depend on season—generally Wed-Sun 12:00-23:00 in summer, closed Mon-Tue; weekends only off-season, tel. 932-117-942, www.tibidabo. cat. For directions, see page 58.

CosmoCaixa

One of Europe's most advanced science museums, CosmoCaixa features hands-on exhibits, many of which are specifically geared toward small children. Youngsters will love *¡Toca toca!* (Touch touch!), an exhibit exploring the natural world, while the newly renovated 3-D planetarium (€4 extra) may entice older kids and teens. Other kid-focused highlights include a jungle greenhouse and a treasure hunt.

Cost and Hours: Kids under 16-free, adults-€4, free on first Sun of the month; Tue-Sun 10:00-20:00, closed Mon; Metro: Tibidabo, then hop on bus #196 for one stop or about a 15-minute walk to the museum, Carrer d'Isaac Newton 26; tel. 932-126-050, www. obrasocial.lacaixa.es.

Barcelona Zoo (Zoo de Barcelona)

This enormous zoo, which gained fame in the 1960s as the home of the only known albino gorilla in the world, *Copito de Nieve* (Snowflake), is inside Citadel Park (see page 73). The zoo features all the kid-recognizable animals such as tigers, hippos, and zebras as well as oddities like Komodo dragons. Daily shows with the dolphins and sea lions in "Aquamara," the small SeaWorld-like marina arena, may impress the young and old.

Cost and Hours: Kids 3-12-€12, adults-€20; hours vary by season, summer hours daily 10:00-20:00; Metro: Barceloneta, Ciutadella-Vila Olímpica, Marina, or Arc de Triomf; tel. 902-457-545, www.zoobarcelona.cat.

Barcelona Aquarium at Port Vell
(L'Aquàrium de Barcelona Port Vell)

Located on the waterfront not far from the Columbus Monument, the aquarium is home to more than 11,000 animals. Its star attraction is the "Oceanarium," a 262-foot underwater glass tunnel that lets you walk beneath schools of deep-sea creatures such as sharks and stingrays. The IMAX Theater next door shows movies in Spanish or Catalan, sometimes with English subtitles. The Port Vell area is an inviting mix of towering sailboats and a steady flow of people on the boardwalk in the midst of daily life; the green space offers room for a picnic or quick rest in between sightseeing.

Cost and Hours: Kids under 3 feet tall are free, kids 3-4.5 feet-€5-€15, kids taller than 4.5 feet and adults-€20; daily 9:30-21:00, July-Aug until 23:00; Metro: Drassanes or Barceloneta, Moll d'Espanya del Port Vell, tel. 932-217-474, www.aquariumbcn.com.

Magic Fountains (Font Màgica)

This popular, free spectacle uses classic and modern tunes—including film scores—as the soundtrack for a fanciful water show. Built for the 1929 World's Fair and renovated before the 1992 Olympics, it's part of a web of ponds and waterfalls on Avinguda Maria Cristina in Montjuïc.

Cost and Hours: Free 20-minute shows start on the half-hour; almost always May-Sept Thu-Sun 21:00-23:30, no shows Mon-Wed; Oct-April Fri-Sat 19:00-21:00, no shows Sun-Thu; these are first and last show times; Metro: Espanya; www.bcn.cat/parcsijardins/fonts, see page 70.

MUSEUMS AND EXHIBITS
Art Museums

A short visit to some of Barcelona's modern and contemporary art museums could dazzle your kids visually. All of the following offer educational programs aimed at children and their families:

Museu d'Art Contemporani (MACBA) houses a vast collection of artwork from the past 50 years and offers lectures, video screenings, and special exhibits covering contemporary culture and art. The museum's square is also a roller-skaters' hangout; it's fun to watch the tricks before going in to see the art (kids under 14-free, adults-€10; Mon and Wed-Fri 11:00-19:30, Sat 10:00-21:00, Sun 10:00-15:00, closed Tue, last entrance 30 minutes before closing, Metro: Universitat or Catalunya, Plaça dels Àngels 1, tel. 934-120-810, www.macba.cat).

CHILDREN

The **Picasso Museum** gives kids a chance to marvel at the artist's early works (see page 48).

If you feel like venturing outside of the city for a surreal experience, a two-hour drive or train ride will take you to the **Salvador Dalí Theater-Museum** in the town of Figueres (see page 255).

Chocolate Museum (Museu de la Xocolata)

Satisfy everyone's sweet tooth while learning the history of traditional Catalan confectionery through a range of kid-friendly exhibits. You'll see chocolate statues of just about anything and everything—including Barcelona soccer players. Family activities may even include painting with chocolate.

Cost and Hours: Kids under 7-free, adults-€5, includes small chocolate bar; Mon-Sat 10:00-19:00 (until 20:00 mid-June-mid-Sept), Sun 10:00-15:00; Metro: Jaume I, Carrer del Comerç 36, tel. 932-687-878, www.museuxocolata.cat; see page 52.

Maritime Museum (Museu Marítim de Barcelona)

While its permanent exhibits are closed for renovation, the museum currently hosts temporary exhibits. When it reopens, the renovated museum will feature the history of Catalunya's rich maritime past from the 13th to the 21st century. Boat aficionados and sailors-to-be enjoy the collection of model boats and seafaring gadgets, as well as the sprawling marina.

A useful audioguide is included in the ticket price. The museum also includes the nearby *Santa Eulàlia* (docked on the Moll de la Fusta quay), a historic three-masted schooner from 1918 that was meticulously restored to its original state. On Saturday mornings, the schooner sails around the harbor—reserve well in advance (Sat 10:00-13:00, adult-€12, children 6-14-€6, tel. 933-429-920, reserves.mmaritim@diba.cat).

Cost and Hours: Museum—usually €5, kids under 7-free, kids 7-16-half price; daily 10:00-20:00, last entry 30 minutes before closing, entrance to the temporary exhibits is free Sun starting at 15:00; *Santa Eulàlia*—€1.50, free with museum admission; April-Oct Tue-Fri and Sun 10:00-20:30, Sat 14:00-20:30, closes at 17:30 in Nov-March, closed Mon year-round; Metro: Drassanes, take the Portal de Santa Madrona exit; Avinguda de la Drassanes, tel. 933-429-920, www.mmb.cat; see page 41.

Blue Museum (Museu Blau)

A good choice for any kid interested in nature, this natural history museum—home to more than three million specimens—celebrates the diversity in flora, fauna, and geology in Catalunya and beyond. Its main exhibit, Planet Earth, follows the birth of our planet and the evolution of life. A special space, the "Science Nest," has activities designed for preschoolers, but you'll need to reserve your visit in advance (closed Aug, though museum is open).

Cost and Hours: Kids under 16-free, adults-€6—free on Sun after 15:00; Tue-Sat 10:00-19:00, Sun 10:00-20:00; closed Mon year-round; Metro: El Maresme-Fòrum, Plaza Leonardo da Vinci 4-5, tel. 932-566-002, www.museublau.bcn.cat.

Botanical Gardens

Montjuïc is the home of the natural history museum's Botanical Gardens and its Botanical Institute as well as the recently reopened Historical Botanical Garden. A network of paths follows the natural terrain, taking visitors past 87 outdoor exhibits known as "phytoepisodes."

Cost and Hours: Kids under 16-free, adults-€3.50; daily June-Aug 10:00-20:00, April-May and Sept 10:00-19:00, Oct-March 10:00-18:00; take bus #193 from Plaça d'Espanya or the Montjuïc funicular from Paral-lel, main entrance between Olympic Stadium and castle—see map on page 62, Carrer Dr. Font i Quer 2; tel. 932-564-160, www.museublau.bcn.cat.

Olympic and Sports Museum
(Museu Olímpic i de l'Esport)

Barcelona hosted the Olympics in 1992 and has never been the same since. Sports-crazed kids might enjoy this museum, as well as exploring what is left of the adjacent, anticlimactic 1992 Olympic Stadium. The mod-yet-tacky museum offers up several kid-friendly multimedia installations, such as a virtual race against an Olympic athlete, but it ultimately appeals only to Olympics fanatics.

Cost and Hours: Kids 14 and under-free, adults-€5.10; April-Sept Tue-Sat 10:00-20:00, Sun 10:00-14:30; shorter hours off-season, closed Mon year-round; Metro: Espanya, Avinguda de l'Estadi 60, tel. 932-925-379, www.museuolimpicbcn.cat; see page 66.

Camp Nou Soccer Stadium

"Barça" is to Barcelona what the Cowboys are to Dallas; the city lives and breathes for this top-ranked soccer team, as evidenced by their motto, "More Than a Club." The team's pricey visitors center has an interactive museum, features memorabilia from past seasons of glory, and includes a behind-the-scenes visit onto the soccer field. An English audioguide helps explain the exhibits—and the city's soccer obsession. The crowded, energetic FC Barcelona superstore *(La FC Botiga)* is a cool spot for kids and teens as well (pick up a scarlet-and-blue jersey or scarf as a souvenir).

Cost and Hours: Kids under 6-free, kids 6-13-€17, adults-€23, audioguide included, mid-April-early Oct Mon-Sat 10:00-20:00 (off-season closes at 18:30), Sun 10:00-14:30; shorter hours on game days, Metro: Maria Cristina or Collblanc, Carrer d'Arístides Mallol 12, toll tel. 902-189-900, www.fcbarcelona.com/camp-nou.

PARKS

Citadel Park (Parc de la Ciutadella)

Barcelona's most central park sprawls its grassy fields and large avenues across the grounds of an old fortress, and offers plenty for curious kids to discover. Attractions include a giant mammoth statue, a small lake with rental rowboats and duck feeding, a large Baroque fountain *(La Cascada)*, and several outdoor events held throughout the year. The Barcelona Zoo is also accessible from the park. Bikes can be rented from the bike-rental shop opposite the entrance to the park on Passeig de Picasso and Avinguda del Marquès de l'Argentera.

Cost and Hours: Free, daily 10:00 until dusk; north of França train station, Metro: Arc de Triomf, Barceloneta, or Ciutadella-Vila Olímpica; see page 73.

Horta Labyrinth Park (Parc del Laberint d'Horta)

Away from the city center in an unassuming location lies the most tranquil green space in town. With barely a tourist in sight, the park holds a handful of Neoclassical and Romantic gardens, highlighted by a small central maze that was used in the filming of Guillermo del Toro's hit, *Pan's Labyrinth* (2006) and Tom Tykwer's *Perfume* (2006). There are more than 20 water features—pools, fountains, reservoirs, canals, and an artificial waterfall—and the tricky labyrinth should provide ample entertainment as youngsters and teens attempt to figure out the puzzle.

Cost and Hours: Kids under 5-free, kids 5-14-about €1.50, adults-about €2.25, free on Wed and Sun; daily May-Sept 10:00-21:00, April 10:00-20:00, March and Oct 10:00-19:00, Nov-Feb 10:00-18:00, last entry one hour before closing; Metro: Mundet then a 15-minute walk, the park is behind a velodrome; www.bcn.cat/parcsijardins/fonts.

BEACHES
Sant Sebastià and Barceloneta Beaches
These are the closest, longest, and busiest beaches (with Sant Sebastià preferred by locals). Both are near the city center, making

them a good stop before or after
sightseeing. A long boardwalk with
food, drink, and ice-cream options
lines both beaches; on the sand,
you'll come upon children's play areas
(including one with a cool climbing
frame). Expect beach sports such as
ping pong, beach volleyball, and the
Basque handball game, *pelota*. Look out on the waves and you'll
also spot a surfer or two. Both beaches are accessible from the Old
City area by bus or Metro (Metro: Barceloneta, walk along Passeig
de Joan de Borbó, streets on the left cut across to the beachfront
or walk all the way to Plaça del Mar to reach the start of Sant Sebastià; bus #36 runs right along the waterfront and will save some
steps; for biking these beaches, see page 73).

Nova Icària Beach
If you don't care for crowds, head instead for the nearby Nova Icària
beach; this more tranquil beach is frequented by families. Nova
Icària is within walking distance of the 1992 Olympic Marina,
a popular place for sailing and boating (Metro: Ciutadella-Vila
Olímpica or Bogatel; bus #36 will get you closer than the Metro).

OTHER EXPERIENCES
Sardana Dance
The easy-to-do *sardana* is a beloved traditional symbol of Catalan unity and pride. Kids might enjoy this spectacle of local culture—and may even be invited to join in. The dances are held in
the square in front of the Cathedral of Barcelona every Sunday at
12:00 and sometimes also on Saturdays at 18:00 (none in Aug); the
performance lasts between one and two hours; see page 45.

Cable Car (El Transbordador Aeri del Port)
This is a fun and scenic ride between the Barcelona waterfront and
Montjuïc, providing spectacular views of the city. Note that the car
is often crowded and very slow-moving; if there's a long line—and
your child is impatient—you may regret waiting. You can also just
take the elevator up the tower in Barceloneta for the views.

Cost and Hours: One-way-€11, round-trip-€16.50, eleva-
tor-€5.50, cash only; 3/hour, daily 11:00-17:30, June-Sept until
20:00, closed in high wind; Metro: Barceloneta or Drassanes; tel.
932-252-718, see page 60.

CHILDREN

SHOPPING IN BARCELONA

Barcelona is a fantastic shopping destination, whatever your taste or budget. The streets of the Barri Gòtic and El Born are bursting with characteristic hole-in-the-wall shops, while the Eixample is the upscale "uptown" shopping district. The area around Avinguda del Portal de l'Angel (at the northern edge of the Barri Gòtic) has a staggering array of department and chain stores.

Store Hours: Most shops are open Monday through Friday from about 9:00 or 10:00 until lunchtime (around 13:00 or 14:00). After the siesta, they reopen in the evening, around 16:30 or 17:00, and stay open until 20:00 or 21:00. Large stores and some smaller shops in touristy zones may remain open through the afternoon—but don't count on it. On Saturdays, many shops are open in the morning only. On Sundays, most shops are closed (though the Maremagnum complex on the harborfront is open).

What to Buy

In this very artistic city, consider picking up prints, books, posters, decorative items, or other keepsakes featuring works by your favorite **artist** (Picasso, Dalí, Miró, Gaudí, etc.). Gift shops at major museums are open to the public (such as the Picasso Museum and Gaudí's La Pedrera) and are a bonanza for art and design lovers. Model-ship builders will be fascinated by the offerings at the Maritime Museum shop.

Foodies might enjoy shopping for local **food items**—olive oil, wine, spices (such as saffron or sea salts), high-quality canned foods and preserves, dried beans, and so on. Remember, food items must be sealed to make it back through US customs (see page 281). Cooks can look for European-style gadgets at **kitchen-supply** stores.

Torró (or *turrón* in Spanish) is the beloved nougat treat that's traditionally eaten around Christmastime, but has become popular anytime. (Consider a visit to *torró* specialty shop, Casa Colomina; see page 207.)

In this design-oriented city, **home decor** shops are abundant and fun to browse, offering a variety of Euro-housewares unavailable back home. For something more classic, look for glassware or other items with a dash of Modernista style.

Department and chain stores can be fun to explore for **clothing**—including fashions you won't find back home.

Decorative **tile** and **pottery** can be a good keepsake. Eixample sidewalks are paved with a few different, distinctive tile patterns, which are sold in some local shops.

An *espardenya* (or *alpargata* in Spanish) is a soft-canvas, rope-soled shoe (known in the US as an espadrille). It originated as humble peasant footwear in the 14th century in the Pyrenean region (including Catalunya, Occitania, and the Basque Country), but has become popular in modern times for its lightweight comfort in hot weather. A few shops in Barcelona (including La Manual Alpargatera, described later) still make these the traditional way.

Jewelry shops are popular here. While the city doesn't have a strictly local style, finding a piece with a Modernista flourish gives it a Barcelona vibe.

Accessories crafted from discarded materials into stylish, useful products (such as handbags) sell well in "green" Barcelona. If you're intrigued by **Catalunya's** culture, consider a Catalan flag (gold and red stripes). And if you're a fan of Catalunyan independence, pick up one with the blue triangle and star.

Sports fans love jerseys, scarves, and other gear associated with the wildly popular **Barça** soccer team. As you wander, you'll likely see official football team shops.

Where to Shop

THE OLD CITY

The Barri Gòtic bursts with shopping opportunities, from international chain stores to creative artisan shops (I'll point out a few on my Barri Gòtic Shopping Walk, below). Neighboring El Born may be the most appealing place in Barcelona for boutique-hopping. My ◐ **El Born Walk** chapter, designed partly as a framework for shoppers, suggests a route through the heart of this district and points you to streets worth exploring.

Barri Gòtic Shopping Walk
(from the Cathedral to the Ramblas)

Most visitors going between the cathedral and the Ramblas follow

Shopping Tips

- If you need **souvenirs,** find a souvenir shop or consult your neighborhood supermarket for that saffron or *torró*—perfect for tucking into your suitcase at the last minute.
- For more elaborate purchases, large **department stores** provide painless one-stop shopping.
- Barcelona—particularly its Old City—is studded with hundreds of delightful neighborhood **boutiques,** the best of which specialize in a unique item and do it well. If you're a collector of anything in particular, do some homework to find the perfect shop.
- Don't leave your shopping for **siesta** time (roughly 14:00-17:00) or **Sunday,** when most stores are buttoned up tight.
- For information on **VAT refunds** and **customs regulations,** see page 280.
- For **clothing size comparisons** between the US and Europe, see page 316 of the appendix.

the straight shot along the wide Carrer de la Portaferrissa. This drag is lined with mostly international clothing stores catering to teens and young adults (H&M, Mango, etc.). For a more characteristic route—leading you through far more interesting streets lined with little local shops—plunge into some lanes just to the south. This brief, U-shaped walk is designed to lead you through some of the Barri Gòtic's most enjoyable shopping streets.

Keep in mind that many shops are closed during the midafternoon siesta and on Sundays. For locations of these shops, see the "Barri Gòtic Walk" map on page 92.

• *Begin on* **Plaça Nova,** *the long square in front of the cathedral. At the west end of that square, stand facing the old Roman towers and the big BARCINO letters. Turn 90 degrees to the right, and just to the left of the restaurant (Bilbao Berria "BB"), head up the tight lane called...*

Carrer de la Palla: This is ideal for antiques, with a half-dozen ancient-feeling shops crammed with mothballed treasures. (You'll also find, on the left, a fenced-in area with fragments of the old Roman walls.) Mixed in are a few contemporary art galleries, offbeat shops (such as **Librería Angel Batlle** at #23, selling books and vintage posters), and a motorcycle museum. Stay on this street until you reach the fork, marked by the building with **Caelum**—a casual but classy-feeling café that sells a wide range of nun-made pastries from convents around Spain. Peruse the boxes of sisterly goodies, and consider sticking around for a coffee—either on the main floor or down in the cellar (open long hours daily, Carrer de la Palla 8).

From here, you could detour left and head down **Carrer dels Banys Nous,** which curves gracefully south as it follows the route of the original Roman wall; while it's out of the way for this walk, it's another great shopping street. Just down this street, on the left at #10, the sprawling **S'Oliver** shop (selling home decor, women's clothing, and accessories) has the remains of an old Arabic bath in the back. Nearby, **Artesania Catalunya,** a large market-space run by the city, features handmade items from Catalan artisans. You can typically find ceramics, jewelry, leather goods, and accessories, but the artisans and merchandise change every few months (Mon-Sat 10:00-20:00, Sun 10:00-14:00, Carrer dels Banys Nous 11).

But to carry on toward the Ramblas, take the right fork past Caelum down Carrer de la Palla to another fine shop, **Oro Líquido** ("Liquid Gold"), which sells a wide range of high-quality olive oils from around Spain (Mon-Sat 10:30-20:30, shorter hours on Sun, Carrer de la Palla 8).

• *After another block, you'll pop out on the charming, café-lined Plaça de Sant Josep Oriol, facing the Church of Santa Maria del Pi (a popular venue for guitar concerts). Skirt around the right side of the church to find...*

Plaça del Pi: While small, this square has some worthwhile shops. Gentlemen enjoy checking out the genteel **Josep Roca,** a *ganiveteria* (cutlery shop) selling knives, shaving gear, and other manly items (Mon-Sat 10:00-20:00 but closes midday, closed Sun, Plaça del Pi 3). Nearby, the **Vaho** shop keeps hipsters happy with "trashion bags" made of recycled fabrics (Mon-Sat 10:30-20:30, closed Sun, many other Vaho stores around town). A couple of doors away, at Plaça del Pi 2, is a small outlet branch of the colorful Barcelona clothing designer, **Custo** (for the full Custo experience, visit their shop on the Ramblas, at #120). On the first and sometimes third Friday and Saturday of each month, local artisanal producers set up stalls in the middle of this square.

• *Head up the street immediately left of Josep Roca...*

Carrer de Petritxol: This fun, narrow, characteristic lane (pronounced peht-ree-CHUHL) runs parallel to the Ramblas. It's a fun combination of art galleries (such as **Sala Parés,** at #5, where Picasso had his first professional exhibition in town), fancy jewelry shops, and simple local places for hot chocolate and churros or other treats (check out **Granja La Pallaresa,** near the end of the street on the left, just after #11—described on page 207). A bit farther along, on the left (at #15), is a fancy sweets shop (specializing in *torró*) called **Vicens.** If you're looking for handmade ballet flats, you'll find them in a rainbow of colors at the family-run **Kokua** (at #18); they also sell bags, with a bigger selection of colors and sizes at their nearby shop at Carrer de la Bouería 30.

• *You'll dead-end onto touristy Carrer de la Portaferrissa. Head one block left to get to the Ramblas, or five blocks right to return to the cathedral. Or retrace your steps, this time poking into side streets to discover more shops.*

More Shops in the Barri Gòtic

The streets described in the above walk are just the beginning. While exploring the many other characteristic lanes of the Barri Gòtic, keep an eye out for these shops.

Sabater Hermanos (abbreviated "Hnos." on the sign) continues a family tradition of making and selling handmade, natural, colorful soaps. The simple but fragrant shop feels like an artisanal Lush. To buy soap and call it a culturally redeemable souvenir, look for the bars shaped like characteristic Barcelona sidewalk tiles (daily 10:30-20:30, Plaça Sant Felip Neri 1—see map on page 92).

Papirum is an inviting, classic, artisan shop selling craft paper, stationery, and hand-bound blank books (Mon-Sat 10:00-20:30, may close at midday, closed Sun, Baixada de la Llibreteria 2—see map on page 92, run by Dolores Crespo and family).

Som Naturals sells earthy baby and toddler clothing, designed and handmade by locals Dora Garriga and Jordi Cugat. They use 100-percent natural burlap and cotton (Mon-Sat 10:00-15:00 & 16:00-20:30, closed Sun, Carrer Santa Anna 37—see map on page 92).

The street called **Carrer de Sant Domènec del Call,** which runs through the old Jewish Quarter (and is described on my Barri Gòtic Walk), is lined with some fun cafés, plus a guitar shop and a leather workshop (Zoen, at #15, described on page 101 of the Barri Gòtic Walk).

La Manual Alpargatera, dating from the 1940s, is a *espardenya* store famous for making and selling these affordable, comfy shoes (Mon-Sat 9:30-20:00, closes at midday, closed Sun, 7 Carrer d'Avinyó, just off of Carrer de Ferran between the Ramblas and Plaça Sant Jaume).

Herbolari Ferran, on Plaça Reial (to the right as you enter the square from the Ramblas), is a fine and aromatic shop of herbs, with fun souvenirs such as top-quality saffron, or *safra* (also a pleasant little café inside, Mon-Fri 9:30-14:00 & 16:30-20:00, closed Sat-Sun, downstairs at Plaça Reial 18).

Carrer Ample, the street one block up from the tapas-loaded Carrer de la Mercè (in the lower part of Barri Gòtic—just above the waterfront), feels local but with little bursts of trendy energy. For example, **Papabubble** is a candy shop where you can watch treats being made the old-fashioned way (daily 10:00-14:00 & 16:00-20:30, Carrer Ample 28).

Other Barri Gòtic streets are loaded with fun shopping opportunities. On the other side of the Ramblas (two blocks below Plaça de Catalunya), stroll down skinny **Carrer de Bonsuccés** (it turns into **Carrer d'Elisabets**) and poke into the little boutiques along the way (such as the tiny, fashionable clothing store, **Passé Composé,** at #12).

THE EIXAMPLE

This ritzy "uptown" district is home to some of the city's top-end shops. In general, you'll find a lot of big international names along **Passeig de Gràcia,** the main boulevard that runs from Plaça de Catalunya to the Gaudí sights—an area fittingly called the "Golden Quarter" (Quadrat d'Or). Appropriately enough, the "upper end" of Passeig de Gràcia has the fancier shops—Gucci, Luis Vuitton, Escada, Chanel, and so on—while the southern part of the street is relatively "low-end" (Zara, Mango, Camper). One block to the west, **Rambla de Catalunya** holds more local (but still expensive) options: fashion, home decor, jewelry, perfume, and so on. The streets that connect Rambla de Catalunya to Passeig da Gràcia are also home to some fine shops.

Vinçon, nearly next door to La Pedrera on Passeig de Gràcia, is a design showroom with a lot of stylish cookware, housewares, lighting, furniture, baby gear, and so on. Combining the practical and the avant-garde, it's a fun place to take a look at Euro-housewares in a sprawling shop that feels like a trendy Spanish Ikea. At the far end of the store, find La Sala Vinçon, with temporary design exhibits and installations. Upstairs, filling the rooms of a fancy old apartment, is a showroom of various living spaces (Mon-Sat 10:00-20:30, closed Sun, Passeig de Gràcia 96).

Cubiñá, three blocks east and a block south, is another highly regarded furniture and home-decor shop—worth a peek for its upscale-mod collection, as well as for the Domènech i Montaner building that houses it (Mon-Sat 10:00-14:00 & 16:30-20:30, closed Sun, Carrer Mallorca 291).

Farther south, the street called **Consell de Cent** has a variety of art galleries (close to Plaça de Catalunya, roughly between Passeig de Gràcia and Carrer d'Enric Granados). And much farther to the west, the broad main boulevard **Diagonal** is another popular shopping zone—especially the stretch between Plaça de Francesc Macià and where it crosses Gran Via de Carles III (at the Maria Cristina Metro stop).

SHOPPING

This neighborhood is also home to some fun kitchen stores: Try **Gadgets & Cuina** (Carrer d'Aragó 249) or **Cooking** (Carrer de Provença 246).

DEPARTMENT AND CHAIN STORES
Avinguda del Portal de l'Angel

Barcelona natives do most of their shopping at big department stores. While most chains have several locations scattered around the city, you'll find the highest concentration on one convenient street, Avinguda del Portal de l'Angel, which connects Plaça de Catalunya with the cathedral. On this street, and throughout town, you'll find all of the following: **El Corte Inglés** is "Macy's-plus," the Spanish answer to one-stop shopping—everything from clothes, housewares, and furniture to electronics, bonsai trees, a travel agency, haircuts, and cheap souvenirs (get the complete list by picking up an English directory at their info desk). The chain **Zara** is focused on clothes. (Shops like Zara can vary from store to store—for example, the one in Barri Gòtic has more casual clothes, while the one along the ritzy Diagonal street emphasizes business attire.) Zara also owns several smaller clothing stores, including **Massimo Dutti** (upscale business attire, like Banana Republic), **Bershka** (teens), and **Pull and Bear** (young adults—sort of the Spanish Gap). The Barcelona-based **Mango** is another popular clothing chain, along with **Desigual** (with boldly colorful designs), the teen-oriented French chain **Pimkie,** and the more sophisticated **Podivm** and **Blanco.** Big international clothing chains include **H&M, Esprit,** and **Benetton. Camper,** which started in Mallorca, sells stylish but comfy shoes. **Yamamay** and **Women's Secret** are the Spanish answer to Victoria's Secret. **Intimissimi,** along with its parent company, **Calzedonia,** are Italian lingerie and swimwear stores. For Spanish fashion, simply walk down the street and dip into any of these that appeal.

At the top of Avinguda del Portal de l'Angel, Plaça de Catalunya has some large shops—including a gigantic **El Corte Inglés** (with a supermarket in the basement and a ninth-floor view café, Mon-Sat 10:00-22:00, closed Sun) and, across the square, **FNAC**—a French department store that sells electronics, music, books, and tickets for major concerts and events (Mon-Sat 10:00-22:00, closed Sun).

Las Arenas

While the shops inside it are nothing special, the Las Arenas shopping mall itself is—since it fills Barcelona's repurposed bullring. After Catalunya outlawed bullfighting in 2010, the former *plaça de toros* was converted into a modern mall with chain stores, a food court, a view terrace on top, and an escalator that trundles all the way up through its wide-open atrium (daily 10:00-22:00, small fee if you take exterior elevator, Gran Via de les Corts Catalanes 373-385). Located on Plaça d'Espanya, it's convenient to combine with a visit to the Montjuïc sights (see page 72).

NIGHTLIFE IN BARCELONA

Like all of Spain, Barcelona is extremely lively after hours. People head out for dinner at 22:00, then bar-hop or simply wander the streets until well after midnight. Some days it seems that more people are out and about at 2:00 in the morning (party time) than at 2:00 in the afternoon (siesta time). The most "local" thing you can do here after sunset is to explore neighborhood watering holes and find your favorite place to nurse a cocktail. I've described several parts of town ideally suited to doing just that. For a musical event, consider taking in a serious performance at a fancy venue (such as the Palace of Catalan Music or the Liceu Opera House), or opt for a jazz, flamenco, or classical guitar show.

Information: The TI hands out a free, monthly, user-friendly *Time Out BCN Guide* (in English, with descriptions of each day's main events and websites for getting tickets). The TI's culture website is also helpful: http://barcelonacultura.bcn.cat. The weekly *Guía del Ocio*, sold at newsstands for €1.20 (or free in some hotel lobbies), is a Spanish-language entertainment listing (with guidelines for English speakers inside the back cover; also available online at www.guiadelocio.com). Although it's in Catalan only, the *Butxaca* monthly cultural agenda includes a detailed schedule that's easy to figure out (available free around town and at Palau de la Virreina —described next, www.butxaca.com). Other resources are the monthly *Barcelona Planning.com* (www.barcelonaplanning.com), quarterly *See Barcelona* (www.seebarcelona.com), and monthly *Barcelona Metropolitan* (www.barcelona-metropolitan.com); all are available for free from the TI.

Palau de la Virreina, an arts-and-culture information office, provides details on Barcelona cultural events—music, opera, and theater (daily 10:00-20:30, Ramblas 99—see map on page 76, tel. 933-161-000, www.lavirreina.bcn.cat). A ticket desk is next door.

Getting Tickets: Most venues have links to booking engines on their websites. The majority of tickets for Barcelona events are booked through www.ticketmaster.es or www.telentrada.com. You can also get tickets through the box offices in the main El Corte Inglés department store or the giant FNAC electronics store (both on Plaça de Catalunya, extra booking fee), or at the ticket desk in Palau de la Virreina Cultura (listed earlier).

Music

SERIOUS CONCERTS

Several classy venues host high-end performances.

The **Palace of Catalan Music** (Palau de la Música Catalana), with one of the finest Modernista interiors in town (see listing on page 49), offers a full slate of performances, ranging from symphonic to Catalan folk songs to chamber music to flamenco (€20-50 tickets, purchase online or in person, box office open daily 9:30-21:00, Carrer Palau de la Música 4, Metro: Urquinaona, box office tel. 902-442-882).

The **Liceu Opera House** (Gran Teatre del Liceu), right in the heart of the Ramblas, is a pre-Modernista, sumptuous venue for opera, dance, children's theater, and concerts (tickets from €10, buy tickets online up to 1.5 hours before the show or in person, Ramblas 51, box office just around the corner at Carrer Sant Pau 1, Metro: Liceu, box office tel. 934-859-913, www.liceubarcelona.cat).

Another, much less architecturally interesting venue for classical music is **L'Auditori,** the home of the city's orchestra (boxy modern building northeast of Old City at Lepant 150; Metro: Glòries, Marina, or Monumental; tel. 932-479-300, www.auditori.cat).

Some of Barcelona's top sights host good-quality concerts. Try **La Pedrera** (described later under "Jazz"), **Fundació Joan Miró** (www.fundaciomiro-bcn.org), and **CaixaForum** (obrasocial. lacaixa.es—choose "CaixaForum Barcelona").

TOURISTY PERFORMANCES OF SPANISH CLICHÉS

Two famously Spanish types of music—flamenco and Spanish guitar—have little to do with Barcelona or Catalunya, but are performed to keep visitors happy. If you're headed for other parts of Spain where these musical forms are more typical (such as Andalucía for flamenco), you might as well wait until you can experience the real deal. But if this is your only stop in Spain, here are some options.

Flamenco: Tarantos, on Plaça Reial in the heart of the Barri Gòtic, puts on cheap, brief (30 minutes), riveting flamenco performances several times nightly. While flamenco is foreign to Catalu-

Sights Open Late

Many of Barcelona's major sights are open well into the evening (and the hop-on, hop-off **Tourist Bus** runs until 20:00 daily in summer). If you'd like to extend your sightseeing day, here's where to do it:

Near the Ramblas

Maritime Museum: Daily until 20:00 (only temporary exhibits open while permanent collection undergoes restoration, likely through 2015)

Palau Güell: April-Oct Tue-Sun until 20:00, closed Mon

La Boqueria Market: Mon-Sat until 20:00, though quiet after about 16:00, closed Sun

Barri Gòtic and El Born

Cathedral of Barcelona: Mon-Fri until 19:30, Sat-Sun until 20:00

Picasso Museum: Tue-Sun until 19:00, Thu until 21:30, closed Mon

Church of Santa Maria del Mar: Daily until 20:00

Eixample and Beyond

Sagrada Família: April-Sept daily until 20:00

La Pedrera (Casa Milà): March-Oct daily until 20:00

Casa Batlló: Daily until 20:00

Park Güell: Daily until 21:30 (Gaudí House Museum: April-Sept daily until 20:00)

Montjuïc and Vicinity

Castle of Montjuïc: April-Sept daily until 21:00

Fundació Joan Miró: Thu until 21:30 year-round, also July-Sept Tue-Wed and Fri-Sat until 20:00

Magic Fountains: May-Sept Thu-Sun 21:00-23:30, Oct-April Fri-Sat 19:00-21:00

CaixaForum: Daily until 20:00

Las Arenas (Bullring Mall): Shops daily until 22:00, terrace restaurants until 24:00

nya (locals say that it's like going to see country music in Boston), this is a fun and easy way to enjoy it. Performances are in a touristy little bar/theater with about 50 seats and reliably good-quality performers (€10, nightly at 20:30, 21:30, and 22:30; Plaça Reial 17, tel. 933-191-789, www.masimas.com/en/tarantos). It's right on Plaça Reial, so it's easy to drop by and get tickets.

Other options include the pricey **Tablao Cordobés** on the Ramblas (€42.50 includes a drink, €78 includes mediocre buffet dinner and better seats, 2-3 performances/day, Ramblas 35, tel. 933-175-711, www.tablaocordobes.com) and **Palau Dalmases,** which also hosts opera and jazz (€20 includes a drink, daily at 19:30 and 21:30, in atmospheric old palace courtyard in heart of El Born, Carrer de Montcada 20, tel. 933-100-673, www.palaudalmases. com).

For flamenco in a concert-hall setting, try one of the Palace of Catalan Music's regular performances (see listing earlier, under "Serious Concerts").

Spanish Guitar: "Masters of Guitar" concerts are offered nearly nightly at 21:00 in the Barri Gòtic's Church of Santa Maria del Pi (€21 at the door, €3 less if you buy at least 3 hours ahead—look for ticket-sellers in front of church and scattered around town, Plaça del Pi 7; sometimes in Sant Jaume Church instead, at Carrer de Ferran 28; tel. 647-514-513, www.maestrosdelaguitarra.com). The same company also does occasional concerts in the Palace of Catalan Music (€28-32).

JAZZ

On summer weekends, a particularly classy option is the **"Summer Nights at La Pedrera"** concerts at Gaudí's Modernista masterpiece in the Eixample. This evening rooftop concert series generally features live jazz and also gives you the chance to see the La Pedrera (Casa Milà) rooftop illuminated (€25, late June-early Sept Thu-Sat 20:30-23:00, book advance tickets online or by phone, tel. 902-101-212, www.lapedrera.com).

Hotel Casa Fuster, a Modernista landmark designed by Lluís Domènech i Montaner, is a luxury hotel that hosts a Woody Allen-inspired jazz night each Thursday (in the basement of Café Vienés, 21:00-23:00, €19 "membership" required, reservations recommended, across Avinguda Diagonal from the Eixample at Passeig de Gràcia 132, tel. 932-553-006, cafevienesjazzclub.blogspot.com).

Jamboree jazz and dance club, right on Plaça Reial, features two jazz sets nightly, at 20:00 and 22:00, in a cellar under brick vaults (€5-20 in advance, a euro or two more at the door, check schedule online or stop by to pick one up, Plaça Reial 17, Metro: Liceu, tel. 933-191-789, www.masimas.com/en/jamboree).

Also consider the divey **Harlem Jazz Club** (€6-10, a couple of blocks off Plaça Reial at Comtessa de Sobradiel 8, tel. 933-100-755, www.harlemjazzclub.es).

After-Hours Hangout Neighborhoods

Most Barcelonans' idea of "nightlife" is hopping from bar to bar with a circle of friends, while nibbling tapas and enjoying a variety of drinks (see "Drinking Words," page 196). The streets are jammed with people. In general, the weekend progression (Thu-Sat) goes like this: dinner at around 22:00; a music club for cocktails and DJ music from midnight; then, at about 2:00 or 3:00 in the morning, hit the discos until dawn. To join this social ritual, here are a few neighborhoods in particular to seek out, and some tips for each one.

EL BORN

Passeig del Born, a broad park-like strip stretching from the Church of Santa Maria del Mar up to the old market hall, is lined with inviting bars and nightspots. The side streets also teem with options. Wander to find a place that appeals to you.

Right on Passeig del Born is **Miramelindo,** a local favorite—mellow yet convivial, with two floors of woody ambience and a minty aura from all those mojitos the bartenders are mashing up (Passeig del Born 15). **Palau Dalmases,** in the atmospheric courtyard of an old palace, slings cocktails when it's not hosting flamenco shows. **La Vinya del Senyor,** one of my recommended eateries, is a fine place for a good glass of wine out on the square in front of the Church of Santa Maria del Mar.

The **Aire de Barcelona** Arab-style thermal baths, across from Citadel Park, are open late. Recently renovated with great style, these are ideal for recovering from a busy day of sightseeing (€29/person for 1.5 hours, massage also possible; reserve ahead—a week ahead for weeknights, a month ahead for weekends; Passeig Picasso 22, tel. 902-555-789, www.airedebarcelona.com).

PLAÇA REIAL AND NEARBY

This elegant-feeling square, just off the Ramblas in the Barri Gòtic, has a trendy charm. It bustles with popular bars and restaurants offering inflated prices at pleasant outdoor tables. While not a great place to eat (the only one worth seriously considering for a meal is the recommended **Les Quinze Nits**), this is a great place to sip a before- or after-dinner drink. **Ocaña Bar,** at #13, has a dilapidated-mod interior, a see-through industrial kitchen, and rickety-chic secondhand tables out on the square (€4-9 tapas, reasonable drinks, open nightly). Or there's always the student option: Buy a cheap €1 beer from a convenience store (you'll find several just off the square, including a few along Carrer dels Escudellers, just south of Plaça Reial), then grab a free spot on the square, either sitting on one of the few fixed chairs, perched along the rim of the fountain, or simply leaning up against a palm tree.

Plaça Reial is also home to the **Tarantos** flamenco bar and **Jamboree** jazz club (both described earlier). You'll find a variety of nightclubs here, including the hip **Sidecar Factory Club** (at #7, often live music, www.sidecarfactoryclub.com) and the hidden, mellow, pipe-happy **Barcelona Pipa Club** (at #3—find and ring the doorbell to get inside, this member's club opens to the public around 22:00, www.bpipaclub.com).

Wandering the streets near the square leads to other nightlife options. **Carrer de Escudellers** is a significantly rougher scene, with a few trendy options mixed in with several sketchy dives. Much closer to the harbor, **Carrer de la Mercè** (described on page 205 of the Eating in Barcelona chapter) has its share of salty sailors' pubs and more youthful bars. The next street up, **Carrer Ample,** has a similar scene.

BARCELONETA

A broad beach stretches for miles from the former fishermen's quarter at Barceloneta to the Fòrum. Every 100 yards or so is a *chiringuito*—a shack selling drinks and light snacks. Originally these sold seafood, but now they keep locals and tourists well-lubricated. It's a very fun, lively scene on a balmy summer evening and a nice way to escape the claustrophobic confines of the city to enjoy some sea air and the day's final sun rays.

Barceloneta itself has a broad promenade facing the harbor, lined with interchangeable seafood restaurants. But the best beach experience is beyond the tip of Barceloneta. From here, a double-decker boardwalk runs the length of the beach, with a cool walkway up above and a series of fine seafood restaurants with romantic candlelit beachfront seating tucked down below. Pricey but well-regarded places featuring high-quality Catalan cuisine are **Agua, Ca la Nuri,** and **Arenal.** Farther along, **Carpe Diem Lounge Club** (a.k.a. CDLC) is a fun Turkish-themed chill-out bar with cozy lounging sofas—ideal for a post-dinner drink; later, it becomes an edgier disco.

Nightclubs: Around Frank Gehry's glittering fish sculpture (at the former Olympic village) are several popular discos, crowded with partying twentysomethings. These get going extremely late—the kind of place where you have to be on the list, look good, and pay upwards of €10 for a drink. One of the most famous—and exclusive—is **Opium Mar,** a haunt of Barça footballers and other celebrities (www.opiummar.com). Beyond the beach, at the Olympic port, you'll find more bars with chill-out music (which later turn into livelier discos).

MONTJUÏC

With a little hustle, in summer it's possible to string together a fun evening of memorable views from the Montjuïc hilltop. Start with sweeping city vistas as you ride the Aeri del Port cable car (catch it at the tip of the Barceloneta peninsula; see page 221) up to the park's Miramar viewpoint. From there, head up to Montjuïc Castle on foot for more breathtaking views. Finally, wind your way around the hilltop to the Catalan Art Museum and reward yourself with a drink at its terrace café—a prime spot for taking in the Magic Fountains show, which makes a dramatic splash every half-hour (Thu-Sun nights in summer; see page 70). For a splurge, consider dinner at the museum's Òleum Restaurant (open until 23:30), which also overlooks the fountains and the entire 1929 Expo site.

Each July the normally peaceful hill pulls an all-nighter for the Montjuïc de Nit festival. Montjuïc Castle, Fundació Joan Miró, and the park's botanic garden are among the venues hosting this night of free musical and other performances (mid-July; see page 27 for details).

THE EIXAMPLE

Barcelona's upscale uptown isn't quite as lively or funky as some other neighborhoods, but a few streets have some fine watering holes. Walk along the inviting, park-like **Rambla de Catalunya,** or a couple of blocks over, along **Carrer d'Enric Granados** and **Carrer d'Aribau** (near the epicenter of the Eixample's gay community); all of these streets are speckled with cocktail bars offering breezy outdoor seating. In the opposite direction (east of Passeig de Gràcia), **Bar Dow Jones**—popular with the American expat student crowd—has a clever gimmick: Drink prices rise and fall like the stock market (Carrer del Bruc 97).

GRÀCIA

A bit farther flung, and more local-feeling because of it, the Gràcia neighborhood sits between the Eixample and Park Güell. Known for its design schools and its international art-house cinema (the Cines Verdi, www.cines-verdi.com/barcelona), it's the unpretentious but intellectual corner of town. Though it lacks the twisty-Gothic-lanes ambience of the Old City, Gràcia feels more like a small town (which it was, before it was swallowed up by an expanding Barcelona). It's popular with students—both local and international—and can be a bit rowdy. The district is even more vibrant in

August, when it hosts the Festa Major de Gràcia, with street music everywhere (see page 27).

The most interesting stretch of Gràcia is squeezed between two Metro stops: Fontana, on the L3 (green) line; and Joanic, on the L4 (yellow) line. Here's a handy bar-crawl route: From the Fontana stop, exit and turn left, heading down the shop-lined Carrer d'Astúries. After crossing the busy Carrer del Torrent de l'Olla, keep going straight two short blocks to **Carrer de Verdi.** You'll find several nightspots up and down this street, and a block over, at **Plaça de la Virreina** (where several places fill the square in front of the church with outdoor tables). From there you can head down Carrer de Torrijos, with more options—including **Café Salambo,** with an Art Deco vibe (at #51, www.cafesalambo.com). A right turn at Carrer de Ramón y Cajal leads you (in three blocks) to your grand finale, **Plaça del Sol,** the epicenter of Gràcia nightlife.

TIBIDABO

Many people enjoy heading up to Tibidabo for drinks with a great view—ideal for watching the sunset. At the top of the Tramvía Blau (blue tram)—which is also the bottom of the Tibidabo funicular—you'll find two places: **Mirabé** (nightly from 19:00, Manuel Arnús 2) and **Mirablau** (Plaça Dr. Andreu). While this probably isn't worth the long trip from downtown (unless you're a panorama seeker), it's handy to combine with a visit to Tibidabo or Park Güell. Come here for a pricey drink with a view—not for dinner.

BARCELONA CONNECTIONS

This chapter covers Barcelona's airports, main train station, cruise port, and main bus station.

I don't advise driving in Barcelona—thanks to its excellent public transportation and taxis, you won't need a car here, and the parking fees are outrageously expensive (for example, the lot behind La Boqueria Market charges upwards of €25/day).

By Plane

Most flights use Barcelona's **El Prat de Llobregat Airport;** a few budget flights use a smaller airstrip 60 miles away, called **Girona–Costa Brava Airport.** Information on both airports can be found on the official Spanish airport website, www.aena-aeropuertos.es.

EL PRAT DE LLOBREGAT AIRPORT

Barcelona's primary airport is eight miles southwest of town (airport code: BCN, info tel. 913-211-000). It has two large terminals, linked by shuttle buses. Terminal 1 serves Air France, Air Europa, American, British Airways, Delta, Iberia, Lufthansa, United, US Airways, Vueling, and others. EasyJet and minor airlines use the older Terminal 2, which is divided into sections A, B, and C.

Terminal 1 and the bigger sections of Terminal 2 (A and B) each have a post office, a pharmacy, a left-luggage office, plenty of good cafeterias in the gate areas, and ATMs (use the bank-affiliated ATMs in the arrivals hall).

Getting Between the Airport and Downtown

To get downtown cheaply and quickly, take the bus or train (about 30 minutes on either).

By Bus: The Aerobus (#A1 and #A2, corresponding with Terminals 1 and 2) stops immediately outside the arrivals lobby of both terminals (and in each section of Terminal 2). In about 30 minutes, it takes you to downtown, where it makes several stops, including Plaça d'Espanya and Plaça de Catalunya—near many of my recommended hotels (departs every 5 minutes, from airport 6:00-1:00 in the morning, from downtown 5:30-24:15, €5.90 one-way, €10.30 round-trip, buy ticket from machine or from driver, tel. 934-156-020, www.aerobusbcn.com).

By Train: The RENFE **train** (on the "R2 Sud" Rodalies line) leaves from Terminal 2 and involves more walking. Head down the long orange-roofed overpass between sections A and B to reach the station (2/hour at about :08 and :38 past the hour, 20 minutes to Sants Station, 25 minutes to Passeig de Gràcia Station—near Plaça de Catalunya and many recommended hotels, 30 minutes to França Station; €4.10 or covered by T10 Card—described on page 28—which you can purchase at automated machines at the airport train station). If you are arriving or departing from Terminal 1, you will have to use the airport shuttle bus to connect with the train station, so leave extra time.

Long term plans call for the RENFE train and eventually the AVE to be extended to Terminal 1, and for the Metro's L9 (orange) line to be extended to both Terminals 1 and 2. Stay tuned.

By Taxi: A taxi between the airport and downtown costs about €35 (including €4.20 airport supplement). For good service, you can round up to the next euro on the fare—but keep in mind that the Spanish don't tip cabbies.

GIRONA–COSTA BRAVA AIRPORT

Some budget airlines, including Ryanair, use this airport, located 60 miles north of Barcelona near Girona (airport code: GRO, tel. 972-186-600, www.aena-aeropuertos.es). Ryanair runs a **bus,** operated by Sagalés, to the Barcelona Nord bus station (€16, departs airport about 20-25 minutes after each arriving flight, 1.25 hours, tel. 902-361-550, www.sagales.com). You can also take a Sagalés bus (hourly, 25 minutes, €2.50) or a taxi (€25) to the town of Girona, then catch a train to Barcelona (at least hourly, 1.25 hours, €15-20). A taxi between the Girona airport and Barcelona costs at least €120.

CHEAP FLIGHTS

Check the reasonable flights from Barcelona to Sevilla or Madrid. **Vueling** is Iberia's most popular discount airline; for example, Barcelona-Madrid flights cost as little as €40 if booked well in advance (tel. 902-333-933, www.vueling.com). These two airlines typically offer €80 flights to Madrid: **Iberia** (tel. 902-400-500, www.iberia.com) and **Air Europa** (tel. 902-401-501 or 932-983-907, www.

aireuropa.com). For more information on flights within Europe, see page 307.

By Train

Virtually all trains end up at Barcelona's **Sants train station,** west of the Old City (described next). AVE trains from Madrid go only to Sants Station and the **Sagrera Station,** far to the northeast. But many other trains also pass through other stations en route, such as **França Station** (between the El Born and Barceloneta neighborhoods), or the downtown **Passeig de Gràcia** or **Plaça de Catalunya** stations (which are also Metro stops—and very close to most of my recommended hotels).

Figure out which stations your train stops at (ask the conductor), and get off at the one most convenient to your hotel.

If departing from the downtown Passeig de Gràcia Station, where three Metro lines converge with the rail line, you might find the underground tunnels confusing. You can't access the RENFE station directly from some of the entrances. Use the northern entrances to this station (rather than the southern "Consell de Cent" entrance, which is closest to Plaça de Catalunya). Train info: tel. 902-320-320, www.renfe.com.

SANTS TRAIN STATION

Barcelona's main train station is vast and sprawling, but manageable. In the large lobby area under the upper tracks, you'll find a TI, ATMs, a world of handy shops and eateries, car-rental kiosks, and, in the side concourse, a classy, quiet Sala Club lounge for travelers with first-class reservations (TV, free drinks, study tables, and coffee bar). Sants is the only Barcelona station with luggage storage (small bag-€3.60/day, big bag-€5.20/day, requires security check, daily 5:30-23:00, follow signs to *consigna,* at far end of hallway from tracks 13-14).

In the vast main hall is a very long wall of ticket windows. Figure out which one you need before you wait in line (all are labeled in English). Generally, windows 1-7 (on the left) are for local commuter and *media distancia* trains, such as to Sitges; windows 8-21 handle advance tickets for long-distance *(larga distancia)* trains beyond Catalunya; the information windows are 22-26—go here first if you're not sure which window you want; and windows 27-31 sell tickets for long-distance trains leaving today. These window assignments can shift during the off-season. The information booths by windows 1 and 21 can help you find the right line and can provide some train schedules. Scattered nearby are two types of train-ticket vending machines. The red-and-gray machines sell tickets for local and *media distancia* trains within Catalunya. The purple machines are for national RENFE trains (be aware that you may have difficulty using a US credit card); these machines can also print out prereserved tickets if you have a confirmation code.

Getting Downtown: To reach the center of Barcelona, take a train or the Metro. To ride the subway, follow signs for the Metro (red *M*), and hop on the L3 (green) or L5 (blue) line, both of which link to a number of useful points in town. Purchase tickets for the Metro at touch-screen machines near the tracks (where you can also buy the cost-saving T10 Card, explained on page 28).

To zip downtown even faster (just five minutes), you can take any Rodalies de Catalunya suburban train from track 8 (R1, R3, or R4) to Plaça de Catalunya (departs at least every 10 minutes). Your long-distance RENFE train ticket comes with a complimentary ride on Rodalies, as long as you use it within three hours before or after your travels. Look for a code on your ticket labeled *Combinat Rodalies* or *Combinado Cercanías*. Go to the red-and-gray commuter ticket machines, touch *Combinat Rodalies*, type in your code, and the machine will print your ticket.

TRAIN CONNECTIONS

Unless otherwise noted, all of these trains depart from Sants Station; however, remember that some trains also stop at other stations more convenient to the downtown tourist zone: França Station, Passeig de Gràcia, or Plaça de Catalunya. Figure out if your train stops at these stations (and board there) to save yourself the trip to Sants.

From Barcelona by Train to Madrid: The AVE train to Madrid is faster than flying (when you consider that you're zipping from downtown to downtown). The train departs at least hourly. The nonstop train is a little more expensive (€130, 2.5 hours) than the slightly slower train that makes a few stops and adds about a half-hour (€110, 3 hours).

Regular reserved AVE tickets can be prepurchased (often with a discount) at www.renfe.com and picked up at the station. If you have a rail pass, you'll pay only a reservation fee of €23 for first class, which includes a meal on weekdays (€10 second class, buy at any train station in Spain). Passholders can't reserve online through RENFE but can make a more expensive reservation at www.raileurope.com for delivery before leaving the US.

For a cheaper, non-AVE option, there's a slow overnight train to Madrid (9 hours, €45, add *litera* or *couchette* for €13).

From Barcelona by Train to: Sitges (departs from both Passeig de Gràcia and Sants, 4/hour, 40 minutes), **Montserrat** (departs from Plaça d'Espanya—*not* from Sants, hourly, 1 hour, €18.80 round-trip, includes cable car or rack train to monastery—see details on page 246), **Figueres** (hourly, 1 hour via AVE or Alvia to Figueres-Vilafant; hourly, 2 hours via local trains to Figueres Station), **Sevilla** (8-9/day, 5.5-6 hours), **Granada** (1/day, 8 hours via AVE and Altaria, transfer in Madrid), **Salamanca** (8/day, 6-7.5 hours, change in Madrid from Atocha Station to Chamartín Station via Metro or *cercanías* train; also 1/day with a change in Valladolid, 8.5 hours), **San Sebastián** (2/day, 6 hours), **Málaga** (8/day direct via AVE, 6-6.5 hours; more with transfer), **Lisbon** (no direct trains, head to Madrid and then catch night train to Lisbon, 17 hours—or fly).

From Barcelona by Train to France: Direct high-speed trains run to **Paris** (2-3/day, 6 hours), **Lyon** (1/day, 5 hours), and **Toulouse** (1/day, 3 hours), and there are more connections with transfers. For a **night train to Paris,** take a regional train to Cerbère and connect with the overnight run to Paris Gare d'Austerlitz (14-16 hours total, may not run Sat).

By Bus

Most buses depart from the Nord bus station at Metro: Arc de Triomf, but confirm when researching schedules (www.barcelonanord. com). Destinations served by Alsa buses (tel. 902-422-242, www. alsa.es) include **Madrid** and **Madrid's Barajas Airport** (nearly hourly, 8 hours), and **Salamanca** (2/day, 11 hours). Sarfa buses (tel. 902-302-025, www.sarfa.com) serve many **coastal resorts,** including **Cadaqués** (2-3/day, 3 hours).

The Mon-Bus leaves from the university and Plaça d'Espanya in downtown Barcelona to **Sitges** (4/day, 1 hour, www.monbus. cat). One bus departs daily for the **Montserrat** monastery, leaving from Carrer de Viriat near Sants Station (see page 246).

By Cruise Ship

Cruise ships arrive in Barcelona at three different ports (all just southwest of the Old City, beneath Montjuïc). If your trip includes cruising beyond Barcelona, consider my guidebook, *Rick Steves Mediterranean Cruise Ports.*

Most American cruise lines put in at **Moll Adossat/Muelle Adosado,** a long two miles from the bottom of the Ramblas. This port has four modern, airport-like terminals (lettered A through D); most have a café, shops, and TI kiosk; some have Internet access and other services. Two other terminals are far less commonly used: the **World Trade Center,** just off the southern end of the Ramblas, and **Moll de la Costa,** tucked just beneath Montjuïc (ride the free, private shuttle bus to World Trade Center; from there, it's a short walk or taxi ride to the Columbus Monument).

Getting Downtown: From any of the cruise terminals, it's easy to reach the Ramblas. **Taxis** meet each arriving ship and are waiting as you exit any of the terminal buildings. The short trip into town (i.e., to the bottom of the Ramblas) runs about €15 (the €4.20 cruise-port surcharge is legit). During high season, a ride into town can take longer and cost €10 more. For a one-way journey to other parts of town, expect to pay these fares: to the Picasso Museum or Plaça de Catalunya—€15; to the Sagrada Família—€20; and to the airport—€35-40.

You can also take a **shuttle bus** from Moll Adossat/Muelle Adosado to the Columbus Monument at the bottom of the Ramblas, then walk or hop on public transportation to various sights. The #T3 shuttle bus (also called Bus Port) departs from the parking lot in front of the terminal—follow *Public Bus* signs (€3.50 round-trip, €2.50 one-way, buses leave every 20-30 minutes, timed to cruise ship arrival, 5-15 minutes, tel. 932-986-000). Pay careful attention to where they drop you off; you'll catch the return bus near here (across the street, heading back toward the port—look for blue-and-white sign). If you're confused, there is usually someone standing by the bus stop to help.

DAY TRIPS FROM BARCELONA

Montserrat • Figueres • Cadaqués • Sitges

Four fine sights are day-trip temptations from Barcelona. Pilgrims with hiking boots head 1.5 hours into the mountains for the most sacred spot in Catalunya: Montserrat. Fans of Surrealism can combine a fantasy in Dalí-land by stopping at the Dalí Theater-Museum in Figueres (one to two hours from Barcelona) and spending a day or two in the classy but sleepy port-town getaway of Cadaqués (pictured above, an hour from Figueres; note that the Salvador Dalí House in Cadaqués requires reservations to visit). Or for a quick escape from the city, head 40 minutes south to the charming and free-spirited beach town of Sitges.

Montserrat

Montserrat—the "serrated mountain"—rockets dramatically up from the valley floor northwest of Barcelona. With its unique rock formations, a dramatic mountaintop monastery (also called Montserrat), and spiritual connection with the Catalan people and their struggles, it's a popular day trip. This has been Catalunya's most important pilgrimage site for a thousand years. Hymns explain how the mountain was carved by little angels with golden saws. Geologists blame nature at work.

    Once upon a time, there was no mountain. A river flowed here, laying down silt that hardened into sedimentary layers of hard rock. Ten million years ago, the continents shifted, and the land around the rock massif sank, exposing this series of peaks that reach upward to 4,000 feet. Over time, erosion pocked the face with caves and cut vertical grooves near the top, creating the famous serrated look.

The monastery is nestled in the jagged peaks at 2,400 feet, but it seems higher because of the way the rocky massif rises out of nowhere. The air is certainly fresher than in Barcelona. In a quick day trip, you can view the mountain from its base, ride a funicular up to the top of the world, tour the basilica and museum, touch a Black Virgin's orb, hike down to a sacred cave, and listen to Gregorian chants by the world's oldest boys' choir.

Montserrat's monastery is Benedictine, and its 30 monks carry on its spiritual tradition. Since 1025, the slogan *"ora et labora"* ("prayer and work") has pretty much summed up life for a monk here.

The Benedictines welcome visitors—both pilgrims and tourists—and offer this travel tip: Please remember that the most important part of your Montserrat visit is not enjoying the architecture, but rather discovering the religious, cultural, historical, social, and environmental values that together symbolically express the life of the Catalan people.

GETTING TO MONTSERRAT

Barcelona is connected to the valley below Montserrat by a convenient train; from there, a cable car or rack railway (your choice) takes you up to the mountaintop. Both options are similar in cost and take about the same amount of time (hourly trains, 1.5 hours each way from downtown Barcelona to the monastery). For ticket options, see the sidebar. Driving or taking the bus round out your options.

Train Plus Cable Car or Rack Railway

By Train: Trains leave hourly from Barcelona's Plaça d'Espanya to Montserrat. Take the Metro to Espanya, then follow signs for Montserrat showing a graphic of a train to the FGC (Ferrocarrils de la Generalitat de Catalunya) underground station. Once there, check the overhead screens to find the track for train line R5 (direction: Manresa, departures at :36 past each hour; additional departures Mon-Fri at 11:56, 13:56, 14:56, and 15:56).

You'll ride about an hour on the train. As you reach the base of the mountain, you have two options: Get out at the Montserrat-Aeri station for the cable car, or continue another few minutes to the next station—Monistrol de Montserrat (or simply "Monistrol de M.")—for the rack railway. (You'll have to make this decision when you buy your ticket in Barcelona—see "Tickets to Montserrat" sidebar.) Hang on to your train ticket; you will need it to exit the FGC station when you return to Plaça d'Espanya.

Cable Car or Rack Train? For the sake of scenery and fun, I enjoy the little German-built cable car more than the rack railway. Departures are more frequent (4/hour rather than hourly on the railway), but because the cable car is small, you might have to wait for a while to get on. If you are afraid of heights, take the rack train. Paying extra (about €5-7) to ride both isn't worthwhile.

By Cable Car, at the Montserrat-Aeri Station: Departing the train, follow signs to the cable-car station (covered by your train or combo-ticket; 4/hour, 5-minute trip, daily March-Oct 9:40-14:00 & 14:35-19:00, Nov-Feb 10:10-14:00 & 14:35-17:45—note the lunch break, www.aeridemontserrat.com). Because the cable car is smaller than the train, don't linger or you may have to wait for the next car. On the way back down,

Tickets to Montserrat

Various combo-tickets cover your journey to Montserrat, as well as some of the sights you'll visit there. All begin with the train from Barcelona's Plaça d'Espanya, and include either the cable car or rack railway—you'll have to specify one or the other when you buy the ticket (same price for either option). You can't go one way and come back the other, unless you pay extra (about €5-7) for the leg that's not included in your ticket.

The basic option is to buy a **train ticket** to Montserrat (€18.80 round-trip, includes the cable car or rack railway to monastery, Eurail pass not valid, tel. 932-051-515, www.fgc. es). Note that if you buy this ticket in Barcelona, then decide at Montserrat that you want to use the funiculars to go higher up the mountain or to the Sacred Cave, you can buy a €10 ticket covering both funiculars at the TI or at either funicular.

If you plan to do some sightseeing once at Montserrat, it makes sense to spend a little more on one of two combo-tickets from the train company: The €27.50 **Trans Montserrat** ticket includes your round-trip Metro ride in Barcelona to and from the train station, the train trip, the cable car or rack railway, unlimited trips on the two funiculars at Montserrat, and entry to the disappointing audiovisual presentation. The €43.70 **Tot Montserrat** ticket includes all of this, plus the good Museum of Montserrat and a self-service lunch (served daily 12:00-16:00). Both tickets are well-explained in the Barcelona TI's online shop (http://bcnshop.barcelonaturisme.com; look for them under the "Near Barcelona" tab).

If you plan to do it all, you'll save at least €5 with either of these combo-tickets. But during the off-season, ask the TI if one of the funiculars or the cable car is closed for maintenance; if so, the combo-ticket may not be worth it.

You can buy any of these tickets from the automated machines at Barcelona's Plaça d'Espanya Station (tourist officials are standing by in the morning to help you figure it out). To use your included round-trip Metro ride to get *to* the station, buy the ticket in advance at the Plaça de Catalunya TI in Barcelona.

cable cars depart from the monastery every 15 minutes; make sure to give yourself enough time to catch the Barcelona-bound trains leaving at :48 past the hour (don't cut it too close, in case the cable car runs late).

By Rack Railway (Cremallera), at the Monistrol de Montserrat Station: From this station you can catch the Cremallera rack railway up to the monastery (covered by your train or combo-ticket; cheaper off-season, hourly, 20-minute trip, www. cremallerademontserrat.com). On the return trip, this train departs the monastery at :15 past the hour, allowing you to catch the Barcelona-bound train leaving Monistrol de Montserrat at :41 past the hour. The last convenient connection back to Barcelona leaves the monastery at 19:15 (Sat-Sun at 20:15). Confirm the schedule when you arrive, as specific times tend to change year to year. Note that there is one intermediate stop on this line (Monistrol-Vila, at a large parking garage), but—going in either direction—you want to stay on until the end of the line.

By Car or Bus

By Car: Once drivers get out of Barcelona (Road A-2, then C-55), it's a short 30-minute drive to the base of the mountain, then a 10-minute series of switchbacks to the actual site (where you can find parking for €5/day). It may be easier to park your car down below and ride the cable car or rack railway up; there is plenty of free parking at the Monistrol-Vila rack-railway station (cable car—€6.60 one-way, €10 round-trip; rack railway—€6 one-way, €9.50 round-trip, €12.90 version also includes Museum of Montserrat).

By Bus: One **bus** per day connects downtown Barcelona directly to the monastery at Montserrat (departs from Carrer de Viriat near Barcelona's Sants Station daily at 9:15, returns from the monastery to Barcelona at 18:00 June-Sept or at 17:00 Oct-May, €5 each way, 1.25- to 1.5-hour trip depending on traffic, operated by Autocares Julià, www.autocaresjulia.es). You can also take a four-hour **bus tour** offered by the Barcelona Guide Bureau (€47, leaves Mon-Sat at 15:00 from Plaça Catalunya; see page 33). However, since the other options are scenic, fun, and relatively easy, the only reason to take a bus is to avoid transfers.

Orientation to Montserrat

When you arrive at the base of the mountain, look up the rock face to find the cable-car line, the monastery near the top, and the tiny building midway up (marking the Sacred Cave).

However you make your way up to the Montserrat monastery, it's easy to get oriented once you arrive at the top. Everything is within a few minutes' walk of your entry point. All of the transit options—including the rack railway and cable car—converge at the big train station. Above those are both funicular stations: one up to the ridge top, the other down to the Sacred Cave trail. Across the street is the TI, and above that (either straight up the stairs, or up the ramp around the left side) is the main square. To the right of the station, a long road leads along the cliff to the parking lot; a humble farmers' market along here sells *mel y mató,* a characteristic Catalan cheese with honey.

Crowd-Beating Tips: Arrive early or late, as tour groups mob the place midday. Crowds are less likely on weekdays and worst on Sundays.

Montserrat

To Montserrat Monastery via road

To Monistrol de Montserrat (Rack Railway) & Manresa

Road down to Monistrol de Montserrat & C-55

To Monistrol de Montserrat Station

Llobregat

BP-1121

C-55

River

CREMALLERA RACK RAILWAY

SANT BENET REFUGE

MONTSERRAT MONASTERY

BASILICA

REST. & PICNIC AREA

HOTEL MUSEUM

P

AERI DE MONTSERRAT CABLE CAR

MONTSERRAT-AERI STATION

P

SANTA COVA FUNICULAR

SANT JOAN FUNICULAR

SACRED CAVE

SANT JOAN

To Barcelona

SANT MIGUEL

C-55

5 Kilometers

3 Miles

To Barcelona

TOURIST INFORMATION

The square below the basilica houses a helpful TI, right across from the rack railway station (daily from 9:00, closes just after last train heads down—roughly 18:45, or 20:15 on weekdays in July-Aug, tel. 938-777-701, www.montserratvisita.com). Pick up the free map and get your questions answered. A good audioguide, available only at the TI, describes the general site and basilica (€6 includes book; €14 includes entrance to museum, bland audiovisual presentation, and book). If you're a hiker, ask for the handout outlining hiking options here. Trails offer spectacular views (on clear days) to the Mediterranean and even (on clearer days) to the Pyrenees.

The audiovisual center (upstairs from the TI) provides some cultural and historical perspective—and an entrance to their big gift shop. The lame interactive exhibition—nowhere near as exciting as the mountains and basilica outside—includes computer touch screens and a short 20-minute video in English. Learn about the mountain's history, and get a glimpse into the daily lives of the

The History of Montserrat

The first hermit monks built huts at Montserrat around A.D. 900. By 1025, a monastery was founded. The Montserrat Escolania, or Choir School, soon followed, and is considered to be the oldest music school in Europe (they still perform—see "Choir Concert" on page 254).

Legend has it that in medieval times, some shepherd children saw lights and heard songs coming from the mountain. They traced the sounds to a cave (now called the Sacred Cave, or Santa Cova), where they found the Black Virgin statue (La Moreneta), making the monastery a pilgrim magnet.

In 1811 Napoleon's invading French troops destroyed Montserrat's buildings, though the Black Virgin, hidden away by monks, survived. Then, in the 1830s, the Spanish royalty—tired of dealing with pesky religious orders—dissolved the monasteries and convents.

But in the 1850s, the monks returned as part of Catalunya's (and Europe's) renewed Romantic appreciation for all things medieval and nationalistic. (Montserrat's revival coincided with other traditions born out of rejuvenated Catalan pride: the much-loved FC Barcelona soccer team; Barcelona's Palace of Catalan Music; and even the birth of local sparkling wine, *cava*.) Montserrat's basilica and monastery were reconstructed and became, once more, the strongly beating spiritual and cultural heart of the Catalan people.

Then came Francisco Franco, the dictatorial leader who wanted a monolithic Spain. To him Montserrat represented Catalan rebelliousness. During Franco's long rule, from 1939 to 1975, the *sardana* dance was still illegally performed here (but with a different name), and literature was published in the outlawed Catalan language. In 1970, 300 intellectuals demonstrating for more respect for human rights in Spain were locked up in the monastery for several days by Franco's police.

But now Franco is history. The 1990s brought another phase of rebuilding (after a forest fire and rain damage), and the Montserrat community is thriving once again, unafraid to display its pride for the Catalan people, culture, and faith.

monastery's resident monks (€5, covered by Trans Montserrat and Tot Montserrat combo-tickets, same hours as TI).

Self-Guided Spin Tour

From the main square in front of the basilica complex, face the main facade and take this spin tour. Like a good pilgrim, face Mary, the high-up centerpiece of the facade. Below her to the left is St. Benedict, the sixth-century monk who established the rules that came to govern Montserrat's monastery. St. George, the symbol of Catalunya, is on the right (amid victims of Spain's Civil War).

Five arches line the base of the facade. The one on the far right leads pilgrims to the high point of any visit, the Black Virgin (a.k.a. La Moreneta). The center arch leads into the basilica's courtyard, and the arch second from left directs you to a small votive chapel filled with articles representing prayer requests or thanks.

Now look left of the basilica, where delicate arches mark the 15th-century monks' cloister. The monks have planted four trees here, hoping to harvest only their symbolism (palm = martyrdom, cypress = eternal life, olive = peace, and laurel = victory). Next to the trees are a public library and a peaceful reading room. The big archway is the private entrance to the monastery. Still turning to your left, then comes the modern hotel and, below that, the glass-fronted museum. Other buildings provide cells for pilgrims. The Sant Joan funicular lifts hikers up to the trailhead (you can see the tiny building at the top). From there you can take a number of fine hikes (described later). Another funicular station descends to the Sacred Cave. And, finally, five arches separate statues of founders of the great religious orders. Step over to the arches for a commanding view (on a clear day) of the Llobregat River, meandering all the way to the Mediterranean.

Sights in Montserrat

▲▲Basilica

Although there's been a church here since the 11th century, the present structure was built in the 1850s, and the facade only dates from 1968. The decor is Neo-Romanesque, so popular with the Romantic artists of the late 19th century. The basilica itself is ringed with interesting chapels, but the focus is on the Black Virgin (La Moreneta) sitting high above the main altar.

Cost and Hours: Free, La Moreneta viewable Mon-Sat 8:00-10:30 & 12:00-18:30, Sun 19:30-20:15; church itself has longer hours and daily services (Mass at 11:00 at the main altar; at 12:00 and 19:30 in side chapels; vespers at 18:45); www.abadiamontserrat.net.

Visiting the Basilica: Montserrat's top attraction is **La Moreneta,** the small wood statue of the Black Virgin, discovered in the Sacred Cave in the 12th century. Legend says she was carved by St. Luke (the gospel writer and supposed artist), brought to Spain by St. Peter, hidden away in the cave during the Moorish invasions, and miraculously discovered by shepherd children. (Carbon dating says she's 800 years old.) While George is the patron saint of Catalunya, La Moreneta is its patroness, having been crowned as such by the pope in 1881. "Moreneta" is usually translated as "black" in English, but the Spanish name actually means "tanned." The statue was originally lighter, but darkened over the centuries from candle smoke, humidity, and the natural aging of its original varnish. Pilgrims shuffle down a long, ornate passage leading alongside the church for their few moments alone with the Virgin (keep an eye on the time if you want to see the statue; there are no visits Mon-Sat 10:30-12:00, or before 19:30 on Sun).

Join the line of pilgrims (along the right side of the church). Though Mary is behind a protective glass case, the royal orb she cradles in her hands is exposed. Pilgrims touch Mary's orb with one hand and hold their other hand up to show that they accept Jesus. Newlyweds in particular seek Mary's blessing.

If you're not ushered right to the exit, immediately after La Moreneta, turn right into the delightful Neo-Romanesque prayer **chapel,** where worshippers sit behind the Virgin and continue to pray. The ceiling, painted in the Modernista style in 1898 by Joan Llimona, shows Jesus and Mary high in heaven. The trail connecting Catalunya with heaven seems to lead through these serrated mountains. The lower figures symbolize Catalan history and culture.

You'll leave by walking along the **Ave Maria Path** (along the outside of the church), which thoughtfully integrates nature and the basilica. Thousands of colorful votive candles are all busy helping the devout with their prayers. Before you leave the inner courtyard and head out into the main square, pop in to the humble little room with the many votive offerings. This is where people leave personal belongings (wedding dresses, baby's baptism outfits, wax replicas of body parts in need of healing, and so on) as part of a prayer request or as a thanks for divine intercession.

Museum of Montserrat

This bright, shiny, and cool collection of paintings and artifacts was mostly donated by devout Catalan Catholics. While it's nothing really earth-shaking, you'll enjoy an air-conditioned wander past lots of antiquities and fine artwork. Head upstairs first to see some lesser-known works by the likes of Picasso, El Greco, Caravaggio, Monet, Renoir, Pissarro, Degas, John Singer Sargent, and some local Modernista artists. One gallery shows how artists have depicted the Black Virgin of Montserrat over the centuries in many different styles. There's even a small Egyptian section, with a sarcophagus and mummy. Down on the main floor, you'll see ecclesiastical gear, a good icon collection, and more paintings, including—at the very end—a Dalí painting, some Picasso sketches and prints, and a Miró.

Cost and Hours: €7, covered by Tot Montserrat combo-ticket, daily July-Aug 10:00-18:45, Sept-June 10:00-17:45, tel. 938-777-745.

▲Sant Joan Funicular and Hikes

This funicular climbs 820 feet above the monastery in five minutes. At the top of the funicular, you are at the starting point of

a 20-minute walk that takes you to the Sant Joan Chapel (follow sign for *Ermita de St. Joan*). Other hikes also begin at the trailhead by the funicular (get details from TI before you ascend; basic map with suggested hikes posted by upper funicular station). For a quick and easy chance to get out into nature and away from the crowds, simply ride up and follow the most popular hike, a 45-minute mostly downhill loop through mountain scenery back to the monastery. To take this route, go left from the funicular station; the trail—marked *Monestir de Montserrat*—will first go up to a rocky crest before heading downhill.

Cost and Hours: Funicular—€5.85 one-way, €9 round-trip, covered by Trans Montserrat and Tot Montserrat combo-tickets, goes every 20 minutes, more often with demand.

Sacred Cave (Santa Cova)

The Moreneta was originally discovered in the Sacred Cave (or Sacred Grotto), a 40-minute hike down from the monastery (then another 50 minutes back up). The path (c. 1900) was designed by devoted and patriotic Modernista architects, including Gaudí and Josep Puig i Cadafalch. It's lined with Modernista statues depicting scenes corresponding to the Mysteries of the Rosary. While the original Black Virgin statue is now in the basilica, a replica sits in the cave. A three-minute funicular ride cuts 20 minutes off the hike. If you're here late in the afternoon, check the schedule before you head into the Sacred Cave to make sure you don't miss the final ride back down the mountain. Missing the last funicular could mean catching a train back to Barcelona later than you had planned.

Cost and Hours: Funicular—€2.20 one-way, €3.50 round-trip, covered by Trans Montserrat and Tot Montserrat combo-tickets, goes every 20 minutes, more often with demand.

Sleep Code

(€1 = about $1.40, country code: 34)

Abbreviations

S = Single, **D** = Double/Twin, **T** = Triple, **Q** = Quad, **b** = bath-room, **s** = shower only.

Price Rankings

$$ Higher Priced—Most rooms €95 or more.

$ Lower Priced—Most rooms less than €95.

Unless otherwise noted, credit cards are accepted, English is spoken, and Wi-Fi is generally free. Some hotels include the 10 percent IVA tax in the room price; others tack it onto your bill. Prices change; verify current rates online or by email. For the best prices, always book directly with the hotel.

Choir Concert

Montserrat's Escolania, or Choir School, has been training voices for centuries. Fifty young boys, who live and study in the monastery itself, make up the choir, which performs daily except Saturday. The boys sing for only 10 minutes, the basilica is jam-packed, and it's likely you'll see almost nothing. Also note that if you attend the evening performance, you'll miss the last train or cable-car ride down the mountain.

Cost and Hours: Free, Mon-Fri at 13:00, Sun at 12:00, and Sun-Thu at 18:45, choir on vacation late June-late Aug.

Sleeping and Eating in Montserrat

An overnight here gets you monastic peace and a total break from the modern crowds. There are ample rustic cells for pilgrim visitors, but tourists might prefer this place:

$$ Hotel Abat Cisneros, a three-star hotel with 82 rooms and all the comforts, is low-key and appropriate for a sanctuary (Sb-€46-70, Db-€80-120, price depends on season, includes breakfast, half- and full-board available, elevator, guest computer, free Wi-Fi, tel. 938-777-701, www.montserratvisita.com, rcscrvcs@larsa-montserrat.com).

Eating: Montserrat is designed to feed hordes of pilgrims and tourists. You'll find a cafeteria along the main street (across from the train station) and a grocery store and bar with simple sandwiches where the road curves on its way up to the hotel. In the other direction, follow the covered walkway below the basilica to reach the Mirador dels Apòstols, with a bar, cafeteria, restaurant, and picnic area. The Hotel Abat Cisneros also has a restaurant. The best option is to pack a picnic from Barcelona, especially if you plan to hike.

Figueres

The town of Figueres (feeg-YEHR-ehs)—conveniently connected by train to Barcelona—is of sightseeing interest only for its Salvador Dalí Theater-Museum. In fact, the entire town seems Dalí-dominated. But don't be surprised if you also find French shoppers bargain-hunting. Some of the cheapest shops in Spain—called *ventas*—are here to lure French visitors.

GETTING TO FIGUERES

Figueres is an easy day trip from Barcelona, or a handy stopover en route to France. It's cheap and convenient to take a regional train to Figueres Station—they depart from Barcelona's Sants Station or from the RENFE station at Metro: Passeig de Gràcia (hourly, 2 hours; the slightly more expensive *media distancia* trains are 20 minutes faster than *regional* trains). If you're in a hurry, consider the high-speed train, which cuts your travel time in half. It departs from Barcelona's Sants Station and stops at the recently opened Figueres-Vilafant Station, on the other side of town (hourly, 1 hour). If you're visiting Figueres on your way to Paris, it's possible to take the high-speed train in the morning, visit the Dalí Theater-Museum, and catch the late afternoon TGV to Paris from the Figueres-Vilafant Station (note that the station does not have baggage storage). For bus connections to Cadaqués, see page 259.

Arrival in Figueres: From Figueres Station, simply follow *Museu Dalí* signs (and the crowds) for the 15-minute walk to the museum. From Figueres-Vilafant Station, it's about a 20-minute walk.

Sights in Figueres

▲▲▲Dalí Theater-Museum (Teatre-Museu Dalí)

This is *the* essential Dalí sight—and, if you like Dalí, one of Europe's most enjoyable museums, period. Inaugurated in 1974, the museum is a work of art in itself. Ever the entertainer and promoter, Dalí personally conceptualized, designed, decorated, and painted it to showcase his life's work. The museum fills a former theater and is the artist's

Salvador Dalí (1904-1989)

When Salvador Dalí was asked, "Are you on drugs?" he replied, "I am the drug...take me."

Labeled by various critics as sick, greedy, paranoid, arrogant, and a clown, Dalí produced some of the most thought-provoking and trailblazing art of the 20th century. His erotic, violent, disjointed imagery continues to disturb and intrigue today.

Born in Figueres to a well-off family, Dalí showed talent early. He was expelled from Madrid's prestigious art school—twice—but formed longtime friendships with playwright Federico García Lorca and filmmaker Luis Buñuel.

After a breakthrough art exhibit in Barcelona in 1925, Dalí moved to Paris. He hobnobbed with fellow Spaniards Pablo Picasso and Joan Miró, along with a group of artists exploring Sigmund Freud's theory that we all have a hidden part of our mind, the unconscious "id," which surfaces when we dream. Dalí became the best-known spokesman for this group of Surrealists, channeling his id to create photorealistic dream images (melting watches, burning giraffes) set in bizarre dreamscapes.

His life changed forever in 1929, when he met an older, married Russian woman named Gala who would become his wife, muse, model, manager, and emotional compass. Dalí's popularity

mausoleum (his tomb is in the crypt below center stage). It's also a kind of mausoleum to Dalí's creative spirit.

Dalí had his first public art showing at age 14 here in this building when it was a theater, and he was baptized in the church just across the street. The place was sentimental to him. After the theater was destroyed in the Spanish Civil War, Dalí struck a deal with the mayor: Dalí would rebuild the theater as a museum to his works, Figueres would be put on the sightseeing map...and the money's been flowing in ever since.

Even the building's exterior—painted pink, studded with golden loaves of bread, and topped with monumental eggs and a geodesic dome—exudes Dalí's outrageous public persona.

Cost and Hours: €12; July-Sept daily 9:00-20:00; March-June and Oct Tue-Sun 9:30-18:00, closed Mon; Nov-Feb Tue-Sun 10:30-18:00, closed Mon; last entry 45 minutes before closing, tel. 972-677-500, www.salvador-dali.org. No flash photography. The free bag check has your belongings waiting for you at the exit.

spread to the US, where he (and Gala) weathered the WWII years.

In his prime, Dalí's work became less Surrealist and more classical, influenced by past masters of painted realism (Velázquez, Raphael, Ingres) and by his own study of history, science, and religion. He produced large-scale paintings of historical events (e.g., Columbus discovering America, the Last Supper) that were collages of realistic scenes floating in a surrealistic landscape, peppered with thought-provoking symbols.

Dalí—an extremely capable technician—mastered many media, including film. *An Andalusian Dog* (*Un Chien Andalou*, 1929, with Luis Buñuel) was a cutting-edge montage of disturbing, eyeball-slicing images. He designed Alfred Hitchcock's big-eye backdrop for the dream sequence of *Spellbound* (1945). He made jewels for the rich and clothes for Coco Chanel, wrote a novel and an autobiography, and pioneered what would come to be called "installations." He also helped develop "performance art" by showing up at an opening in a diver's suit or by playing the role he projected to the media—a super-confident, waxed-mustached artistic genius.

In later years, Dalí's over-the-top public image contrasted with his ever-growing illness, depression, and isolation. He endured the scandal of a dealer overselling "limited editions" of his work. When Gala died in 1982, Dalí retreated to his hometown, living his last days in the Torre Galatea of the Theater-Museum complex, where he died of heart failure.

Dalí's legacy as an artist includes his self-marketing persona, his exceptional ability to draw, his provocative pairing of symbols, and his sheer creative drive.

Coin-Op Tip: Much of Dalí's art is movable and coin-operated—bring a few €1 coins.

◗ Self-Guided Tour: The museum has two parts: the theater-mausoleum and the "Dalí's Jewels" exhibit in an adjacent building. There's no logical order for a visit (that would be un-Surrealistic), and the museum can be mobbed at times. Naturally, there's no audioguide. Dalí said there are two kinds of visitors: those who don't need a description, and those who aren't worth a description. At the risk of offending Dalí, I've written this loose commentary to attach some meaning to your visit.

Stepping through or around the courtyard, go into the **theater** (with its audience of statues) and face the stage—and Dalí's unmarked crypt. You know how you can never get a cab when it's raining? Pop a coin into Dalí's personal 1941 Cadillac, and it rains inside the car. Look above, atop the tire tower: That's the boat Dalí enjoyed with his soul mate, Gala—his emotional life preserver, who kept him from going overboard. When she died, so did he (for his last seven years). Blue tears made of condoms drip below the boat.

Up on the **stage,** squint at the big digital Abraham Lincoln, and president #16 comes into focus. Approach the painting to find that Abe's facial cheeks are Gala's butt cheeks. Under the painting, a door leads to the **Treasures Room,** with the greatest collection of original Dalí oil paintings in the museum. (Many of the artworks on the walls are prints.) You'll see Cubist visions of Cadaqués and dreamy portraits of Gala. Crutches—a recurring Dalí theme—represent Gala, who kept him supported whenever a meltdown threatened.

The famous **Homage to Mae West room** is a tribute to the sultry seductress. Dalí loved her attitude. Saying things like, "Why marry and make one man unhappy, when you can stay single and make so many so happy?" Mae West was to conventional moral-ity what Dalí was to conventional art.

Climb to the vantage point where the sofa lips, fireplace nostrils, painting eyes, and drapery hair come together to make the face of Mae West.

Dalí's art can be playful, but also disturbing. He was passionate about the dark side of things, but with Gala for balance, he managed never to go off the deep end. Unlike Pablo Casals (the Catalan cellist) and Pablo Picasso (another local artist), Dalí didn't go into exile under Franco's dictatorship. Pragmatically, he accepted both Franco and the Church, and was supported by the dictator. Apart from the occasional *sardana* dance (see sidebar on page 45), you won't find a hint of politics in Dalí's art.

Wander around. You can spend hours here, wondering, is it real or not real? Am I crazy, or is it you? Beethoven is painted with squid ink applied by a shoe on a stormy night. Jesus is made with candle smoke and an eraser. It's fun to see the Dalí-ization of art classics. Dalí, like so many modern artists, was inspired by the masters—especially Velázquez.

The former theater's **smoking lounge** is a highlight, displaying portraits of Gala and Dalí (with a big eye, big ear, and a dark side) bookending a Roman candle of creativity. The fascinating ceiling painting shows the feet of Gala and Dalí as they bridge earth and the heavens. Dalí's drawers are wide open and empty, indicating that he gave everything to his art.

Leaving the theater, keep your ticket and pop into the adjacent **"Dalí's Jewels"** exhibit. It shows sketches and paintings of jewelry Dalí designed, and the actual pieces jewelers made from those sur-real visions: a mouth full of pearly whites, a golden finger corset, a fountain of diamonds, and the breathing heart. Explore the ambiguous perception worked into the big painting titled *Apotheosis of the Dollar*.

Cadaqués

Since the late 1800s, Cadaqués (kah-dah-KEHS) has served as a haven for intellectuals and artists alike. The fishing village's craggy coastline, sun-drenched colors, and laid-back lifestyle inspired Fauvists such as Henri Matisse and Surrealists such as René Magritte, Marcel Duchamp, and Federico García Lorca. Even Picasso, drawn to this enchanting coastal haunt, painted some of his Cubist works here.

Salvador Dalí, raised in nearby Figueres, brought international fame to this sleepy Catalan port in the 1920s. As a kid Dalí spent summers here in the family cabin, where he was inspired by the rocky landscape that would later be the backdrop for many Surrealist canvases. In 1929, he met his future wife, Gala, in Cadaqués. Together they converted a fisherman's home in nearby Port Lligat into their semi-permanent residence, dividing their time between New York, Paris, and Cadaqués. And it was here that Dalí did his best work.

In spite of its fame, Cadaqués is mellow and feels off the beaten path. If you want a peaceful beach-town escape near Barcelona, this is a good place. From the moment you descend into the town, taking in whitewashed buildings and deep blue waters, you'll be struck by the port's tranquility and beauty. Join the locals playing chess or cards at the cavernous Casino Coffee House (harborfront, with games and Internet access). Have a glass of *vino tinto* or *cremat* (a traditional rum-and-coffee drink served flambé-style) at one of the seaside cafés. Savor the lapping waves, brilliant sun, and gentle breeze. And, for sightseeing, the reason to come to Cadaqués is the Salvador Dalí House, a 20-minute walk from the town center at Port Lligat.

GETTING TO CADAQUÉS

Reaching Cadaqués is very tough without a car. There are no trains and only a few buses a day.

By Car: It's a twisty drive from Figueres (figure 45-60 minutes). In Cadaqués, drivers should park in the big lot just above the city—don't try to park near the harborfront. To reach the Salvador Dalí House, follow signs near Cadaqués to Port Lligat (easy parking).

By Bus: Sarfa buses serve Cadaqués from **Figueres** (3/day, 1 hour) and from **Barcelona** (2-3/day, 3 hours). You can buy bus tickets to Cadaqués at Barcelona TIs on Plaça de Catalunya, Plaça Sant Jaume, and at the Columbus Monument. Bus info: Barcelona toll tel. 902-302-025, Cadaqués tel. 972-258-713, Figueres tel. 972-674-298, www.sarfa.com.

TOURIST INFORMATION

The TI is at Carrer Cotxe 2 (July-Sept Mon-Sat 9:00-21:00, Sun 10:00-13:00 & 17:00-20:00, shorter hours off-season plus closed for lunch, tel. 972-258-315, www.visitcadaques.org).

Sights near Cadaqués

▲▲▲Salvador Dalí House
(Casa Museu Salvador Dalí)

Once Dalí's home, this house in Port Lligat (a 20-minute walk from town) gives fans a chance to explore his labyrinthine compound. This is the best artist's house I've toured in Europe. It shows how a home can really reflect the creative spirit of an artistic genius and his muse. The ambience, both inside and out, is perfect for a Surrealist hanging out with his creative playmate. The bay is ringed by sleepy islands. Fishing boats are jumbled on the

beach. After the fishermen painted their boats, Dalí asked them to clean their brushes on his door—creating an abstract work of art he adored (which you'll see as you line up to get your ticket).

The interior is left almost precisely as it was in 1982, when Gala died and Dalí moved out. See Dalí's studio (the clever easel cranks up and down to allow the artist to paint while seated, as he did eight hours a day); the bohemian-yet-divine living room (complete with a mirror to reflect the sunrise onto their bed each morning); the phallic-shaped swimming pool, which was the scene of orgiastic parties; and the painter's study (with his favorite mustaches all lined up). Like Dalí's art, his home is offbeat, provocative, and fun.

Cost and Hours: €11; mid-June-mid-Sept daily 9:30-21:00; mid-Feb-mid-June and mid-Sept-early Jan Tue-Sun 10:30-18:00, closed Mon; closed early Jan-mid-Feb. Last tour departs 50 minutes before closing. No bags of any kind are allowed in the house; the baggage check is free.

Reservations: You must reserve in advance—call or use the website (tel. 972-251-015, www.salvador-dali.org). In summer, book a week in advance. You must arrive 30 minutes early to pick up your ticket, or they'll sell it.

Visiting the House: Only 8-10 people are allowed in (no large groups) every 10 minutes. Once inside, there are five sections, each with a guard who gives you a brief explanation in English, and then turns you loose for a few minutes. The entire visit takes 50 minutes. Before your tour, enjoy the 15-minute video that plays in the waiting lounge (with walls covered in Dalí media coverage) just across the lane from the house.

Getting There: Parking is free nearby. There are no buses or taxis. The house is a 20-minute, one-mile walk over the hill from Cadaqués to Port Lligat. (The path, which cuts across the isthmus, is much shorter than the road.)

Sleeping and Eating in Cadaqués

$$ Hotel Llané Petit, with 32 spacious rooms (half with view balconies), is a small resort-like hotel with its own little beach, a 10-minute walk south of the town center (Db-€128 mid-July-Aug, €98 in shoulder season, €79 in winter, seaview rooms-about €30-50 more, breakfast-€12, air-con, elevator, Wi-Fi, parking-€10, Dr. Bartomeus 37, tel. 972-251-020, www.llanepetit.com, info@llanepetit.com). Reserve direct with this book for a free breakfast (not valid on weekends in high season and long weekends in shoulder season).

$ Hotel Nou Estrelles is a big, concrete exercise in efficient, economic comfort. Facing the bus stop a few blocks in from the waterfront, this family-run hotel offers 15 rooms at a great value (Db-€85-98 in high season, €68-76 in shoulder season, €57-60 in winter, extra bed-€10-15, breakfast-€7, air-con, elevator, Wi-Fi, Carrer Sant Vicens, tel. 972-259-100, www.hotelnouestrelles.com, reservas@hotelnouestrelles.com, Emma).

$ Hostal Marina is a cheap, low-energy place, with 27 rooms and a great location a block from the harborfront main square (high season: D-€55, Db-€90; low season: D-€40, Db-€50-60; balcony rooms-€10 extra, no breakfast, no elevator, Riera 3, tel. 972-159-091).

Eating: There are plenty of eateries along the beach. A lane called Carrer Miguel Rosset (across from Hotel La Residencia) also has several places worth considering. At **Casa Anita,** you'll sit with others around a big table and enjoy house specialties such as *calamares a la plancha* (grilled squid) and homemade *helado* (ice cream). Finish your meal with a glass of sweet Muscatel (Calle Miquel Rosset 16, tel. 972-258-471, Joan and family).

Sitges

Sitges (SEE-juhz) is one of Catalunya's most popular resort towns. Because the town beautifully mingles sea and light, it's long been an artists' colony. Here you can still feel the soul of the Modernistas...in the architecture, the museums, the salty sea breeze, and the relaxed rhythm of life.

Today's Sitges is a world-renowned vacation destination among the gay community. Despite its jet-set status, the Old Town has managed to retain its charm. With a much slower pulse than Barcelona, Sitges is an enjoyable break from the big city.

If you visit during one of Sitges' two big **festivals** (St. Bartholomew on Aug 24 and St. Tecla on Sept 23), you may see teams of *castellers* competing to build human pyramids.

Getting There: Southbound **trains** depart Barcelona from the Sants and Passeig de Gràcia stations (take Rodalies train on the dark-green line R2 toward Sant Vincenç de Calders, 4/hour, 40 minutes). From the train station, exit straight ahead (past a TI kiosk—open in summer) and walk down Carrer Francesc Gumà. When it dead-ends, continue right onto Carrer de Jesús, which takes you to the town's tiny main square, Plaça del Cap de la Villa. (Keep an eye out for directional signs.) From here, turn left down Carrer Major ("Main Street"), which leads you past the old market hall (now an art gallery) and the town hall, to a beautiful terrace next to the main church. Poke into the Old Town or take the grand staircase down to the beach promenade.

The Mon-Bus Company runs an easy and direct **bus** route from downtown Barcelona (with stops near the university and Plaça d'Espanya) that stops at Barcelona's airport en route to Sitges (4/day, 1 hour from Barcelona, 45 minutes from airport, www.monbus.cat).

Tourist Information: The TI, a couple of blocks northwest of the train station, hands out a good town map and museum brochures; the staff can also help you find a room (open daily, closed Sun afternoon, Sínia Morera 1, tel. 938-944-251, www.sitgestur.cat).

Visiting Sitges: Sitges basically has two attractions: its tight-and-tiny Old Town (with a few good museums) and its long, luxurious beaches.

Take time to explore the **Old Town's** narrow streets. They're crammed with cafés, boutiques, and all the resort staples. The focal point, on the waterfront, is the 17th-century Baroque-style **Sant Bartomeu i Santa Tecla Church.** The terrace in front of the church will help you get the lay of the land.

As an art town, Sitges has seen its share of creative people—some of whom have left their mark in the form of appealing museums. Walking along the water behind the church, you'll find two of the town's three museums (all closed Mon, www.museusdesitges.com). The **Museu Maricel** displays the eclectic artwork of a local collector, including some Modernista works, pieces by Sitges artists, and a collection of maritime-themed works. The **Museu Cau Ferrat,** which may be closed for restoration, bills itself as a "temple of art," as collected by local intellectual Santiago Rusiñol. In addition to paintings and drawings, it has ironwork, glass, and ceramics. Also on this square, you'll see **Palau Maricel**—a sumptuous old mansion that's sometimes open to the public for concerts in the summer (ask at TI). The third museum is the **Museu Romàntic.** Offering a look at 19th-century bourgeois lifestyles (and a collection 400 antique dolls) in an elegant mansion, it's a few blocks up (one block west of main square: Head out of the square on the main pedestrian street, then take the first right turn, to Sant Gaudenci 1).

Nine **beaches,** separated by breakwaters, extend about a mile southward from town. Stroll down the seaside promenade, which stretches from the town to the end of the beaches. Anyone can enjoy the sun, sea, and sand; or you can rent a beach chair to relax like a pro. The crowds thin out about halfway down, and the last three beaches are more intimate and cove-like. Along the way, restaurants and *chiringuitos* (beach bars) serve tapas, paella, and drinks. If you walk all the way to the end, you can continue inland to enjoy the nicely landscaped **Terramar Gardens** (Jardins de Terramar; free, long hours daily).

Sleeping in Sitges: Hotel values are not much better in this swanky beach resort than in Barcelona. As this is a party town, expect some noise after hours (request a quiet room). If staying overnight, consider **$$ Hotel Celimar,** a mid-sized place with small but modern rooms in a classic Modernista building facing the

beach (Paseo de la Ribera 20, tel. 938-110-170, www.hotelcelimar.
com, info@hotelcelimar.com) or the larger **$$ Hotel Romàntic,**
an old-fashioned-elegant, quirky, family-run place in an old villa,
a few blocks from the beach (some rooms in annex—Hotel de la
Renaixença, Sant Isidre 33, tel. 938-948-375, www.hotelromantic.
com, romantic@hotelromantic.com).

BARCELONA: PAST AND PRESENT

Barcelona has thrived for 2,500 years. Its location is ideal: on a gently sloping plain facing the Mediterranean, where east-west sea trade meets the natural north-south highway to northern Europe. In its day, Barcelona has been a Roman retirement colony, a maritime power, a dynamo of the Industrial Age, and a cradle for all things modern. Today it cobbles together all these elements into a one-of-a-kind culture.

Keep in mind that Catalunya's history is quite distinct from that of the rest of Spain. Catalans pride themselves on their different language and independent traditions. When the rest of Spain was riding high, Catalunya was often in the doldrums, and vice versa.

The painter Joan Miró said, "We Catalans believe that you must plant your feet firmly on the ground in order to jump high in the air." This optimistic Catalan spirit—earthy but creative—has blossomed again and again through their history. Free spirits like Picasso, Dalí, Miró, Gaudí—and even Wilfred the Hairy—have all come from this small corner of Europe.

PREHISTORY AND ROMAN ORIGINS (C. 500 B.C.-A.D. 500)

The original Iberian inhabitants settled atop Barcelona's hills overlooking the harbor, creating settlements on Montjuïc and around today's Plaça de Sant Jaume. They called their town "Barkeno." The name may (or may not) derive from the famous family of

Hannibal Barca—the Carthaginian general who passed through the area with his war elephants en route to attacking Rome, in 218 B.C.

In 19 B.C., the (future) Roman Emperor Augustus conquered Iberia. The Romans made "Hispania" their agricultural breadbasket to feed the vast Empire. In Catalunya, they planted grapes on large farming estates and shipped the wine abroad from Barcelona's busy port. Roman "Barcino"—a pleasant, sun-bathed valley with Mediterranean breezes—became a retirement colony for soldiers.

Like most Roman cities, Barcino had a forum in the center of town (today's Plaça de Sant Jaume) and a grid pattern of streets. It was a tight, 30-acre town of some 4,000 inhabitants contained within a wall (the area around today's cathedral). More broadly, the Romans brought Barcelona the Latin language (which became modern Catalan) and a connection to the wider world.

Related Sights
- Barcelona History Museum (with Roman ruins in basement)
- Temple of Augustus
- Big, sculpted BARCINO letters on Plaça Nova
- Remnants of the Roman wall (especially the towers on Plaça Nova, near the cathedral)
- Roman necropolis near the Ramblas

MEDIEVAL (500-1000)

As the Roman Empire crumbled, Barcelona made a peaceful transition, coming under the protection of Christian Visigoths from

Germany who had strong Roman ties. Christianity had entered Barcelona during Rome's last years (when martyrs such as Saint Eulàlia were persecuted). The feisty Christians built their cathedral—the core of today's cathedral—atop the Roman Temple of Jupiter.

In 711, the Moors (Muslim invaders from North Africa) swept through Spain, and Barcelona surrendered without a fight. While Moorish culture went on to dominate much of Spain for the next 700 years, its impact on Catalunya was minimal. In 801, Barcelona was liberated by Charlemagne's son, who made it part of the Frankish empire under the rule of Frankish "Counts." When Count Wilfred the Hairy (so called because he was; ruled 878-898) declared himself independent of the Franks, he launched a golden age in Barcelona.

Related Sights
- Cathedral (with its original fourth-century font)
- St. Eulàlia's tomb and silver statue in the cathedral

THE KINGDOM OF ARAGON (1000-1500)

Wilfred the Hairy's heirs sprouted and grew into powerful sea-traders who connected Catalunya to the world. When Count Ramon of Barcelona married Petronila of Aragon in 1137, it united their two realms, creating the powerful kingdom of Aragon.

King Jaume I the Conqueror (1208-1276) led Aragon's powerful army and navy in acquiring rich trading ports in the Mediterranean. He also established the Catalan Generalitat, one of Europe's first parliaments, which still governs the region today. By 1450, the Crown of Aragon ruled a mercantile empire that stretched across the Mediterranean, from eastern Spain to southern Italy to Greece. Barcelona flourished.

In 1469 came another powerful marriage: King Ferdinand II of Aragon married Isabel of Castile. This power couple—the so-called Catholic Monarchs—united the peninsula's two largest kingdoms. They drove the last Moors out of Granada, expelled the Jews, and created a unified nation-state. They sent Christopher Columbus to explore new lands under the Spanish flag. And where did Columbus come first to debrief the Catholic Monarchs upon his return? To Barcelona.

Related Sights
- The medieval legacy lives on in lots of Neo-Gothic and medieval motifs in Modernisme (especially the city symbol of St. George slaying the dragon)
- The El Born neighborhood, which flourished during this time
- Catalan Art Museum (excellent Romanesque collection)
- Columbus Monument
- Plaça del Rei and the Royal Palace, where Columbus met Ferdinand and Isabel
- The coffin of Count Ramon in the cathedral
- Generalitat building and statue of Jaume I on Plaça de Sant Jaume
- The churches of Santa Maria del Mar, Santa Maria del Pi, and the Chapel of St. Agatha (at the Royal Palace), plus the *extra muro* ("outside the walls") Church of Santa Anna
- Montserrat monastery, dating from medieval times

Church Architecture

History comes to life when you visit a centuries-old church. Even if you don't know your apse from a hole in the ground, learning a few simple terms will enrich your experience. Note that not every church will have every feature, and a "cathedral" isn't a type of architecture, but rather a designation for a church that's a governing center for a local bishop.

Aisles: The long, generally low-ceilinged arcades that flank the nave.

Altar: The raised area with a ceremonial table (often adorned with candles or a crucifix), where the priest prepares and serves the bread and wine for Communion.

Apse: The space beyond the altar, generally bordered with small chapels.

Barrel Vault: A continuous round-arched ceiling that resembles an extended upside-down U.

Choir: A cozy area, often screened off, located within the church nave and near the high altar, where services are sung in a more intimate setting.

Cloister: Covered hallways bordering a square or rectangular open-air courtyard, traditionally where monks and nuns got fresh air.

Facade: The exterior surface of the church's main (west) entrance, generally highly decorated.

Groin Vault: An arched ceiling formed where two equal barrel vaults meet at right angles. Less common usage: term for a medieval jock strap.

Narthex: The area (portico or foyer) between the main entry and the nave.

Nave: The long, central section of the church (running west to east, from the entrance to the altar) where the congregation sits or stands during the service.

Transept: In a traditional cross-shaped floor plan, the transept is one of the two parts forming the "arms" of the cross. The transepts run north-south, perpendicularly crossing the east-west nave.

West Portal: The main entry to the church (on the west end, opposite the main altar).

DECLINE (1500-1800)

Ironically, the glorious age of Ferdinand and Isabel also sowed the seeds of Barcelona's decline. Columbus' discoveries opened new Atlantic trade routes that made Barcelona's Mediterranean trade routes obsolete. Meanwhile, the center of royal power slowly shifted from Barcelona to the region midway between Aragon and Castile—the growing city of Madrid. While the rest of Spain enjoyed an unprecedented Golden Age of fabulous New World wealth and influence (producing artists such as El Greco, Velázquez, Goya, and Murillo), Barcelona became a poor and forgotten backwater.

On September 11, 1714—a date that is still marked by Catalunya's most sobering holiday—Catalan independence ended. Barcelona found itself on the losing end in the War of Spanish Succession (1701-1714), having sided against the eventual winner, the French-backed King Philip V. On September 11, Philip's forces overran the city walls and massacred those who had stood against him.

For more than a century, the Spanish crown centered in Madrid would punish the rebellious Catalans. They suppressed the Catalan language, culture, and institutions. The Generalitat was disbanded. Trade with the Americas was forbidden. For surveillance and control, the Castilians built an imposing citadel on one side of town and a fortress atop Montjuïc on the other, and ordered that nothing could be built beyond the reach of the fort's cannons. Barcelona spiraled down into a dirty, cramped city contained within its medieval wall.

Related Sights
- Monument to Catalan Independence in El Born (honoring the victims of September 11, 1714)
- Castle of Montjuïc
- Citadel Park (previously the site of the citadel)
- Barceloneta fishermen's quarter (built to house those displaced by Citadel construction)
- Betlem Church on the Ramblas (rare example of Baroque)

INDUSTRIAL REVIVAL AND CULTURAL RENAISSANCE (1800-1900)

In the 1800s, another revolution was brewing—the Industrial Revolution. Blessed with soft coal and rushing rivers from the Pyrenees, Barcelona harnessed the power to stoke textile mills. Having finally been given permission to trade with the Americas (1788), they imported cotton and shipped the finished cloth abroad from their busy harbor. Workers flocked in from the countryside, drawn by good-paying jobs. Barcelona's population doubled, reaching a million, and it created a thriving middle class.

By 1850—while the rest of Spain stagnated as a fading colonial power—Catalunya was humming. In 1854, Queen Isabella II finally loosened Madrid's death-grip, allowing the growing city to tear down the medieval wall and expand northward, creating the Eixample neighborhood of modern boulevards. They used new technology to make life better for everyday citizens, bringing in modern plumbing, streetlights, and the first rail line in Spain. The city hosted a World's Fair in 1888 that renovated the city (and gave us the Columbus Monument and other urban improvements).

There was a cultural renaissance of the Catalan language and the arts. Historians divide the movement (somewhat arbitrarily) into two parts. The Renaixença (roughly 1840-1880) was a rediscovery of Catalunya's historic roots and national identity, similar to the Romantic movements sweeping all of Europe. Suddenly, people were embracing the language and traditions of their forebears. Writers wrote in Catalan, and artists revived the medieval motifs of Barcelona's 14th-century glory days. This energy flowed naturally into Modernisme (roughly 1890-1910), which continued the love affair with Catalunya's traditions while championing all things modern—things like streetcars and electric lights. The new technology was also meant to be beautiful, and Modernisme is Barcelona's version of the curvy, wistful Art Nouveau style found elsewhere in Europe. As the old city walls came down, Modernista architects like Antoni Gaudí remade the city with fanciful buildings—made of a modern concrete-and-iron substructure but decorated with colorful, playful, medieval motifs.

Related Sights

- The Eixample neighborhood, with the Block of Discord, La Pedrera, and other buildings
- Sagrada Família
- Other Gaudí and Modernista sights (see sidebar on page 144)

TURBULENT 20TH CENTURY

By the turn of the 20th century, Barcelona was seething with change. Industrialization had made factory owners rich, but the working class was still poor, living in dirty slums, and working in unsafe factories. Barcelona's Socialists fought for the right to bathroom breaks, while anarchists bombed the Liceu Opera House. The unrest culminated in the bloody riots of "Tragic Week" (1909),

Catalans You May Know

Catalans invented the submarine, assassinated Leon Trotsky, and founded San Diego. Here are a few names you may be familiar with.

Pablo Picasso (1881-1973)—Though he was born in Andalucía (to Spanish, not Catalan, parents) and spent his adult life in France, Picasso's formative teenage years were spent in Barcelona's Barri Gòtic.

Salvador Dalí (1904-1989)—The master Surrealist was born in Figueres, spent holidays in Cadaqués, and passed his formative years in Barcelona, where he exhibited his early works and soaked up Gaudí's dreamlike architecture.

Joan Miró (1893-1983)—Raised in the Barri Gòtic, he divided his adulthood living between Barcelona and Paris. His whimsical sculptures and ceramics adorn Barcelona.

Antoni Gaudí (1852-1926)—Resident of the Barri Gòtic (in his youth), the Eixample (in young adulthood), and Park Güell (in his twilight years). Gaudí's buildings are the iconic symbols of Barcelona's Modernista revival.

Pau (Pablo) Casals (1876-1973)—A world-class cellist who's often described as one of the best musicians ever to pick up the instrument, he retired to French Catalunya in protest against Franco.

Bacardi Rum Family—The world-famous rum company was founded in Cuba in 1814 by a man from Sitges; it's now run by his great-great-grandson.

Juan Antonio Samaranch (1920-2010)—The longtime president of the International Olympic Committee (r. 1980-2001) was born and raised in Barcelona.

Ferran Adrià (b. 1962)—This celebrity chef revolutionized cuisine with his innovations in molecular gastronomy at the (now-closed) Costa Brava restaurant El Bulli.

Antoni Tàpies (1923-2012)—Spain's best-known postwar artist is most famous for his distinctive mud-caked canvases.

Pau Gasol (b. 1980) and **Marc Gasol** (b. 1985)—Basketball-playing brothers who gained fame in the NBA.

Rafael Nadal (b. 1986)—The "King of Clay," a world-ranked tennis player and frequent Grand Slam winner, is from the Catalan-speaking island of Mallorca.

during which dozens of churches were vandalized and demonstrators were shot in the streets.

Barcelona developed a reputation across Spain as a breeding ground for liberals, troublemakers, and nonconformists. In the art world, young Pablo Picasso captured the plight of society's disenfranchised (in his Blue Period), then moved to Paris and—with fellow artist Georges Braque—broke all the rules of art by pioneering Cubism. Joan Miró perplexed the masses with his childlike doodles, and Salvador Dalí shocked and astonished with his Surrealistic dreamscapes.

When Spain splintered into its bitter Civil War (1936-1939)—pitting democratic Republicans against fascist Nationalists—left-leaning Barcelona became the natural capital of the Republican side. The fascists, under General Francisco Franco (1892-1975), invited Mussolini's Italian air force to bomb Barcelona, killing a thousand citizens. When Barcelona finally fell in 1939, the war was effectively over. For the next four decades, Franco would rule Spain with an iron fist.

Catalunya was punished. The Generalitat was abolished after having been restored just a few years earlier, and the Catalan president was executed by firing squad. Franco began a program of Castilianization to assimilate the region into greater Spain. The Catalan language and traditions were suppressed. You couldn't buy a newspaper in Catalan or hear the people's language spoken on TV. You couldn't dance the *sardana*. Simultaneously, the region was flooded with poor, Castilian-speaking farmers from the rest of Spain, looking for work. The city expanded way too fast, throwing up dusty gray concrete buildings amid suburban sprawl.

But Catalunya kept the flame alive with underground newspapers and a president-in-exile living in France. Finally, Franco died in 1975, and—on September 11, 1977—millions of Catalan patriots flooded the streets to demand they get their culture back.

It ushered in a third golden age for Catalunya. The Generalitat and Catalan president returned. Catalan became the sole official language in schools. Barcelona reinvented itself, spiffing up old quarters with new buildings and expanding the Metro system. The Sagrada Família, after nearly a century of false starts, made dramatic progress. In 1992, a revived Barcelona hosted the Summer Olympic Games—for which they rebuilt Montjuïc and the waterfront—and put on a modern face for the world.

Related Sights

- Picasso Museum
- Fundació Joan Miró, plus Liceu mosaic in the Ramblas, *Woman and Bird* sculpture, and other public works by Miró
- Figueres, hometown of Salvador Dalí
- Cadaqués, a mecca for modern artists
- 1929 World Expo Fairgrounds, including Magic Fountains (at the base of Montjuïc, near Plaça d'Espanya)
- Fresh-looking Montjuïc (with Olympic Stadium) and the rejuvenated waterfront

- *Barcelona Head* sculpture by Roy Lichtenstein, on the waterfront

CATALUNYA TODAY: FEISTY AND PROUD

Today Catalunya speeds into the future on a course that may diverge from the rest of Spain. With each visit, I seem to hear more Catalan and less Spanish spoken in the streets. With a population of 1.6 million, Barcelona is Spain's second city.

Along with the rest of Spain, Catalunya has suffered from the global economic downturn that began in 2008. Spain's real-estate bubble burst, banks stopped lending, and unemployment soared. So many young Spaniards are out of work that a new name was coined to describe them: *"generación ni-ni"* (the neither-nor generation). Under pressure from the European Union, Spain is working to dig itself out of debt.

Barcelona continues its legacy of feisty independence. Regular massive demonstrations fill Plaça de Catalunya, as the people fight to regain their cultural heritage. As if to underscore their cultural distance from greater Spain, in 2010 Barcelona outlawed the widely popular Spanish pastime of bullfighting. The Las Arenas bullring is now a shopping mall.

With pro-independence parties holding a majority in the Catalunya parliament, politicians scheduled a vote on leaving Spain for late 2014—300 years after the massacre that ended independence. But the national government contended any vote was illegal under the Spanish constitution and vowed to block the special election. While the outcome remains unclear, it's certain that the proud Catalan people will continue to push for more autonomy.

Related Sights
- *Sardana* dances in front of the cathedral
- The red-and-gold flag of Catalunya flapping in the breeze

For more on history, consider *Europe 101: History and Art for the Traveler*, written by Rick Steves and Gene Openshaw (available at www.ricksteves.com).

PRACTICALITIES

Contents

This chapter covers the practical skills of European travel: how to get tourist information, pay for purchases, sightsee efficiently, use technology wisely, and get between destinations smoothly. To study ahead and round out your knowledge, check out "Resources" for a summary of recommended books and films.

Tourist Information

Spain's national tourist office **in the US** will fill brochure requests and answer your general travel questions by email (newyork. information@tourspain.es). Scan their website (www.spain.info) and Barcelona's (www.barcelonaturisme.cat) for practical information and sightseeing ideas; you can download many brochures free of charge from the national website.

In Barcelona, your best first stop is at any of its tourist information offices (see page 21). TIs are good places to pick up a city map and get information on public transportation (including bus and train schedules), walking tours, special events, and nightlife.

While TIs are eager to book you a room, use their room-finding service only as a last resort. They are unable to give hard opinions on the relative value of one place over another. The accommodations stakes are too high to go potluck through the TI. Even if there's no "fee," you'll save yourself and your host money by going direct with the listings in this book.

Websites: In addition to the TI websites listed above, try www.barcelonaplanning.com, www.guiadelocio.com/barcelona, and www.butxaca.com. The latter two sites focus on events and are in Spanish and Catalan, respectively, but are decipherable.

Travel Tips

Emergency and Medical Help: In **Spain,** dial 091 or 092 for police help and 112 in any emergency (medical or otherwise). If you get sick, do as the Spanish do and go to a pharmacist for advice. Or ask at your hotel for help—they'll know the nearest medical and emergency services.

Theft or Loss: To replace a passport, you'll need to go in person to an embassy or consulate (see page 313). If your credit and debit cards disappear, cancel and replace them (see "Damage Control for Lost Cards" on page 279). File a police report, either on the spot or within a day or two; you'll need it to submit an insurance claim for lost or stolen rail passes or travel gear, and it can help with replacing your passport or credit and debit cards. Precautionary measures can minimize the effects of loss—back up your digital photos and other files frequently. For more information, see www.ricksteves.com/help.

Thieves target tourists throughout Spain, especially in Barcelona. While hotel rooms are generally safe, thieves break into cars, snatch purses, and pick pockets. Thieves zipping by on motorbikes grab handbags from pedestrians or even from cars in traffic (by reaching through open car windows at stoplights). A fight or commotion is created to enable pickpockets to work unnoticed. Be on guard, use a money belt, and treat any disturbance around you as a smoke screen for theft. Don't believe any "police officers" looking for counterfeit bills.

Time Zones: Spain, like most of continental Europe, is generally six/nine hours ahead of the East/West Coasts of the US. The exceptions are the beginning and end of Daylight Saving Time: Europe "springs forward" the last Sunday in March (two weeks after most of North America), and "falls back" the last Sunday in October (one week before North America). For a handy online time converter, try www.timeanddate.com/worldclock.

Business Hours: For visitors, Spain is a land of strange and frustrating schedules. Many businesses respect the afternoon siesta. When it's 100 degrees in the shade you'll understand why. The

PRACTICALITIES

biggest museums stay open all day. Smaller ones often close for a siesta. From Monday through Friday, shops generally open at 9:00 or 10:00, close at lunchtime (around 13:00 or 14:00), reopen at 16:30 or 17:00, then close at 20:00 or 21:00. On Saturdays, many shops are open only in the morning. On Sundays, many shops are closed, including La Boqueria and Santa Caterina markets, but sightseeing attractions are generally open. Banking hours are generally Monday through Friday from 9:00 to 14:00.

Watt's Up? Europe's electrical system is 220 volts, instead of North America's 110 volts. Most newer electronics (such as laptops, battery chargers, and hair dryers) convert automatically, so you won't need a converter, but you will need an adapter plug with two round prongs, sold inexpensively at travel stores in the US. Avoid bringing older appliances that don't automatically convert voltage; instead, buy a cheap replacement at a Barcelona department store (see the Shopping in Barcelona chapter).

Discounts: Discounts are not listed in this book. However, many sights offer discounts for youths (up to age 18), students (with proper identification cards, www.isic.org), families, seniors (loosely defined as retirees or those willing to call themselves seniors), and groups of 10 or more. Always ask. Some discounts are available only for citizens of the European Union (EU).

Online Translation Tip: You can use Google's Chrome browser (available free at www.google.com/chrome) to instantly translate websites. With one click, the page appears in (very rough) English translation. You can also paste the URL of the site into the translation window at www.google.com/translate.

Money

This section offers advice on how to pay for purchases on your trip (including getting cash from ATMs and paying with plastic), dealing with lost or stolen cards, VAT (sales tax) refunds, and tipping.

WHAT TO BRING

Bring both a credit card and a debit card. You'll use the debit card at cash machines (ATMs) to withdraw local cash for most purchases, and the credit card to pay for larger items. Some travelers carry a third card, in case one gets demagnetized or eaten by a temperamental machine.

For an emergency stash, bring several hundred dollars in hard cash in $20 bills. If you need to exchange bills, go to a bank; avoid using currency-exchange booths because of their lousy rates and/or outrageous fees.

> # Exchange Rate
>
> ### 1 euro (€) = about $1.40
>
> To convert prices in euros to dollars, add about 40 percent: €20 = about $28, €50 = about $70. (Check www.oanda.com for the latest exchange rates.) Just like the dollar, one euro (€) is broken down into 100 cents. Coins range from €0.01 to €2, and bills from €5 to €500.

CASH

Cash is just as desirable in Europe as it is at home. Small businesses (B&Bs, mom-and-pop cafés, shops, etc.) prefer that you pay your bills with cash. Some vendors will charge you extra for using a credit card, and some won't take credit cards at all. Cash is the best—and sometimes only—way to pay for cheap food, bus fares, taxis, and local guides.

Throughout Europe, ATMs are the standard way for travelers to get cash. To withdraw money from an ATM (known as a *cajero automático* in Spanish and *caixer automàtic* in Catalan), you'll need a debit card (ideally with a Visa or MasterCard logo for maximum usability), plus a PIN code. Know your PIN code in numbers; there are only numbers—no letters—on European keypads. For increased security, shield the keypad when entering your PIN code, and don't use an ATM if anything on the front of the machine looks loose or damaged (a sign that someone may have attached a "skimming" device to capture account information). Try to withdraw large sums of money to reduce the number of per-transaction bank fees you'll pay.

When possible, use ATMs located outside banks—a thief is less likely to target a cash machine near surveillance cameras, and if your card is munched by a machine, you can go inside for help. Stay away from "independent" ATMs such as Travelex, Euronet, Moneybox, Cardpoint, and Cashzone, which charge huge commissions, have terrible exchange rates, and may try to trick users with "dynamic currency conversion" (described at the end of "Credit and Debit Cards," next).

Although you can use a credit card for ATM transactions, it only makes sense in an emergency, because it's considered a cash advance (borrowed at a high interest rate) rather than a withdrawal.

While traveling, if you want to monitor your accounts online to detect any unauthorized transactions, be sure to use a secure connection (see page 294).

Pickpockets target tourists. To safeguard your cash, wear a money belt—a pouch with a strap that you buckle around your waist like a belt and tuck under your clothes. Keep your cash, credit cards, and passport secure in your money belt, and carry only a day's spending money in your front pocket.

CREDIT AND DEBIT CARDS

For purchases, Visa and MasterCard are more commonly accepted than American Express. Just like at home, credit or debit cards work easily at larger hotels, restaurants, and shops. I typically use my debit card to withdraw cash to pay for most purchases. I use my credit card only in a few specific situations: to book hotel reservations by phone, to cover major expenses (such as car rentals, plane tickets, and long hotel stays), and to pay for things near the end of my trip (to avoid another visit to the ATM). While you could use a debit card to make most large purchases, using a credit card offers a greater degree of fraud protection (because debit cards draw funds directly from your account).

Ask Your Credit- or Debit-Card Company: Before your trip, contact the company that issued your debit or credit cards.

• Confirm that your **card will work overseas,** and alert them that you'll be using it in Europe; otherwise, they may deny transactions if they perceive unusual spending patterns.

• Ask for the specifics on transaction **fees.** When you use your credit or debit card—either for purchases or ATM withdrawals—you'll often be charged additional "international transaction" fees of up to 3 percent (1 percent is normal) plus $5 per transaction. If your card's fees seem high, consider getting a different card just for your trip: Capital One (www.capitalone.com) and most credit unions have low-to-no international transaction fees.

• If you plan to take out cash from ATMs, confirm your daily **withdrawal limit,** and if necessary, ask your bank to adjust it. Some travelers prefer a high limit that allows them to take out more cash at each ATM stop (saving on bank fees), while others prefer to set a lower limit in case their card is stolen. Note that foreign banks also set maximum withdrawal amounts for their ATMs. Also, remember that you're withdrawing euros, not dollars—so if your daily limit is $300, withdraw just €200. Many frustrated travelers walk away from ATMs thinking their cards have been rejected, when actually they were asking for more cash in euros than their daily limit allowed.

• Get your bank's emergency **phone number** in the US (but not its 800 number, which isn't accessible from overseas) to call collect if you have a problem.

• Ask for your credit card's **PIN** in case you need to make an emergency cash withdrawal or encounter Europe's "chip-and-PIN" system; the bank won't tell you your PIN over the phone, so allow time for it to be mailed to you.

Chip and PIN: While much of Europe is shifting to a "chip-and-PIN" security system for credit and debit cards, Spain mostly uses the old magnetic-swipe technology. (European chip-and-PIN cards are embedded with an electronic security chip, and require the purchaser to punch in a PIN rather than sign a receipt.) If you happen to encounter chip and PIN, it will probably be at payment machines, such as those at train stations, toll roads, or self-serve gas pumps. On the outside chance that a machine won't take your card, find a cashier who can make your card work (they can print a receipt for you to sign), or find a machine that takes cash. But don't panic. Most travelers who are carrying only magnetic-stripe cards don't run into problems. You can always use an ATM to withdraw cash with your magnetic-stripe card, even in countries where people predominantly use chip-and-PIN cards.

Dynamic Currency Conversion: If merchants offer to convert your purchase price into dollars (called dynamic currency conversion, or DCC), refuse this "service." You'll pay even more in fees for the expensive convenience of seeing the amount in dollars. "Independent" ATMs (such as Travelex and Moneybox) may try to confuse customers by presenting DCC in misleading terms. If an ATM offers to "lock in" or "guarantee" your conversion rate, choose "proceed without conversion." Other prompts might state, "You can be charged in dollars: Press YES for dollars, NO for euros." Always choose the local currency in these situations.

DAMAGE CONTROL FOR LOST CARDS

If you lose your credit, debit, or ATM card, you can stop people from using your card by reporting the loss immediately to the respective global customer-assistance centers. Call these 24-hour US numbers collect: Visa (tel. 303/967-1096, toll-free number in Spain is 900-991-124); MasterCard (tel. 636/722-7111); and American Express (tel. 336/393-1111). In Spain, to make a collect call to the US, dial 900-99-0011. Press zero or stay on the line for an English-speaking operator. European toll-free numbers (listed by country) can be found at the websites for Visa and MasterCard.

Providing the following information will allow for a quicker cancellation of your missing card: full card number, whether you are the primary or secondary cardholder, the cardholder's name exactly as printed on the card, billing address, home phone number, circumstances of the loss or theft, and identification verification (your birth date, your mother's maiden name, or your Social Security number—memorize this, don't carry a copy). If you are the secondary cardholder, you'll also need to provide the primary cardholder's identification-verification details. You can generally receive a temporary card within two or three business days in Europe (see www.ricksteves.com/help for more).

If you report your loss within two days, you typically won't be responsible for any unauthorized transactions on your account, although many banks charge a liability fee of $50.

TIPPING

Tipping in Spain isn't as automatic and generous as it is in the US. For special service, tips are appreciated, but not expected. As in the US, the proper amount depends on your resources, tipping philosophy, and the circumstances, but some general guidelines apply.

Restaurants: If you order a meal at a counter—as you often will when sampling tapas at a bar—there's no need to tip (though if you buy a few tapas, you can round up the bill a few small coins). At restaurants with table service, most Spaniards tip nothing or next to nothing; a service charge is generally included in the bill (*servei inclós* in Catalan, or *servicio incluido* in Spanish). If you like to tip for good service, give up to 5 percent extra. If service is not included (*servei no inclós* in Catalan, or *servicio no incluido* in Spanish), you could tip up to 10 percent. At most places, you can leave the tip on the table. But if you're eating at an outdoor café, hand the tip to your server to avoid having it swiped by a passerby. Also, it's best to tip in cash even if you pay with your credit card. Otherwise the tip may never reach your server.

Taxis: Spanish people rarely give tips in taxis, unless it's to round up to the next full euro (if the fare is €4.85, they'll give €5). If the cabbie hauls your bags and zips you to the airport to help you catch your flight, you might want to toss in a little more. But if you feel like you're being driven in circles or otherwise ripped off, skip the tip.

Services: In general, if someone in the service industry does a super job for you, a small tip of a euro or two is appropriate...but not required. If you're not sure whether (or how much) to tip for a service, ask your hotelier or at the TI.

GETTING A VAT REFUND

Wrapped into the purchase price of your Spanish souvenirs is a Value-Added Tax (VAT) of 21 percent (in Spain, it's called IVA—*Impuesto sobre el Valor Añadido*). You're entitled to get most of that tax back if you purchase more than €90.15 (about $125) worth of goods at a store that participates in the VAT-refund scheme. Typically, you must ring up the minimum at a single retailer—you can't add up your purchases from various shops to reach the required amount.

Getting your refund is usually straightforward and, if you buy a substantial amount of souvenirs, well worth the hassle. If you're lucky, the merchant will subtract the tax when you make your purchase. (This is more likely to occur if the store ships the goods to your home.) Otherwise, you'll need to:

Get the paperwork. Have the merchant completely fill out the necessary refund document. You'll have to present your passport at the store. Get the paperwork done before you leave the store to ensure you'll have everything you need (including your original sales receipt).

Get your stamp at the border or airport. Process your VAT document at your last stop in the European Union (such as at the airport) with the customs agent who deals with VAT refunds. Arrive an additional hour early before you need to check in for your flight, to allow time to find the local customs office—and to stand in line. It's best to keep your purchases in your carry-on. If they're too large or dangerous to carry on (such as knives), pack them in your checked bags and alert the check-in agent. You'll be sent (with your tagged bag) to a customs desk outside security, which will examine your bag, stamp your paperwork, and put your bag on the belt. You're not supposed to use your purchased goods before you leave. If you show up at customs wearing your new flamenco outfit, officials might look the other way—or deny you a refund.

Collect your refund. You'll need to return your stamped document to the retailer or its representative. Many merchants work with a service, such as Global Blue or Premier Tax Free, that has offices at major airports, ports, or border crossings (either before or after security, probably strategically located near a duty-free shop). These services, which extract a 4 percent fee, can refund your money immediately in cash or credit your card (within two billing cycles). If the retailer handles VAT refunds directly, it's up to you to contact the merchant for your refund. You can mail the documents from home or, more quickly, from your point of departure (using an envelope you've prepared in advance or one that's been provided by the merchant). You'll then have to wait—it can take months.

CUSTOMS FOR AMERICAN SHOPPERS

You are allowed to take home $800 worth of items per person duty-free, once every 30 days. You can take home many processed and packaged foods: vacuum-packed cheeses, dried herbs, jams, baked goods, candy, chocolate, oil, vinegar, mustard, and honey. Fresh fruits and vegetables and most meats are not allowed. However, canned meat is allowed if it doesn't contain any beef, veal, lamb, or mutton. As for alcohol, you can bring in one liter duty-free (it can be packed securely in your checked luggage, along with any other liquid-containing items).

PRACTICALITIES

To bring alcohol (or liquid-packed foods) in your carry-on bag on your flight home, buy it at a duty-free shop at the airport. You'll increase your odds of getting it onto a connecting flight if it's packaged in a "STEB"—a secure, tamper-evident bag. But stay away from liquids in opaque, ceramic, or metallic containers, which usually cannot be successfully screened (STEB or no STEB).

To check customs rules and duty rates, visit www.cbp.gov.

Sightseeing

Sightseeing can be hard work. Use these tips to make your visits to Barcelona's finest sights meaningful, fun, efficient, and painless.

PLAN AHEAD

Set up an itinerary that allows you to fit in all your must-see sights. For a one-stop look at opening hours, see "Barcelona at a Glance" (page 38; also see "Daily Reminder" on page 20). Most sights keep stable hours, but you can easily confirm the latest by checking with the TI or visiting museum websites.

Don't put off visiting a must-see sight—you never know when a place will close unexpectedly for a holiday, strike, or restoration. Many museums are closed or have reduced hours at least a few days a year, especially on holidays such as Christmas, New Year's, and Labor Day (May 1). A list of holidays is on page 314; check museum websites for possible closures during your trip. Off-season, many museums have shorter hours.

Going at the right time helps avoid crowds. This book offers tips on the best times to see specific sights. Try visiting popular sights very early or very late. Evening visits are usually peaceful, with fewer crowds. The Picasso Museum keeps evening hours year-round, and the Sagrada Família and La Pedrera stay open late in peak season (for an overview, see "Sights Open Late" on page 232).

Study up. To get the most out of the sight descriptions in this book, read them before you visit. Gaudí seems less gaudy if you understand his artistic vision.

AT SIGHTS

Here's what you can typically expect:

Entering: Be warned that you may not be allowed to enter if you arrive 30 to 60 minutes before closing time. And guards start ushering people out well before the actual closing time, so don't save the best for last.

Some important sights have a security check, where you must open your bag or send it through a metal detector. Some sights require you to check daypacks and coats. (If you'd rather not check your daypack, try carrying it tucked under your arm like a purse as you enter.)

At churches—which often offer interesting art (usually free) and a cool, welcome seat—a modest dress code (no bare shoulders or shorts) is encouraged though rarely enforced.

Photography: If the museum's photo policy isn't clearly posted, ask a guard. Generally, taking photos without a flash or tripod is allowed. Some sights ban photos altogether.

Temporary Exhibits: Museums may show special exhibits in addition to their permanent collection. Some exhibits are included in the entry price, while others come at an extra cost (which you may have to pay even if you don't want to see the exhibit).

Expect changes: Artwork can be on tour, on loan, out sick, or shifted at the whim of the curator. To adapt, pick up a floor plan as you enter, and ask museum staff if you can't find a particular item. Say the title or artist's name, or point to the photograph in this book, and ask, "Where is?" by saying "*¿Dónde está?*" (dohn-day ay-stah).

Audioguides: Many sights rent audioguides, which generally offer dry-but-useful recorded descriptions in English (about €3-4). If you bring your own earbuds, you can enjoy better sound and avoid holding the device to your ear. To save money, bring a Y-jack and share one audioguide with your travel partner. Increasingly, museums are offering apps (often free) that you can download to your mobile device.

Services: Important sights may have an on-site café or cafeteria (usually a handy place to rejuvenate during a long visit). The WCs at sights are free and generally clean.

Before Leaving: At the gift shop, scan the postcard rack or thumb through a guidebook to be sure that you haven't overlooked something that you'd like to see.

Every sight or museum offers more than what is covered in this book. Use the information in this book as an introduction—not the final word.

Communicating

"How can I stay connected in Europe?"—by phone and Internet—may be the most common question I hear from travelers. You have three basic options:

1. "Roam" with your US mobile device. This is the easiest option, but likely the most expensive. It works best for people who won't be making very many calls, and who value the convenience of sticking with what's familiar (and their own phone number). In recent years, as data roaming fees have dropped and free Wi-Fi has become easier to find, the majority of travelers are finding this to be the best all-around option.

2. Use an unlocked mobile phone with European SIM cards. This is a much more affordable option if you'll be making lots of calls, since it gives you 24/7 access to low European rates. Although remarkably cheap, this option does require a willingness to grapple with the technology and do a bit of shopping around for the right phone and card. Savvy travelers who routinely use SIM cards swear by them.

3. Use public phones and get online with your hotel's guest computer and/or at Internet cafés. These options can work in a pinch, particularly for travelers who simply don't want to hassle with the technology, or want to be (mostly) untethered from their home life while on the road.

Each of these options is explained in greater detail in the following pages. Mixing and matching works well. For example, I routinely bring along my smartphone for Internet chores and Skyping on Wi-Fi, but also carry an unlocked phone and buy cheap SIM cards for affordable calls on the go.

For an even more in-depth explanation of this complicated topic, see www.ricksteves.com/phoning.

HOW TO DIAL

Many Americans are intimidated by dialing European phone numbers. You needn't be. It's simple, once you break the code.

Dialing Within Spain

The following instructions apply whether you're dialing from a Spanish mobile phone or a landline (such as a pay phone or your hotel-room phone). If you're roaming with a US phone number, follow the "Dialing Internationally" directions described later.

About half of all European countries use area codes; the other half, including Spain, use a direct-dial system without area codes.

Land lines start with 9, and mobile lines start with 6. All phone numbers in Spain are nine digits (no area codes) that can be dialed direct throughout the country. For example, the phone number of one of my recommended Barcelona hotels is 933-015-151. That's exactly what you dial, whether you're calling the hotel from the Barcelona train station or from Madrid.

In Spain, numbers that start with 900 are toll-free; numbers that start with 901 and 902 have per-minute fees (about €0.04-0.07/minute from a landline; more from a mobile). Note that you can't call Spain's toll-free numbers from America, nor can you count on reaching America's toll-free numbers from Spain.

Hurdling the Language Barrier

Spain already presents the English-speaking traveler with one of the most formidable language barriers in Western Europe, and Barcelona adds its own twist to the challenge. About 75 percent of Barcelonans speak Catalan, the language unique to the Catalunya region. Though all Barcelonans speak Spanish, many locals insist on speaking Catalan first.

Many Barcelonans—especially those in the tourist trade—speak English, but still, many people don't. Locals visibly brighten when you know and use some key Catalan or Spanish words (see "Catalan Survival Phrases" on page 321 and "Spanish Survival Phrases" on page 319). Learn the key phrases. Travel with a phrase book, particularly if you want to interact with the people. You'll find that doors open more quickly and with more smiles when you can speak a few words of the language.

Dialing Internationally to or from Spain

Always start with the **international access code**—011 if you're calling from the US or Canada, 00 from anywhere in Europe. If you're dialing from a mobile phone, simply insert a + instead (by holding the 0 key). Dial the **country code** of the country you're calling (34 for Spain, or 1 for the US or Canada). Then dial the local number, keeping in mind that calling many countries requires dropping the initial zero of the phone number. (The European calling chart lists specifics per country.)

Calling from the US to Spain: To call the Barcelona hotel from the US, dial 011 (US access code), 34 (Spain's country code), then 933-015-151.

Calling from any European country to the US: To call my office in Edmonds, Washington, from anywhere in Europe, I dial 00 (Europe's access code), 1 (US country code), 425 (Edmonds' area code), and 771-8303.

More Dialing Tips

The chart on the next page shows how to dial per country. For online instructions, see www.countrycallingcodes.com or www.howtocallabroad.com.

Remember, if you're using a mobile phone, dial as if you're in that phone's country of origin. So, when roaming with your US phone number in Spain, dial as if you're calling from the US. But if you're using a European SIM card, dial as you would from that European country.

Note that calls to a European mobile phone are substantially more expensive than calls to a fixed line. Off-hour calls are generally cheaper.

For tips on communicating with someone who speaks another language, see sidebar above.

USING YOUR SMARTPHONE IN EUROPE

Even in this age of email, texting, and near-universal Internet access, smart travelers still use the telephone. I call TIs to smooth out sightseeing plans, hotels to get driving directions, museums to confirm tour schedules, restaurants to check open hours or to book a table, and so on.

Most people enjoy the convenience of bringing their own smartphone. Horror stories about sky-high roaming fees are dated and exaggerated, and major service providers work hard to avoid surprising you with an exorbitant bill. With a little planning, you can use your phone—for voice calls, messaging, and Internet access—without breaking the bank.

Start by figuring out whether your phone works in Europe. Most phones purchased through AT&T and T-Mobile (which use the same technology as Europe) work abroad, while only some phones from Verizon or Sprint do—check your operating manual (look for "tri-band," "quad-band," or "GSM"). If you're not sure, ask your service provider.

Roaming Costs

"Roaming" with your phone—that is, using it outside of its home region, such as in Europe—generally comes with extra charges, whether you are making voice calls, sending texts, or reading your email. The fees listed here are for the three major American providers—Verizon, AT&T, and T-Mobile; Sprint's roaming rates tend to be much higher. But policies change fast, so get the latest details before your trip. For example, as of mid-2014, T-Mobile waived voice, texting, and data roaming fees for some plans.

Voice calls are the most expensive. Most US providers charge from $1.29 to $1.99 per minute to make or receive calls in Europe. (As you cross each border, you'll typically get a text message explaining the rates in the new country.) If you plan to make multiple calls, look into a global calling plan to lower the per-minute cost, or buy a package of minutes at a discounted price (such as 30 minutes for $30). Note that you'll be charged for incoming calls whether or not you answer them; to save money ask your friends to stay in contact by texting, and to call you only in case of an emergency.

Text messaging costs 20 to 50 cents per text. To cut that cost, you could sign up for an international messaging plan (for example, $10 for 100 texts). Or consider apps that let you text for free (iMessage for Apple, Google Hangouts for Android, or WhatsApp for any device); however, these require you to use Wi-Fi or data roaming. Be aware that Europeans use the term "SMS" ("short message service") to describe text messaging.

Data roaming means accessing data service via a cellular network other than your home carrier's. Prices have dropped dramatically in recent years, making this an affordable way to bridge gaps between Wi-Fi hotspots. You'll pay far less if you set up an international data roaming plan. Most providers charge $25-30 for 100-120 megabytes of data. That's plenty for basic Internet tasks—100 megabytes lets you view 100 websites or send/receive 1,000 text-based emails, but you'll burn through that amount quickly by streaming videos or music. If your data use exceeds your plan amount, most providers will automatically kick in an additional 100- or 120-megabyte block for the same price. (For more on Wi-Fi versus data roaming—including strategies for conserving your data—see "Using Wi-Fi and Data Roaming," later.)

Setting Up (or Disabling) International Service

With most service providers, international roaming (voice, text, and data) is disabled on your account unless you call to activate it. Before your trip, call your provider (or navigate their website), and cover the following topics:

- Confirm that your phone will work in Europe.
- Verify global roaming rates for voice calls, text messaging, and data roaming.
- Tell them which of those services you'd like to activate.
- Consider any add-on plans to bring down the cost of international calls, texts, or data roaming.

When you get home from Europe, be sure to cancel any add-on plans that you activated for your trip.

Some people would rather use their smartphone exclusively on Wi-Fi, and not worry about either voice or data charges. If that's you, call your provider to be sure that international roaming options are deactivated on your account. To be double-sure, put your phone in "airplane mode," then turn your Wi-Fi back on.

Using Wi-Fi and Data Roaming

A good approach is to use free Wi-Fi wherever possible, and fill in the gaps with data roaming.

Wi-Fi—Internet access through a wireless router—is readily available throughout Europe. But just like at home, the quality of the signal may vary. Be patient, and don't get your hopes up. At accommodations, access is often free, but you may have to pay a fee, especially at expensive hotels. At hotels with thick stone walls, the Wi-Fi signal from the lobby may not reach every room. If Wi-Fi is important to you, ask about it when you book—and be specific ("In

PRACTICALITIES

PRACTICALITIES

European Calling Chart

Just smile and dial, using this key:
AC = Area Code, LN = Local Number.

European Country	Calling long distance within ...	Calling from the US or Canada to ...	Calling from a European country to ...
Austria	AC + LN	011 + 43 + AC (without initial zero) + LN	00 + 43 + AC (without initial zero) + LN
Belgium	LN	011 + 32 + LN (without initial zero)	00 + 32 + LN (without initial zero)
Bosnia-Herzegovina	AC + LN	011 + 387 + AC (without initial zero) + LN	00 + 387 + AC (without initial zero) + LN
Croatia	AC + LN	011 + 385 + AC (without initial zero) + LN	00 + 385 + AC (without initial zero) + LN
Czech Republic	LN	011 + 420 + LN	00 + 420 + LN
Denmark	LN	011 + 45 + LN	00 + 45 + LN
Estonia	LN	011 + 372 + LN	00 + 372 + LN
Finland	AC + LN	011 + 358 + AC (without initial zero) + LN	999 (or other 900 number) + 358 + AC (without initial zero) + LN
France	LN	011 + 33 + LN (without initial zero)	00 + 33 + LN (without initial zero)
Germany	AC + LN	011 + 49 + AC (without initial zero) + LN	00 + 49 + AC (without initial zero) + LN
Gibraltar	LN	011 + 350 + LN	00 + 350 + LN
Great Britain & N. Ireland	AC + LN	011 + 44 + AC (without initial zero) + LN	00 + 44 + AC (without initial zero) + LN
Greece	LN	011 + 30 + LN	00 + 30 + LN
Hungary	06 + AC + LN	011 + 36 + AC + LN	00 + 36 + AC + LN
Ireland	AC + LN	011 + 353 + AC (without initial zero) + LN	00 + 353 + AC (without initial zero) + LN
Italy	LN	011 + 39 + LN	00 + 39 + LN

European Country	Calling long distance within ...	Calling from the US or Canada to ...	Calling from a European country to ...
Latvia	LN	011 + 371 + LN	00 + 371 + LN
Montenegro	AC + LN	011 + 382 + AC (without initial zero) + LN	00 + 382 + AC (without initial zero) + LN
Morocco	LN	011 + 212 + LN (without initial zero)	00 + 212 + LN (without initial zero)
Netherlands	AC + LN	011 + 31 + AC (without initial zero) + LN	00 + 31 + AC (without initial zero) + LN
Norway	LN	011 + 47 + LN	00 + 47 + LN
Poland	LN	011 + 48 + LN	00 + 48 + LN
Portugal	LN	011 + 351 + LN	00 + 351 + LN
Russia	8 + AC + LN	011 + 7 + AC + LN	00 + 7 + AC + LN
Slovakia	AC + LN	011 + 421 + AC (without initial zero) + LN	00 + 421 + AC (without initial zero) + LN
Slovenia	AC + LN	011 + 386 + AC (without initial zero) + LN	00 + 386 + AC (without initial zero) + LN
Spain	LN	011 + 34 + LN	00 + 34 + LN
Sweden	AC + LN	011 + 46 + AC (without initial zero) + LN	00 + 46 + AC (without initial zero) + LN
Switzerland	LN	011 + 41 + LN (without initial zero)	00 + 41 + LN (without initial zero)
Turkey	AC (if there's no initial zero, add one) + LN	011 + 90 + AC (without initial zero) + LN	00 + 90 + AC (without initial zero) + LN

PRACTICALITIES

- The instructions above apply whether you're calling to or from a European landline or mobile phone.

- If calling from any mobile phone, you can replace the international access code with "+" (press and hold 0 to insert it).

- The international access code is 011 if you're calling from the US or Canada.

- To call the US or Canada from Europe, dial 00, then 1 (country code for US and Canada), then the area code and number. In short, 00 + 1 + AC + LN = Hi, Mom!

the rooms?"). Get the password and network name at the front desk when you check in.

When you're out and about, your best bet for finding free Wi-Fi is often at a café. They'll usually tell you the password if you buy something. Or you can stroll down a café-lined street, smartphone in hand, checking for unsecured networks every few steps until you find one that works. Some towns have free public Wi-Fi in highly trafficked parks or piazzas. You may have to register before using it, or get a password at the TI.

Data roaming is handy when you can't find usable Wi-Fi. Because you'll pay by the megabyte (explained earlier), it's best to limit how much data you use. Save bandwidth-gobbling tasks like Skyping, watching videos, or downloading apps or emails with large attachments until you're on Wi-Fi. Switch your phone's email settings from "push" to "fetch." This means that you can choose to "fetch" (download) your messages when you're on Wi-Fi rather than having them continuously "pushed" to your device. And be aware of apps—such as news, weather, and sports tickers—that automatically update. Check your phone's settings to be sure that none of your apps is set to "use cellular data."

I like the safeguard of manually turning off data roaming on my phone whenever I'm not actively using it. To turn off data and voice roaming, look in your phone's settings menu—try checking under "cellular" or "network," or ask your service provider how to do it. If you need to get online but can't find Wi-Fi, simply turn on data roaming long enough for the task at hand, then turn it off again.

Figure out how to keep track of how much data you've used (in your phone's menu, look for "cellular data usage"; you may have to reset the counter at the start of your trip). Some companies automatically send you a text message warning if you approach or exceed your limit.

There's yet another option: If you're traveling with an unlocked smartphone (explained later), you can buy a SIM card that also includes data; this can be far cheaper than data roaming through your home provider.

USING EUROPEAN SIM CARDS

Using your American phone in Europe is easy, but it's not always cheap. And unreliable Wi-Fi can make keeping in touch frustrating. If you're reasonably technology-savvy, and would like to have the option of making lots of affordable calls, it's worth getting comfortable with European SIM cards.

Here's the basic idea: With an unlocked phone (that works with different carriers), get a SIM card—the microchip that stores data about your phone—once you get to Europe. Slip in the SIM,

---

Internet Calling

To make totally free voice and video calls over the Internet, all you need are a smartphone, tablet, or laptop; a strong Wi-Fi signal; and an account with one of the major Internet calling providers: Skype (www.skype.com), FaceTime (preloaded on most Apple devices), or Google+ Hangouts (www.google. com/hangouts). If the Wi-Fi signal isn't strong enough for video, try sticking with an audio-only call. Or...wait for your next hotel. Many Internet calling programs also work for making calls from your computer to telephones worldwide for a very reasonable fee—generally just a few cents per minute (you'll have to buy some credit before you make your first call).

---

turn on the phone, and bingo! You've got a European phone number (and access to cheaper European rates).

Getting an Unlocked Phone

Your basic options are getting your existing phone unlocked, or buying a phone (either at home or in Europe).

Some phones are electronically "locked" so that you can't switch SIM cards (keeping you loyal to your carrier). But in some cases it's possible to unlock your phone—allowing you to replace the original SIM card with one that will work with a European provider. Some US carriers are beginning to offer phones/tablets whose SIM card can't be swapped out in the US but will accept a European SIM without any unlocking process.

You may already have an old, unused mobile phone in a drawer somewhere. Call your service provider and ask if they'll send you the unlock code. Otherwise, you can buy one: Search an online shopping site for an "unlocked quad-band phone," or buy one at a mobile-phone shop in Europe. Either way, a basic model typically costs $40 or less.

Buying and Using SIM Cards

Once you have an unlocked phone, you'll need to equip it with a SIM card. Note that the smaller SIM-card variation called a "micro-SIM" or "nano-SIM"—which is used in most iPhones—is less widely available in Europe.

SIM cards are sold at mobile-phone shops, department-store electronics counters, and newsstands for $5-10, and usually include about that much prepaid calling credit (making the card itself virtually free). Because SIM cards are prepaid, there's no contract and no commitment; I routinely buy one even if I'm in a country for only a few days.

However, an increasing number of countries—including Spain—require you to register the SIM card with your passport (an antiterrorism measure). This takes only a few minutes longer: The shop clerk will ask you to fill out a form, then submit it to the service provider. Sometimes you can register your own SIM card online. Either way, an hour or two after submitting the information, you'll get a text welcoming you to that network.

When using a SIM card in its home country, it's free to receive calls and texts, and it's cheap to make calls—domestic calls average 20 cents per minute. You can also use SIM cards to call the US—sometimes very affordably (Lebara and Lycamobile, which operate in multiple European countries, let you call a US number for less than 10 cents a minute). Rates are higher if you're roaming in another country. But if you bought the SIM card within the European Union, roaming fees are capped no matter where you travel throughout the EU (about 25 cents/minute to make calls, 7 cents/minute to receive calls, and 8 cents for a text message).

While you can buy SIM cards just about anywhere, I like to seek out a mobile-phone shop, where an English-speaking clerk can help explain my options, get my SIM card inserted and set up, and show me how to use it. When you buy your SIM card, ask about rates for domestic and international calls and texting, and about roaming fees. Also find out how to check your credit balance (usually you'll key in a few digits and hit "Send"). You can top up your credit at any newsstand, tobacco shop, mobile-phone shop, or many other businesses (look for the SIM card's logo in the window).

To insert your SIM card into the phone, locate the slot, which is usually on the side of the phone or behind the battery. Turning on the phone, you'll be prompted to enter the "SIM PIN" (a code number that came with your card).

If you have an unlocked smartphone, you can look for a European SIM card that covers both voice and data. This is often much cheaper than paying for data roaming through your home provider.

LANDLINE TELEPHONES AND INTERNET CAFÉS

If you prefer to travel without a smartphone or tablet, you can still stay in touch using landline telephones, hotel guest computers, and Internet cafés.

Landline Telephones

Phones in your **hotel room** can be great for local calls and for calls using cheap international phone cards (described in the sidebar). Many hotels charge a fee for local and "toll-free" as well as long-

Types of Telephone Cards

Europe uses two different types of telephone cards. Both types are sold at post offices, newsstands, street kiosks, tobacco shops, and train stations.

Insertable Phone Cards: These cards can only be used at pay phones. Simply take the phone off the hook, insert the card, wait until the digital display says *"Marque número,"* and dial away. Dial slowly and deliberately. Push the square R button to get a dial tone for a new call. The phone displays your credit ticking down as you talk. Each European country has its own insertable phone card—so your Spanish card won't work in a French phone.

International Phone Cards: These prepaid cards can be used to make inexpensive calls—within Europe, or to the US, for pennies a minute—from nearly any phone, including the one in your hotel room. The cards come with a toll-free number and a scratch-to-reveal PIN code. If the voice prompts aren't in English, experiment: Dial your code, followed by the pound sign (#), then the phone number, then pound again, and so on, until it works.

You can buy an international phone card, called *tarjeta telefónica con código,* at most kiosks and newsstands, but the best selection is usually at little shops catering to immigrants, who are the leading experts on calling home cheaply. You can also find them at call centers *(locutorios).* Buy a low denomination in case the card is a dud.

distance or international calls—always ask for the rates before you dial. Since you'll never be charged for receiving calls, it can be more affordable to have someone from the US call you in your room.

While **public pay phones** are on the endangered species list, you'll still see them in post offices and train stations. Pay phones generally come with multilingual instructions. Most public phones work with insertable phone cards (described in the sidebar).

You'll see many cheap **call shops** that advertise low rates to faraway lands, often in train-station neighborhoods. While these target immigrants who want to call home cheaply, tourists can use them, too. Before making your call, be completely clear on the rates.

Internet Cafés and Public Internet Terminals

Finding public Internet terminals in Europe is no problem. Many hotels have a computer in the lobby for guests to use. Otherwise, head for an Internet café, or ask the TI or your hotelier for the nearest place to access the Internet.

European computers typically use non-American keyboards. A few letters are switched around, and command keys are labeled in the local language. Many European keyboards have an "Alt Gr" key (for "Alternate Graphics") to the right of the space bar; press this to insert the extra symbol that appears on some keys. Spanish keyboards are a little different from ours; to type an @ symbol, press the "Alt Gr" key and 2 at the same time. If you can't locate a special character (such as the @ symbol), simply copy it from a Web page and paste it into your email message.

SECURITY OVER THE INTERNET

Whether you're accessing the Internet with your own device or at a public terminal, using a shared network or computer comes with the potential for increased security risks. Ask the hotel or café for the specific name of their Wi-Fi network, and make sure you log on to that exact one; hackers sometimes create a bogus hotspot with a similar or vague name (such as "Hotel Europa Free Wi-Fi"). It's better if a network uses a password (especially a hard-to-guess one) rather than being open to the world.

While traveling, you may want to check your online banking or credit-card statements, or take care of other personal-finance chores, but Internet security experts advise against accessing these sites entirely while traveling. Even if you're using your own computer at a password-protected hotspot, any hacker who's logged on to the same network can see what you're up to. If you need to log on to a banking website, try to do so on a hard-wired connection (i.e., using an Ethernet cable in your hotel room), or if that's not possible, use a secure banking app on a cellular telephone connection.

If using a credit card online, make sure that the site is secure. Most browsers display a little padlock icon, and the URL begins with *https* instead of *http*. Never send a credit-card number over a website that doesn't begin with *https*.

If you're not convinced a connection is secure, avoid accessing any sites (such as your bank's) that could be vulnerable to fraud.

MAIL

You can mail one package per day to yourself worth up to $200 duty-free from Europe to the US (mark it "personal purchases"). If you're sending a gift to someone, mark it "unsolicited gift." For details, visit www.cbp.gov and search for "Know Before You Go."

The Spanish postal service works fine, but for quick transatlantic delivery (in either direction), consider services such as DHL (www.dhl.com).

Transportation

If your trip will cover more of Spain than just Barcelona, you'll need to decide whether to rent a car or take public transportation. Cars are best for three or more traveling together (especially fami-

Buying Train Tickets

Trains can sell out, so it's smart to buy your tickets a day in advance, even for short rides. You have four options for buying train tickets: at the station, at a travel agency, online, or by phone. Since station ticket offices can get very crowded, most travelers will find it easiest to go to a travel agency, most of which charge only a nominal service fee.

At the Station: You will likely have to wait in a line to buy your ticket. First find the correct line—at bigger stations, there might be separate windows for short-distance, long-distance, advance, and "today" (*para hoy*) tickets. To avoid wasting time in the wrong line, read the signs carefully, and ask a local (or a clerk at an information window) which line you need. You might have to take a number—watch others and follow their lead. While clerks accept regular US credit cards, most RENFE ticket machines only take chip-and-PIN credit cards (described on page 279).

As another option, you could buy tickets or reservations at the RENFE offices located in more than 100 city centers. These are more central and multilingual—also less crowded and confusing—than the train station.

Travel Agency: The best choice for most travelers is to buy tickets at an English-speaking travel agency. The El Corte Inglés department stores (with locations in most Spanish cities) often have handy travel agencies inside. I've recommended these and other travel agencies throughout this book. Look for a train sticker in agency windows.

Online: Although the website www.renfe.com is useful for confirming schedules and prices, you cannot dependably buy tickets online unless you have a European credit card. The website rejects nearly every attempt to use a US card, but may accept PayPal payments. With patience and enough Spanish language skill, you might nab an online discount of up to 60 percent (available two weeks to two months ahead of travel). Online vendors based in the US include www.raileurope.com and www.petrabax.com (higher fees).

By Phone: You can purchase your ticket by phone with an American Express card (tel. 902-240-202), then pick it up at the station by punching your confirmation code (*localizador*) into one of the automated machines. Discounts up to 40 percent off are offered a week or more ahead by phone (and at stations).

You can also reserve tickets by phone, then buy them at the station, which you must do a few days before departure (at a ticket window, usually signed "*venta anticipada*"). You can't pay for reserved tickets at the station on your day of travel.

The Fine Print: First-class tickets cost 50 percent more than second class—often as much as a domestic flight. Discounted tickets come with restrictions, such as being nonrefundable and nonchangeable. Be sure to read all the details carefully at time of purchase.

PRACTICALITIES

lies with small kids), those packing heavy, and those scouring the countryside. Trains and buses are best for solo travelers, blitz tourists, city-to-city travelers, those with an ambitious, multi-country itinerary, and those who don't want to drive in Europe. While a car gives you more freedom, trains and buses zip you effortlessly and scenically from city to city, usually dropping you in the center, often near a TI. Cars are an expensive headache in places like Barcelona.

TRAINS

You can buy a Eurail Spain "flexi" rail pass that allows travel for a given number of days over a longer period of time, but you'll pay separately ($10-35) for seat reservations on all trains. Buying individual train tickets in advance or as you go in Spain can be less expensive, and gives you better access to seat reservations (which are limited for rail-pass holders). Some individual ticket prices already include seat reservations when required (for instance, for fast trains). RENFE also offers their own, eticketed "Renfe Spain Pass," which works entirely differently. It counts trips instead of calendar days, requires reservations to be made in chronological order, and is only sold on their website.

If your trip also includes a neighboring country, consider the Eurail France-Spain, Portugal-Spain, or Italy-Spain passes (see chart in this chapter). A Eurail Select pass lets you travel even farther. These passes are sold only outside Europe. Even if you have a rail pass, use buses when they're more convenient and direct than the trains. Remember to reserve ahead for the fast AVE trains and overnight journeys.

RENFE (the acronym for the Spanish national train system) used to mean "Really Exasperating, and Not For Everyone," but it has moved into the 21st century. For information and reservations, dial RENFE's national number (toll tel. 902-320-320) from anywhere in Spain, or visit www.renfe.com. For tips on buying tickets, see the sidebar.

Spain categorizes trains this way:

The high-speed train called the **AVE** (AH-vay, stands for *Alta Velocidad Española*) whisks travelers between Barcelona and Madrid in three hours or less, and Barcelona and Sevilla in 5.5 hours. For decades, Spain's trains didn't fit on Europe's tracks, but AVE trains run on standard European-gauge rails. AVE trains can be priced differently according to their time of departure. Peak hours *(punta)* are most expensive, followed by *llano* and *valle*

PRACTICALITIES

Rail Passes

Prices listed are for 2014 and are subject to change. For the latest prices, details, and train schedules (and easy online ordering), see www.ricksteves.com/rail.

"Saver" prices are per person for two or more people traveling together. "Youth" means under age 26. The fare for children 4–11 is half the adult individual fare or Saver fare. Kids under age 4 travel free.

SPAIN PASS

	1st Class	2nd Class
3 days in 2 months	$319	$256
Extra rail days (max 10)	41-48	33-39

SPAIN-PORTUGAL PASS

	Individual 1st Class	Saver 1st Class
3 days in 2 months	$364	$310
Extra rail days (max 7)	45-48	38-41

Map key:
Approximate point-to-point one way second-class rail fares in US dollars. First class costs 50 percent more. Add up fares for your itinerary to see whether a railpass will save you money. Dashed lines are buses and ferries (not covered by passes).

PRACTICALITIES

SELECTPASS

This pass covers travel in four adjacent countries, not including France.

	Individual 1st Class	Saver 1st Class	Youth 2nd Class
5 days in 2 months	$582	$495	$379
6 days in 2 months	635	540	414
8 days in 2 months	739	629	482
10 days in 2 months	845	719	551

FRANCE–SPAIN PASS

	Individual 1st Class	Individual 2nd Class	Saver 1st Class	Saver 2nd Class	Youth 2nd Class
4 days in 2 months	$439	$374	$374	$318	$287
Extra rail days (max 6)	45-51	38-44	38-44	33-37	29-33

ITALY–SPAIN PASS

Does not cover travel through France.

	Individual 1st Class	Individual 2nd Class	Saver 1st Class	Saver 2nd Class	Youth 2nd Class
4 days in 2 months	$439	$374	$374	$318	$287
Extra rail days (max 6)	45-51	38-44	38-44	33-37	29-33

(quietest and cheapest times). AVE is almost entirely covered by the Eurail pass (but book ahead).

A related high-speed train, the **Alvia,** runs on AVE lines but can switch to Iberian track without stopping.

Avant trains are also high-speed—typically about as fast as AVE—but designed for shorter distances. They also tend to be cheaper than AVE, even on the same route. Rail-pass reservations also cost about half as much for Avant as for AVE. If you're on a tight budget, compare your options before buying.

The **Talgo** is fast, air-conditioned, and expensive, and runs on AVE rails. **Intercity** and **Electro** trains fall just behind Talgo in speed, comfort, and expense. **Rápido, Tranvía, Semidirecto,** and **Expreso** trains are generally slower. **Cercanías** and **Rodalies** are commuter trains for big-city workers and small-town tourists. **Regional** and **Correo** trains are slow, small-town milk runs. Trains get more expensive as they pick up speed, but all are cheaper per mile than their northern European counterparts. Spain loves to name trains, so you may encounter types of trains not listed here. The names **Euromed, Alaris, Altaria,** and **Arco** all indicate faster trains that require reservations. These can cost significantly less than AVE on some routes and yet may be just as fast. Ask about the travel time for each option when buying your tickets.

Salidas means "departures," and *llegadas* is "arrivals." On train schedules, "LMXJVSD" stands for the days of the week in Spanish, starting with Monday. A train that runs "LMXJV-D" doesn't run on Saturdays. *Laborables* can mean Monday through Friday or Monday through Saturday.

Overnight Trains: For long trips, you can usually go overnight on the train (or consider flying—domestic shuttle flights are generally less than $100). Overnight trains (and buses) are generally less expensive and slower than the daytime rides, not counting any sleeper fees. Most overnight trains have berths and beds that you can rent (not included in the cost of your train ticket or rail pass). A sleeping berth *(litera* or *couchette)* costs extra, with the price depending on the route and type of compartment. Night trains are popular, so it's smart to reserve in advance, even from home. Travelers with first-class reservations are entitled to use comfortable "Intercity" lounges in train stations in Spain's major cities.

Night Trains to France: You can take a cheap train trip that involves a transfer at the Spanish border (at Cerbère, up the coast from Barcelona, or at Irún on Madrid-Paris runs that travel a few days per week). You'll connect to a normal night train with $35 sleeping berths *(literas/couchettes)* on one leg of the trip. This plan is more time-consuming, and may take two days of a flexipass.

For more detailed advice on figuring out the smartest rail pass options for your train trip, visit the Trains & Rail Passes section of my website at www.ricksteves.com/rail.

BUSES

Spain's bus system is confusing (www.movelia.es is a good place to begin researching schedules and carriers). There are a number of different bus companies (though usually clustered within one building), sometimes running buses to the same destinations and using the same transfer points. If you have to transfer, make sure to look for a bus with the same name/logo as the company you bought the ticket from. The larger stations have a consolidated information desk with all the schedules. In smaller stations, check the destinations and schedules posted on each office window. (If your connection requires a transfer to another company's bus in a different city, don't count on getting help from the originating clerk to figure out the onward connection.) Bus service on holidays, Saturdays, and especially Sundays can be less frequent.

If you arrive in a city by bus and plan to leave by bus, stick around the station upon your arrival to check your departure options and buy a ticket in advance if necessary (and possible). If you're downtown, need a ticket, and the bus station isn't central, save time by asking at the tourist office about travel agencies that sell bus tickets.

You can (and most likely will be required to) stow your luggage under the bus. Your ticket comes with an assigned seat; if the bus is full, you should take that seat, but if it's uncrowded, most people just sit where they like. For longer rides, give some thought to which side of the bus will get the most sun, and sit on the opposite side, even if the bus is air-conditioned and has curtains. Your ride likely will come with a soundtrack: taped Spanish pop music, radio, or sometimes videos. If you prefer silence, bring earplugs. Buses are non-smoking.

Drivers and station personnel rarely speak English. Buses generally lack WCs, but they stop every two hours or so for a break (usually 15 minutes, but can be up to 30). Drivers announce how long the stop will be, but if in doubt, ask the driver, "How many minutes here?" *("¿Cuántos minutos aquí?")*, so you know if you have time to get out. Listen for the bus horn as a final call before departure. Bus stations have WCs (rarely with toilet paper) and cafés that offer quick and slightly overpriced food.

TAXIS

Most taxis are reliable and cheap. Drivers generally respond kindly to the request, "How much is it to _____, more or less?" *("¿Cuánto cuesta a _____, más o menos?")*. Spanish taxis have extra supplements (for luggage, nighttime, Sundays, train/bus-station or airport pickup, and so on). Rounding up the fare (maximum of 10 percent) is adequate for a tip, though locals usually don't tip in taxis. City rides cost €4-6. Keep a map in your hand so the cabbie knows (or thinks) you know where you're going. Big cities have plenty of taxis. In many cases, couples travel

by cab for little more than the cost of two bus or subway tickets.

RENTING A CAR

If you're renting a car in Spain, bring your driver's license. You're also required to have an International Driving Permit—an official translation of your driver's license (sold at your local AAA office for $15 plus the cost of two passport-type photos; see www.aaa.com). While that's the letter of the law, I've often rented cars without having this permit. If all goes well, you'll likely never be asked to show the permit—but it's a must if you end up dealing with the police.

Rental companies require you to be at least 21 years old and to have held your license for one year. Drivers under the age of 25 may incur a young-driver surcharge, and some rental companies do not rent to anyone 75 and over. If you're considered too young or old, look into leasing (covered later), which has less-stringent age restrictions.

Research car rentals before you go. It's cheaper to arrange most car rentals from the US. Call several companies or look online to compare rates.

Most of the major US rental agencies (including Avis, Budget, Hertz, and Thrifty) have offices throughout Europe. Also consider the two major Europe-based agencies, Europcar and Sixt. It can be cheaper to use a consolidator, such as Auto Europe/Kemwel (www. autoeurope.com) or Europe by Car (www.ebctravel.com), which compares rates at several companies to get you the best deal. But because you're working with a middleman, it's especially important to ask in advance about add-on fees and restrictions.

Regardless of the car-rental company you choose, always read the fine print carefully for add-on charges—such as one-way drop-off fees, airport surcharges, or mandatory insurance policies—that aren't included in the "total price." You may need to query rental agents pointedly to find out your actual cost.

For the best deal, rent by the week with unlimited mileage. To save money on fuel, ask for a diesel car. I normally rent the smallest, least-expensive model with a stick shift (generally much cheaper than an automatic). Almost all rentals are manual by default, so

PRACTICALITIES

if you need an automatic, request one in advance; be aware that these cars are usually larger models (not as maneuverable on narrow, winding roads).

Figure on paying roughly $250-450 for a one-week rental. Allow extra for insurance, fuel, tolls, and parking. For trips of three weeks or more, look into leasing (explained later); you'll save money on insurance and taxes.

Big companies have offices in most cities; ask whether they can pick you up at your hotel. Small local rental companies can be cheaper but aren't as flexible.

Compare pickup costs (downtown can be less expensive than the airport) and explore drop-off options. Always check the hours of the location you choose: Many rental offices close from midday Saturday until Monday morning and, in smaller towns, at lunchtime.

When selecting a location, don't trust the agency's description of "downtown" or "city center." In some cases, a "downtown" branch can be on the outskirts of the city—a long, costly taxi ride from the center. Before choosing, plug the addresses into a mapping website. You may find that the "train station" location is handier. But returning a car at a big-city train station or downtown agency can be tricky; get precise details on the drop-off location and hours, and allow ample time to find it.

When you pick up the rental car, check it thoroughly and make sure any damage is noted on your rental agreement. Find out how your car's lights, turn signals, wipers, radio, and fuel cap function, and know what kind of fuel the car takes (diesel vs. unleaded). When you return the car, make sure the agent verifies its condition with you. Some drivers take pictures of the returned vehicle as proof of its condition.

Navigation Options

When renting a car in Europe, you have several alternatives for your digital navigator: Use your smartphone's online mapping app, download an offline map app, or rent a GPS device with your car (or bring your own GPS device from home).

Online mapping apps used to be prohibitively expensive for overseas travelers—but that was before most carriers started offering affordable international data plans. If you're already getting a data plan for your trip, this is probably the way to go (see "Using Your Smartphone in Europe," earlier).

A number of well-designed apps allow you much of the convenience of online maps without any costly demands on your data plan. City Maps 2Go is one of the most popular of these; OffMaps, Google Maps, and Navfree also offer good, zoomable offline maps for much of Europe (some are better for driving, while others are better for navigating cities).

PRACTICALITIES

Public Transportation Routes in Iberia

Some drivers prefer using a dedicated GPS unit—not only to avoid the data-roaming fees, but because a stand-alone GPS can be easier to operate (important if you're driving solo). The major downside: It's expensive—around $10-30 per day. Also, your car's GPS unit may only come loaded with maps for its home country—if you need additional maps, ask. Make sure your device's language is set to English before you drive off. If you have a portable GPS device at home, you can take that instead. Many American GPS devices come loaded with US maps only—you'll need to buy and download European maps before your trip. This option is far less expensive than renting.

Car Insurance Options

When you rent a car, you are liable for a very high deductible,

Driving in Spain

FRANCE

Santiago de Compostela — 285M·6H — Comillas
Santillana del Mar
80M·1.5H — Bilbao — St-Jean-de-Luz
20M·.75H
San Sebastián
200M·4.5H
95M 2.5H 10M·.25H Potes
125M 2.5H
60M 1.25H 95M·1.5H

140M·2.5H
270M·5.5H
León
120M·2H 50M 1.5H
35M·.25H
125M·2.25H (VIA VITORIA)
Pamplona
Barcelona to Cerbère (French border) 110m·2h

Porto
75M·1.25H
150M·3H
210M·3H
150M·3H
Burgos
115M 2H
115M·3H

220M·4H
Salamanca
60M 1.5H 55M 1H
Segovia
Zaragoza
205M 3.5H
Barcelona

Coimbra
185M·4H
Ávila
60M 1.25H Madrid
220M·3.5H

PORTUGAL
520M·9H
70M·1.5H
45M 1H
225M·3.5H

Lisbon
125M·2H
315M·5.5H
Toledo
Valencia

Évora
85M 1.5H
200M·3.5H
220M 3H

195M·3.5H
180M·3H
90M·2H Córdoba
100M·3H
225M 3.5H
330M·5.5H

Salema
Sevilla
155M·3H
Granada

55M·1.5H Arcos
Ronda
120M·2H
65M·1.25H

70M·2H
50M·1.25H
70M·1.5H
Nerja

Tarifa
.5H FERRY
60M·1.75H
Gibraltar

Tangier

m = miles	
h = hours	
···· = ferry	

NOTE: YOUR TIMES MAY VARY BASED ON TRAFFIC, CONSTRUCTION & ROAD CONDITIONS.

sometimes equal to the entire value of the car. Limit your financial risk by choosing one of these three options: Buy Collision Damage Waiver (CDW) coverage from the car-rental company, get coverage through your credit card (free, if your card automatically includes zero-deductible coverage), or get collision insurance as part of a larger travel-insurance policy.

CDW includes a very high deductible (typically $1,000-1,500). Though each rental company has its own variation, basic CDW costs $10-35 a day (figure roughly 30 percent extra) and reduces your liability, but does not eliminate it. When you pick up the car, you'll be offered the chance to "buy down" the basic deductible to zero (for an additional $10-30/day; this is sometimes called "super CDW" or "zero-deductible coverage").

If you opt for **credit-card coverage,** there's a catch. You'll technically have to decline all coverage offered by the car-rental company, which means they can place a hold on your card (which can be up to the full value of the car). In case of damage, it can be time-consuming to resolve the charges with your credit-card company. Before you decide on this option, quiz your credit-card company about how it works.

If you're already purchasing a travel-insurance policy for your trip, adding collision coverage is an option. For example, Travel

Guard (www.travelguard.com) sells affordable renter's collision insurance as an add-on to its other policies; it's valid everywhere in Europe except the Republic of Ireland, and some Italian car-rental companies refuse to honor it, as it doesn't cover you in case of theft.

For more on car-rental insurance, see www.ricksteves.com/cdw.

Leasing

For trips of three weeks or more, consider leasing (which automatically includes zero-deductible collision and theft insurance). By technically buying and then selling back the car, you save lots of money on tax and insurance. Leasing provides you a brand-new car with unlimited mileage and a 24-hour emergency assistance program. You can lease for as little as 21 days to as long as five and a half months. Car leases must be arranged from the US. One of many companies offering affordable lease packages is Europe by Car (www.europebycar.com/lease).

DRIVING

Driving in rural Spain is great—traffic is sparse and roads are generally good. But a car is a pain in big cities such as Barcelona. Drive defensively. If you're involved in an accident, you will be in for a monumental headache.

Good maps are available and inexpensive throughout Spain. In smaller towns, following signs to *centro ciudad* will get you to the heart of things.

Freeways and Tolls: Spain's freeways come with tolls, but save huge amounts of time. Each toll road *(autopista de peaje)* has its own pricing structure, so tolls vary. Near some major cities, you must prepay for each stretch of road you drive; on other routes, you take

a ticket where you enter the freeway, and pay when you exit. Payment can be made in cash or by credit or debit card (credit-card-only lanes are labeled *vias automáticas;* cash lanes are *vias manuales).*

Because road numbers can be puzzling and inconsistent, be ready to navigate by city and town names. Memorize some key road words: *salida* (exit), *de sentido único* (one way), *despacio* (slow), *adelantamiento prohibido* (no passing). Mileage signs are in kilometers (see page 316 for conversion formula into miles).

Road Rules: Seatbelts are required by law. Children under 12 must ride in the back seat, and children up to age 3 must have a child seat. You must put on a reflective safety vest any time you get out of your car on the side of a highway or unlit road (most rental-car companies provide one—but check when you pick up the car). Those who use eyeglasses are required by law to have a spare pair in the car. It is illegal to talk on a cell phone while driving (unless using a fully hands-free system).

Drivers must turn on headlights during daylight hours if visibility is poor. Spain does not allow a right turn at a red light. On expressways it's illegal to pass drivers on the right. Ask your car-rental company about these rules, or check the US State Department website (www.travel.state.gov, search for your country in the "Learn about your destination" box, then click on "Travel and Transportation").

AND LEARN THESE ROAD SIGNS

50 Speed Limit (km/hr)	Yield	No Passing	End of No Passing Zone
DIRECCIÓN ÚNICA One Way	Intersection	Main Road	Expressway
Danger	No Entry	Cars Prohibited	All Vehicles Prohibited
No Through Road	Restrictions No Longer Apply	Yield to Oncoming Traffic	No Stopping
Parking	No Parking	Customs	Peace

Traffic Cops: Watch for traffic radar and expect to be stopped for a routine check by the police (be sure your car-insurance form is up-to-date). Small towns come with speed traps and corruption. Tickets, especially for foreigners, are issued and paid for on the spot. Insist on a receipt *(recibo)*, so the money is less likely to end up in the cop's pocket.

Fuel: Gas and diesel prices are controlled and the same everywhere—about $7 a gallon for gas, less for diesel (gas is priced by the liter in Spain). Unleaded gas *(gasolina sin plomo)* is either *normal* or *super*. Note that diesel is called *diesel* or *gasóleo*—pay attention when filling your tank.

Theft: Choose parking places carefully. Stow valuables in the trunk during the day and leave nothing worth stealing in the car overnight. While you should avoid parking lots with twinkly asphalt, thieves break car windows anywhere, even at stoplights. If your car's a hatchback, take the trunk cover off at night so thieves can look in without breaking in. Try to make your car look locally owned by hiding the "tourist-owned" rental-company decals and putting a local newspaper in your front or back window. Parking attendants all over Spain holler, *"Nada en el coche"* ("Nothing in the car"). And they mean it. Ask your hotelier for advice on parking. In cities you can park safely but expensively in guarded lots.

FLIGHTS

The best comparison search engine for both international and intra-European flights is www.kayak.com. For inexpensive flights within Europe, try www.skyscanner.com or www.hipmunk.com; for inexpensive international flights, try www.vayama.com.

Flying to Europe: Start looking for international flights four to five months before your trip, especially for peak-season travel. Off-season tickets can be purchased a month or so in advance. Depending on your itinerary, it can be efficient to fly into one city and out of another. If your flight requires a connection in Europe, see our hints on navigating Europe's top hub airports at www.ricksteves.com/hub-airports.

Flying within Europe: If you're considering a train ride that's more than five hours long, a flight may save you both time and money. When comparing your options, factor in the time it takes to get to the airport and how early you'll need to arrive to check in.

Well-known cheapo airlines include easyJet (www.easyjet.com) and Ryanair (www.ryanair.com).

Be aware of the potential drawbacks of flying on the cheap: nonrefundable and nonchangeable tickets, minimal or nonexistent customer service, treks to airports far outside town, and stingy baggage allowances with steep overage fees. If you're traveling with lots of luggage, a cheap flight can quickly become a bad deal. To avoid unpleasant surprises, read the small print before you book.

Resources

RESOURCES FROM RICK STEVES

Rick Steves Barcelona is one of many books in my series on European travel, which includes country guidebooks, city guidebooks (Rome, Florence, Paris, London, etc.), Snapshot Guides (excerpted chapters from my country guides), Pocket Guides (full-color little books on big cities, such as Barcelona), and my budget-travel skills handbook, *Rick Steves' Europe Through the Back Door*. Most of my titles are available as ebooks. My phrase books—for Italian, French, German, Spanish, and Portuguese—are practical and budget-oriented. My other books include *Europe 101* (a crash course on art and history designed for travelers); *Mediterranean Cruise Ports* and *Northern European Cruise Ports* (how to make the most of your time in port); and *Travel as a Political Act* (a travelogue sprinkled with tips for bringing home a

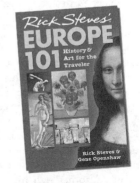

PRACTICALITIES

global perspective). A more complete list of my titles appears near the end of this book.

Video: My public television series, *Rick Steves' Europe,* covers European destinations in 100 shows, with eight episodes on Spain (including one on Barcelona and Catalunya). To watch full episodes online for free, see www.ricksteves.com/tv. Or to raise your travel IQ with video versions of our popular classes, such as the one on Spain, see www.ricksteves.com/travel-talks.

Audio: My weekly public radio show, *Travel with Rick Steves,* features interviews with travel experts from around the world. All of this audio content is available for free at Rick Steves Audio Europe, an extensive online library organized by destination. Choose whatever interests you, and download it via the Rick Steves Audio Europe app, www.ricksteves.com/audioeurope, iTunes, or Google Play.

MAPS

The black-and-white maps in this book are concise and simple, designed to help you locate recommended places and get to local TIs, where you can pick up more in-depth maps of cities or regions (usually free). Better maps are sold at newsstands and bookstores. Before you buy a map, look at it to be sure it has the level of detail you want. Drivers will want to pick up a good, detailed map in Europe (I'd recommend a 1:200,000- or 1:300,000-scale map).

RECOMMENDED BOOKS AND MOVIES

Barcelona bristles with history, art, and culture. To deepen your knowledge of the city's past and present, check out some of these books and films.

Nonfiction

Dense and detailed, Robert Hughes' *Barcelona* is an opinionated journey through the city's tumultuous history, with a focus on art and architecture. *Barcelona: The Great Enchantress,* a more condensed version of his earlier book, is Hughes' love song to his favorite city.

Barcelona: A Thousand Years of the City's Past (Fernandez-Armesto) gives a historical and artistic perspective on Barcelona's culture while detailing the tensions between the city and the rest of Spain. Another rich history of Barcelona is *Homage to Barcelona* (Toibin), which includes the author's anecdotes from his time there since the 1970s.

Begin Your Trip at
www.RickSteves.com

My **website** is *the* place to explore Europe. You'll find thousands of fun articles, videos, photos, and radio interviews on European destinations; money-saving tips for planning your dream trip; monthly travel news; my travel talks and travel blog; my latest guidebook updates (www.ricksteves.com/update); and my free Rick Steves Audio Europe app. You can also follow me on Facebook and Twitter.

Our **Travel Forum** is an immense, yet well-groomed collection of message boards, where our travel-savvy community answers questions and shares their personal travel experiences (www.ricksteves.com/forums).

Our **online Travel Store** offers travel bags and accessories that I've designed specifically to help you travel smarter and lighter. These include my popular bags (rolling carry-on and backpack versions), money belts, totes, toiletries kits, adapters, other accessories, and a wide selection of guidebooks, planning maps, and DVDs.

Choosing the right **rail pass** for your trip—amid hundreds of options—can drive you nutty. Our website will help you find the perfect fit for your itinerary and your budget: We offer easy, one-stop shopping for rail passes, seat reservations, and point-to-point tickets.

Want to travel with greater efficiency and less stress? We organize **tours** with more than three dozen itineraries and more than 800 departures reaching the best destinations in this book...and beyond. Our Spain tours include Barcelona and Madrid in 8 days, the Basque Country of Spain and France in 9 days, a My Way: Spain "unguided" tour in 11 days, and Spain in 14 days. You'll enjoy great guides, a fun bunch of travel partners (with small groups of 24 to 28 travelers), and plenty of room to spread out in a big, comfy bus when touring between towns. You'll find European adventures to fit every vacation length. For all the details, and to get our Tour Catalog and a free Rick Steves Tour Experience DVD (filmed on location during an actual tour), visit www.ricksteves.com or call us at 425/608-4217.

George Orwell traveled to Barcelona, where he traded his press pass for a uniform, fought against Franco's Fascists in the Spanish Civil War of 1936-1939 (and was nearly killed), and then wrote a gripping account of his experiences in *Homage to Catalonia*. The political climate during the Civil War is chronicled in *The Battle for Spain* (Beevor).

Spain has undergone incredible changes since the death of Franco in 1975 and the end of his nearly four-decade dictatorship.

The New Spaniards (Hooper) is a survey of all aspects of modern Spain, including its politics, economy, demographics, education, religion, and popular culture.

James Michener traveled to Spain for several decades, and his tribute, *Iberia,* describes how Spain's dark history created a contradictory and passionately beautiful land.

Travelers' Tales: Spain (McCauley) offers dozens of essays about Spain and its people from numerous authors.

Penelope Casas has written many popular books on the food of Spain, including tapas, paella, and regional cooking. Her *Discovering Spain: An Uncommon Guide* blends references to history, culture, and food with travel information.

Fiction

Carmen Laforet's *Nada* details the experiences of an orphaned university student in the 1940s who discovers the haunting reality of post-Civil War Barcelona.

Ernest Hemingway's *For Whom the Bell Tolls,* a tale of idealism and harsh reality, is set against the complexity of the Spanish Civil War. That ugly period of Spanish history is also the subject of *The Carpenter's Pencil* (Rivas), an unsentimental tale of an imprisoned revolutionary haunted by his past.

Set in the early 20th century, Josep M. de Sagarra's *Vida Privada* (*Private Life*) exposes dark events and scandal among Barcelona's bourgeoisie.

Themes of power, greed, and money permeate *The City of Marvels* (Mendoza), about a young man who rises from poverty in Barcelona.

The best-selling thriller *The Shadow of the Wind* (Zafón) takes place in 1950s Barcelona; sequels include *The Angel's Game* and *The Prisoner of Heaven.*

Cathedral of the Sea (Falcones) tells the story of a humble medieval *bastaixo* who toils to build the Church of Santa Maria del Mar in El Born and gradually climbs the social ladder of medieval Barcelona.

Films

In *The Mystery of Picasso* (1956), Picasso is filmed painting from behind a transparent canvas, allowing a unique look at his creative process.

L'auberge Espagnole (2002) tells the story of the loves and lives of European students sharing an apartment in Barcelona.

In *Barcelona* (1994), two Americans in Spain try to navigate the Spanish singles scene and the ensuing culture clash.

Woody Allen's *Vicky Cristina Barcelona* (2008) stars Javier Bardem as a macho Spanish artist romancing two American women, when suddenly his stormy ex-wife (Penélope Cruz, in an Oscar-winning role) re-enters his life.

Pedro Almodóvar's piquant films about relationships in the post-Franco era have garnered piles of international awards. Spanish actors Bardem, Cruz, and Antonio Banderas have starred in his films. Almodóvar's best-known films include *Women on the Verge of a Nervous Breakdown* (1988), *All About My Mother* (1999), *Talk to Her* (2002), *Volver* (2006), and *Broken Embraces* (2009).

Salvador (2006) uses Barcelona as a backdrop for its story about the life of Salvador Puig Antich, an anarchist and bank robber executed by Franco in the 1970s.

Manuale d'Amore (2007), a love story starring Monica Bellucci, illuminates the cities of Barcelona and Rome as several couples come together across four episodes.

APPENDIX

Contents

Useful Contacts

Emergency Needs
Police: Tel. 091 (nationwide), tel. 092 (local)
Ambulance or Any Emergency: Tel. 112

Consulates
US Consulate: Tel. 932-802-227, after-hours emergency tel. 915-872-200, passport services Mon-Fri 9:00-13:00, closed Sat-Sun (Passeig Reina Elisenda de Montcada 23, http://barcelona. usconsulate.gov)
Canadian Consulate: Tel. 932-703-614, after-hours emergency tel. in Ottawa—call collect 613-996-8885 (Plaça de Catalunya 9, www.spain.gc.ca, click on "Contact Us," then "Consulate of Canada in Barcelona")

Directory Assistance
In Spain, dial 11811 (€0.40/min) or 11818 (€0.55/call from private numbers, free from phone booths).

Holidays and Festivals

This list includes selected festivals in Barcelona, plus national holidays observed throughout Spain. Many sights and banks close on national holidays—keep this in mind when planning your itinerary. Before planning a trip around a festival, verify its dates by checking the festival's website or TI sites (www.spain.info). For more on Barcelona's festivals and feast days, see "City of Festivals" sidebar on page 27.

Be prepared for big crowds during these holiday periods: Holy Week (Semana Santa) and Easter weekend; Labor Day; Ascension; Pentecost weekend; Assumption weekend; Spanish National Day; Constitution Day, followed closely by the Feast of the Immaculate Conception—both the previous and following weekends may be busy; and Christmas and New Year's. Look out for any local holiday that falls on a Tuesday or Thursday—the Spanish will often take Monday or Friday off as well to have a four-day weekend.

Jan 1	New Year's Day
Jan 6	Epiphany (Día de los Reyes Magos)
Mid-Feb	Les Festes de Santa Eulàlia (parades, kid-friendly activities)
March 29-April 4 in 2015, March 20-26 in 2016	Holy Week
April 5 in 2015, March 27 in 2016	Easter
April 6 in 2015, March 28 in 2016	Easter Monday
April 23	St. George's Day
May 1	Labor Day (closures)
May 14 in 2015, May 5 in 2016	Ascension
May 23-24 in 2015, May 14-15 in 2016	Pentecost weekend
May-Sept (Saturdays)	La Festa Catalana (local folk traditions)
June 4 in 2015, May 26 in 2016	Corpus Christi
June-Aug	Música als Parcs (jazz, classical music)

June 23	Festival of St. John the Baptist (bonfires, fireworks)
July	Grec Festival (music, arts)
Mid-July	Montjuïc de Nit (music, arts)
Mid-Aug	Festes de Sant Roc (street festival)
Mid-Aug	Festa Major de Gràcia (music, dancing, food, and drink)
Aug 15	Assumption of Mary (religious festival)
Aug 21-27	St. Bartholomew Festival, Sitges (carnival, traditional Catalan entertainments)
Sept 23	St. Tecla Festival, Sitges (fireworks, castellers)
Late Sept	La Mercè Festival (fireworks, parades, music)
Oct 12	Spanish National Day
Nov 1	All Saints' Day
Dec 6	Constitution Day
Dec 8	Feast of the Immaculate Conception
Dec 13	Feast of Santa Lucía
Dec 25	Christmas
Dec 31	New Year's Eve

APPENDIX

Conversions and Climate

NUMBERS AND STUMBLERS

- Europeans write a few of their numbers differently than we do. 1 = 1 , 4 = 4 , 7 = 7 .
- In Europe, dates appear as day/month/year, so Christmas 2016 is 25/12/16.
- Commas are decimal points and decimals are commas. A dollar and a half is $1,50, one thousand is 1.000, and there are 5.280 feet in a mile.
- When counting with fingers, start with your thumb. If you hold up your first finger to request one item, you'll probably get two.
- What Americans call the second floor of a building is the first floor in Europe.
- On escalators and moving sidewalks, Europeans keep the left "lane" open for passing. Keep to the right.

METRIC CONVERSIONS

A kilogram is 2.2 pounds, and 1 liter is about a quart, or almost four to a gallon. A kilometer is six-tenths of a mile. I figure kilometers to miles by cutting them in half and adding back 10 percent of the original (120 km: 60 + 12 = 72 miles, 300 km: 150 + 30 = 180 miles).

1 foot = 0.3 meter	1 square yard = 0.8 square meter
1 yard = 0.9 meter	1 square mile = 2.6 square kilometers
1 mile = 1.6 kilometers	1 ounce = 28 grams
1 centimeter = 0.4 inch	1 quart = 0.95 liter
1 meter = 39.4 inches	1 kilogram = 2.2 pounds
1 kilometer = 0.62 mile	32°F = 0°C

CLOTHING SIZES

When shopping for clothing, use these US-to-European comparisons as general guidelines (but note that no conversion is perfect).
- Women's dresses and blouses: Add 30
  (US size 10 = European size 40)
- Men's suits and jackets: Add 10
  (US size 40 regular = European size 50)
- Men's shirts: Multiply by 2 and add about 8
  (US size 15 collar = European size 38)
- Women's shoes: Add about 30
  (US size 8 = European size 38-39)
- Men's shoes: Add 32-34
  (US size 9 = European size 41; US size 11 = European size 45)

BARCELONA'S CLIMATE

First line, average daily high; second line, average daily low; third line, average days without rain. For more detailed weather statistics for destinations in this book (as well as the rest of the world), check www.wunderground.com.

J	F	M	A	M	J	J	A	S	O	N	D
55°	57°	60°	65°	71°	78°	82°	82°	77°	69°	62°	56°
43°	45°	48°	52°	57°	65°	69°	69°	66°	58°	51°	46°
26	23	23	21	23	24	27	25	23	22	24	25

FAHRENHEIT AND CELSIUS CONVERSION

For Weather   For Health

Europe takes its temperature using the Celsius scale, while we opt for Fahrenheit. For a rough conversion from Celsius to Fahrenheit, double the number and add 30. For weather, remember that 28°C is 82°F—perfect. For health, 37°C is just right. At a launderette, 30°C is cold, 40°C is warm (usually the default setting), 60°C is hot, and 95°C is boiling.

Packing Checklist

Whether you're traveling for five days or five weeks, you won't need more than this. Pack light to enjoy the sweet freedom of true mobility.

Clothing

- ❑ 5 shirts: long- & short-sleeve
- ❑ 2 pairs pants or skirt
- ❑ 1 pair shorts or capris
- ❑ 5 pairs underwear & socks
- ❑ 1 pair walking shoes
- ❑ Sweater or fleece top
- ❑ Rainproof jacket with hood
- ❑ Tie or scarf
- ❑ Swimsuit
- ❑ Sleepwear

Money

- ❑ Debit card
- ❑ Credit card(s)
- ❑ Hard cash ($20 bills)
- ❑ Money belt or neck wallet

Documents & Travel Info

- ❑ Passport
- ❑ Airline reservations
- ❑ Rail pass/train reservations
- ❑ Car-rental voucher
- ❑ Driver's license
- ❑ Student ID, hostel card, etc.
- ❑ Photocopies of all the above
- ❑ Hotel confirmations
- ❑ Insurance details
- ❑ Guidebooks & maps
- ❑ Notepad & pen
- ❑ Journal

Toiletries Kit

- ❑ Toiletries
- ❑ Medicines & vitamins
- ❑ First-aid kit
- ❑ Glasses/contacts/sunglasses (with prescriptions)
- ❑ Earplugs
- ❑ Packet of tissues (for WC)

Miscellaneous

- ❑ Daypack
- ❑ Sealable plastic baggies
- ❑ Laundry soap
- ❑ Spot remover
- ❑ Clothesline
- ❑ Sewing kit
- ❑ Travel alarm/watch

Electronics

- ❑ Smartphone or mobile phone
- ❑ Camera & related gear
- ❑ Tablet/ereader/media player
- ❑ Laptop & flash drive
- ❑ Earbuds or headphones
- ❑ Chargers
- ❑ Plug adapters

Optional Extras

- ❑ Flipflops or slippers
- ❑ Mini-umbrella or poncho
- ❑ Travel hairdryer
- ❑ Belt
- ❑ Hat (for sun or cold)
- ❑ Picnic supplies
- ❑ Water bottle
- ❑ Fold-up tote bag
- ❑ Small flashlight
- ❑ Small binoculars
- ❑ Insect repellent
- ❑ Small towel or washcloth
- ❑ Inflatable pillow
- ❑ Some duct tape (for repairs)
- ❑ Tiny lock
- ❑ Address list (to mail postcards)
- ❑ Postcards/photos from home
- ❑ Extra passport photos
- ❑ Good book

Spanish Survival Phrases

Spanish has a guttural sound similar to the J in Baja California. In the phonetics, the symbol for this clearing-your-throat sound is the italicized *h*.

English	Spanish	Pronunciation
Good day.	*Buenos días.*	**bway**-nohs **dee**-ahs
Do you speak English?	*¿Habla Usted inglés?*	ah-blah oo-**stehd** een-**glays**
Yes. / No.	*Sí. / No.*	see / noh
I (don't) understand.	*(No) comprendo.*	(noh) kohm-**prehn**-doh
Please.	*Por favor.*	por fah-**bor**
Thank you.	*Gracias.*	**grah**-thee-ahs
I'm sorry.	*Lo siento.*	loh see-**ehn**-toh
Excuse me.	*Perdóneme.*	pehr-**doh**-nay-may
(No) problem.	*(No) problema.*	(noh) proh-**blay**-mah
Good.	*Bueno.*	**bway**-noh
Goodbye.	*Adiós.*	ah-dee-**ohs**
one / two	*uno / dos*	**oo**-noh / dohs
three / four	*tres / cuatro*	trays / **kwah**-troh
five / six	*cinco / seis*	**theen**-koh / says
seven / eight	*siete / ocho*	see-**eh**-tay / **oh**-choh
nine / ten	*nueve / diez*	**nway**-bay / dee-**ayth**
How much is it?	*¿Cuánto cuesta?*	**kwahn**-toh **kway**-stah
Write it?	*¿Me lo escribe?*	may loh ay-**skree**-bay
Is it free?	*¿Es gratis?*	ays **grah**-tees
Is it included?	*¿Está incluido?*	ay-**stah** een-kloo-**ee**-doh
Where can I buy / find...?	*¿Dónde puedo comprar / encontrar...?*	**dohn**-day **pway**-doh kohm-**prar** / ayn-kohn-**trar**
I'd like / We'd like...	*Quiero / Queremos...*	kee-**ehr**-oh / kehr-**ay**-mohs
...a room.	*...una habitación.*	**oo**-nah ah-bee-tah-thee-**ohn**
...a ticket to ___.	*...un billete para ___.*	oon bee-**yeh**-tay **pah**-rah ___
Is it possible?	*¿Es posible?*	ays poh-**see**-blay
Where is...?	*¿Dónde está...?*	**dohn**-day ay-**stah**
...the train station	*...la estación de trenes*	lah ay-stah-thee-**ohn** day **tray**-nays
...the bus station	*...la estación de autobuses*	lah ay-stah-thee-**ohn** day ow-toh-**boo**-says
...the tourist information office	*...la oficina de turismo*	lah oh-fee-**thee**-nah day too-**rees**-moh
Where are the toilets?	*¿Dónde están los servicios?*	**dohn**-day ay-**stahn** lohs sehr-**bee**-thee-ohs
men	*hombres, caballeros*	**ohm**-brays, kah-bah-**yay**-rohs
women	*mujeres, damas*	moo-**heh**-rays, **dah**-mahs
left / right	*izquierda / derecha*	eeth-kee-**ehr**-dah / day-**ray**-chah
straight	*derecho*	day-**ray**-choh
When do you open / close?	*¿A qué hora abren / cierran?*	ah kay **oh**-rah **ah**-brehn / thee-**ay**-rahn
At what time?	*¿A qué hora?*	ah kay **oh**-rah
Just a moment.	*Un momento.*	oon moh-**mehn**-toh
now / soon / later	*ahora / pronto / más tarde*	ah-**oh**-rah / **prohn**-toh / mahs **tar**-day
today / tomorrow	*hoy / mañana*	oy / mahn-**yah**-nah

In a Spanish Restaurant

English	Spanish	Pronunciation
I'd like / We'd like...	Quiero / Queremos...	kee-**ehr**-oh / kehr-**ay**-mohs
...to reserve...	...reservar...	ray-sehr-**bar**
...a table for one / two.	...una mesa para uno / dos.	oo-nah **may**-sah **pah**-rah oo-noh / dohs
Non-smoking.	No fumador.	noh foo-mah-**dohr**
Is this table free?	¿Está esta mesa libre?	ay-**stah** ay-stah **may**-sah **lee**-bray
The menu (in English), please.	La carta (en inglés), por favor.	lah **kar**-tah (ayn een-**glays**) por fah-**bor**
service (not) included	servicio (no) incluido	sehr-**bee**-thee-oh (noh) een-kloo-**ee**-doh
cover charge	precio de entrada	**pray**-thee-oh day ayn-**trah**-dah
to go	para llevar	**pah**-rah yay-**bar**
with / without	con / sin	kohn / seen
and / or	y / o	ee / oh
menu (of the day)	menú (del día)	may-**noo** (dayl **dee**-ah)
specialty of the house	especialidad de la casa	ay-spay-thee-ah-lee-**dahd** day lah **kah**-sah
tourist menu	menú turístico	meh-**noo** too-**ree**-stee-koh
combination plate	plato combinado	**plah**-toh kohm-bee-**nah**-doh
appetizers	tapas	**tah**-pahs
bread	pan	pahn
cheese	queso	**kay**-soh
sandwich	bocadillo	boh-kah-**dee**-yoh
soup	sopa	**soh**-pah
salad	ensalada	ayn-sah-**lah**-dah
meat	carne	**kar**-nay
poultry	aves	**ah**-bays
fish	pescado	pay-**skah**-doh
seafood	marisco	mah-**ree**-skoh
fruit	fruta	**froo**-tah
vegetables	verduras	behr-**doo**-rahs
dessert	postres	**poh**-strays
tap water	agua del grifo	**ah**-gwah dayl **gree**-foh
mineral water	agua mineral	**ah**-gwah mee-nay-**rahl**
milk	leche	**lay**-chay
(orange) juice	zumo (de naranja)	**thoo**-moh (day nah-**rahn**-hah)
coffee	café	kah-**feh**
tea	té	tay
wine	vino	**bee**-noh
red / white	tinto / blanco	**teen**-toh / **blahn**-koh
glass / bottle	vaso / botella	**bah**-soh / boh-**tay**-yah
beer	cerveza	thehr-**bay**-thah
Cheers!	¡Salud!	sah-**lood**
More. / Another.	Más. / Otro.	mahs / **oh**-troh
The same.	El mismo.	ehl **mees**-moh
The bill, please.	La cuenta, por favor.	lah **kwayn**-tah por fah-**bor**
tip	propina	proh-**pee**-nah
Delicious!	¡Delicioso!	day-lee-thee-**oh**-soh

For hundreds more pages of survival phrases for your trip to Spain, check out *Rick Steves' Spanish Phrase Book.*

Catalan Survival Phrases

Catalan may look similar to Spanish (*castellano*), but there are important variations in pronunciation. The letters **c** and **z** before vowels are pronounced as "s" (unlike the Spanish "th" sound). The letters **b**, **d**, **r**, or **t** at the end of a word are usually not pronounced (unless the final syllable is stressed). An **s** between two vowels sounds like a "z."

English	Catalan	Pronunciation
Hello.	Hola.	**oh**-lah
Do you speak English?	¿Parles anglès?	**par** luhs ahn **glays**
Yes. / No.	Sí. / No.	see / noh
I (don't) understand.	(No) entenc.	(noh) ahn-**tehnk**
Please.	Si us plau.	see oos plow
Thank you (very much).	(Moltes) Gràcies.	(**mohl**-tehs) **grah**-see-ehs
I'm sorry.	Ho sento.	oo **sehn**-too
Excuse me.	Perdó.	pehr-**doh**
(No) problem.	(Cap) problema.	(kahp) proh-**blay**-mah
Good.	Bé.	bay
Goodbye.	Adéu.	ah-**day**-oo
one / two / three	uno / dos / tres	**oo**-noo / dohs / trehs
four / five / six	quatre / cinc / sis	**kwah**-trah / seenk / sees
seven / eight	set / vuit	seht / **voo**-eet
nine / ten	nou / deu	**noh**-oo / **deh**-oo
How much?	¿Quant és?	kwahn ehs
Write it?	¿M'ho escriu?	moh ah-**skree**-oo
Is it free?	¿És gratis?	ehs **grah**-tees
Is it included?	¿Està inclós?	ah-**stah** in-**klohs**
Where can I find / buy...?	¿On puc trobar / comprar...?	ohn pook troo **bah** / koom **prah**
I'd like / We'd like...	Voldria / Voldríem...	vool-**dree**-ah / vool-**dree**-ahm
...a room.	...una habitació.	**oo**-nah ah-bee-tah-see-**oh**
...a ticket to ___.	...una entrada per___.	**oo**-nah ahn-**trah**-dah pehr ___
Is it possible?	¿És possible?	ehs poo-**see**-blah
Where is...?	¿On està...?	ohn ah-**stah**
...the train station	...l'estació del tren	lah-stah-see-**oh** dahl trehn
...the bus station	...l'estació d'autobuses	lah-stah-see-**oh** dow-toh-**boo**-zehs
...the tourist information office	...l'oficina de turisme	loo-fee-**see**-nah deh too-**rees**-meh
Where are the toilets?	¿On estan els serveis?	ohn ah-**stahn** ehls sehr-**vays**
men / women	homes / dones	**oh**-mehs / **doh**-nehs
left / right	esquerre / dreta	ehs-**keh**-reh / **dreh**-tah
straight	dret	dreht
At what time does this open / close?	¿A quina hora obre / tanca?	ah **kwee**-nah **oh**-rah **oh**-brah / **tahn**-kah
Just a moment.	Un moment.	oon moo-**mehn**
now / soon / later	ara / aviat / més tard	**ah**-rah / ah-vee-**aht** / mehs tahr
today / tomorrow	avui / demà	ah-**voo**-ee / deh-**mah**
Long live Catalunya!	¡Visca Catalunya!	**vee**-skah kah-tah-**loon**-yah

In a Catalan Restaurant

English	Catalan	Pronunciation
I'd like / We'd like...	Voldria / Voldríem...	vool-**dree**-ah / vool-**dree**-ahm
...to reserve...	...reservar...	reh-zehr-**vah**
...a table for one / two.	...una taula per una / dues.	oo-nah tow-lah pehr oo-nah / doo-ehs
Is this table free?	¿Està lliure aquesta taula?	eh-**stah yoo**-rah ah-**kwehs**-tah **tow**-lah
The menu (in English), please.	La carta (en anglés), si us plau.	lah **kar**-tah (ehn ahn-**glays**) see oos plow
service (not) included	servei (no) inclòs	sehr-**vay**-ee (noh) in-**klohs**
cover charge	preu d'entrada	**preh**-oo dahn-**trah**-dah
to go	per emportar	pehr ehm-por-**tah**
with / without	amb / sense	ahm / **sehn**-seh
and / or	i / o	ee / oh
tapas (small plates)	tapes	**tah**-pahs
daily special	plat del dia	plah dahl **dee**-ah
tourist menu	menú turístic	mah-**noo** too-**ree**-steek
specialty of the house	especialitat de la casa	eh-spah-see-ah-lee-**tah** dah lah **kah**-zah
combination plate	plat combinat	plah koom-bee-**nah**
half portion	mitja porció	**meet**-yah poor-see-**oh**
appetizers	entrants	ehn-**trahns**
bread	pà	pah
cheese	formatge	foor-**mah**-jeh
sandwich	entrepà	ehn-trah-**pah**
soup	sopa	**soh**-pah
salad	amanida	ah-mah-**nee**-dah
meat	carn	karn
poultry	aviram	ah-vee-**rahm**
fish	peix	paysh
seafood	marisc	mah-**rees**
fruit	fruita	**froo**-ee-tah
vegetables	verdures	vehr-**doo**-rehs
dessert	postres	**poh**-strehs
tap water	aigua (de l'aixeta)	**eye**-gwah (deh lah-**shay**-tah)
mineral water	aigua mineral	**eye**-gwah mee-nah-**rahl**
milk	llet	yeht
(orange) juice	suc (de taronja)	soo (dah tah-**rohn**-zhah)
coffee	cafè	kah-**feh**
tea	te	teh
wine	vi	vee
red / white	negre / blanc	**neh**-greh / blahnk
glass / bottle	copa / ampolla	**koh**-pah / ahm-**poy**-yah
beer	cervesa	sehr-**veh**-zah
Cheers!	¡Salut!	sah-**loo**
More. / Another.	Més. / Un altre.	mehs / oon **ahl**-treh
The same.	El mateix.	ahl mah-**taysh**
The bill, please.	El compte, si us plau.	ahl **kohmp**-teh see oos plow
tip	propina	proo-**pee**-nah
Delicious!	Boníssim!	boo-**nee**-zeem

INDEX

MAP INDEX

Our website enhances this book and turns

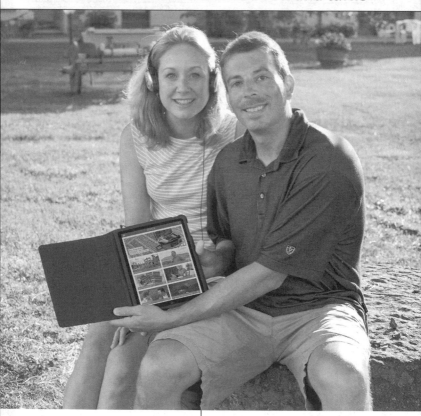

Explore Europe

At ricksteves.com you can browse through thousands of articles, videos, photos and radio interviews, plus find a wealth of money-saving travel tips for planning your dream trip. And with our mobile-friendly website, you can easily access all this great travel information anywhere you go.

TV Shows

Preview the places you'll visit by watching entire half-hour episodes of Rick Steves' Europe (choose from all 100 shows) on-demand, for free.

ricksteves.com

your travel dreams into affordable reality

Radio Interviews

Enjoy ready access to Rick's vast library of radio interviews covering travel

tips and cultural insights that relate specifically to your Europe travel plans.

Travel Forums

Learn, ask, share! Our online community of savvy travelers is a great resource for first-time travelers to Europe, as well as seasoned pros. You'll find forums on each country, plus travel tips and restaurant/hotel reviews. You can even ask one of our well-traveled staff to chime in with an opinion.

Travel News

Subscribe to our free Travel News e-newsletter, and get monthly updates from Rick on what's happening in Europe.

Audio Europe™

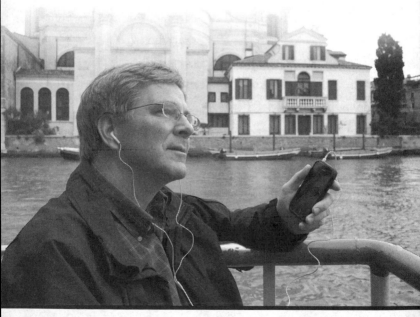

Pack Light and Right

Gear up for your next adventure at ricksteves.com

Light Luggage

Pack light and right with Rick Steves' affordable, custom-designed rolling carry-on bags, backpacks, day packs and shoulder bags.

Accessories

From packing cubes to moneybelts and beyond, Rick has personally selected the travel goodies that will help your trip go smoother.

Rick Steves has

Experience maximum Europe

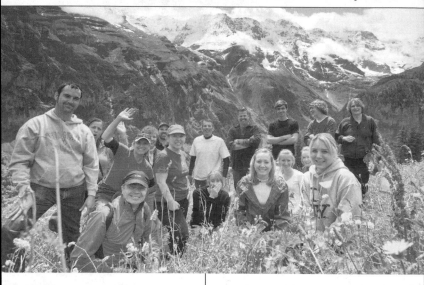

Save time and energy

This guidebook is your independent-travel toolkit. But for all it delivers, it's still up to you to devote the time and energy it takes to manage the preparation and logistics that are essential for a happy trip. If that's a hassle, there's a solution.

Rick Steves Tours

A Rick Steves tour takes you to Europe's most interesting places with great

great tours, too!

with minimum stress

guides and small groups of 28 or less. We follow Rick's favorite itineraries, ride in comfy buses, stay in family-run hotels, and bring you intimately close to the Europe you've traveled so far to see. Most importantly, we take away the logistical headaches so you can focus on the fun.

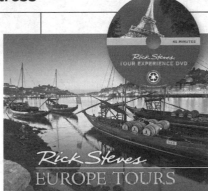

customers—along with us on 40 different itineraries, from Ireland to Italy to Istanbul. Is a Rick Steves tour the right fit for your travel dreams? Find out at ricksteves.com, where you can also get Rick's latest tour catalog and free Tour Experience DVD.

Join the fun

This year we'll take 18,000 free-spirited travelers—nearly half of them repeat

Europe is best experienced with happy travel partners. We hope you can join us.

See our itineraries at ricksteves.com

EUROPE GUIDES

Best of Europe
Eastern Europe
Europe Through the Back Door
Mediterranean Cruise Ports
Northern European Cruise Ports

COUNTRY GUIDES

Croatia & Slovenia
England
France
Germany
Great Britain
Ireland
Italy
Portugal
Scandinavia
Spain
Switzerland

CITY & REGIONAL GUIDES

Amsterdam, Bruges & Brussels
Barcelona
Budapest
Florence & Tuscany
Greece: Athens & the Peloponnese
Istanbul
London
Paris
Prague & the Czech Republic
Provence & the French Riviera
Rome
Venice
Vienna, Salzburg & Tirol

SNAPSHOT GUIDES

Basque Country: Spain & France
Berlin
Bruges & Brussels
Copenhagen & the Best of
   Denmark
Dublin
Dubrovnik
Hill Towns of Central Italy
Italy's Cinque Terre
Krakow, Warsaw & Gdansk
Lisbon
Madrid & Toledo
Milan & the Italian Lakes District
Munich, Bavaria & Salzburg
Naples & the Amalfi Coast
Northern Ireland
Norway
Scotland
Sevilla, Granada & Southern Spain
Stockholm

POCKET GUIDES

Amsterdam
Athens
Barcelona
Florence
London
Paris
Rome
Venice

Rick Steves guidebooks are published by Avalon Travel,
a member of the Perseus Books Group.

NOW AVAILABLE:
eBOOKS, DVD & BLU-RAY

TRAVEL CULTURE

Europe 101
European Christmas
Postcards from Europe
Travel as a Political Act

eBOOKS

Nearly all Rick Steves guides are available as ebooks. Check with your favorite bookseller.

RICK STEVES' EUROPE DVDs

11 New Shows 2013–2014
Austria & the Alps
Eastern Europe
England & Wales
European Christmas
European Travel Skills & Specials
France
Germany, BeNeLux & More
Greece, Turkey & Portugal
Iran
Ireland & Scotland
Italy's Cities
Italy's Countryside
Scandinavia
Spain
Travel Extras

BLU-RAY

Celtic Charms
Eastern Europe Favorites
European Christmas
Italy Through the Back Door
Mediterranean Mosaic
Surprising Cities of Europe

PHRASE BOOKS & DICTIONARIES

French
French, Italian & German
German
Italian
Portuguese
Spanish

JOURNALS

Rick Steves Pocket Travel Journal
Rick Steves Travel Journal

PLANNING MAPS

Britain, Ireland & London
Europe
France & Paris
Germany, Austria & Switzerland
Ireland
Italy
Spain & Portugal

RickSteves.com 🅕🅣 @RickSteves

Rick Steves books and DVDs are available at bookstores
and through online booksellers.

Photo © Patricia Feaster

Credits

RESEARCHERS
To help update this book, Rick relied on...

Amanda Buttinger

Amanda moved to Madrid in 1998, thinking she'd be there a year. Since then she's found many reasons to stay, from learning more Spanish to guiding for Rick Steves' Europe and travel writing to the best of all—sunny city walks with her boys and dog.

Suzanne Kotz

Suzanne, an editor with Rick Steves' Europe, began her travel career riding in a station wagon with her six siblings from Michigan to Florida. A librarian by training and a longtime editor of art publications, she lives in Seattle with her husband and son.

CONTRIBUTORS
Cameron Hewitt

Cameron writes and edits guidebooks for Rick Steves, specializing in Eastern Europe. For this book, he gorged on Gaudí, bored into El Born, marveled at Miró, aced the Eixample, and sashayed the *sardana* in front of the cathedral. When he's not traveling, Cameron lives in Seattle with his wife Shawna.

Gene Openshaw

Gene is the co-author of a dozen Rick Steves guidebooks. For this book he wrote material on art, history, and culture for several of the neighborhood walks, and museum and church tours. When not traveling, Gene enjoys composing music, recovering from his 1973 trip to Europe with Rick, and living everyday life with his daughter.